Land, Power, and Poverty

Thematic Studies in Latin America

Gilbert W. Merkx

Series Editor

*Land, Power, and Poverty: Agrarian Transformation and
Political Conflict in Central America,* Second Edition,
Charles D. Brockett

*The Women's Movement in Latin America:
Participation and Democracy,* Second Edition,
edited by Jane S. Jaquette

Land, Power, and Poverty

*Agrarian Transformation
and Political Conflict
in Central America*

SECOND EDITION

Charles D. Brockett
The University of the South

WestviewPress
A Division of HarperCollins*Publishers*

Thematic Studies in Latin America

Copyright © 1998 by Westview Press, A Division of HarperCollins Publishers, Inc.

Published in 1998 in the United States of America by Westview Press, 5500 Central Avenue, Boulder, Colorado 80301-2877, and in the United Kingdom by Westview Press, 12 Hid's Copse Road, Cumnor Hill, Oxford OX2 9JJ

Library of Congress Cataloging-in-Publication Data
Brockett, Charles D., 1946–
   Land, power, and poverty : agrarian transformation and political
conflict in Central America / Charles D. Brockett. — 2nd ed.
      p.   cm. — (Thematic studies in Latin America)
   Includes bibliographical references (p.   ) and index.
   ISBN 0-8133-8695-0 (pb)
   1. Agriculture—Economic aspects—Central America.   2. Land use—
Central America.   3. Land tenure—Central America.   4. Land reform—
Central America.   5. Elite (Social sciences)—Central America.
6. Poor—Central America.   7. Central America—Rural conditions.
I. Title.   II. Series.
HD1797.B76   1998
333.3'09728—dc21
                                                                        98-5451
                                                                        CIP

10   9   8   7   6   5   4   3   2   1

Contents

Tables and Figures

Acronyms

ACASCH	Social Christian Peasant Association of Honduras
AIFLD	American Institute for Free Labor Development
ALCOSA	Alimentos Congelados Monte Bello, S.A.
ANACH	National Association of Honduran Peasants
ANC	National Peasant Association
APP	area of people's property
ARENA	Nationalist Republican Alliance
ATC	Association of Rural Workers
BPR	Popular Revolutionary Bloc
CAAP	Private Agricultural and Agroindustrial Council
CAS	Sandinista production cooperatives
CAT	certificate of tax payment
CCS	credit and service cooperatives
CCUC	Central Committee of Peasant Unity
CEPA	Evangelistic Committee for Agrarian Promotion
CIA	Central Intelligence Agency
CINDE	Costa Rica Trade and Investment Center, Costa Rican Coalition for Development Initiatives
CNCG	National Confederation of Peasants of Guatemala
CNUS	National Committee of Trade Union Unity
CONIC	National Coordinator of Indigenous and Peasants
CUC	Committee for Peasant Unity
EC	European Community
ECLA/CEPAL	United Nations Economic Commission for Latin America
EGP	Guerrilla Army of the Poor
ENABAS	Nicaraguan Agency for Basic Foods
FAO	Food and Agriculture Organization of the United Nations
FAPU	United Popular Action Front
FAR	Rebel Armed Forces
FCG	Campesino Federation of Guatemala
FDN	Democratic National Front
FDN	Nicaraguan Democratic Front

FDR	Democratic Revolutionary Front
FECCAS	Christian Federation of Salvadoran Peasants
FECORAH	Federation of Honduran Agrarian Reform Cooperatives
FENACH	National Federation of Honduran Peasants
FENAGH	National Federation of Farmers and Cattlemen
FINATA	National Financial Institution for Agricultural Lands
FMLN	Farabundo Martí National Liberation Front
FSLN	Sandinista National Liberation Front
GDP	gross domestic product
GNP	gross national product
IMF	International Monetary Fund
INA	National Agrarian Institute
IRCA	International Railways of Central America
ISTA	Salvadoran Institute of Agrarian Transformation
LAAD	Latin American Agribusiness Development Corporation
MNR	National Revolutionary Movement
MRP-Ixim	Revolutionary Movement of the People
NAFTA	North American Free Trade Agreement
NTAEs	nontraditional agricultural exports
NTXs	nontraditional exports
OAS	Organization of American States
ORDEN	Nationalist Democratic Organization
ORIT	Inter-American Regional Organization of Labor
ORPA	Organization of People in Arms
PAN	National Nutritional Plan
PCN	National Conciliation Party
PDC	Christian Democratic Party
PGT	Guatemalan Workers' Party
PLN	National Liberation Party
UCS	Salvadoran Communal Union
UNAG	National Union of Farmers and Ranchers
UNC	National Peasant Union
UNO	National Opposition Union, United Nicaraguan Opposition
UPA	National Union of Small Agriculturists
UPANIC	Union of Nicaraguan Agricultural Producers
URNG	National Guatemalan Revolutionary Unity
USAID	U.S. Agency for International Development
UTC	Union of Rural Workers

Preface to Second Edition

There have been major changes in Central America since the late 1980s, many of them for the good. When I wrote the first edition of this book, El Salvador, Guatemala, and Nicaragua were engulfed in civil conflicts, tragic upheavals that claimed the lives of over 200,000 people and disrupted the lives of millions of others. Not only has each of these conflicts ended, but some significant efforts at reconciliation also have been undertaken. The challenges, of course, remain substantial. But there is more cause for hope in the region now than often was the case in the past.

Given the extent of the changes in the years since the first edition appeared, this volume is necessarily a significant revision. Furthermore, during this time scholarship on the region has blossomed. I have attempted to learn as much as I could from this literature and to incorporate it here. The scope of this work is very broad, covering not just five countries but issues (and their separate literatures) that range from rural development to export development models to popular mobilization to public policy. I have attempted to strengthen my arguments in each of these areas, focusing on two in particular. First, I challenge not the agro-export model itself but rather the mistaken confidence in this model as the answer to mass poverty in highly unequal societies. Second, I do not claim a direct link between agrarian transformation and political conflict but instead see their connection as highly conditioned by political factors, especially the role of outside agents and the response of the state.

In taking on the challenge of this new edition, I have benefited from much encouragement, not just from students and other friends but also from colleagues previously unknown to me. To each of you my great gratitude. I am also most grateful to Sherry Cardwell for her outstanding work on the tables and figures. The following individuals took time from their own busy schedules and critiqued at least one chapter for me, gaining my substantial appreciation: Gordon Bowen, Alfred Cuzán, Charles Davis, Roland Ebel, Mark Everingham, Robert Gottfried, Yasmeen Mohiuddin, Tommie Sue Montgomery, Donald Schulz, Kenneth Sharpe, Rose Spalding, and Scott Wilson. In addition, I have learned much from Sidney Tarrow that has strengthened my analysis. Students in my seminar on contemporary Central America gave a big boost to this project; many thanks especially to Jennifer Hamilton as well as to Chris Cairns, Maggie Giel, Charles Hodgkins, Ryan McConnell, Heather Manning, Wilbur Matthews, Jeff Peters, and Joe Sumpter. A number of trips to rural Costa Rica deepened my understanding of the issues I deal with in this book, particularly because of the interactions with my traveling companions Robert Gottfried and William Davis. My appreciation also to the University of the South for its financial support for these trips and to the National Endowment for the Humanities for a summer stipend and a summer seminar. Everyone at Westview Press has been most supportive and understanding; my thanks to each of them, especially Alice Colwell for her wonderful copyediting.

Finally, I offer this edition in appreciation of all the people who have heightened my awareness of what it means to ensure that "the children get fed first," specifically and generally, and to all of the people who work to restructure societies in accordance with this principle.

And a reminder to us all: Ideology can be a useful guide for social criticism, but worldviews, be they of the right or the left, are dangerous models for public policy when they trick policymakers into relying on concepts in their heads, which are infinitely malleable, instead of people's experiences, which are constrained by infinite uniqueness.

Charles D. Brockett

Preface to First Edition

This study represents the confluence of two previously separate projects. The first concerns the political crisis that has engulfed Central America since—to pick a somewhat arbitrary starting point—the beginning of the end for the Somoza dynasty in Nicaragua in the late 1970s. The second is the tragic persistence of hunger generally, and in Central America specifically.

Eventually, I came to realize that these were different starting points leading me to the same story: a series of socioeconomic transformations occurring over the course of centuries that have advantaged some groups but that have created and perpetuated the disadvantage of others. This book is not intended to tell all of that story; instead, its focus is on the aspects concerned with rural life. Central American societies are still primarily rural, and they were substantially so in the not-so-distant past. The changes that have occurred in the region's rural areas are not only central to understanding the causes of widespread hunger and malnutrition; they also are fundamental to comprehending the politics of the last few decades, including revolution, civil war, reformism, and repression.

Students of Latin American politics are necessarily led to appreciate how closely political life is connected to its socioeconomic context and to realize the importance of viewing politics from a historical perspective. Sadly, much of the North American discussion of contemporary Central America has not been enlightened by these perspectives, especially when its subjects are the causes of the region's conflicts or possible solutions to them. This work is presented in the hope of underscoring the importance of perceiving Central America in light of its own history, especially the development of its fundamental socioeconomic structures. It is offered with the conviction that a sensitivity to this history is necessary, if not sufficient, for the achievement to solutions that facilitate the realization of peace and justice.

Although my training is as a political scientist, this study makes extensive use of the works of anthropologists, economists, historians, and sociologists. Considerable effort has been made to integrate the vocabularies of a number of disparate disciplines, fields, and schools of thought into one language intelligible to all, including undergraduates. Similarly, I have attempted to write a theoretically informed work—and one that offers its own theoretical contributions—without becoming diverted by issues and debates tangential to my primary objectives.

This is a work of synthesis. I have been impressed by the quantity and quality of field studies, published and unpublished, available on particular aspects of Central American life. At the same time, I have been disappointed by the lack of good works of interdisciplinary synthesis, on individual countries and especially for the region as a whole. Because this is a work of synthesis, my debts are substantial. As the reference section indicates, I have made use of a great number of studies by both Central American and North American scholars. A study such as this one is dependent on the quality of libraries and the helpfulness of librarians. During separate summers of research, I developed significant debts to the staffs at the following institutions: the University of North Carolina at Chapel Hill; the University of Denver; and, at the University of Wisconsin at Madison, the Land Tenure Center, the main library, and the agricultural library. Research on a more limited basis was undertaken at the libraries of Duke University, the University of Tennessee at Knoxville, and Vanderbilt University. The crucial financial support for my summer research ventures was provided by several grants from the University of the South Faculty Research Fund.

My debt to Robert Trudeau is substantial. His encouragement and example over many years were critical to my decision to undertake this effort, and his suggestions on the organization of Part 1 were almost all incorporated, with a great improvement as the result. Robin Gottfried also offered useful advice for portions of the manuscript. Gilbert Merkx, the editor of this series, provided many good suggestions that helped me to produce a more coherent volume. Laura de la Torre Bueno's superb copyediting eliminated many errors and helped to add some grace to my prose. Earlier versions of parts of this study were presented as papers at professional meetings and published in academic journals. My understanding and treatment of the issues discussed here have been substantially strengthened by the comments of a number of panelists and reviewers; to them I again express my gratitude. I am pleased to distribute credit widely but do accept full responsibility for any of this work's shortcomings.

This book is dedicated to my children, Aaron and Kate. Their love, confidence, and support have inspired and sustained me throughout the project.

C.D.B.

Chapter One

Introduction: Agrarian Transformation and Political Conflict

The extraordinary concentration of landownership and the entrenched position of a small but powerful land-based elite long have been regarded by both reformers and revolutionaries in Central America as primary causes of the impoverishment of the rural population and as fundamental obstacles to the sustained, just development of their societies. Agrarian issues such as land use and distribution have consequently been central to the platforms of progressive movements and to their policies when they are in power and even to their survival. For example, agrarian reform programs and proposals were major catalysts of the overthrow of progressive governments in Guatemala in 1954 and Honduras in 1963. Contrasting agrarian reform programs were at the heart of the different developmental models pursued in the 1980s by the governments of El Salvador and Nicaragua. More recently, land issues have been among the most intractable in the 1990s as national reconciliation is pursued through peace processes in these two countries, as well as Guatemala.

Conservative groups in Central America also have been preoccupied with agrarian issues. Since the days when the region was a Spanish colony, the profit-generating sector of the economy has been oriented toward the export of agricultural commodities. Whether in the nineteenth century or in the post–World War II period, most conservatives have favored the expansion of agricultural exports as the preferred model of economic development, as have other groups, especially when they have had direct interests in this expansion themselves (for example, as landowners or exporters). Historically, elites attracted to this agro-export development model have been concerned with securing sufficient land

and labor to implement the model successfully. Until recent decades they were invariably able to utilize public power to achieve their goals.

For their part, the rural majority have seldom been in a position to determine development policy; instead, they have been the subjects of policy and, too often, its victims. Particularly during those periods when export agriculture expanded rapidly, peasants have been thrown into unequal competition against more powerful interests for control of fertile land. They were even coerced at times into laboring for those interests. Peasants have resisted their dispossession and subjugation across the centuries, but ultimately with little success. During the 1970s and 1980s, conflict and resistance intensified, above all in Guatemala, El Salvador, and Nicaragua. In addition, the peasant cause was embraced by armed revolutionaries, who found support from some politicized peasants. As a result, government counterinsurgency programs targeted innocent peasants, a form of repression that grew especially ferocious in Guatemala and El Salvador.

Agrarian structures, issues, and conflicts, then, are central to understanding contemporary Central America. This study divides the pursuit of such an understanding into two parts. Part 1 discusses the succession of transformations that created contemporary agrarian society and evaluates their impact on the lives of the rural population. Part 2 examines in separate country chapters the political response of peasants, political movements, and governments to postwar agrarian change.

This book begins on the regionwide level and becomes more specific to individual countries as it proceeds. During the colonial period, what are now the countries of Costa Rica, El Salvador, Guatemala, Honduras, and Nicaragua were unified under an administrative structure headquartered in Guatemala. Many of the central political conflicts of the nineteenth century were generated by contradictory impulses toward national autonomy and regional unity. Because of their small sizes and therefore proximity, the Central American countries have been subjected to many similar influences. Discussion at the regional level often will be most fitting for Part 1, but care will be taken to distinguish country-specific patterns where appropriate. Part 2 has a more explicitly political focus; since variations among countries are more prominent here, the discussion is organized by country. Several manifestations of regional characteristics, including both similarities and differences among countries, are provided in Table 1.1, which indicates some of the region's demographic trends from 1960 to 1994.

Agrarian Transformation

The primary focus of Part 1 is the transformation that occurred in rural Central America after World War II as a result of the rapid spread of commercial, especially export, agriculture. Although the region had produced

TABLE 1.1   Demographic Profile

	Population[a]		Rural Population[b]		Infant Mortality[c]	
	1960	*1994*	*1960*	*1994*	*1960*	*1994*
Costa Rica	1.2	3.3	63	51	85	13
El Salvador	2.6	5.5	62	55	130	41
Guatemala	4.0	10.3	68	59	125	45
Honduras	1.9	5.5	77	57	145	40
Nicaragua	1.5	4.0	60	38	141	48

[a]In millions.
[b]As percentage of total population.
[c]Infant deaths in first year per thousand live births.
SOURCE: UNDP 1997:166, 192, 194.

for international markets since the colonial period, before the mid-twentieth century most peasants[1] toiled for their own subsistence largely outside of the market economy. They seldom purchased agricultural inputs (such as seeds or fertilizer) or produced more than at most a minimal amount for commercial markets. Until recently, Central American agriculture was accurately characterized as dualistic: Multitudes of peasants worked small plots, essentially for their own consumption, alongside large, often huge, estates that produced for consumption in urban centers and overseas. Outside of the banana enclaves owned by foreign enterprises, most of these large haciendas operated under neofeudal conditions, using both land and labor inefficiently.

As a result of numerous interrelated changes, such as the opening of new international markets, technological innovations, and the increased availability of credit, traditional agricultural structures and practices have altered substantially in recent decades, as Chapter 3 details. Haciendas became commercial farms as new incentives encouraged established landowners and new investors to pursue opportunities for financial gain. Sharecroppers were replaced by wage laborers, whereas large commercial enterprises devoted to such export commodities as cotton, sugar, beef, and more recently other fruits and vegetables such as melons and snow peas spread throughout the countryside. Similarly, small and medium-sized landholdings producing for urban markets became more commonplace. The market economy, then, has penetrated rural society. Through this commercialization of agriculture, the share of the region's land, farms, and production that is devoted to commercial sales rose dramatically.[2]

When this contemporary agrarian transformation is placed in a historical perspective, it is clear that it is but the latest in a series of similar agrarian changes that extend all the way back to the Spanish conquest of the sixteenth century. Across the centuries, the results of the agro-export development model have been much less than its promise, as Chapters 2 and 4 demonstrate. As often as they have invested their profits in developmental enterprises, elites have used them for the purchase of luxury goods imported from industrial countries. Sometimes the profits have been returned even more directly to the affluent trading partners, either because Central American elites protected their gains in foreign banks or because the production and export of a crop was controlled by First World companies to begin with. Furthermore, the expansion of export agriculture often has had a direct, negative effect on the lives of rural people. From the colonial expansion of cacao and indigo exports to the coffee boom of the nineteenth and early twentieth centuries and on to the spread of commercial agriculture after World War II, peasants have lost their land to more powerful interests that have wanted it for export production. Systems of domination have been created to coerce labor from peasants so that the export crops could be produced. When land and autonomy have been lost, domestic food production usually has suffered, resulting in an inadequate food supply for the rural poor. Rather than bringing progress for all sectors of society, then, the expansion of export agriculture in Central America has resulted for many rural people in an adverse and often devastating disruption of their lives.

Part 1 ends with an evaluation of the agro-export development model in Central America. A fairly extensive literature has documented that in situations of great inequality the promotion of commercial agriculture through the adoption of modern productive technology exacerbates that inequality.[3] Similar concerns have been raised about the economic and social consequences of the agro-export development model, although the issues are complex given the export-based successes of East Asian countries such as South Korea and Taiwan.[4] Upon considering this evidence, Part 1 concludes by challenging the viability of the agro-export development model for countries with substantial rural inequality and underdeveloped domestic markets.

Central America entered the postwar period with most of its population living in terrible poverty and with the possibilities for improvement in the quality of life constrained by pronounced inequalities in social structures. Although the agrarian transformation of the following decades provided new alternatives and promises for many Central Americans, it actually diminished economic security for many others. As a result, substantial pressures developed on governments in the region to address the needs of millions of desperate people.

Political Conflict

The reaction of rural people to the impact of the postwar agrarian transformation on their lives has taken many forms, from passivity to migration to political activity. Many of those who benefited from these changes have organized in order to defend and advance their interests. These groups include not only large producers but also farmers with medium and small commercial operations. Many others, largely peasants with insufficient land or none, experienced serious threats to their economic security, creating the motivation for a significant degree of grassroots political activity.

A substantial body of literature exists concerning the sources of peasant passivity, politicization, and mobilization.[5] In Part 2 I use the following model, abstracted from this scholarship, to guide the analysis of peasant mobilization and demobilization in each of the Central American countries. Peasants in this region, like peasants virtually everywhere, traditionally were politically passive, although they certainly did not lack for grievances. As Brown (1971) has pointed out, "There is probably enough despair, anger, perceived relative deprivation and 'consciousness' to start an uprising in most any traditional rural community in Latin America on any given day" (p. 194). Self-assertion is dangerous, however, for those with little power, wealth, or protection. This reality is well captured by Huizer's (1972) concept of a "culture of repression."[6] Consequently, successful peasant mobilization requires, at a minimum, two changes in social relations. First, traditional patronage relationships must be weakened, for they are the personalized manifestation of peasants' subordination within the status quo. Second, new ties of solidarity must be forged among the peasants themselves.

There have been two major agents of such changes in social relations: economic transformations and outside organizers. The commercialization of agriculture has diminished economic security for many rural people while eroding traditional patronage relationships. As a consequence, it increases the incentives for mobilization while reducing one of its major constraints. To the extent that the commercialization of agriculture transforms individualistic small landholders into wage-earning farm laborers working in teams, it also facilitates rural organizing. Yet at the same time, some other peasants manage to benefit from the spread of commercial agriculture. Their gain in economic security can reduce their vulnerability to traditional elites and patrons and foster a desire for enhanced roles in society. Under certain conditions, these newly secure peasants join their economically insecure counterparts as forces for change.

Significant peasant mobilization, though, is seldom self-generated. Outside organizers, including religious workers, union organizers, revolutionary guerrillas, political party activists, and development workers, have been important to the political changes of recent decades in the Central American countryside, as seen in the country chapters of Part 2. Such organizers help to break down the domination of traditional patrons by offering alternative sources of economic assistance and protection. They are able to promote peasant mobilization not only through their organizational expertise but also because with their resources they can facilitate the transformation of attitudes from the powerlessness manifested by isolated individuals to the solidarity and strength that are made possible with collective action.

The actual form that peasants' activity will take rests of course on a number of variables. Whether they will organize peaceful marches, initiate land seizures, support insurgents, or become revolutionaries depends in part on internal factors such as the depth and scope of their discontent, the level of their organization, and their perception of the legitimacy of the regime and system. Equally important are external conditions, especially the response of government and private elites to peasant mobilization. In Part 2 I give considerable attention to the agrarian policies of the five Central American governments. Responses have ranged from mild distributive policies such as land colonization programs to major redistributive actions such as extensive land expropriations and division. Tragically, though, the government response in Central American too often has been a violent one.

Several attempts at agrarian reform have been made in Central America during the postwar period, but there have been great variations among them, especially in the scope and seriousness of intent.[7] I have left my conception of agrarian reform broad and loose in order to encompass these diverse approaches.[8] Some reforms have envisioned major alterations in tenure relations, whereas others have required little disruption in prevailing structures; some have been central to the purposes of committed popular governments, whereas others appear to have been primarily symbolic actions intended to pacify a restive peasantry.

Through this diversity, three general patterns emerge. In Guatemala a substantial reform effort in 1944–1954 was followed by counterreform and repression—a repression that reached extraordinary levels in the late 1970s and early 1980s. Second, Nicaragua and El Salvador shared the pattern of elite obstruction of agrarian reform up to the end of the 1970s. Hated tyrants were overthrown in both countries in 1979, transforming not only domestic political life but also regional politics. The Nicaraguan insurgency, nurtured in rural areas, regarded agrarian issues as fundamental. Once in power, the Sandinista government made agrarian reform central to its program for the transformation of society. Similarly, the agrarian reform initiated in El Salvador in 1980 had far-reaching consequences. The 1980s were dominated by civil conflicts in both countries, as in Guatemala. The results were catastrophic for the three: over 200,000 dead, millions displaced, economies battered, and societies disrupted. Fortunately, peace processes have prevailed in each in the 1990s. Finally, a third pattern applies to Honduras and Costa Rica, which have pursued intermittent, mild reforms over more than three decades but with very different results.

This study includes no separate chapter on international influences. The intent is not to minimize their role; on the contrary, the impact of foreign influences is a major topic throughout these chapters. Central America has been tied to the international economic system through agricultural exports since the early colonial period. To a significant extent, Part 1 tells the story of the increasing impact of this connection up to the present time. Other aspects of the internationalization of Central American agriculture are also examined in depth, such as the role of foreign actors in promoting the agrarian transformation of the contemporary period. Part 2 documents the critical role that the United States has played in agrarian politics in Central America in recent decades, from promoting certain peasant organizations and guiding and financing some agrarian reform programs to working to destroy others.

By the end of this study, it should be clear that no lasting stability can be created in Central America without significant change in the social structures that have perpetuated poverty and suffering for much of the region's rural population. Given the strength of these structures and of the elites who are advantaged by them, such change requires major popular mobilization as well as committed governments. It also should be clear, however, that in Central America such movements and governments frequently have encountered the stiff resistance of the United States. Accordingly, the last chapter and the study conclude with a discussion of the role and interests of the United States in Central America.

Notes

1. I employ the terms "peasant" and "peasantry" loosely in this study, generally conforming to the authoritative definition in the Latin American context provided by Landsberger and Hewitt (1970) of the peasant as "any rural cultivator who is low in economic and political status" (p. 560). This usage does not assume any particular set of values or agricultural practices. As appropriate, I use more descriptive terms, such as "rural people," "small farmer," "wage earner," "sharecropper," "plantation worker," and so on. For a good description of traditional peasant agricultural practices in Central America prior to World War II, see Tax (1963:47–49); for various types of agricultural practices in the 1950s at several locations in the region, see Dozier (1958).

2. The commercialization of agriculture is of course part of the larger process of the capitalist transformation of agriculture, or the development of agrarian capitalism. This transformation involves not only penetration by the market economy and the profit motive but also the restructuring of class relations as, for example, sharecroppers are replaced by wage laborers (a process often referred to as the

"proletarianization of the peasantry"). Because this study focuses on the first set of transformations but gives only limited attention to the second, "the commercialization of agriculture" is a more accurate characterization of the transformation under examination. The expansion of export agriculture obviously is generated by the profit motive, but it can occur with little disturbance to precapitalist class relations (as will become clear in Chapter 2). For good discussions of the theoretical issues involved in the capitalist transformation of agriculture in Latin America, see Arroyo (1978), Duncan and Rutledge (1977), and de Janvry (1981).

3. On the relationship between rural inequality and capitalist modernization, see Barkin (1982), von Braun and Kennedy (1994), Carter and Barham (1996), Feder (1977), Griffin (1978), Hewitt de Alacantara (1973–1974, 1976), de Janvry (1981), Kay (1995), Pearse (1980), and Tomich et al. (1995).

4. For discussions of the agro-export development model, see Adams and Behrman (1982), Barham et al. (1992), Bulmer-Thomas (1987, 1994), Carter et al. (1996), Conroy et al. (1996), Goldberg (1981), Hillman (1981), Kent (1984), Lappé and Collins (1978), Paus (1988), Payer (1975), Pelupessy (1991), and Thrupp (1995).

5. Especially helpful for this study have been the following: Migdal (1974), Paige (1975), Popkin (1979), Scott (1976, 1985, 1990), Singelmann (1981), and White (1977); also see Anderson (1994), Booth and Seligson (1979), Brown (1971), and Huizer (1972). For reviews of some of this literature, see Colburn (1982) and Skocpol (1982); for reviews combined with case studies of Guatemala and Peru, respectively, see Paige (1983) and McClintock (1984). For more thorough elaborations of models similar to the one sketched here, see Brockett (1991b) and Tilly (1978).

6. Huizer (1972:x, 19, 27, 52–61); also see Scott (1985:317–345).

7. Among the many comparative studies of agrarian reform that include at least some Latin American cases, see Alexander (1974), Barraclough (1973), Dorner (1971, 1992), Ghose (1983), Grindle (1986), King (1977), Meyer (1989), Tai (1974), Thiesenhusen (1989, 1995), and Tuma (1965). Other useful studies of agrarian reform include Barraclough (1970), Berry and Cline (1979), Dorner (1972), El-Ghonemy (1990), Herring (1983), Jacoby (1971), de Janvry (1981), Sobhan (1993), and Smith (1965).

8. Some argue that agrarian reform is meaningful only when it involves significant land redistribution and the provision of adequate supportive services, such as technical assistance and credit. Others, especially government officials in the region and in the United States, have found value in more limited programs, such as colonization and land titling. In order to be inclusive, agrarian reform is understood in this study to mean changes brought about by public policy in land distribution and/or land tenure relations. Such changes will vary from the narrowly distributive to the broadly redistributive.

Part One

Agrarian Transformation

Chapter Two

Agrarian Transformation Before 1950

The fundamental cause of the current crisis in Central America is the system of domination elites established over the centuries in order to pursue their material goals.[1] The objectives of Part 1 are to outline the essential features of the historical development of this repressive social order and to assess its human consequences. The central organizing concept is that of an agrarian transformation, that is, a major change in the organization of agrarian society.[2] The results of the transformations that occurred before 1950 limit present possibilities; they are important determinants of the demands faced by contemporary society, the resources available for meeting those demands, and the distribution of political power that restricts possible solutions.

This chapter begins with brief descriptions of indigenous Central American society, the devastating impact of the conquest, and the creation of the colonial agrarian system. Following national independence in the early nineteenth century, socioeconomic change continued at a slow pace until the Liberal reforms and the coffee boom of the second half of the century, both of which I give substantial attention. The final topic of this chapter is the coming of the great banana companies and the creation of banana enclaves around the beginning of the twentieth century. A major purpose is to assess the impact of the agrarian transformations of each period on the lives of rural people.

The objectives of development-oriented Central American elites have been constrained across the centuries by the availability of markets, land, and labor. Elites often have sought their wealth through the development of primary—usually agricultural—exports. Adequate foreign markets, though, have been a recurrent problem for four centuries. Sufficient land

and labor also have been problematic, but over these factors elites have had more control. Central to most of the transformations of the past has been the expropriation of land and labor from the peasantry in order that elites might pursue their objectives. Although the implementation of the agro-export development model in Central America has brought great wealth to some, for much of the peasantry it has represented the loss of land, food supply, and autonomy.

Pre-Columbian Central America

Pre-Columbian Central America was a meeting and mixing ground for indigenous peoples from Mexico, the Caribbean, and South America.[3] As a result of migration, wars of conquest, and trade, many different linguistic and cultural groups had been created and had settled in the area. These various indigenous groups are usually divided into two types: those of the more complex Meso-American culture and those of the less advanced groups of South American ancestry. The former occupied the more hospitable areas of what is now Guatemala[4] and the western portion of Honduras, as well as the Pacific coast of Nicaragua and northern Costa Rica. The remainder of Central America is more tropical and less conducive to settled agricultural communities. Although inhabitants of these latter regions did raise some crops, especially corn and tubers, they were just as likely to pursue fishing, hunting, and gathering activities. Their descendants can still be found today in Caribbean Nicaragua and the proximate part of Honduras. Historically isolated from the rest of their countries and living in remote, "undesirable" surroundings, they continue to resist incorporation into national life. The contemporary manifestation of this tension is the recent conflict between the Sandinista government and the Miskito Indians.

Before the conquest, northern Central America had a substantial population living in well-developed, complex societies. Many of its inhabitants were descendants of the great Mayan civilization, whose core was in the lowlands of the Petén region of northern Guatemala, in western Honduras, and on the Yucatan Peninsula. The accomplishments of this civilization in science and mathematics, art and architecture, and commerce and construction often rivaled those of contemporary Europe. Although it had been in a long decline before the conquest, its influence remained throughout the area.

As civilizations developed and declined in the Mexican plateau, Indians migrated into Central America from the north, usually intermixing with the indigenous populations they subjugated. One notable example was a group that arrived in the Guatemalan highlands about 1250, mixed with the local population, and adopted the local language by which they became known. The Quiché Empire then expanded through conquest until it reached its peak two centuries later with a total population of about 1 million people.

The Quiché and similar groups were organized into stratified societies. Nobles lived in cities supported by the agricultural production of vassals. Production techniques were often relatively advanced; for example, cacao groves of thousands of trees requiring careful attention were cultivated along the Pacific coast. A substantial commerce was maintained within the empire as well as with other regions. The Quiché overextended their empire, however. After 1450, subject tribes were in revolt, and in the years leading up to the Spanish invasion the Quiché were involved in a number of protracted wars.

Tribal divisions and warfare were only some of the factors that facilitated the Spanish conquest of Central America. Lacking immunity to many potentially lethal European diseases, the indigenous population was often weakened, physically and psychologically, by infections that invaded in advance of their European carriers. Pedro de Alvarado, "infamous for his cruelty and inhuman treatment of his foes" (Morley and Brainerd 1983:576), entered the region from the north in 1524, as did Pedrarias Dávila a few years earlier from the south. They quickly subjugated the area in behalf of the Spanish Crown and their own personal fortunes.

The Impact of the Conquest

It is now generally acknowledged that in 1492 the population of the Americas was greater than that of Europe and Russia combined.[5] The 5 million or so inhabitants of Central America, however, were quickly reduced in numbers by a series of epidemics that swept the region throughout the colonial period. The indigenous population of the Caribbean lowlands of Guatemala and Honduras soon disappeared, as did that of Costa Rica. The Indians of Honduras and Nicaragua (and to a lesser extent those of El Salvador and Guatemala) were further decimated by a second horror: slavery. Able-bodied adults were captured and exported to labor in Panama and Peru. When the slave trade ended by 1550, "there were simply no Indians left to send" in Nicaragua and Honduras (MacLeod 1973:54); as many as 200 to 500,000 Indian slaves might have been shipped out of Nicaragua alone. The most recent scholarship suggests that the populations of Nicaragua, Honduras, and along the Pacific coast of Guatemala were cut to about one-twentieth of their preconquest numbers. Although the decimation was less in the Guatemalan highlands, the rates were still extraordinarily high: Anywhere from four-fifths to seven-eighths of the population disappeared. Several hundreds of years later, on the eve of independence, the population of Central America in the early nineteenth century was still only about one-fifth of its size at the time of the conquest.[6]

Where indigenous communities were more advanced and productive, most notably in Guatemala, the conquerors superimposed themselves at the top of the existing social structure, redirecting tribute into their own hands. The direct labor of Indians was also obtained through the *encomienda* system (from *encomendar,* "to entrust"). Large numbers of Indians were "entrusted" to conquerors in reward for their services and in order that they might be "civilized" and Christianized. The usual result was virtual slavery.

The tragedy the indigenous peoples of Central America suffered was of terrible proportions. Whole villages disappeared. In those that survived, much of the remaining population was enfeebled and incapable of producing an adequate food supply. Consequently, to the horrors of conquest, enslavement, and disease was added famine. The plight of the Indians provoked many in the clergy and Spanish Crown to action. Although impossible to enforce effectively, beginning with the New Laws of 1542 slavery was prohibited and the use of the *encomienda* was restricted. Theoretically, Indians became free vassals; not surprisingly, however, they were reluctant to sell their labor to the Spaniards. The colonists accordingly continued to rely on systems of domination to ensure for themselves an adequate cheap labor supply. Especially important to that end were the concentration of villages and the *repartimiento.*

Because of the decimation of the indigenous population and the ever present threat of rebellion, some social restructuring was thought necessary in order to maintain both order and access to sufficient labor after the first few decades following the conquest. Better access to the indigenous population would also facilitate the religious mission of the clergy. Crucial to the accomplishment of these objectives was the resettlement of about one-half of the Indians remaining in Guatemala into centralized villages during the 1540s. More than 400 years later and for many of the same reasons, descendants of these Mayas would once again be subjected to a similar resettlement program in Guatemala, as discussed in Chapter 5.

The *repartimiento* (from *repartir,* "to divide up") provided another effective way to guarantee a labor supply. Each indigenous village was to fill a labor quota, generally one-quarter of the men between sixteen and sixty in the village each week. In practice, however, the demand was often greater in both numbers and duration. The conquered were assigned to work not only in religious and public institutions but also for private individuals, sometimes at long distances from their homes. Consequently, their ability to produce subsistence for their own families was diminished, heightening their susceptibility to the periodic epidemics. The travails of the indigenous Central Americans under this system, which continued to the end of the colonial period, are well portrayed in the account of a contemporary observer:

> They go to the farms and other places of work, where they are made to toil from dawn to dusk in the raw cold of morning and afternoon, in wind and storm, without other food than the rotten or dried-out tortillas, and even of this they have not enough. They sleep on the ground in the open air, naked, without shelter. Even if they wish to buy food with their pitiful wages they could not, for they are not paid until they are laid off. . . .
>
> So the Indian returns home worn out from his toil, minus his pay and his mantle, not to speak of the food that he brought with him. He returns home famished, unhappy, distraught, and shattered in health. For these reasons pestilence always rages among the Indians. . . . The Indians will all die out very quickly if they do not obtain relief from these intolerable conditions. (quoted in Sherman 1979:207)

The Search for Exports

The primary motive governing the creation of the Spanish colony in Central America was the enrichment of the Crown, colonists, and colonial administrators.[7] In the early years, this was achieved through what MacLeod (1973:63) aptly terms "looting," that is, the expropriation of slaves and surface gold. Once these resources were exhausted, however, new sources of wealth had to be discovered. Many commodities were tried, but with little gain.

The cacao trade was the first to be developed successfully, in part because it was just a few steps beyond looting. Large cacao orchards were maintained by the indigenous peoples on both coasts before the conquest. Cacao beans were used for money and in religious rituals, and the beverage produced from them was an aristocratic drink. Following the conquest, Central America continued to supply cacao to Mexican Indians. Chocolate caught on in Europe, and a demand was created for the region's first transatlantic agricultural export. This demand was met in Central America by production primarily along the Pacific coast extending from north of present-day Guatemala down to western El Salvador.

Outside of the Salvadoran region, the cacao plantations were taken over by the Spaniards, with Indians forced to provide the labor. Weakened by the demanding work, they were vulnerable to disease and died in great numbers. The colonists in their greed compounded the problem by forcing the conversion of too much land to cacao production. Lacking land and time, the subjugated Indians were unable to raise sufficient food; a serious famine resulted in 1570. To meet their labor needs, the colonists then brought indigenous people down from the highlands to work on the plantations. Not only did the new arrivals experience the same problems as their predecessors, but their stress was aggravated by the difficulty of adjusting to a severely different climate. The highland Indians apparently died as fast as they could be replaced.

In El Salvador the effects were similar, though the indigenous villages retained ownership of their orchards, some of which numbered up to 15,000 trees. The colonists obtained their wealth through unfair trade practices and tribute demands. Initially the Salvadoran Indians enjoyed some benefits from the cacao boom; but as time passed they, too, suffered from disease and famine, and their production fell as a result of depopulation. Nonetheless, these villages were able to preserve their relative independence, making the southwestern part of El Salvador the one place in that country where an indigenous culture persisted. Browning (1971:65) accords this situation substantial significance in explaining why Salvadoran peasant rebellions of the late nineteenth century and the major uprising of 1932 (see Chapter 6) were centered in this region.

By the close of the sixteenth century, the cacao boom had ended. High death rates prevented the maintenance of an adequate labor supply. Cacao production required specialized knowledge, which was possessed not at all by the Spaniards and by fewer of the Indians as time passed. The indigenous people had little incentive to preserve or replenish healthy orchards. Essentially, then, the existing orchards were plundered rather than cultivated by the Spaniards. As the orchards were depleted, so was the soil. When cacao production arose elsewhere, the Central American colonists were therefore unequal to that competition.

As Central America's cacao boom turned into a bust, the search for alternative export crops accelerated. The colonists tried various possibilities but centered their attention on a dye extracted from the leaves of the indigo plant. Despite enough suitable land to create a prosperous indigo industry, commercial hopes were constantly frustrated by both scarce labor and insufficient markets. Indigo production did not have the year-round labor requirement of cacao production, but for a few months the labor demands were heavy. Indigo planters relied on a variety of techniques to ensure an adequate labor supply, but it was a constant challenge because of both depopulation and colonial laws. Some regulations were general in scope, affecting all of colonial society in an effort to halt the most grievous exploitation of the Indians. Others were directed specifically at the indigo works because of the reputation they soon gained as death traps. For example, one priest wrote in 1636:

> I have seen large Indian villages . . . practically destroyed after indigo mills have been erected near to them. For most Indians that enter the mills will soon sicken as a result of the forced work and the effect of the piles of rotting indigo they make. . . . As most of these wretches have been forced to abandon their homes and plots of maize, many of their wives and children die also. (quoted in Browning 1971:73)

Regulations, however, could be ignored, and officials bribed. More intractable was the problem of markets. The early-seventeenth-century acceleration of indigo production along the Pacific coast from Nicaragua to Guatemala was stifled by 1630 because of the inability of Spain, then in economic decline, to stimulate a healthy trade. Since the beginning of its empire, Spain had attempted to prevent trade between its colonies and other countries. Consequently, when European demand for indigo increased at the end of the seventeenth century, direct Central American access to those markets was possible only through contraband trade, and even this alternative was hindered by inadequate transportation. Central American economic development did improve in the eighteenth century as the new Bourbon dynasty eased trade restrictions and rationalized colonial administration. The region (especially El Salvador and Guatemala) thus was better situated to take advantage of growing dye demand when European textile industrialization took off at midcentury. Indigo exports increased through much of the eighteenth century, only to decline again at the start of the new century in the face of international competition (e.g., India) and the disruptions caused by the Napoleonic Wars, the struggles for Latin American independence, and the conflicts of postindependence political consolidation.

Insufficient export development was not the only agricultural problem facing colonial society, nor even the most serious. As disease and famine depleted Indian numbers and the size of the Spanish population continued to climb, a meager food supply became an increasingly serious problem in the late sixteenth century. It was aggravated, of course, when the conquered inhabitants were forced to cultivate nonfood commodities. With this twin failure of the colonial economic system, many colonists were forced to leave the cities, some departing the region altogether but most taking to the countryside. It was at this time that the haciendas long so characteristic of the area first developed.

The expansion of the hacienda had both positive and negative ramifications for indigenous people. Up to that point they had been exploited for their labor, but they had confronted only minimal competition for their use of the land. Now, as colonists found urban life too expensive and turned to the countryside, Indians began to lose land to their conquerors. This loss was felt most seriously in those areas close to cities and trade routes and where the climate was most hospitable to the colonists. As Spanish penetration of these regions hastened Indian depopulation, they soon became ladino (non-Indian in culture) if not mestizo (racially mixed) in composition. Significant autonomy and continuity with the indigenous past, then, were retained by Indian peoples only in areas that were remote and/or inhospitable: in the tropical Caribbean lowlands from northeastern Honduras to Panama, in the high mountains of parts of Honduras, and most important in the western highlands of Guatemala.

Even in the highlands, the impact of the conquest and colonial structures was extensive through depopulation by death and enslavement and
through the enforced destruction of much of traditional culture. Furthermore, highland Indians were compelled to pay tribute to the Crown and
the local colonial governments; as late as 1748, over 80 percent of royal
revenues came from tribute (Wortman 1982:146). Some of the most seriously eroded and sterile soils in Guatemala today are located in the highlands. Where indigenous people were forced to pay their tribute in wool
products, the excessive demands led to the overgrazing of sheep, thereby
resulting not only in soil destruction but also in an insufficient food supply, even though the population was only one-half of that at the time of
the conquest (Veblen 1978).

Because village life left Indians vulnerable to oppressive tribute demands and the excesses of the *repartimiento*, the hacienda provided many
with an alternative—if not attractive, at least less burdensome. Hacienda
owners were often rich in land and sometimes in labor, once depopulation
reversed, but they usually lacked capital and markets. Until markets could
be found (a discovery that was centuries in coming for many), there was little incentive for efficient use of the land. As economic life stagnated in the
seventeenth century, many haciendas slipped into a semifeudal existence.

One exception to this pattern was Costa Rica, whose atypical characteristics today can be traced back in part to its unique colonial development.
Its indigenous population, less numerous than elsewhere in the region to
begin with, was largely exterminated by the pandemic of 1576–1581.[8]
Lacking a labor supply and any exploitable mineral wealth, as well as remote from the cities of the colonial administration, Costa Rica attracted
few colonists. Those who did settle in this area had to farm for themselves, usually on a subsistence basis. With few indigenous people to sub-
jugate or convert, neither did it attract much of a military or clerical presence, thereby escaping from the worst features of those systems of
domination that were widely instituted in the rest of the region. Consequently, Costa Rica's central plateau was slowly populated by the "yeo-
man farmer, independent, self-sufficient, and poor" (Seligson 1980a:7).

In summary, when the Spaniards conquered Central America, the region was rich in resources that they could exploit in order to materialize
their goals. Soon, however, the indigenous population was decimated by
disease, both because it lacked immunities and because of overwork, periodic famines, and the psychological impact of sudden subjugation. The
effect of the colonial agrarian transformation on the rural population,
then, was devastating, ranging from the widespread loss of land, culture,
and autonomy to death on an extraordinary scale. As a result, access to an
adequate labor supply was a constant preoccupation of rural elites
throughout the colonial period and continued as a major concern into the
twentieth century. The colonists came to the region not with the intention

of retiring to a sleepy pastoral life but with the goal of self-enrichment. The expansion of agricultural exports has always been limited, however, by the ability to produce and market on a competitive basis goods desired by others, especially people in the more developed countries.

Coffee and the Liberal Reforms

Central America gained its independence in 1823. Some aspects of life changed , but economic structures that had evolved over the previous 300 years remained intact.[9] Agricultural production continued to be primarily for self-consumption or domestic use. The major exports at the time and for the next few decades, although minor contributors to the overall economy, were the two dyes, indigo and cochineal (a red dye produced from insects that thrive on a particular type of cactus; it takes 70,000 insects to yield 1 pound of dye). Inadequate earners of foreign exchange even at their peak, these products could not compete with the new synthetic dyes developed in Europe at midcentury. Consequently, the search for new and better exports intensified. The result was the creation of a booming coffee economy that transformed the lives of many rural inhabitants, some for the better but many for the worse.

Coffee had received some governmental promotion during the colonial period, but inadequate transportation retarded its development as a trade item then and in the decades immediately following independence. Costa Rica, where export dye production had been proscribed during the colonial period, was the first to step up its production, which boomed when development of steamships and completion of the Panama Railway in 1855 facilitated transportation of coffee to growing European and North American markets. Impressed by the example and needing an alternative to cochineal, Guatemalans expanded their plantings, and coffee became their leading export by 1870. The revolution then hit El Salvador in that decade (as indigo had remained competitive a little longer than cochineal) and Nicaragua in the next; in Honduras export coffee has been largely a post–World War II development. These and other longitudinal and comparative trends are portrayed in Table 2.1, which gives coffee production figures for each country from 1885 to 1914 and coffee export figures from 1909 to 1945. The impact of the coffee boom was substantial everywhere in the region, though once again the Costa Rican experience needs to be differentiated from that of its neighbors.

Guatemala

The initial expansion of coffee growing in Guatemala was due to market stimulation without the support of the Conservative government, which was allied with the cochineal interests. This lack of support was a primary

TABLE 2.1   The Central American Coffee Boom

	Costa Rica	El Salvador	Guatemala	Honduras	Nicaragua
Coffee Production, 1885–1914[a]					
1885–1890	24.5	17.1	39.3	4.1	9.3
1890–1895	26.9	29.5	49.7	4.4	12.6
1895–1899	31.1	17.2	64.0	2.3	9.0
1900–1904	45.7	47.2	67.9	2.6	18.5
1905–1909	31.1	64.3	80.0	2.5	19.9
1910–1914	30.9	66.6	106.3	.9	18.1
Coffee Exports, 1909–1945[b]					
1909–1913	28.4	64.6	86.6	1.1	19.0
1914–1918	31.1	75.2	84.6	1.1	22.9
1919–1923	31.3	83.8	95.6	1.1	25.8
1924–1928	38.3	97.4	103.4	3.0	32.7
1929–1933	49.6	112.8	96.4	3.4	29.1
1934–1938	51.2	119.4	104.2	3.6	33.7
1939–1943	46.4	116.2	99.6	3.7	30.9
1944–1945	44.8	133.2	110.5	5.1	28.0

[a]Average annual production within each period, reported in millions of pounds. The coffee year is not equivalent to the calendar year; for convenience, years are listed here as, for example, 1885–1890 rather than 1884/1885–1889/1890.

[b]Average annual exports within each period, reported in millions of pounds.

SOURCE: Condensed from Torres Rivas 1971:283–287.

factor leading to the seizure of power in 1871 by the Liberals, the other leading party in the nineteenth century. The Liberal administration of Justo Rufino Barrios had been unsuccessfully anticipated earlier in the 1830s, during the Liberal presidency of Mariano Gálvez. Unlike Conservatives, the Liberals in Central America sought in the nineteenth century to create modern societies in place of the anachronistic structures of colonial society. The privileged position of the Catholic Church was to be destroyed and the isolation of the Indians ended. Reinforcing their anticlerical position were some 900 haciendas and sugar mills said to be owned by the church throughout Central America. Liberals tended to see Indians as an inferior race blocking the development of the nation. Under both Gálvez and Barrios, they tried to dilute the indigenous presence by encouraging European and North American immigration and by assimilating Indians into a free market system. Given Central America's marginal position in the world economy and their own espousal of the doctrine of comparative advantage, Liberals were strong believers in the expansion of agricultural exports as the best route to developing a prosperous society.

Gálvez acted too quickly, however, provoking not only a Conservative reaction but also a peasant rebellion that brought the Conservatives back to power for the next three decades. Peasants were left alone by the state during this period to a degree unmatched since the sixteenth century. Conditions were more conducive to the Liberal program in the 1870s, though, and Barrios was more politically astute. The new government undertook the direct promotion of coffee growing through financial incentives, infrastructure development, the dissemination of agricultural information, and land and labor reforms. The program was successful; coffee production and exports skyrocketed. The new coffee elite was enriched, and associated commercial interests and service providers benefited as well; much of the peasantry, however, lost once again.

Prime coffee-growing land is at moderate elevations, but most such land was already claimed in Guatemala by subsistence peasants (as it often was in the rest of the region). Consequently, Indians gradually lost much of their communal lands in areas coveted for coffee growing as land titling reforms were instituted to foster coffee growing and to promote and protect the European concept of private property. This notion was alien to the preconquest societies of Central America. Generally in these cultures, individual use of village property for family sustenance was frequent and access to such plots even inheritable; however, the land continued to belong to the community. From the earliest days of the colonial period, the state had promoted the titling of uncontested indigenous communal lands, sometimes to protect them from greedy colonists but also as the basis for the tribute payments that were a major source of the state's financial support. Some indigenous communities closer to the lines of colonial administration and in areas of growing land pressures availed themselves of this form of self-protection. But such titling was less likely in more remote areas.

Indian land tenure patterns grew more complex as time passed. Beyond its core holdings, a village might rent outlying land, even to ladino commercial farmers. Furthermore, many highland villages claimed lands in the Pacific piedmont that were used on a seasonal basis. The Liberal reforms of the late nineteenth century sometimes solidified Indian possession of the lands at the core of their villages, especially outside of the coffee regions, but at the expense of accelerating the long-standing processes by which they lost access to other traditional lands. Most vulnerable at that time were the good coffee-growing lands, but these private property reforms also provided the legal basis for parallel losses to growers of later commercial crops long into the twentieth century.

Even more critical to the dreams of the coffee growers was the labor of the Indians. The potential for coffee export expansion was great, but the limiting factor was the labor supply. Rather than providing the necessary financial and other incentives to attract workers (who in fact did not want to work for them), the growers depended on coercion. Initially, they turned to the *mandamiento* (an updated version of the colonial *repartimiento*), which had been little utilized in previous decades because of depressed economic activity. The legitimacy of such coerced Indian labor was reaffirmed by President Barrios in 1876, who stated that all development efforts would otherwise be doomed to failure because of the "deceit of the Indians" and negligence (quoted in Whetten 1961:119). This anachronistic quasi slavery, however, proved to be tough to defend in the face of growing criticism and was outlawed in 1894. It then returned, supposedly on a temporary basis, but actually continued into the 1920s, albeit at times in submerged form.

The *mandamiento* met the pressing needs of growers in the early period of the coffee boom, but as time progressed other methods to secure labor evolved, making the more archaic form less necessary. Indeed, a work-force of both resident and seasonal workers often was obtained from Indians who saw these forms of exploitation as a lesser evil compared to the forced work draft, especially since the *mandamiento* frequently was relied on to conscript labor for the most hazardous work. As an alternative to the *mandamiento*, labor could be secured through debt peonage. A wage advance in excess of the work that they were then credited for left Indians in bondage to the coffee *finca* (farm). There also were other methods for creating indebted workers; for example, as one observer pointed out, "It used to be customary during times of labor shortage to imprison large numbers of Indians for small offenses, especially for drunkenness, and to impose heavy fines. Obligadores [labor bosses] from some plantation would pay this fine . . . and the Indian was turned over to the plantation to work off the debt" (quoted in Dessaint 1962:339).

This system of labor extraction was regulated through a series of laws beginning in 1877 that required workers to labor for employers to whom they were indebted until the debt was paid. Upon their deaths, debts were even transferred to family members if personal property had been used as collateral. Particular victims of this system were poorer Indians, who had little or no land other than their communal lands. The appropriation of those lands left many of them helpless in the face of the determination of elites to guarantee an adequate labor supply. As one government official later admitted about a 1894 law, it kept the Indian in a "status similar to slavery" (quoted in Jones 1966:153). Nonetheless, growers still complained of labor shortages, which they believed could not be alleviated without compulsion.

A different form of labor coercion was created in 1934 as long-term debt labor was prohibited and replaced with a new vagrancy law with a much broader reach than its predecessors. To work is an obligation, that law stated, and the amount of work one had to provide depended upon the amount of land one owned (under the assumption that those with little or no land would be underemployed). Peasants were forced to provide their labor for 100 to 150 days a year to someone who would give them the "opportunity" to discharge their "debt to society." As Jones (1966) observes, the law's "main object was to shift the basis of regulation of Indian labor from the obligation of the laborer to work to pay his debts to an obligation to work whether he was in debt or not" (p. 162). As exploitive as this system was, it still represented an improvement for at least some: Wealthier Indians could avoid coerced labor, the work requirement could be met locally if opportunities were available, and its application applied to poor ladinos as well. This law in turn was abolished as one of the first targets of the progressive revolution of 1944.

The developmental model pursued in Guatemala effectively turned the countryside into a forced labor camp for much of the Indian population. Such a system of domination necessarily contaminates the rest of society, as it is inherently predisposed toward reliance on coercion as the preferred method of dealing with dissent and challenge. The following description of Guatemala in 1918, during the twenty-two-year rule of Manuel Estrada Cabrera, bears chilling resemblance to the Guatemala of six decades later:

> The administration firmly maintains its authority by means of a large standing army and police force, and promptly and mercilessly checks the slightest manifestation of popular dissatisfaction. An elaborate secret service attempts, with a large measure of success, to inform itself fully of everything which occurs in the Republic. Supposed enemies of the party in power are closely watched. . . . Persons who fall under suspicion are imprisoned or restricted in their liberty, or even mysteriously disappear. The ruthless execution of large numbers of persons, many of whom were probably innocent, have followed attempts to revolt or to assassinate the President. This reign of terror is approved by many influential natives and by the majority of the foreigners in the country on the ground that only a very strong government can prevent revolution and maintain order; and there is no doubt that the life and property of foreigners, at least, has been safer in Guatemala than in some of the other Central American countries. (Munro 1918:53–54)

El Salvador

Labor power was more readily available in El Salvador, which was the core zone for indigo production, had the highest population density in the region, and had become substantially ladino during the colonial period. There, too, though, labor shortages led to vagrancy laws following independence and constrained coffee production in the first decades of its development as an export crop. Later, labor accessibility increased, especially as the country's population almost tripled between 1878 and 1931. With the growing labor surplus, real wages at the turn of the century were lower than at midcentury. Accordingly, when government officials

encouraged coffee production after the mid-nineteenth century, their preoccupation was more land than labor—specifically, the coffee-growing
potential of the one-quarter of the national territory still held commu-
nally by Indians and either devoted to the production of basic food crops
or rented to commercial growers.

Ladinos had long coveted these lands out of a mix of Liberal ideology,
racism, and individual greed. Their ambitions had been checked, though,
by the power of indigenous communities, combined with the backing of the
Conservative government in Guatemala. The Liberal "revolution" in Guatemala changed the political context in El Salvador. The first Liberal attack
on communal lands in El Salvador was a decree in 1878 mandating that access to common lands was no longer a right and that private title to such
lands could be received upon the cultivation of specified (export) crops.
Many villages attempted to comply with the law, but they were hampered
by the greater capital requirements of coffee compared to those of other
crops. Development-minded elites were impatient, however, and by decrees in 1881 and 1882 all common lands were abolished. The Salvadoran
"land reform," then, was more far-reaching than in Guatemala and more
devastating for the indigenous population. Some small and medium-sized
farms did emerge through this transformation; primarily, though, the land
was consolidated into the hands of a few growers with holdings substantial
enough to make them the backbone of the small oligarchy that ruled El Salvador until recently—the fabled "fourteen families," actually seventy-five
families in fourteen groups. Peasants did resist; there were a number of up-
risings in the next few decades, but they were successfully repressed as the
Salvadoran state rapidly bolstered its repressive capability.

The expansion of coffee holdings continued through the next several
decades. The 1920s saw notable growth until coffee prices crashed along
with the world economy at the end of the decade. The impact of this conversion of land to coffee growing is well described in contemporary accounts. The following observation by a journalist concerns the Indians in
the southwestern part of the country, close to the cacao- and indigo-grow-
ing regions discussed earlier: "The conquest of territory by the coffee industry is alarming. It has already occupied all the high ground and is
now descending to the valleys, displacing maize, rice, and beans. It goes
in the manner of the conquistador, spreading hunger and misery, reducing the former proprietors to the worst conditions—woe to those who sell
out!" (quoted in Durham 1979:34).

Nicaragua

Except for its retarded development, the spread of coffee cultivation in
Nicaragua manifested most of the characteristics of its neighbors. In

Nicaragua more than in the other countries, coffee expansion was limited by poor transportation and civil wars. Even more problematic was the meddling of the United States and Great Britain in the country's affairs. The Liberal cause in Nicaragua was severely damaged by its association with the U.S. adventurer William Walker, who fought his way to the presidency in 1856. Following his forced departure the next year, the Liberals were out of power until 1893, when José Santos Zelaya established his rule. Once again, though, foreign interference led to a Liberal setback; the U.S. government was centrally involved in Zelaya's overthrow in 1909 and in subsequent efforts to keep his political heirs out of office. This active intervention by the United States in behalf of Conservatives was a critical factor in retarding the rise in Nicaragua of a modernizing agrarian bourgeoisie such as was occurring in Costa Rica, El Salvador, and Guatemala (Deere and Marchetti 1981:44). Even after it developed, the Nicaraguan coffee elite still was unable to gain control of the state because of the creation and perpetuation of the Somoza dynasty, which again was a manifestation of substantial U.S. interference (Paige 1985:94).

Fortunately for coffee growers, some of the Conservative presidents before Zelaya were willing to adopt portions of the reforms elsewhere identified with the Liberals. An agrarian law in 1877 was especially directed at the communal and public lands of the north central highlands. Still held by indigenous communities, these were prime coffee-growing lands. The law required the privatization of land, with those working it at the time given the first opportunity to purchase it. If they did not pay, then the land could be auctioned. In the face of efforts to draft their labor, as well as to this threat to their land and communities, Indians rose up in 1881 in one of the region's most significant rebellions. They attacked the regional governmental headquarters of Matagalpa twice, first with a force of about 1,000 and then about five months later with a force of up to 7,000. In the end the Indians lost, 1,000–2,000 were killed, fierce repression followed, and their lands were gradually lost to private coffee estates. Coffee production, though, was still retarded by labor shortages. Instead of working on the coffee farms, peasants preferred to move deeper into the ample agricultural frontier. Finally, vagrancy laws were passed in 1894 and 1901 and the state's repressive capacity for their enforcement enhanced.

Other land became available under Zelaya as church lands were expropriated and national lands sold. Conservative governments between 1910 and 1920 continued the sale of national lands, some of which were worked by small and medium-sized farmers with no legal titles, who were accordingly expelled. Some of these peasants were able to get their lands back when the nationalist rebel army of Augusto Sandino established control over parts of the northern region of the country during the late 1920s and early 1930s. Later they were the primary victims of the rural repression by the national guard that followed the guard's assassination of Sandino in 1934.

Costa Rica

Unlike the rest of Central America, rural Costa Rica was populated largely by independent small farmers, and it was the better off of these who initiated Costa Rica's coffee boom. Their ability to meet the expanding international coffee demand, however, was limited by labor shortages, since the sparsely populated country had an ample frontier. Consequently, small to medium farms dominated coffee production in Costa Rica with relatively high wages offered in order to attract help during harvesting. Technological innovation provided a partial solution to the labor supply problem. The importation of newly invented processing machinery at midcentury allowed the rapid expansion of production for larger farmers who could raise the necessary capital. As the decades progressed, labor shortages eventually became less of a problem as population growth, higher land prices in the Central Valley, and some bankruptcies created a growing landless rural population. The development of the coffee economy in Costa Rica, then, benefited both elites and masses throughout the nineteenth century and fostered the development of a strong rural middle class, explaining in part the uniqueness of Costa Rican political life today.[10] Still, by the early twentieth century the expansion of coffee production for export markets in Costa Rica was associated with land concentration, a decline in food production, and social stratification. Contemporary data can be used to support both images of Costa Rica: In the early 1990s about 92 percent of coffee farms were under 12.4 acres and produced about 40 percent of the crop; yet the largest 1.7 percent of coffee *fincas* (those with over 50 acres) produced almost as much: 37 percent of the total (*Tico Times*, May 22, 1992:4; June 25, 1993:22).

Summary

The expansion of coffee production in Central America had a differential impact upon various social groups. A wealthy agrarian bourgeoisie arose in each country because of the export boom, whereas many peasants (especially Indians) lost their access to land and were coerced, by the marketplace and/or by law, to supply their labor to others. Some of the most fertile land was switched from raising basic food crops to producing for export, with deleterious effects on food supplies. One scholar's careful study of this process in an Indian region of Guatemala led him to the following characterization, which applies almost equally well to the coffee-growing regions of El Salvador and Nicaragua: Elites created and "controlled a virtual fascist state" (Carmack 1983:243).

As coffee exports and earnings increased, a substantial amount of money entered the region. Some was productively employed in such areas as public works, education, and the beginnings of a textile industry. Contrary to the boldest Liberal dreams, however, coffee earnings did not spark an industrial revolution. Much of the profit paid for imports to meet the rising consumerist aspirations of the elites and the growing urban middle sectors, and considerable sums were reinvested abroad (Woodward 1976:163–164). Many of the merchants who handled the coffee trade were of foreign origin, as in fact were many of the owners of the coffee *fincas*, especially in Nicaragua and Guatemala. In a number of cases, then, the coffee boom benefited Europeans and North Americans attracted to the region, not Central Americans. In Guatemala, for example, a slump in coffee prices in 1897 left a number of native planters bankrupt and unable to prevent their German creditors from taking over their *fincas*; by 1914, 170 German planters produced almost one-third of the Guatemalan coffee crop (Jones 1966:207).

The unsettling experience of world market slumps, like the coffee crisis of 1897, reinforced the commitment of government officials and commercially oriented farmers to diversify export production. Dependence on the export of essentially one commodity obviously leaves a country highly vulnerable to world market fluctuations over which it has little control or influence if it is a minor producer—and Central America has never produced more than 15 percent of the world's coffee. Finding a new export proved to be much easier this time, however, than it had been during the past four centuries.

The Coming of the Banana Companies

Few issues concerning the history of Central American political and economic life have generated more intense controversy than the role of the great U.S. banana companies.[11] To some, the story is one of heroic entrepreneurs struggling against tremendous odds and risks to bring civilization and economic opportunity to the inhospitable tropical lowlands of the Caribbean coast. In pursuit of their vision and their self-interest, some lost their lives, others went broke, but some made vast fortunes. In the process, they provided good jobs and relatively high incomes for tens of thousands of Central Americans, built schools and hospitals, and provided much-needed export earnings for the underdeveloped countries of the area.

Others see the story instead as that of two U.S. corporations, United Fruit Company and Standard Fruit Company, that gained monopoly power over what had been a developing domestic industry through their control of shipping and marketing operations, their more highly developed business skills, their size, and their ruthless practices.[12] Through corruption and political intrigue, backed at times by U.S. military power, the banana companies were able to obtain from vulnerable Central American governments extraordinary concessions that allowed them to capture and maintain control over an important sector of the region's economy and vast sections of its countryside.

Actually, there is little essential contradiction between these two very different stories. Although the first has validity, much of it is irrelevant to an evaluation of the role of the fruit companies in Central America. The dominating presence of the companies is incontrovertible, especially United Fruit, which was always the largest, controlling at least one-half of the U.S. market, for example, for much of the first half of the twentieth century. At its peak in 1950, United Fruit owned or leased 3 million acres, cultivating 138,910 of those, and operated 1,500 miles of railroads and thirty-six ships, with a total net worth of just under $.33 billion (Dosal 1993:6). The most important issues we must explore in evaluating "the Octopus" and its competitors are first, the balance between the positive contributions of the companies and their negative consequences, and second, the balance between this cost-benefit analysis and the benefits enjoyed by the companies themselves. The systematic exploration of these questions is still to be performed; what follows is a brief account of the evidence that is available.

The development of the banana industry in Central America is intimately tied to the building of railroad lines in the region, though this relationship varied from country to country. Railroad construction in Costa Rica led to the banana industry, whereas in Honduras the relationship was essentially the reverse. In Guatemala an existing rail line facilitated the expansion of United Fruit operations. Bananas are grown in Nicaragua, but their importance has been considerably less; they are unimportant in El Salvador.[13] In addition to their obvious importance as an infrastructure necessary for economic development, railroads were an important symbol of modernity in the second half of the nineteenth century. Central American countries wanted railroads for both reasons. They were willing to pay a high price, and they generally did, both in bad loans and in the alienation of extraordinary amounts of land to foreign interests. Costa Rica's first loans with European bankers left it with a debt of £2.4 million, even though it had received only about half a million (Seligson 1980a:51). Honduras ran up a debt in the late 1800s of almost £6 million to pay for a rail line that was incompetently built and left uncompleted. Yet Honduras actually received only about £3 million, and about half of that was paid out to bankers (Ross 1975:78). The country was unable to pay off the loans; by 1912 it had the highest per capita national debt in the world (Williams 1994:92), and by 1926 high interest charges had increased the debt to an incredible $125 million (Kepner and Soothill 1967:104–105).

Costa Rica contracted in 1871 with the famous railroad builder Henry Meiggs to construct its line, following its receipt of his £100,000 bribe. He then turned the contract over to his nephew Henry Meiggs Keith, who in turn brought in his younger brother, Minor, to help with the job. The project faced much greater hardships than foreseen, and Henry soon died in the effort, as did a younger brother later, as well as perhaps 5,000 other workers. Work plodded on slowly, and consequently the line was more expensive than planned. Minor Keith founded a banana-producing enterprise in order to provide the railroad with income while work continued on the segment from the Caribbean coast to the central plateau and its coffee groves, which were intended to be its major cargo. Keith's banana-growing efforts coincided with rising prices in the United States as demand continued to exceed supply. By 1890 his Costa Rican operation was the largest banana producer in the world. In 1900, the year after United Fruit was formed through Keith's merger with other interests, the new company owned almost .25 million acres in six countries; by the end of 1918 it owned or leased 1.25 million acres of land and operated about 1,000 miles of railroad lines (Wilson 1968:118, 196). This land came very cheaply, much of it free of charge. Costa Rica signed the Soto-Keith contract in 1894, under the terms of which Keith committed himself to finish the railway and to absorb the attendant £2.4 million debt. In return Costa Rica granted him 800,000 acres of state lands in any part of the country he chose, a ninety-nine-year lease on the railroad, a twenty-year exemption from land taxes, and an exemption from import duties for construction materials related to the railroad project. Although the inducement was excessive, Costa Rica did get a railroad linking its inland capital with the Atlantic coast.

The Honduran experience, by contrast, was less fortunate. Before the turn of the century, there were hundreds of small banana producers in Honduras (as there were in Costa Rica) who sold their produce to U.S. trading interests. The Honduran government, however, desired to expand the banana industry rapidly and retained hopes of constructing a railroad to the capital, which was separated from the Caribbean coast by rugged, mountainous terrain. Government officials believed that foreign capital and technicians would be necessary to achieve both goals, and the banana companies seemed to provide the solution. At the same time, the U.S. interests were ready to expand from trading bananas to producing their own supplies on their own plantations. Within a short period of time, three of these interests came to dominate Honduran production: United Fruit, Cuyamel (which was bought out by United in 1930), and Vacarro Brothers (which became Standard Fruit).

Honduras offered the companies concessions similar to those granted United Fruit in Costa Rica as incentives to expand their operations into the country. Especially notable were generous land grants in return for railroads the fruit companies were to construct. By 1924 United's two subsidiaries possessed 400,000 acres, at least 175,000 of them obtained without cost as subsidies for railroad construction. Honduran officials intended for the rail lines to serve national needs by linking interior cities to the coast, but the 1,000 miles of tracks the banana companies built were designed to meet their needs instead. Each company's coastal enclave was laced with tracks that neither penetrated into the interior nor even linked adjacent enclaves. Because of the vulnerability of officials in the weak Honduran government to ambitious and omnipresent foes, the companies often were able to manipulate the political process to obtain deadline extensions or stifle attempts to institute meaningful sanctions for noncompliance (Kepner and Soothill 1967:140–152).

Honduras had intended to prevent the banana companies from developing larger enclaves. The lands granted were in alternating lots, with those in between retained by the nation to be rented to Honduran citizens for a small fee. The banana companies later bought many of these leases from their individual possessors, however, thereby expanding and consolidating their holdings.

Guatemala demonstrates a third pattern in the relationship between bananas and railroads. A substantial amount of railroad construction had been completed in various parts of the country before United Fruit obtained its first concession in 1900. In addition to investors from the United States, Germany, Britain, and France, domestic public and private investment financed this construction as well. Political leaders and coffee producers hoped that Guatemalans would be able to control their railways. These nationalist dreams were doomed, though, by a severe ten-year economic crisis beginning in 1897 and by the replacement of Liberal administrations with the brutal and corrupt Estrada Cabrera dictatorship beginning the next year. These preexisting tracks were considerable for the region at the time but had one major gap: The rail line up from the Caribbean fell about 60 miles short of the capital, Guatemala City.

In 1904 the energetic Minor Keith obtained a contract for its completion. In return, he received control of the entire line for ninety-nine years, including all of the Caribbean port facilities at Puerto Barrios; 168,000 acres of good agricultural land; the right to acquire and build railways throughout the rest of the country; and freedom from regulation. This enterprise changed its name in 1912 to International Railways of Central America (IRCA) as it merged with the other railroad in the country, about 200 miles of U.S.-business-owned track in the west. Because of Keith's interest in both operations, it is no surprise that mutual preferential treatment existed between IRCA and United Fruit, giving the latter great advantage over rival banana producers. Nor was it a surprise when United

Fruit eventually absorbed IRCA, as it did formally in 1936. Estrada Cabrera's take in return for selling out his country cannot be specified, but the presumption has always been that it was considerable.

From today's perspective, the huge tracts granted to the banana companies often look shocking. At the turn of the century, however, the Caribbean lowlands were largely unsettled and were viewed by most Central Americans (especially urban elites) as inhospitable to civilized habitation. Population densities were still quite low; the common belief was that Central America was blessed with bountiful land. Therefore, unlike the coffee planters or the growers of new export crops after World War II, the banana companies could gain enormous landholdings without making much impact on land tenure patterns or rural class structures. But once land pressures developed in the postwar period, the size of those holdings became both a significant obstacle to meeting the land needs of a growing population locally and nationally and a pressing political issue, as discussed in Part 2.

As their operations expanded, the companies hired thousands of workers, making them the largest employers in each of the countries. In the early days, most of the workers were of African heritage, often from Jamaica. Frequently misled by labor importers, they found themselves working under the harshest conditions for wages far worse than expected and usually under the racist control of white supervisors from the southern United States. Thousands died under the brutal labor and environmental conditions associated with building the railroads and establishing the banana plantations. As working conditions improved, though, the banana companies provided important job opportunities for domestic workers displaced when the expansion of coffee growing resulted in diminished land access and food supplies in Costa Rica, Guatemala, and even El Salvador, the Salvadorans migrating to the Honduran banana fields. Wages paid by the U.S. banana companies have almost always been higher than those offered by domestic employers, and at a relatively early date the companies began to provide housing and educational, medical, and recreational facilities. Nevertheless, workers have had a number of reasons for serious discontent, including inadequate pay, extortionist company store prices, poor working conditions, and racism. The collective nature of their work has facilitated their organization, and the banana workers' unions have been among the most militant in each of the countries. Their activities have influenced both rural and national politics, especially in Guatemala and Honduras, as discussed in later chapters.

The most important issue concerning the impact of the fruit companies, however, is their contribution to the development of the Central American economies through the generation of export earnings. As discussed in previous sections of this chapter, across the centuries Central American elites had seen the diversification and expansion of agricultural exports as the key to their own enrichment and their countries' development. The banana companies were welcomed to the region with generous concessions because of the promise they offered of achieving these goals.

It is uncontroversial today to assert that in the first decades (say, up to 1940) this contribution was much less than it should have been. Indeed, United Fruit's public relations director of the early 1970s admitted as much, writing that the "values of the era allowed the company to take without giving back in reasonable proportions" (McCann 1976:160). Nor did the presence of the banana companies stimulate the development of the local economies to the extent that might be expected. Despite their substantial infrastructure, many company operations were impermanent. When forced by disease or declining productivity to relocate, the entire operation, including even the railroad tracks, often would be moved to the next area to be cultivated.[14]

In addition to the wages the companies disbursed, their direct contribution to the domestic economy was based on goods and services purchased domestically and on taxes and duties paid. Generally, though, the needs of the companies were met by imports from the United States. Indeed, since the banana enclaves were isolated from the rest of the country, large portions of the workers' wages were spent in company stores that sold imported goods. Although duties on these imports were an important generator of income, they were reduced by concessions that let the companies import duty-free materials necessary for construction. "Necessity" often has been interpreted broadly; United Fruit was still successfully importing liquor duty free into Costa Rica in 1970, arguing that it was necessary for the improvement of labor relations (Seligson 1980a:61).

Potentially more important were the export taxes that could be levied on the bananas as they left the country. As part of the initial package of inducements, however, the companies were usually guaranteed a number of years of operation free from any export duties; United Fruit in Costa Rica, for example, had an exemption that lasted eleven years; the original exemption in Guatemala was for thirty-five years. Once taxes were levied on the exports of the foreign-owned banana companies, the rates were substantially below those paid by domestic coffee growers. In 1928 the export tax on bananas in Guatemala was 1.97 percent of total valuation, but it was 8.7 percent on coffee; in Costa Rica the comparable figures were 1.4 percent for bananas and 11.8 percent for coffee (Kepner and Soothill 1967:213). Eventually, the companies were hit with other taxes, such as various types of land taxes. From 1918 to 1927, United Fruit in Costa Rica annually paid $2,000 on its vast uncultivated lands; in Guatemala its 1929 land tax was $6,500 (Kepner and Soothill 1967:214). As late as 1952, one study estimated that United Fruit's tax bill in Guatemala was still one-half of what it would have been without the exemptions granted in the original contracts (Adler, Schlesinger, and Olson 1952:124).

Such generous concessions proved to be very difficult to amend. The banana companies grew to be the largest landowners, employers, and generators of foreign exchange in the three countries. They were huge, stable, profitable, and backed by the government of the United States. The Central American governments, by contrast, were weak, unstable, and chronically short of revenues; in fact, when facing insolvency, the Honduran government often accepted loans from Standard Fruit. Central American officials were understandably apprehensive about pressuring the companies to contribute more for fear that they might respond by asserting their substantial economic leverage, perhaps cutting back on exports or production or even shifting operations to other countries. Such fears were reinforced by action on a number of occasions, as when United Fruit in 1930 successfully persuaded Costa Rica to modify proposed changes in the export tax by threatening to withdraw from the country (Kepner and Soothill 1967:79–80) or when in Honduras in 1920 United and Cuyamel threatened lockouts in support of Vacarro (Standard Fruit), which was experiencing serious labor difficulties (Karnes 1978:67). Furthermore, the historical record is full of examples of the companies' using their substantial power and income to intervene directly in Central American politics in order to protect their interests.

The period of the banana companies' expansion in Central America (the first third of the twentieth century) corresponded with the most interventionist stage of U.S. policy toward the region. The U.S. government did not always back the position of the companies, but its military penetration of the region generally, and incidents of its military support for the companies specifically, had an obvious effect on Central American governments. Public officials were reluctant to press confrontation with the companies when the U.S. Navy appeared offshore. The U.S. military also intervened at times in behalf of the companies to help squelch labor strikes, such as the Puerto Barrios strike in Guatemala in 1923.

Domestic elements conspiring to overthrow a Central American government invariably dreamed of the advantage to be gained by enlisting the support of a banana company and/or the United States to their cause. As a result of the dominating position of the companies and of the U.S. government (whose military forces occupied Honduras and Nicaragua during part of this period), Central American politics had little autonomy. Two somewhat extreme examples make the point well. A loser in the 1923 Honduran presidential election launched a revolt, with the support of United Fruit, against the government, which had substantial financial ties to Cuyamel Fruit. The following year U.S. troops were landed to protect lives and property, a role that soon brought them into armed conflict with the

United Fruit–backed rebels. The conflict was then mediated by the U.S. State Department (LaFeber 1984:62). This antagonism in turn occurred within the context of a dispute between the two banana companies over access to the Montagua River and its right bank, an area of contesting sovereignty claims between Honduras and Guatemala. The intrigues of the two banana companies aggravated tensions between the two countries, leading on several occasions to violence and the possibility of war (Dosal 1993).

Slowly, though, the dominating position of the banana companies eroded. Central American governments stabilized, their economies grew, urban middle sectors expanded, and the nationalist voice became more prominent in domestic politics. The U.S. government became less overtly interventionist by the 1930s, and there arose a new generation of business managers who had greater concern for the image of their firms, both at home and abroad. As the configuration of power altered, contracts and taxes were amended to be less disadvantageous to the Central American countries. Accordingly, the evaluation of the economic contribution of the banana industry to Central America since about 1940 is complex.

As a preface to the discussion of the recent period, it is important to keep in mind that the erosion of the companies' dominant position has been slow and relative; they continue to enjoy a substantial ability to protect their interests through their economic leverage in the three countries. The prime example, of course, is United Fruit's role in the overthrow of the progressive government of Guatemala in 1954, to be discussed in Chapter 5. Two decades later, in 1975, a $1.25 million bribe United Brands (as United Fruit was then known) paid to Honduran officials was successful in minimizing a proposed increase in the banana export tax (UNECLA 1979:72–95, 139–150). The previous year the banana-exporting countries of the isthmus had banded together in a union in hopes of equalizing their bargaining status with the fruit companies. They optimistically increased their export taxes, especially Costa Rica. However, because of the relative ease with which the companies can reduce production in one area and shift production emphasis to others, the countries remained too vulnerable. Between 1978 and 1985, each of the region's three major banana-exporting countries lowered or eliminated taxes levied on the multinational companies (Baer 1973:44–45; CAR 1986:114; Torres-Rivas and Deutscher 1988).

Labor unions face the same dilemma. Assertive wage demands have been met enough times with reduced production and the dismissal of workers to make credible threats such as that issued in late 1991 by the Chiquita subsidiary in Honduras that it would need to dismiss 650 workers as part of the reduction of "unprofitable" operations. The announcement came during the midst of wage negotiations. Following several years of labor strife, the company closed down several operations in 1994 and fired over 3,000 workers. To give themselves greater flexibility, in some areas the banana companies have eliminated their own plantations (and unionized workforce), marketing instead bananas purchased from small domestic producers. This is characteristic of Standard's operations in Costa Rica, for example, where it has not had a labor contract since 1986.[15]

There have been several empirical attempts to evaluate the economic impact of the banana companies in Central America relative to their profits, but all are methodologically inadequate.[16] Furthermore, even complete access to the companies' accounting statements, as Clairmonte (1975:114) points out, would tell us little because of the integrated nature of their operations. Until recently, each company controlled the railway and shipping lines it utilized, and therefore profits could be hidden under transportation costs. Another illustration of this difficulty is provided by a former United Fruit official. McCann (1976:40) explains that in 1952 the company's 300 stores generated a 16 percent gross profit of almost $3 million—in itself, he claims, an understatement of actual profits. Yet after the accounts were juggled, the books showed an operating loss of about $50,000 for the stores. In sum, a conclusive statement well grounded in empirical analysis cannot yet be made concerning the economic impact of the banana companies relative to their gains.

There is, however, some useful evidence concerning foreign exchange earnings. The annual percentage of export earnings converted to local currency (a measure of the proportion of fruit company earnings benefiting the local economy) fluctuated between 40 and 65 percent in Honduras from 1961 to 1974, with the average for the period at 53 percent (Ellis 1983:204). This evidence is reinforced by a 1966 Alliance for Progress estimate that about half of foreign exchange earnings from bananas were converted into local currency for direct expenditure in Honduras.

Foreign exchange earnings have been depressed, though, by declining real prices for bananas on the world market. The real retail price of bananas fell 44 percent in the United States and 59 percent in West Germany between 1950 and 1972; they then recovered somewhat, but world prices in 1986 were still only about 65 percent those of thirty-six years earlier (Clairmonte 1975:135; Torres-Rivas and Deutscher 1988:30).

But higher real prices and expanding markets would not represent a great windfall for individual banana growers because only a small portion of what the foreign consumer pays comes back to the producer. Clairmonte (1975:138–139) estimates that growers get only about 11.5 cents for each dollar spent by foreign consumers, whereas retailers' gross costs amount to 31.9 cents. Even when all other domestic costs (e.g., transportation) are added, only a quarter of the price paid by the consumer is generated in the banana-producing country. Given the nature of the Central American banana industry, most of even that small amount is incurred by U.S.-based multinational corporations, not by domestic growers or businesses. For such reasons, a study by the United Nations Economic Commission for Latin America (UNECLA 1979:116) came to the following conclusion: "Given this uneven balance of bargaining capacity the benefits derived from the [banana] industry were appropriated mainly by [transnational corporations]. The linkages with the domestic economy and the tax revenues extracted by the host governments were relatively insignificant."

However, it is important to realize that the traditional U.S. banana companies do not dominate Central America as they did in the past. Not only do they face periodic incursions from European firms, but, more important, they now are competing with Latin American companies. Costa Rica provides perhaps the best example. In 1963 virtually all banana exports were controlled by United Fruit and Standard, with the first alone providing about 70 percent. In 1973 United Fruit was down to 31 percent, Standard was up to 37, and the newer competitor, Del Monte, was at 23 percent. Two decades later, though, there had been great upheaval. Del Monte's operation, by then Mexican owned, along with Standard/Dole, each controlled about 31 percent of Costa Rican banana exports, with Chiquita down to around 15 percent, about par with a Colombian firm (Banaco), then followed at close to 6 percent by another Colombian firm (Turbana). At the same time, the Costa Rican government was subsidizing the expansion of domestic producers (Garnier, González, and Cornick 1988:101; *Tico Times,* December 11, 1992:30).

But one enduring characteristic of Central American export agriculture does not change: insufficient world demand relative to production capacity. In anticipation of greater access to European markets when internal market restrictions were lifted inside the European Community (EC), Central American producers rapidly expanded their area under banana cultivation. Instead, however, the EC slapped quotas on Latin American banana imports at the end of 1992 in order to protect the less efficient production from their own former colonies. The loss was double: Bananas bring a higher price in Europe, and sale of the surplus resulting from reduced European access knocked down prices elsewhere. Within the first two years of the new system, Costa Rica estimated it had lost over $100 million in export earnings and 9,000 jobs. And it actually fared better under the system than many of the other Latin American banana producers (*Chronicle,* June 6 and November 2, 1995).

Conclusion: Export Agriculture and Comparative Advantage

The history of rural Central America is marked by tension and at times conflict between two different conceptions of the role of the land. The first sees it as provider and source of security. Often the human-land relationship takes on religious overtones; in any case, the attachment is invariably strong. The second view values the land for its commercial possibilities: The tie is functional. The first conception is obviously that of peasants everywhere, whereas the second is characteristic of both rural and urban elites with commercial and/or developmental goals.

Because domestic commercial possibilities were minor following the Spanish conquest of Central America, profit-minded colonists not surprisingly turned their attention toward the world market. As theirs was a conquest society, the structures they created exploited for their enrichment not only the land but also the indigenous people. This domination and exploitation of the native population reinforced the bias toward export agriculture because too few in society benefited sufficiently to promote the development of stronger domestic markets. After independence, this rigidly unequal social structure continued, and along with it the bias toward export agriculture. While elites placed great hopes on export diversification and expansion and made efforts toward these goals, basic food production received little attention and fewer resources. Development-oriented elites continued to value the land and the labor of the peasantry for their commercial potential.

The bias toward commercial export agriculture was justified in the nineteenth century by the spread of Liberal ideology, which was in part a manifestation and defense of the expanding international capitalist economic system. Adam Smith's "invisible hand" rationalized both the external and the internal components of that system. Internationally, the doctrine of comparative advantage taught that the mutual wealth of nations would be maximized by free trade between countries that specialized in the production of those commodities for which they enjoyed a relative advantage. In the years between independence and the Great Depression, this theory was understood (largely without controversy) to mean that Central America should concentrate on the development of exportable agricultural products. The capital accumulated through such trade would in turn promote domestic development that eventually would materially advance everyone, allowing for a more internally generated growth. The invisible hand, then, also worked its magic at home; although elites were obviously pursuing their own self-interest in developing export agriculture, the fruits of their efforts would eventually spread through all of society.

As this chapter's brief survey of agrarian transformations in Central America from the conquest to World War II has demonstrated, the actual results of the implementation of the agro-export development model during this period were much less than promised. The dependence of Central

American economies and governments on the export earnings of a few agricultural commodities left them tightly bound to, and therefore vulnerable to, an international economic system over which they had only the most minimal influence. The revenues obtained from the expansion of agricultural exports have been less than desired and expected, and the amount of capital actually employed in promoting further development has also been substantially less than anticipated.

Furthermore, the negative consequences of the great agricultural transformations of the past have been substantial. The expansion of export crop production during the colonial cacao and indigo booms and the coffee boom of the late nineteenth century had a devastating impact on the peasantry. During the first transformation, the land and labor of Indians were expropriated, with death the frequent result. The coffee transformation extended the domination of the agro-elite as more lands were confiscated and coercive labor systems were expanded and tightened. For the affected peasantry, the results were a further loss of land, autonomy, and food supply. In Central America, then, the model might more correctly be termed "the repressive agro-export development model"; it has been most repressive in Guatemala and El Salvador and least so in Costa Rica.

Because bananas are grown in what used to be remote areas, their initial cultivation did not have similar adverse consequences. Once land pressures did develop, however, the banana companies' enormous landholdings (obtained at little or no cost) contributed to a rapidly expanding pool of landless peasants. The foreign companies have made a number of important contributions, such as helping to eradicate tropical diseases, developing railroads and ports (held under their control), and building schools and hospitals. But their tremendous size gave them a dominating political position that allowed them to make minimal financial contributions to the Central American countries, especially during the first third of the century, while reaping great profits. Furthermore, the continual involvement of such giant enterprises in domestic affairs served to distort Central American politics and retard the region's political maturation.

When following World War II development became an even greater imperative in the region, the diversification and expansion of agricultural exports was once again believed by many to be the key to realizing Central America's aspirations.[17] Although the developments of the previous 400 years were not encouraging, the renewed reliance on export agriculture should not be surprising. A small (though now larger) elite still controlled economies too underdeveloped to stimulate independently their own rapid development. And the same ideological beliefs continued to rationalize the defense of privilege and the pursuit of self-interest as fundamental to the achievement of the greater good.

Notes

1. For similar but briefer arguments, see Weeks (1986) and Woodward (1984) on Central America and Grindle (1986:25–46) on Latin America as a whole.

2. The more general concept of an agrarian transformation is utilized in this study to avoid the problematic and tangential controversies associated with defining "modes of production" in rural societies and identifying changes from one to another.

3. Helpful in preparing this section were Fox (1978), Harrison and Turner (1978), Linares (1979), Morley and Brainerd (1983), Orellana (1984), West and Augelli (1976), and Woodward (1976).

4. To facilitate discussion, geographical references will utilize postindependence national boundaries.

5. Especially useful in preparing this section were MacLeod (1973) and Sherman (1979). I consulted as well Herring (1964), Lovell and Lutz (1994), MacLeod and Wasserstrom (1983), Newson (1982, 1985), Orellana (1984), Stannard (1992), Weaver (1994), Woodward (1976), and Wortman (1982).

6. See Lovell and Lutz (1994:8) and Newson (1982, 1985:44). It is important for North American readers to realize that similar depopulation occurred throughout their region, with the indigenous population of North America subjected to the same inhumane treatment experienced to the south. Stannard (1992) effectively discusses this holocaust for all of the Americas.

7. This section draws heavily on MacLeod (1973); also useful were Browning (1971), McCreery (1994), Seligson (1980a), Smith (1956), Weaver (1994), Woodward (1976), and Wortman (1982).

8. For further information on Costa Rican Indians, see the special issue of *América Indígena* (1974), Hall (1985:32–50), and Saenz Maroto (1970).

9. For Costa Rica, this section draws on Gudmundson (1983, 1986) and Seligson (1980a); for El Salvador, on Browning (1971), Durham (1979), and Lindo-Fuentes (1990); for Nicaragua, on Wheelock Román (1980). More resources are available on Guatemala: See especially McCreery (1994), as well as Cambranes (1985), Carmack (1983), Dessaint (1962), Griffith (1965), Jones (1966), McCreery (1976, 1983), Mosk (1955), Naylor (1967), and Whetten (1961). For discussions of the entire region, see especially Williams (1994), as well as Torres Rivas (1971), Weaver (1994), and Woodward (1976).

10. Although Costa Rican politics are unique in the region, the difference should not be overstated. Of the first forty-four presidents after independence (through 1982), thirty-three were descendants of three families. Just one of these families (the Vazquez de Coronados) has given the nation eighteen presidents and 230 parliamentary deputies (Dunkerley 1982:8).

11. The best-known positive accounts of the role of the U.S. banana companies are May and Plaza (1958) and Wilson (1968); their leading critical counterparts are Bauer Paíz (1956) and Kepner and Soothill (1967). Also useful in preparing this section were Baer (1973), Chomsky (1996), Dosal (1993), Ellis (1983), Karnes (1978), LaBarge (1968), LaFeber (1984), Ross (1975), Seligson (1980a), Strouse (1970), UNECLA (1979), and Woodward (1976).

12. The United Fruit Company was formed in 1899 through the merger of the Boston Fruit Company, several other trading and marketing companies, and Minor Keith's Costa Rican operation. It became United Brands in 1970 after being taken over by the AMK Corporation (a story well told by McCann [1976]) and now is known as Chiquita. Wilson (1968) offers an uncritical but most readable account of its fascinating pioneering days. A third U.S. agribusiness giant, Del Monte, entered the Central American banana industry in 1968 to avoid a United Fruit takeover effort (United Fruit is legally enjoined in the United States from absorbing competing banana companies following the resolution of an antitrust suit filed by the U.S. Justice Department in 1954). In 1992 Del Monte's tropical fruit division was bought out by the Mexican firm Grupo Empresarial Agrícola Mexicano.

Standard Fruit was built by the Vacarro brothers and was named after them until 1923. Between 1964 and 1968, it was absorbed by Castle & Cooke and now markets its Central American fruit under the brand name of Dole. A scholarly history of the company is provided by Karnes (1978).

13. As Karnes (1978:119) notes, "Generally, Nicaragua has played a minor role in the banana industry, but periodically the land is 'rediscovered,' its prospects exaggerated, and its problems and previous failures ignored."

14. One observer described the impact of this impermanence still in the 1950s in Honduras: "Probably more development would evolve along the route of the railway if people knew that it would remain. There is an overdependence and complacency because of the Fruit Company being around, and there is no incentive to establish roots because it may soon be gone, together with all of its facilities" (Dozier 1958:42).

15. See *Update* (November 29, 1991), *Chronicle* (April 25, 1996), and *Tico Times* (October 9, 1992).

16. The most favorable judgment is provided by May and Plaza (1958:118–120, 157–158), who claim that United Fruit's dividends for operations in six countries in 1954–1955 were only 11.4 percent, not "immoderate by any standards" (p. 120). This study has limited usefulness, however, because of its brief time span and omission of relevant data. Its shortcomings become clear when the study is compared to the highly critical evaluation of United Fruit's contribution to the Guatemalan economy during 1950–1953 by Bauer Paíz (1956:328–331), minister of labor and economy during that period. The more complete data compiled by Bauer Paíz, though again covering only a short period of time, indicate profits for that period averaging 47.6 percent. A contrasting view of United Fruit's impact on Guatemala for 1946–1953 is provided by LaBarge (1968). Using data sets as extensive as those of Bauer Paíz but with a different focus, LaBarge (1960:25) claims that United Fruit's operations added 2.5 percent annually to Guatemala's gross national product during the period examined. The conclusions of these two studies, of course, are not mutually exclusive.

17. The expansion of the internal market through the development of the Central American Common Market to promote industrialization was the important alternative during this period.

Chapter Three

The Postwar Transformation of Central American Agriculture

The desire of public and private elites in Central America to find new agricultural exports intensified after World War II. The traditional export commodities of coffee and bananas (and minerals in Nicaragua and Honduras) had enriched some people and had brought sorely needed capital to the region. They had not, however, promoted sufficient development of the region's economies. Each of the countries remained at a low level of economic development, with most of the peasantry living at subsistence level. Furthermore, both of the major export crops had faced years of difficulties. With the Great Depression, the price of coffee fell by 80 percent relative to the price of gold. The important markets of Europe were closed by the war and remained shut for a period after its end. Eventually, prices began to climb, even rapidly, but they peaked by 1954 as overproduction once again plagued the world's coffee producers. Banana cultivation had long been troubled by devastating diseases that often required the abandonment of huge sections of plantations. Furthermore, the banana sector continued to be controlled by the U.S. fruit companies.

A revolution of rising aspirations hit urban Central America by mid-century. The region's economic growth, even if less than desired, had created a growing middle sector and a limited industrial working class. These groups wanted an improvement in their standard of living, and they hoped it would be dramatic and soon. Accordingly, rapid economic development was an imperative for them. On occasion middle-sector groups were able to participate directly in the formulation of public policy when popular movements brought progressive governments to power, as happened in Costa Rica and Guatemala in the 1940s. At other times such groups were able to influence policy as the social base of dominant political institutions—such as the military in El Salvador and the political parties in Honduras—became more inclusive in the postwar period. As the influence of the middle sectors increased, many elites came to share their commitment to economic development, viewing an expanding economic pie as the solution that would satisfy the mounting aspirations of those below them without sacrificing their own material advantages (Anderson 1961).

Once again many people saw the diversification and expansion of agricultural exports as the keys to the region's development, and for essentially the same reasons as in earlier periods. Hopes also were placed on industrialization, but internal markets were too small and underdeveloped to promote sufficient economic development; they remained so even with the establishment of the Central American Common Market during the 1960s.[1] Furthermore, internally oriented growth strategies collided with the seriously skewed distribution of such critical resources as land and with the systems of labor domination that had evolved over the centuries, both of which left most people too poor to play the role of marketplace consumer.

Strategies based on export agriculture not only avoided these constraints but in addition were congruent with existing socioeconomic structures and their attendant ideologies. The primary constraint on export agriculture in Central America had always been external, especially as structures for controlling the internal problems of land and labor were developed during the colonial and coffee transformations. Once international postwar recovery began, the external limitation, too, seemed to vanish with the expansion of foreign markets. Furthermore, new international agencies had been created that came to Central America with advice and financial credits to assist in the quest for economic development. Soon great expanses of land were given over to the production of the new export commodities: cotton, sugar, and beef.[2] Later, as it became clear that neither were these commodities sufficient to spur the region's sustained development, the search continued for new "nontraditional" exports. It is necessary, then, to examine the merits of the agro-export model itself. Evidence of its accomplishments and limitations are presented throughout this and the next chapter; I take a strong position in the conclusion to Chapter 4.

New Exports and the Drive for Development

Honduras has traditionally been the least developed of the Central American countries, largely for geographical reasons. Its mountainous terrain is the region's most difficult to traverse, and its central location has made it a frequent site of conflict between the region's contending forces from the early nineteenth century through the 1980s. As the least developed of the five countries, Honduras provides a good illustration of the forces at work in the early postwar period. The portrait of these forces may be given finer detail through a brief examination of Nicaragua, which stood ahead at midcentury of the other countries (except Costa Rica) on most indicators of socioeconomic development.

The Honduran government played virtually no role in the nation's economy up to midcentury except for its dealings with the banana companies, discussed in the previous chapter.[3] Excluding the banana enclave, which was largely isolated from the rest of the country, Honduras was still characterized by the traditional dualistic agricultural economy: a subsistence peasantry toiling alongside large landholdings utilizing land and labor inefficiently. Indeed, a study mission to the country in the early 1950s called the prevailing level of agricultural development "as primitive as can be comprehended within the meaning of the term 'agriculture'" (Checchi 1959:52).

At the same time, though, other international study missions were laying the framework for the transformation of Honduran agriculture. Advisers from the International Monetary Fund (IMF) played an important role in drafting an income tax, which was implemented in 1949, and in the founding of the central bank and the national development bank in the following year. In 1951 an agricultural extension service was formed under U.S. auspices and staffed by personnel from both countries. This service in turn stimulated the creation of the agricultural ministry the next year. The income tax provided revenues that could be used for developmental purposes, and the new banks provided the instruments necessary for a direct governmental role in the economy. In the early 1950s, construction of the Pan American Highway through the southern part of Honduras, along with that of connecting highways to Tegucigalpa in the interior and San Pedro Sula in the northern coastal region, more effectively integrated the country, broadening the internal market and better linking agricultural producers to international markets. At the same time, the government began through its development bank to provide credits to encourage the expansion of commercial agricultural production, especially that aimed at the export market. Indeed, Posas and del Cid (1981:87) credit the bank with the creation of an agrarian bourgeoisie in Honduras.

Similar developments occurred in neighboring Nicaragua,[4] where they were earlier, stronger, and closely connected to the personal fortune of the dictator, Anastasio Somoza. As he consolidated his political power from 1934 on, Somoza undertook the completion of the Liberal project in Nicaragua. Through strict autocratic rule, he attempted to modernize the country by promoting economic growth. His efforts were not without self-interest: His family, which in 1934 owned no land, was the largest landowner in the country by the 1950s. Somoza built his empire in the industrial sector as well. In Nicaragua, unlike Honduras, much of the necessary government infrastructure was in place and therefore ready to take advantage of postwar opportunities. Somoza's agricultural modernization campaign began in 1936. He soon created a ministry of agriculture, an overseas trading company, and a national bank, the latter becoming an important source of agricultural credit by 1938. Working through these three institutions, Somoza cooperated with the leading cattlemen and coffee growers' associations to stimulate agricultural modernization.

The First Round: Cotton and Sugar

Although in 1954 coffee and bananas still accounted for about 80 percent of foreign exchange earnings in each country except Nicaragua, this was soon to change. Table 3.1 portrays the diversification of the Central American agricultural sector during the postwar period, giving the percentage change for the area planted in the major export and food crops between 1948–1952 and 1976–1978, that is, up to the eve of the political convulsions that shook the region throughout the following decade.[5] A few explanatory comments are required before this and later tables can be discussed. They include not all crops but only the major ones: beans, corn, and rice as the principal food crops; bananas, coffee, cotton, sorghum, and sugar as the major export crops. Furthermore, the distinction between the two categories is not a clean one; all of the export crops are also consumed domestically, especially sugar and in recent years sorghum (which is still primarily fed to livestock, much of which is meant for the export market). Large quantities of corn also are used as animal feed (for example, over one-quarter of domestic supply in Honduras in 1982) and therefore indirectly related to the export market. It should be noted, too, that the lands held by the banana companies are many times greater than the crop sizes reported here would seem to indicate. It has been the companies' traditional (and controversial) practice to hold reserves substantially greater than the land actually planted in bananas or any other crop.

The big increases shown in Table 3.1 for banana cultivation are primarily the result of a resurgence in this crop after the difficult days when plantations were abandoned in the face of spreading disease. Otherwise, the essential pattern is the same in each country: The largest gains are registered by cotton, followed by sugar, regardless of end date. The gains for these two export crops are greater than those for all food crops in every case, with the exception of rice in Costa Rica (a commercial crop there). Consequently, the ratio of land devoted to export crops in comparison to

TABLE 3.1 Agricultural Land Use: Percentage Change in Area Devoted to Various Food and Export Crops, 1948–1952 to 1976–1978

	Costa Rica	El Salvador	Guatemala	Honduras	Nicaragua
Food Crops[a]					
Beans	−4	72	111	48	100
Corn	−22	36	8	53	105
Rice	204	−7	75	36	14
Total Food	34	35	20[b]	52	92
Export Crops[a]					
Bananas	156	–	264	−12	4,100
Coffee	63	31	60	92	57
Cotton	600	300	2,080	1,400	780
Sorghum	–	36	110	0	47
Sugar	129	223	419	168	169
Total Export	127	71	153	51	219

[a]Figures are for percentage change in area harvested for annual averages from 1948–1952 to 1976–1978.
[b]Guatemala's total food production also includes wheat.
SOURCE: Calculated from UNFAO, *Production Yearbook,* various years.

food crops increased. This change has been dramatic, as Table 3.1 shows, especially in Guatemala, Costa Rica, and Nicaragua.

Cotton had received some attention in the nineteenth century as a possible commercial crop, at least in El Salvador, where at midcentury the government offered various financial incentives to potential planters.[6] But conditions were not conducive to its cultivation for another century. Although the Pacific lowlands of Central America are ideal for cotton growing, diseases introduced at the conquest, such as malaria and yellow fever, had made them inhospitable to human habitation. Following the decimation of the indigenous people in the sixteenth century, these areas remained sparsely populated up to the mid-twentieth century. Their primary importance had been as a frontier destination for peasants dispossessed of their land elsewhere, for instance, by the spread of coffee cultivation on the more temperate mountain slopes. These areas were also the site of large haciendas devoted to low-density cattle ranching.

Technological change was one of the keys to opening up the Pacific lowlands. The development of chemical pesticides and small airplanes to spray them conveniently over large expanses of territory permitted the management of disease-carrying mosquitoes and the ravenous enemies of the cotton plant. The construction of highways and feeder roads made the region accessible and facilitated property management by growers who preferred to continue to live in the cities of the interior. Finally, the necessary international markets were available; this was a period of growing world demand and rising prices.

Because the Caribbean lowlands are too wet for cotton growing, cultivation spread most rapidly in the three countries with the most extensive lowlands on the Pacific coast: Nicaragua, El Salvador, and Guatemala. Governments eagerly encouraged its expansion, from the progressive administration of Arbenz in Guatemala to the autocratic regime of Somoza in Nicaragua. The result was a cotton boom; between 1950 and 1964 the total area of Central America planted in cotton increased tenfold, especially in Nicaragua, where by the 1960s cotton had become the largest sources of rural employment and foreign exchange earnings.

In later years, though, cotton went through boom-bust cycles driven largely by profit fluctuations. Most cotton is produced on large commercial holdings using modern techniques. Since cotton (unlike coffee or bananas) is an annual crop, its production can be expanded or contracted relatively easily in response to profit possibilities. Many cotton growers have therefore had a more speculative orientation than have growers of other export crops. A "get-rich-quick" attitude, especially prevalent during the 1950s and early 1960s, led to an indiscriminate use of pesticides and a lack of attention to soil fertility and conservation. As insect resistance increased and soil fertility declined, input costs climbed because more pesticides and fertilizer were required (Murray 1994). Rising input costs coupled with less attractive cotton prices caused a downturn in production in the late 1960s (see Figure 3.1). Production then recovered in the 1970s, reaching new levels of output in each of the three major producer countries. But then came the crash. By the end of the decade, the same factors, reinforced by the political upheavals to be discussed in Part 2, provoked a decline in cotton production so severe that by the early 1990s production levels were below those of thirty years before.

When commercial farmers shifted out of cotton production, they usually turned to corn for urban markets or sugarcane for export. Accordingly, sugar growing tended to expand most rapidly during the periods when cotton was least attractive, especially in Guatemala and Honduras. Since the latest crash of cotton, conversion of land to sugar cultivation has been particularly prevalent in Guatemala, which now has by far the most land devoted to sugar in the region.

The expansion of cotton and sugar cultivation did not come at the expense of coffee growing; the amount of land allocated to coffee has continued to rise throughout the contemporary period. One useful way of gauging this increase is to compare the relative fortunes of coffee, still the leading export crop, to corn, by far the most important food crop. The percentage of the increase in land devoted to coffee is greater than for corn in Costa Rica, Guatemala, and Honduras and close in El Salvador.

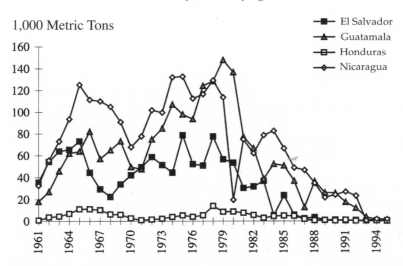

FIGURE 3.1   The Cotton Export Boom and Bust

SOURCE: Calculated from UNFAO database at <http://www.fao.org>.

The most significant expansion of coffee growing came in Honduras, where the amount of coffee land almost doubled. The coffee boom starting in the late nineteenth century largely bypassed Honduras, but following World War II the development of the coffee sector became a primary concern of Honduran elites. New conditions—political stability, a more adequate transportation system, available credit, and rising world prices—made the materialization of their interest possible. By the late 1960s, Honduran coffee earnings were approaching those of Nicaragua, which it surpassed for the first time in 1973.

The major instrument available to governments to promote export development has been the provision of credit, often using capital obtained from international lenders. In some cases laws needed to be changed first; in Nicaragua, for example, reforms in 1941, 1949, and 1952 removed impediments such as a credit ceiling of 173 acres (Belli 1970:390). As a result, by 1951–1952 almost 80 percent of the national bank lending for agriculture in Nicaragua went to a few hundred producers of cotton, sugar, and sesame (IBRD 1953:292). More generally, almost two-thirds of total bank loans for agriculture in Nicaragua in 1952 went to coffee and cotton producers; by 1956 cotton growers alone were receiving about the same proportion, as they still were in 1970 (Wheelock Román 1980:204). Similarly in El Salvador, the relevant institutions consistently lent over three-quarters of their credit between 1961 and 1975 to planters of the same two crops (Burke 1976:485). In Honduras the proportion of agricultural credit allocated to cotton and coffee from 1950 to 1974 varied between 52 and 68 percent (Posas 1979:49).

Cotton has been unimportant in Costa Rica,[7] where the more important new export was beef, as discussed below. In the late 1960s, the production of coffee and beef received about two-thirds of Costa Rica's total agricultural credits (Kriesberg, Bullard, and Becraft 1970:38). By 1972 the cattle sector in Costa Rica received more credits than the rest of agriculture combined (Barahona Riera 1980:53). The following year it got even more than the industrial sector: 31.4 percent of all national banking system credit went to the expansion of the cattle industry that year (Guess 1979:44). And the terms were easy; for most of the 1970s cattle credit in Costa Rica was provided at interest charges below the inflation rate. Some investors took their credit granted for cattle grazing and instead put it into saving certificates or bought more land (Edelman 1992:250).

Little of the postwar credit in the region went to the smallholder, although there were important country differences. Lenders were less likely to discriminate on the basis of farm size in Costa Rica and Honduras but were likely to do so in the other three countries, where most of the credit went to large farms, even though they were just a small minority of all farms. In El Salvador in the 1970s, for example, large farms received up to double the national average of credit per cropped acre, but the smallest ones received only about one-twentieth of the average (Daines 1977:9; also see Adams, Graham, and Von Pischke 1984 and Hatch, Ames, and Davis 1977). These huge disparities in access to agricultural credit made it easier for the largeholder to expand farm size and made it harder for smallholders to retain their farms. Consequently, agricultural lending policies facilitated the concentration of land in the postwar era, often utilizing funds obtained from international sources such as the United States.

Raising Cattle for Export

Cattle grazing had been traditional on the underutilized lands of the larger estates of Central America since the early colonial period.[8] Demand for meat was weak, however, because the domestic market was limited in such poor countries. Whether for domestic or minor export trade, cattle were usually sold live by the head rather than by weight, minimizing incentives for improvements in herd quality. Expanding domestic and especially international beef markets during the postwar period, though, changed the cattle business in Central America into a major commercial operation. Pastures and herds expanded and practices modernized. The most important stimulus was the growth in demand for the "industrial-quality" beef used in fast foods for sale in restaurants and in frozen food aisles of grocery stores in the United States. The United States imported almost no beef in 1960; by 1980 nearly 10 percent of the beef consumed

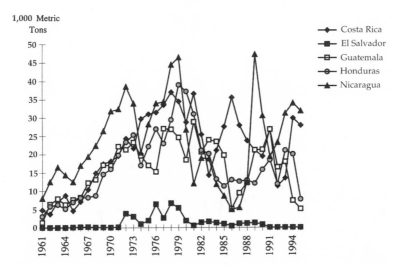

FIGURE 3.2   Beef Exports, 1961–1995

SOURCE: Calculated from UNFAO database at <http://www.fao.org>.

was imported. Although only about one-eighth of this amount comes from Central America (the major suppliers are Australia and New Zealand), this trade nevertheless became one of the more important earners of foreign exchange for the region. Grass-fed cattle and old dairy cows are too tough for U.S. steak standards but fine for fast-food uses. Even high-quality steer meat from Central America, though, still gets classified—and sells—at the lower, industrial-level prices (Edelman 1992:194).

The development of the Central American cattle industry received substantial assistance from international actors. One study, for example, estimates that over half of the loans made to the region during the 1960s and 1970s by the World Bank and the Inter-American Development Bank for agriculture and rural development promoted the production of beef for export (Keene 1980:2).[9] Substantial loans from the United States also played a major role by facilitating herd expansion and improvement and building packing plants for the export trade. Credit during these expansionary years disproportionately went to the larger ranchers, with repayment often subsidized and on lenient terms. Private foreign capital has been involved as well. In Honduras, for instance, foreign capital initiated the beef export industry and for a period controlled the two largest packing plants, providing about three-quarters of all exports (Slutzky 1979:166–169).

The development of this trade is portrayed in Figure 3.2. Excluding El Salvador, where beef exports have been unimportant, there is a common pattern up to about 1983. The volume of beef exports climbed steadily through the 1960s, dropped temporarily in the early 1970s before rising to

Percent

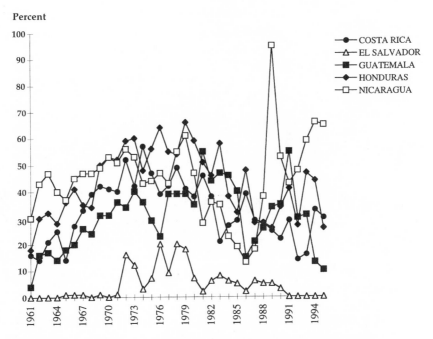

FIGURE 3.3   Beef Exports as a Percentage of Production, 1961–1995

SOURCE: Calculated from UNFAO database at <http://www.fao.org>.

new levels of exports, followed by a steep decline into the early 1980s. At this point two sets of patterns diverge sharply. Beef exports have returned to high levels for Costa Rica and Nicaragua (with the impact of domestic events in Nicaragua in both the late 1970s and 1980s clearly shown in these data). Meanwhile, exports have fallen to a low level in Guatemala. Honduras could be placed in either set, depending on whether the last two data points are the beginning of the Guatemalan trend or a few aberrant years within essentially the first trend.

A major reason the growth of Central American beef exports has been controversial is that it was based not just on expanded production but also on an increasing percentage of production for export rather than domestic consumption. This can be seen most clearly in Figure 3.3. At the start of the 1960s, all of the countries exported less than 20 percent of production, except for Nicaragua, which was just below 30 percent. The export share of production then rose, reaching at least 50 percent at some point for each country (again excluding El Salvador) and averaging around at least 40 percent into the early 1980s for Nicaragua and into the mid-1980s for the other three. The record in more recent years has been erratic. However, if data for the past few years are averaged out, each country is exporting about 10 percent more of production than it was in 1961, except for Nicaragua, which in the hyperinflation year of 1989 exported almost all production and where the export percentage remains at a historically high level.

A second reason for the controversy surrounding the expansion of the Central American beef industry has been its role in the massive deforestation of the region. Most pastureland in the region was once covered by forest; much of it should have remained in forest as land unsuited for sustainable pasture—an issue to be discussed more fully in the next chapter.

It is clear that recent years have been problematic for the beef export industry. The U.S. market has not continued to expand as rapidly as has the Central American export potential. Indeed, U.S. imports peaked in 1979 as beef consumption declined from 92 pounds per person in 1977 to an estimated 77 pounds in 1985 (*World Development Forum* 1985:2). Access to the U.S. market was governed from 1964 to 1979 by a system of voluntary export restraints and since then by mandatory quotas that set each country's share of the U.S. market below its export capacity.[10] An additional problem has been pesticide contamination, usually the result of promiscuous spraying by cotton planters. In order to export to the United States, a processing plant must pass periodic inspections. With substantial frequency during the late 1970s and early 1980s, inspectors temporarily suspended permission to export to the United States. Such suspensions were a major factor, for example, behind the fall in Guatemalan exports for the early 1980s, shown in Figure 3.2.

Central American officials have attempted to get their quotas increased, but the quota system was established by the U.S. Congress largely in response to the considerable pressure from the U.S. cattle industry, which wants to restrict access in order to protect prices. Because relatively low beef prices have prevailed in recent years, any significant increase in quotas is unlikely unless the market situation changes. Indeed, real international meat prices in 1990 were half what they had been in the peak year of 1970 and far lower even than those of 1960 (Kaimowitz 1996:26). As a result of these difficulties, Central American exporters have been looking for other markets, with partial success. Mexico in particular has been an important market alternative to the United States, but the North American Free Trade Agreement (NAFTA), once it is fully implemented, is expected to undercut Central American exporters (Kaimowitz 1996:28).

Export Expansion and Land Use Patterns

The increasing allocation of agricultural land to the production of the major export crops to the detriment of major food crops is clearly portrayed for each Central American country in Figure 3.4 (precisely how this came at the expense of food crops is documented in the next chapter). The

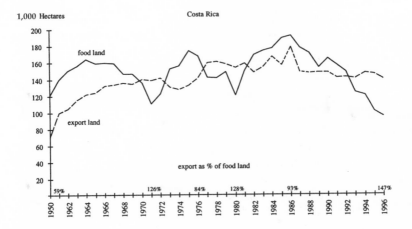

1,000 Hectares — Costa Rica

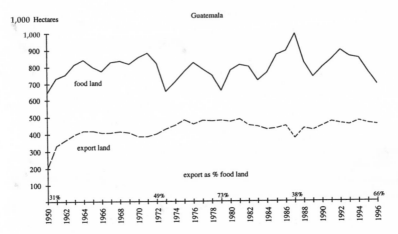

1,000 Hectares — Guatemala

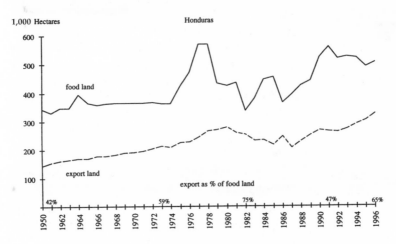

1,000 Hectares — Honduras

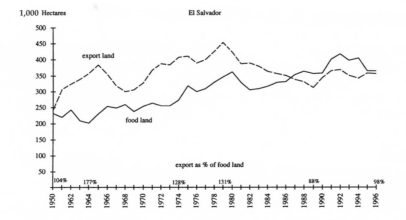

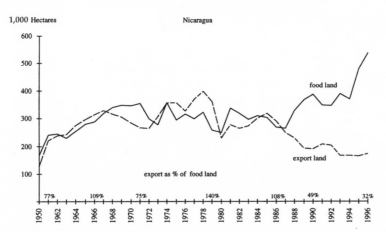

FIGURE 3.4   Land Use Changes, 1950–1996

NOTE: Total amount of land planted in basic food crops and export crops; 1950 is annual average for 1948–1952.

SOURCE: Calculated from UNFAO database at <http://www.fao.org> except statistics for 1948–1952, which are calculated from UNFAO, *Production Yearbook,* various years.

amount of land devoted to the four major export crops (these data in-clude neither land for banana cultivation nor cattle grazing)[11] steadily ex-panded in each country from the late 1940s through the late 1970s, whereas the amount of land in food crops featured greater fluctuations. What is significant, though, is that the ratio of export to food land (shown along the horizontal axis of each chart in Figure 3.4) increased in each country to the late 1970s, usually by a substantial amount.

At this point interesting differences occur among the countries. In the two that went through the greatest political strife and policy changes in the 1980s, El Salvador and Nicaragua, the amount of land devoted to ex-port crops declined, whereas that allocated to food crops rose, with these changes especially prominent in Nicaragua. Consequently, these two countries by the mid-1990s had a lower export-to-food-land ratio than they did at the beginning of the dataset, early in the postwar period.

Conversely, the other three countries have a higher proportion of land in export production at the end of the dataset than they did at the beginning of the era, and substantially so. Costa Rica, Guatemala, and Honduras also featured roughly similar patterns during the 1980s, when export land re-mained relatively constant while food land fluctuated generally in an up-ward direction. Then in the 1990s the export ratio grew, although as a result of different trends within each country. The actual increase in the propor-tion of agricultural land devoted to export crops in these three is undoubt-edly even greater. For one reason, these are the banana-producing coun-tries, and Costa Rica and Honduras are reported to have significantly expanded banana area under cultivation in recent years. And second, these countries have moved most aggressively into the export of new agricul-tural crops (especially Costa Rica and Guatemala), land that is not included in this data (but an issue that is addressed later in this chapter).

Stepping back and looking across the whole time period for the region, we can divide the postwar era into three stages. In the first, running from the beginning of the era to the late 1970s, land devoted to export crops ex-panded more rapidly than that devoted to food crops, and consequently the proportion of land in export production climbed, usually by a notable margin. During the second stage, that is, the 1980s, the trend reversed, and the export land ratio fell. This trend continues into the present for El Salvador and Nicaragua, although the other three countries entered a new stage in the 1990s of increasing bias toward export crops.

Critical factors in explaining the reversal between the first two stages were the armed conflicts in Guatemala, Nicaragua, and El Salvador and the subsequent changes in agrarian policy in the latter two. The relation-ship between political constraints and land use patterns, however, also runs in the opposite direction. As shown in Part 2, the postwar agrarian transformation was a primary underlying cause of the armed conflicts and therefore of the policy changes that followed. That is to say, the transformation associated with the expansion of postwar export agriculture generated new forces that then limited its further expansion.

International constraints were clearly at work as well. Market limits were reached in the 1970s for all of Central America's major agricultural exports; the future seemed to promise at best only slowly growing international markets and uncertain prices. Cotton illustrates the point well. Because it is the most speculative of the commercial crops, the amount of land planted in cotton fluctuated widely over the years in response to changing prices. Except for a few good years in the 1970s, real cotton prices have declined steadily since 1951 (Edelman 1992:316). By contrast, the costs of the imported inputs necessary for mechanized cotton growing continued to rise relentlessly. International forces also are related to the renewed export expansion of the most recent period, as the region desperately attempts to earn sufficient foreign exchange to meet its crushing international debts, as discussed below.

Nontraditional Agricultural Exports Today

A team of agricultural experts counseled the Guatemalan government in 1970 that "the fairly bleak prospects which coffee and cotton are facing on the world demand side make it unlikely that the crops can continue to be the dynamic and propulsive forces in the growth of the overall economy" (Fletcher et al. 1970:49; also see OAS 1974:90–91). Their advice was correct and applied not only to these two crops but to bananas, sugar, and meat as well. The region's ability to produce its export crops has been far greater than the world market's ability to absorb that production. Furthermore, at the end of the 1970s the real world price for each of these commodities (with the qualified exception of coffee) was below the 1970–1974 average; except for sugar, the 1979 real price was also below annual averages for 1965–1969 (Kessing 1981:32). Coffee's higher price was due to a frost that limited Brazil's huge exports and therefore was only temporary. And the problem continues. In 1993 real prices were below those of 1980 for each of the five with the exception of bananas (Conroy et al. 1996:18). Export expansion through diversification, then, continued to be an imperative for Central American development even after the export boom of the first decades of the postwar era. By the early 1980s, a new imperative was added: Because of rapidly escalating foreign debts, the search for new, or "nontraditional," exports (NTXs) to provide the necessary foreign exchange to service these debts became a major concern of Central Americans, as well as international advisers and lenders.[12]

Most attention in Central America has been given to the cultivation of fruits and vegetables to be sold in the United States, either fresh (during

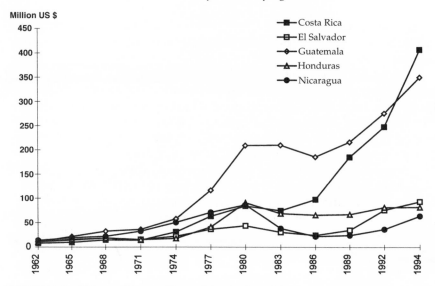

FIGURE 3.5   Value of Nontraditional Agricultural Exports, 1961–1995

NOTES: Annual averages for three-year periods.

SOURCE: Calculated from UNFAO database at <http://www.fao.org>.

the winter season) or frozen. Many of these are attractive because their return is substantially higher than traditional crops; in fact one study estimated that 247 acres in flowers could earn more than 49,400 acres in cotton or sugarcane (Thrupp 1995:60). Efforts at export diversification have been undertaken by private individuals both on their own initiative and with governmental encouragement. The task has often been more difficult than anticipated, and many efforts have resulted in failure (Belli 1977; Conroy et al. 1996; Goldberg and Wilson 1974). Nonetheless, eventually significant successes were registered, as is clear from Figure 3.5, which operationalizes nontraditional agricultural exports (NTAEs) as the remainder when the traditional five commodities are subtracted from the value of all agricultural exports.[13]

The development and expansion of nontraditional agricultural exports has received considerable assistance from the United States, going as far back as the late 1960s, when the U.S. Agency for International Development (USAID) encouraged the government of Guatemala to establish an export promotion center and to adopt legislation that would provide incentives to attract foreign investors to export industries (NACLA 1974:11–15). This was followed in 1970 by a USAID loan of $8.5 million to encourage the expansion of new vegetable and fruit crops, as well as flowers, aimed at regional and international markets (USAID 1970). More

USAID loans came in the second half of the 1980s, a period when the Guatemalan government also sought through its policy instruments to more effectively promote NTX expansion (Colindres 1993). The results of these efforts are vividly apparently in Figure 3.5: The value of Guatemalan NTAEs took off earlier than elsewhere in the region, shooting up sharply throughout the 1970s and again since the latter part of the 1980s. By the mid-1990s, NTAEs in Guatemala provided about 22 percent of all export value (the highest percentage for the region), up from about 9 percent in the early 1960s.

One of the best-known efforts in Guatemala is Alimentos Congelados Monte Bello, S.A. (ALCOSA), now a subsidiary of Hanover Brands. ALCOSA was developed with considerable financial assistance from the Latin American Agribusiness Development Corporation (LAAD), which in turn received USAID loans in the 1970s of at least $17 million. LAAD is a private company organized in 1970 to finance and develop agribusiness projects in Latin America and the Caribbean; its shareholders have included Bank of America, Cargill, Castle & Cooke, and Chase Manhattan Bank. Some of its early projects were criticized for promoting upper-status domestic consumption or export expansion instead of the interests of the "small man" (Lappé and Collins 1978:423–424). In contrast, ALCOSA was designed to fulfill later USAID guidelines to benefit the rural poor. By 1979 it had purchased 11 million pounds of cauliflower, broccoli, brussels sprouts, snow peas, and okra from 2,000 farmers, 95 percent of them "very small," for export to the United States (Kusterer et al. 1981:6). Whether it succeeded in its social objectives, though, is a matter of some controversy, as discussed in the following chapter.

The development of U.S. programs to benefit the poor directly was characteristic of the "new directions" of the middle to late 1970s. More typical of U.S. policy during the Republican administrations that followed was direct attention to the stimulation of export production itself, especially through private initiatives. This approach was taken up particularly by USAID, which began a "private-sector initiative" and created a new Bureau for Private Enterprise.[14] Throughout the decade and into the 1990s, USAID aggressively recommended to Central American governments the necessity of rapid NTX expansion.

Honduras probably received the most attention from the United States in this regard during the early 1980s. Previous efforts by the Honduran government to promote exports were characterized by USAID as "sporadic and relatively unsuccessful," but through "policy dialogue" between the two governments and through USAID assistance, the Honduran government in 1983 passed an export incentives law, one manifestation of its becoming "more committed to altering its policies to favor exports" (USAID 1984:9). In the following year, the United States initiated an export promotion and services project, similarly aimed at boosting nontraditional exports by Honduran entrepreneurs.[15] This eventually expanded into a five-year program with a $23.5 million budget (Thrupp 1995:22). In 1984 USAID also established a $20 million Honduran Agricultural Research Foundation to provide applied research activities for both export and food crops (USAID 1985:115–123). But in the end U.S. assistance for agricultural research and extension took on a clear bias toward export crops over crops for domestic consumption (Murray 1994:112). The same bias was found in the Honduran government, even to the point of its refusing credits when an agrarian reform collective farm attempted to return to basic grain production after growing cotton and melons for export (Boyer 1982:192–194).

This new round of export cropping in Honduras, however, did not enjoy the same success as in Guatemala. Through the last half of the 1970s, NTAE values rose rapidly in Honduras, Nicaragua, and Costa Rica, taking all three to roughly the same level in 1980. But that proved to be the high point for the first two, not surprising for Nicaragua, given the events of the following decade. What is remarkable is the contrasting experience of Honduras and Costa Rica. As late as 1982–1984, NTAE value was at the same level for the two countries. But although it stagnated in Honduras, the boom in Costa Rica has been extraordinary, with total value quadrupling in essentially one decade and NTAEs' contribution to total export value doubling since the early 1960s (in Honduras it actually declined by five percentage points and in Nicaragua showed no change).

During this time USAID had been hard at work in Costa Rica. These efforts, along with substantial funding, led to the formation of a private-sector business association for export promotion in 1983; two years later this became the Private Agricultural and Agroindustrial Council (CAAP). To assist its export promotion work, CAAP received $35 million from USAID between 1986 and 1990 (although about 90 percent of that was in local currency [Sojo 1992:62]); in at least one of those years this was more than the entire budget of Costa Rica's agricultural ministry. At the same time that subsidies and assistance to small farmers were being cut in Costa Rica, substantial subsidies to export producers—usually larger farmers—helped to fuel the recent boom in NTAEs. The United States also was at the heart of a "private" export-promotion center, the Costa Rican Coalition for Development Initiatives (CINDE), that was founded in 1983 to foster nontraditionals, in part through promoting new government incentives for exporters. Funded by the United States in the beginning with the local equivalent of almost $12 million, USAID remained the sole financial benefactor of CINDE until 1991 (Clark 1997). Although not at the same levels, the United States provided similar subsidies to export producers throughout the region, for example, funding a $20 million agribusiness development project in El Salvador from 1987 through 1992 (Conroy et al. 1996:69–90; Thrupp 1995:22).

Central American governments often did what they could as well through national policy changes to encourage export expansion (albeit sometimes under pressure from international lenders). Some of these policies were mandated for more general reasons related to structural adjustment agreements, such as more realistic exchange rates and other macroeconomic policies intended to reduce inflationary pressures. Others, though, were specifically targeted to NTX promotion, especially exemption from or reduction of taxes and duties, free trade zones, and reduced restrictions on profit repatriation. Direct subsidies also were provided, such as Costa Rica's certificate of tax payment (CAT), a tax credit awarded to NTX producers. At an estimated cost of 8 percent of the total government budget in 1990, CATs were phased out in the early 1990s because of both their cost and controversy concerning their concentration in the hands of larger companies—1.5 percent of recipients received 27 percent of benefits, with Del Monte's pineapple operation receiving the most, and over half of these benefits went to foreign enterprises (Barham et al. 1992:55–56, 67–71; Sojo 1992:62; Thrupp 1995:29–34).

Central America and the Internationalization of Agriculture

The postwar expansion of Central American export agriculture is the latest in a sequence of stages that have reinforced the region's linkage to the international economic system. Trade in agricultural commodities was part of preconquest economic life. Spanish colonialism internationalized this trade, carrying it beyond Middle America to the Iberian peninsula and eventually to other parts of Europe. The development of the coffee and banana trades in the nineteenth and early twentieth centuries further tied Central America to the international system. Although this linkage was crucial to the interests of economic elites and governments, many of the region's people worked apart from this international connection, in subsistence agriculture.

The postwar expansion of agricultural exports furthered the region's integration into the international system as a larger share of the population became more dependent on the success of agricultural exports and/or the availability of agricultural imports, from wheat to fertilizer. With the growth of cotton, sugar, and beef exports and the further expansion of coffee cultivation, an increasing proportion of the population grew dependent on the response of foreign markets. This dependency is not limited to commercial farmers and their employees; peasants in Honduran agrarian reform settlements and on their individual plots in the Guatemalan highlands now produce fruits and vegetables that are consumed in the United States. Meanwhile, increasing numbers of farmers, small as well as large, make at least some use of imported fertilizer, seeds, or expertise.

Concurrent with the greater importance of export production has been the growing reliance on food imports, consumed largely in urban areas. Their availability also affects price levels of domestic farm goods. Central America's integration into the world food system has been furthered by the foreign-based multinational corporations that are often involved in the importation of agricultural inputs and commodities and in the processing and marketing of agricultural production. The internationalization of Central American agriculture, then, includes not only the expanded scope of the international connection (the relative share of land, workers, and consumers involved) but also the region's penetration by international actors, from development agency advisers to multinational agribusiness.

From the perspective of traditional notions of comparative advantage, the internationalization of Central American agriculture is regarded as a positive development. Through the production and export of certain commodities of which it enjoys a comparative advantage over other countries, Central America is able to maximize its trading potential and, accordingly, promote its economic development.[16] Rising export earnings can mean more funds for investment—both private investment of profits and public investment of monies from taxes on exports and income. Finally, a growing export sector can foster the development of new enterprises through backward linkages (producers of goods and services consumed in production) and forward linkages (processing and marketing of the export crops). As a result, expanding export production also can provide more employment and income for rural workers.

The doctrine of comparative advantage has long had its dissenters, especially in Latin America. Their arguments tend to focus on two issues brought to the fore around midcentury particularly by the Argentine economist Raúl Prebisch and other scholars associated with the United Nations Economic Commission for Latin America (ECLA/CEPAL). This position claims, first, that the prices Central America has received for its agricultural exports have declined relative to the cost of the manufactured goods it imports from its industrialized trading partners. There is significant evidence to support this claim for Central America depending on the period examined, but its more general application is still the subject of some controversy.[17] The second claim of this position is easier to demonstrate. The prices of primary commodities are very unstable, and as they rise and fall dramatically, so, too, do export earnings. Such instability is especially traumatic for countries, such as those of Central America, that are dependent on the export of only a few primary commodities. Great price instability hinders rational economic planning by both private individuals and governments, and substantial economic (and therefore social and political) havoc can be created when prices fall. It is not surprising, then, that export diversification has been a major goal in Central America.

Central American Export Expansion: A Preliminary Assessment

Positive results from the regionwide effort at export diversification and expansion can be seen in the following tables. The importance of coffee is clear in part A of Table 3.2. On the eve of World War I, coffee constituted at least 80 percent of the exports of El Salvador and Guatemala and almost two-thirds of those of Nicaragua. Coffee had composed 88 percent of Costa Rica's exports as recently as 1892 (Cardoso 1977:189), but the 1914 figure demonstrates the considerable impact on that nation of the banana trade (which was of lesser importance at the next date, however, because of disease problems). The continuing need to diminish reliance on coffee exports is shown by the figures for 1937; just prior to World War II, coffee still contributed the bulk of the region's export earnings. Substantial success at export diversification is shown by parts B and C of Table 3.2, which provide the share of the top two exports for each country and then the traditional five exports. Indeed, in the mid-1990s the share of export earnings of the five traditional exports was significantly less than that of the top two in 1961 and less than just coffee earnings alone in 1937 (with the exception of Honduras).

During the first decades of the postwar period, the Central American economies performed reasonably well. Although growth slowed during the 1970s, for the period 1961 to 1980 each country's gross national product (GNP) per capita expanded, as Table 3.3 indicates, notably in Costa Rica and Guatemala. Exports grew steadily during this period, averaging an annual increase of 6.7 percent for the five countries, with Costa Rica again in the lead (Weeks 1985:64). As can be seen in Figure 3.6, export values peaked in the late 1970s and then stagnated during the difficult years of the 1980s. Although all of the countries have registered successes with export diversification, Figure 3.6 shows that the larger goal of export expansion has had only mixed results across the past two decades or so. It is perhaps not surprising that export earnings in El Salvador and Nicaragua in 1995 were still not back to their pre–civil conflict levels. Probably more noteworthy is that this recovery of their 1980 peak was not reached in either Guatemala or Honduras until the mid-1990s. In contrast, Costa Rica reached this turnaround point in 1986 and has enjoyed a sustained boom in export earnings since; a decade latter it had the second highest exports per capita in Latin America (Chile having the highest).[18]

The dismal export performance of the 1980s is mirrored by the more general economic growth data. The worst part of the decade was the first half; growth slowly resumed thereafter. Nonetheless, each economy contracted for the entire "lost decade." Costa Rica was the first to pull out of this tailspin in 1986, as Honduras and Guatemala did the following year,

TABLE 3.2   Structure of Exports

	Costa Rica	El Salvador	Guatemala	Honduras	Nicaragua
Coffee Exports as a Percentage of Total Exports					
1914	35	80	85	–	63
1937	53	91	66	–	44
1954	41	88	71	26	46
1965[a]	41	50	46	16	17
Top Two Exports as a Percentage of Total Exports[b]					
1962	73	76	69	61	56
1971	57	60	44	59	38
1986	54	67	45	62	62
1994	37	33	24	39	20
Traditional Five Exports as a Percentage of Total Exports[c]					
1962	82	77	82	66	69
1971	72	66	59	67	60
1980	60	69	56	63	67
1986	61	70	58	67	74
1994	40	37	43	43	41

[a]Beginning with 1962, three-year annual averages.

[b]Top two exports in the 1960s. Coffee for each plus bananas for Costa Rica and Honduras; cotton for El Salvador, Guatemala, and Nicaragua.

[c]Coffee, bananas, cotton, beef, and sugar.

SOURCES: For 1914, Woodward 1976:160; for 1937, International Institute of Agriculture 1947; for 1954, Herring 1964:825; for other years, calculated from UNFAO database at <http://www.fao.org>.

TABLE 3.3   Growth Rate of GDP per Capita

	1961–1980[a]	1981–1985	1980–1990	1990–1993	1988 as % of 1980[b]
Costa Rica	2.6	–2.6	–0.6	2.6	94
El Salvador	1.5	–2.9	–1.8	2.6	85
Guatemala	2.7	–3.9	–2.0	1.2	80
Honduras	2.2	–2.5	–0.8	1.1	89
Nicaragua	.4	–2.7	–4.3	–3.4	71

[a]All figures indicate annual averages for the periods shown.

[b]GDP per capita in 1988 as percentage of 1980.

SOURCE: IDB 1989:tables 11-3 and B-1 and 1994:239.

but El Salvador was not able to until 1990, and in Nicaragua the decline did not end until 1994. Picking a midpoint from this record, Table 3.3 gives 1988 per capita income as a percentage of that in 1980—lower in every case. In fact, 1987 Costa Rican per capita gross domestic product (GDP) had fallen back to the level of 1974; for Honduras, it had regressed back to 1973; for Guatemala, back to 1971; for El Salvador, 1964; and for

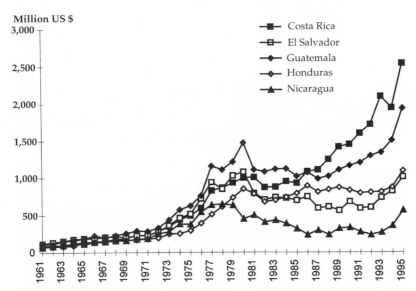

FIGURE 3.6   Total Export Value, 1961–1995

SOURCE: Calculated from UNFAO database at <http://www.fao.org>.

Nicaragua, all the way back to the level of 1960, according to the Inter-
American Development Bank (*Times of the Americas*, September 20,
1989:16).

The causes of this miserable performance were both external and internal. With their economies based on the export of a small number of commodities, the Central American countries continued to be vulnerable to
variations in the international system—a system on which these weak
economies have virtually no impact. A major cause of the economic stagna-
tion of the region during the first half of the 1980s was the severe worldwide recession at the decade's beginning. In addition, the recession-
induced reduction of demand for Central American products was
paralleled by deteriorating terms of trade, as the relative costs of imports
outpaced the value of regional exports. The terms of trade dropped for each
country through the decade to 1985. Although they recovered by 1988 for
three of the countries, the terms of trade then fell again through 1992, least
for Costa Rica, most for El Salvador (IDB 1989; UNDP 1995:180).

Starting in the 1960s, the Central American countries began receiving
sizable loans from international agencies to promote the expansion of
exports, as well as for other developmental objectives. The growth of the
region's economies and exports, however, was not proportional to the
foreign debts incurred, as Figure 3.7 clearly demonstrates. As a result,

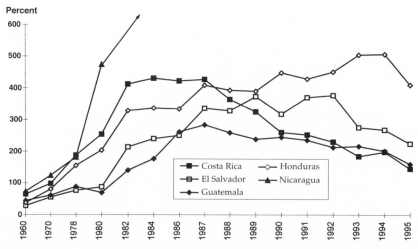

FIGURE 3.7   Outstanding Foreign Debt as a Percentage of Export Earnings

SOURCES: For 1960–1984, IDB 1982, 1986; for 1960 and 1970, exports from UN 1985. For debt, 1986–1995 from IDB database at <http://www.iadb.org>; for export earnings, UNFAO database at <http://www.fao.org>.

Nicaragua entered the 1970s with its foreign debt larger than its annual export earnings; by the later part of the decade both Costa Rica and Honduras crossed this unfortunate threshold, joined in the early 1980s by El Salvador and Guatemala.

These data indicate, then, that the Central American countries already were in debt difficulties before the political strife and economic "lost decade" hit around 1980; when they did, the results were disastrous.

Export earnings dropped in the conflict-torn nations of El Salvador and Nicaragua and grew only minimally for the rest during these years of recession and declining terms of trade. Beginning around 1978–1980 the debt-to-export ratio rose precipitously in each country, climbing above the 400 percent mark in Costa Rica and Honduras and almost to that level in El Salvador. In Nicaragua the result was catastrophic: The debt-to-export ratio skyrocketed from almost 500 percent in 1980 to over 1,000 percent in 1984 to a peak of almost 4,800 percent in 1992 before dropping back to 1,700 percent in 1995. Meanwhile Costa Rica developed the fourth highest per capita foreign debt in the world.

Central Americans, then, found themselves in the 1980s locked into a situation where a high and increasing percentage of their export earnings had to be used to pay their foreign debts. Indeed, in some years just the service payments made on the debt consumed most of the year's export earnings. Consequently, a new imperative for export expansion was created: Exports had to be expanded to pay foreign creditors. Ironically, as the example of Costa Rican cattle suggests, at least some of that debt was created by loans used to stimulate earlier rounds of export expansion—an expansion that did not always pay its own way. The final irony is that the guidelines governing loans from the United States ensured that they did benefit U.S. interests, which provided the goods and services they purchased (see, for example, Dosal 1985).

Eventually, though, economies began to grow again, and the debt-to-export ratio improved, first in Costa Rica and Guatemala by 1988, last in Honduras. None of the countries, however, are close to where they were in 1970, except for Costa Rica, whose export boom of recent years has dramatically cut its debt-to-export ratio by two-thirds.

Conclusion

Many features of the postwar agrarian transformation in Central America are well summarized by two terms: "commercialization" and "internationalization." The traditional dualistic system of subsistence peasantry and inefficient haciendas (joined more recently by banana plantations) has been replaced by a highly differentiated agrarian structure in which even the most remote peasants are touched by the monetized commercial system. This transformation has been promoted by new commercial opportunities both in growing urban areas and overseas. Export markets have been especially important to development-minded elites, who have continued into the present era to seek their objectives through the expansion of agricultural trade. One result has been the further linkage of Central America to the international system. The developmental objective has been elusive, however. Although individuals have prospered, the keys to sustained rapid economic development have yet to be found.

This assessment of the agro-export development model is still incomplete for Central America, however, because its impact on rural society has yet to be examined. The historical overview of the previous chapter and the work of other scholars suggest that the implementation of the model in unequal societies such as those of Central America would undermine the economic security of much of the rural population. The claim to be examined is that access to land, food, and employment for many rural people will have been reduced by the implementation of this model. The objective of the following chapter is to evaluate this hypothesis for the postwar experience in Central America, with its rapid agricultural export expansion.

Notes

1. For background information, see Bulmer-Thomas (1987) and Torres Rivas (1993).

2. For a detailed discussion of the development of the cotton and beef industries in Central America, see Williams (1986). More generally, see Bulmer-Thomas

(1987). Among the case studies of individual countries that parallel at least parts of this chapter, see Grindle (1986) for Brazil, Colombia, and Mexico; Galli (1981) for Colombia; Caballero (1984) for Peru; Feder (1981) and Sanderson (1986) for Mexico; and McSpirit Alas (1994) for El Salvador and Guatemala.

3. Background on Honduras during this period may be found in Blutstein et al. (1971), Checchi (1959), Posas (1979), and Posas and del Cid (1981).

4. For background on Nicaragua during this period, see OAS (1966), Deere and Marchetti (1981), IBRD (1953), Laird (1974), Lethander (1968), and Núñez Soto (1981).

5. Of course, it must be remembered that almost all the figures provided in this book should be regarded as approximate, given the difficulties of collecting reliable data in poor countries, especially for the earlier time periods.

6. Major sources for this section include Adams (1970), Belli (1970), Browning (1971), Deere and Marchetti (1981), DeWitt (1977), Harness and Pugh (1970), IBRD (1953), Laird (1974), Lethander (1968), Murray (1994), Place (1981), Quiros Guardia (1973), Satterthwaite (1971), and Williams (1986).

7. Cotton production has proven to be too risky on the Pacific lowlands of Costa Rica because rainfall is more unpredictable than for the countries to the north (Edelman 1992:318).

8. Useful in preparing this section were Allen, Dodge, and Schmitz (1983); Edelman (1992); *Foreign Agriculture* (1960); Guess (1979); Kaimowitz (1996); Metrinko (1978); Myers (1981); Parsons (1965); Roux (1978); Shane (1980); Spielmann (1972); USDA (various issues); and Williams (1986).

9. More specifically, between 1974 and 1978 World Bank loans included $55.6 million to Costa Rica, $40.6 million to Honduras, and $24.3 million to Nicaragua for livestock development programs; Inter-American Development Bank livestock lending between 1961 and 1977 included $16.8 million for Costa Rica, $4.4 million for Guatemala, $36.9 million for Honduras, and $9.1 for Nicaragua (Shane 1980:36–37, 41–42).

10. Although the United States has encouraged Central American export growth, it also pursues policies that restrict that growth, such as beef and sugar import quotas and cotton dumping to lower world prices. For further discussions, see Brooks (1967) and Pastor (1982).

11. The Food and Agriculture Organization of the United Nations (FAO) stopped reporting the amount of land in banana production in the mid-1970s, and the data reported for pasture are too constant across the years to be taken seriously. The absence of these data reduces the meaningfulness of the export-food ratio in any one year, especially for the major banana-producing countries. For periods when banana area under cultivation and pasture are relatively constant, patterns across the period are valid. This underreporting of export land is most serious for Costa Rica, which is the only country that is one of the top two producers in both categories. How much land in Costa Rica is under banana cultivation is a matter of controversy: González (1993:58) indicates a decline from 1973 to 1988 down to 21,000 hectares; in the early 1990s the general manager of the government banana corporation cited 33,500 hectares; and environmental groups claimed closer to 50,000 (*Update,* July 10, 1992).

12. A nontraditional export is usually defined as a commodity not previously exported, either because it was not produced at all or was produced only for domestic use (Barham et al. 1992:42). Some definitions also would include new markets for already exported commodities, but this seems of a different category. For Central America, contemporary nontraditional exports largely have been agricultural in nature, although certainly new industrial exports are a major goal of current efforts as well.

13. Although this definition includes as NTAE some commodities that long had been exported on a minor basis, this causes little distortion since, as can be seen from Figure 3.5, in the early 1960s the total value of all NTAE was quite low.

14. For a discussion and criticism of this approach, see Newfarmer (1983).

15. Intended to provide both technical assistance and foreign exchange, the project was characterized as "a massive technology transfer" utilizing "the accumulated experience of highly experienced trade executives" from the United States budgeted at a cost of about $100,000 per year per adviser (USAID 1984:42).

16. For sophisticated treatments of the concept of comparative advantage, see Chenery (1979) and Streeten (1990).

17. Among the many discussions, see especially Bulmer-Thomas (1987:334; 1994:264–275) and Barham et al. (1992:58–59), as well as de Janvry (1981:158–162); Ffrench-Davis and Tironi (1982:49–125); Gordon-Ashworth (1984); Lofchie and Commins (1982); Meier (1984:502–505); Payer (1975); Streeten (1974); and UNECLA (1950).

18. Costa Rican foreign trade minister José Rossi, address to the Canadian Council for the Americas, Toronto, Canada, May 17, 1996, <http://www.cinde.or.cr/discurso.html>,

Chapter Four

Agrarian Transformation and Rural Economic Security

After three decades of export expansion and commercialization in the agricultural sector following World War II, most of Central America's rural population remained very poor. In fact, the number of rural people with insufficient access to food, employment, and land had increased dramatically up to the outbreak of the civil conflicts beginning in the late 1970s. Many public officials and international advisers continued to recommend further expansion of agricultural exports as the best solution to this continuing tragedy; others pointed to the obvious role played by the area's rapidly growing population. Although descriptive accounts had been offered of the connection between the expansion of commercial, and especially export, agriculture in the postwar period and increasing rural misery, it was not until the publication in 1979 of William Durham's *Scarcity and Survival in Central America* that the issue received its first careful, systematic analysis for the region.

In this landmark study Durham (1979:21–51) demonstrated that the pressing problems of land and food scarcity in El Salvador were not primarily the result of a high population growth rate. Rather, these scarcities were largely the consequence of the concentration of landownership that occurred with expanding production of crops for the export market. In 1971, for example, 21.8 percent of the agriculturally active population of El Salvador had access to no land, and 29 percent more had access to less than 2.5 acres. Durham's analysis indicated that for this slight majority of the agricultural sector, "it was not so much the rapid growth of the population after 1892 as the simultaneous trend toward land concentration that created the scarcity of land" they faced (p. 48). The underlying cause of this concentration was the development of new opportunities for export crops, first coffee and then cotton and sugar. As landownership was consolidated and land switched to export production, basic food production suffered; although per capita food production declined in El Salvador from 1950 to 1970, the amount of land per capita devoted to export crops actually increased.

In this chapter, following the lead of Durham and pursuing the historical patterns identified in Chapter 2, I analyze the impact of the expansion of commercial agriculture on the rural population of Central America in the postwar period. Through an integration of descriptive accounts with an analysis of empirical data, I discuss the impact of this transformation on the following aspects of rural economic security: access to land, food, employment, and income; and environmental quality.[1] This discussion is largely restricted to the antecedents of the political conflicts of the late 1970s–1980s, with more recent trends to be examined in the individual country chapters that follow in Part 2. The chapter concludes with an evaluation of the merits of the agro-export development model in countries with gross disparities in the distribution of key resources.

Access to Land

Central America entered the contemporary period with land distributions that were grossly unequal. Most of the rural population lived on small subsistence plots, and most of the private land was owned by a small percentage of the landholders. Pressure on land supply already existed in El Salvador and in the most densely settled portions of the other countries. Because much of the region's land is not suitable for cultivation and because population has grown at rapid rates, it can be assumed that eventually population growth alone would progressively erode access to land for rural people. But this has not been the only force with which peasants have had to contend.

As commercial agricultural possibilities expanded in the postwar period, peasants found themselves in competition with more powerful groups. Sometimes the competition has been financial; as the commercial boom in agriculture developed, land values climbed. New profit-making opportunities attracted affluent urban groups to speculative agriculture, thereby increasing the demand for land and, again, inflating land values. As values have gone up, poor rural people have found themselves priced out of the market. On occasion, the competition has been settled by force as peasants have been dispossessed of land whose use they had enjoyed. This usurpation in turn has led to land invasions and occupations by angry peasants and, as a result, violence among peasants, large landholders, and sometimes the state.[2]

Traditionally, small landholders in Central America have had an insecure claim to the land that they worked, whether they were sharecroppers, renters, or "owners." An agricultural census in Honduras in the
mid-1960s, for example, found that the probability of producer ownership steadily increased with farm size; only 14 percent of the smallest
farmers (under 3.5 acres) owned their land, whereas 94 percent of the
largest (over 1,500 acres) were owners (Fonck 1972:30–31). More recently,
a USAID report in 1982 found that three-quarters of Honduran farmers
still had insecure tenancy (USAID 1982:1).

In one tenure pattern typical of traditional agricultural systems in Latin
America, peasants lived and worked on land that belonged to a large
landowner, using it in return for a contribution of their labor or a share of
their production. This arrangement between families may have gone back
for generations, but it has been swept aside in many cases by the spread
of modern commercial agriculture. The peasants have been turned out to
make way for more intensive cotton or sugar growing or cattle grazing. A
primary location of this transformation has been the Pacific lowlands. In
his description of the change in this part of El Salvador from subsistence
tenant farming mixed with low-density cattle grazing to mechanized cotton cultivation, Browning (1971:236) noted the cancellation of tenant relationships and the eviction of squatters. If they remained in the area, the
only income-earning opportunity for the dispossessed came during the
short cotton-picking season. They were reduced to living in straw huts
built on the public right-of-way along roads and riverbeds.

A similar fate has befallen many renters. Surveys in both Honduras and
Nicaragua in the 1960s found that most rental contracts were unwritten
and usually covered less than one year (Fonck 1972:31; Lethander
1968:185). Although such relationships might have been stable in the past,
as commercial alternatives opened to owners, renters often were pushed
aside. Sometimes contracts were not renewed; on other occasions rental
prices were escalated too rapidly for peasants to afford (Parsons
1976:11–15). One technique that has been applied throughout the region
has been to rent out uncleared land at a nominal price for a short duration. At the end of the contract, the land, by then cleared by the renter, is
converted to cattle grazing. No longer needed, the former renter must
move on to find new land.

The major source of conflict, however, has been the use of land where
access rights are in dispute. Despite the impact of the Liberal reforms of
the nineteenth century, public lands remained in all of the countries, especially Honduras. Furthermore, ownership of land in previously remote
areas is frequently unclear. Peasants have often enjoyed use of such lands
for years, even generations, without challenge. The expansion of export
markets in the contemporary period, however, has made these lands at-

tractive to elites, and it is here that peasant and elite interests have collided directly.

This conflict has been most intense, and best documented, in Guatemala. Lands isolated from the well-populated highlands and from good coffee-growing areas had long been an important frontier region for land-poor peasants. This was true, for example, of the Pacific lowlands, which were of little interest to elites until after World War II. As described in the previous chapter, new export possibilities (cotton), insect and disease control, and improved transportation opened the area to commercial use. Peasants were pushed aside in what has been called a "massive displacement" (Quiros Guardia 1973:87), as vast landholdings came to monopolize the area. Today the highest degree of land concentration in Guatemala is found in the Pacific lowlands; by 1964 the largest 3.7 percent of farms in that region occupied an incredible 80.3 percent of the land (Graber 1980:20). Although not in such an extreme degree, the same pattern can be found in Nicaragua; there, too, land concentration was the greatest in the Pacific region, where 1.6 percent of the farms held 55.8 percent of the land in the mid-1960s (Taylor 1969:19).

More recently, the pattern has been replicated throughout the Northern Transversal Strip, a lowland area that runs across the neck of Guatemala from the Caribbean to the Mexican border. This area was well settled by Indians prior to the conquest but then depopulated by the introduction of malaria and other tropical diseases. As land pressures mounted in the highlands centuries later, Indians returned, especially in recent decades. As long as elites perceived this area to be remote and unattractive, Indians could settle freely on public lands, lands thought to be public, and private lands with or without the (absentee) owner's consent. Peasant access to this land began to be challenged by the late 1960s, however, as road construction and the possibilities of mineral wealth made the area of interest to elites (Carter 1969:309; Lassey et al. 1969:6–42).

One of the first large-scale manifestations of this conflict occurred in 1978 in the town of Panzós when over 100 Kekchi Indians, including at least twenty-five women and five children, were massacred by soldiers. Families of many of the Indians in this area had worked their land for the previous forty to 100 years, but without legal title. In recent years, though, entire communities of Indian peasants have been displaced by developers attracted by discoveries of oil and nickel deposits and by the booming real estate market along the road (IWGIA 1978:11; Aguilera Peralta 1979). A statement issued by priests and nuns from the Diocese of La Verapaz (which includes Panzós) claimed that in their attempts to gain more land, landowners would "resort to semilegal manoeuvres and all sorts of pressures, without excluding violence" (IWGIA 1978:45). Peasants in the area had been working without success to obtain legal titles.

On May 29, 1978, some 700 peasants from a number of outlying communities traveled to Panzós, some in protest, others to learn of documents that they had been told had arrived from the capital concerning their efforts to work through government channels to protect their interests. In response to a very minor provocation, soldiers apparently thought they were being attacked by the peasants. The statement by the La Verapaz religious workers describes the result:

> Soldiers . . . started to blaze away; some of them climbed onto the town hall building and shot from there on the crowd of men, women and children. At the same time, there were trigger-happy individuals at different spots, some even from private houses, who joined the general shooting, firing at those who tried to run away in different directions. . . .
>
> The utterly terrified peasants, trying to escape in turmoil, found death in the park, in the streets, in the neighboring cornfields, and some who got seized by panic flung themselves into the river and drowned before reaching the other side. (IWGIA 1978:47)

The Northern Transversal Strip had been officially designated for colonization by landless Indians. By 1979, however, it was reported that "much of the best land has already fallen into the hands of wealthy farmers and army officers" (*NY Times,* April 5, 1979:A2). In fact, former presidents General Kjell Laugerud and General Romeo Lucas García were reported to possess large estates in the area, which came to be known as "the zone of the generals" (*NY Times,* April 5, 1979:A2).[3]

To the north and even less developed but facing similar pressures is El Petén. Both it and the strip have been viewed as important new sites for cattle grazing. Through the mid-1970s, 60 percent of the country's cattle were grazed in the south, but because of competition from export crops and pesticide contamination from cotton spraying, forecasts were that the north would become the country's major cattle region (Hemphill 1976:3). Consequently, the government offered handsome incentives for settlement in the remote area. Despite the serious landlessness problem chronic to Guatemala, much of the land was sold in large parcels to buyers often selected because of their good connections. Nonetheless, tens of thousands of poor farmers have migrated to the area, settling in abandoned or unclaimed lands, setting the scene for what are predicted to be "major and probably violent land conflicts" (Kaimowitz 1995:25).

Although the violence has not been as pervasive or as excessive in the other countries of the region, similar dynamics have occurred elsewhere as well. No less an authority than the second Somoza president, Luis, attested to the dispossession of peasants in Nicaragua. He told an agrarian reform symposium in 1965 that rapid agricultural development since 1955 caused "a violent displacement of the campesinos who traditionally worked the lands in periods of unemployment. Before my eyes I saw lands cleared and many people leave, permanent workers, sharecroppers, and squatters—by the force of the plow and machinery" (quoted in Taylor 1969:19).

Similarly, in Honduras observers have described the impact of the spread of commercial agriculture on the peasantry as an "enclosure movement" (e.g., Parsons 1976:11–15). This characterization is particularly apt for that country, which, uniquely in the region, entered the contemporary period with much of its land public—in 1974 still about one-third of all land. Although Honduras has a low population density, good agricultural land is increasingly scarce. Consequently, as land values have increased in recent decades, peasant access to public lands has been contested by other interests who have been willing to use physical force. As is elaborated in Part 2, there is a direct relationship between the widespread violence in recent years in rural Central America and the intensified competition for land between peasants and large growers, a result of the spread of commercial agriculture.

Peasants' efforts to defend their interests—whether through peaceful petition, land invasions and occupations, or the creation of peasant organizations—have often been perceived by elite groups as a challenge to their priorities. This perception strengthens intensely when radical guerrilla movements advocating structural transformations in behalf of the poor appear in rural areas. The result in El Salvador, Guatemala, and Nicaragua was repression directed at the rural population—repression that reached extraordinary levels in the early 1980s in the first two countries.

An indication of the extreme disparity in access to land in the region is provided by Tables 4.1 and 4.2. Table 4.1 gives the findings of all of the region's official landownership surveys. The most recent results show that in the 1970s in El Salvador the largest 1.5 percent of holdings had 49.5 percent of the land; in Guatemala 2.6 percent of holdings had 65.5 percent; in Honduras 4.2 percent of holdings had 56 percent; in Nicaragua 1.8 percent of holdings had 46.8 percent; and even in Costa Rica 9.1 of holdings had 67.2 percent of the land.

These figures are not directly comparable among countries because they come from different years and because the size categories used in the surveys vary. Table 4.2 standardizes the data so as to allow intercountry comparisons and to facilitate comparisons within individual countries over time. It presents a coefficient of inequality for both the smallest and the largest farms during the latest agricultural census (sometime in the 1970s).[4]

Looking first at the small farms, we see that for both time periods they had only about 4 percent of what would be an equal share of land in Guatemala, Honduras, and Nicaragua. Although their share improved marginally over time in the first two countries, it declined in Nicaragua,

TABLE 4.1   Land Distribution by Farm Size, 1950s–1970s

Country and Size (Hectares)	Percentage of All Farms			Percentage of Land		
	1950s	1960s	1970s	1950s	1960s	1970s
Costa Rica	(1955)	(1963)	(1973)	(1955)	(1963)	(1973)
1 < 10	51.0	49.8	47.8	5.1	4.7	3.8
10 < 20	15.1	15.0	14.0	5.3	5.1	3.9
20 < 100	28.0	28.2	29.1	28.3	27.8	25.1
100 < 1,000	5.5	6.6	8.6	31.6	36.6	42.0
1,000+	0.4	0.4	0.5	29.7	25.8	25.2
El Salvador		(1961)	(1971)		(1961)	(1971)
< 1	–	47.2	48.8	–	3.9	4.8
1 < 10	–	44.2	43.9	–	18.0	22.5
10 < 50	–	6.7	5.8	–	20.6	23.2
50 < 200	–	1.5	1.2	–	19.8	21.1
200+	–	0.5	0.3	–	37.7	28.4
Guatemala	(1950)	(1964)	(1979)	(1950)	(1964)	(1979)
< .7	21.3	20.4	31.4	.8	1.0	1.3
.7 < 3.5	54.9	54.6	47.0	8.2	10.6	9.2
3.5 < 7	12.2	12.5	9.7	5.3	7.0	5.7
7 < 44.8	9.5	10.4	9.3	13.5	18.9	18.7
44.8 < 450	1.9	1.9	2.3	21.9	26.5	30.7
450 < 900	0.2	0.1	0.2	9.5	10.0	12.8
900+	0.1	0.1	0.1	40.8	26.0	21.6
Honduras	(1952)		(1974)	(1952)		(1974)
< 1	10	–	17	0.4	–	0.8
1 < 5	47	–	47	8	–	8
5 < 10	18	–	15	8	–	8
10 < 50	21	–	18	27	–	28
50 < 100	3	–	2	11	–	12
100 < 500	2	–	2	18	–	22
500 < 1,000	0.2	–	0.1	8	–	7
1,000+	0.1	–	0.1	20	–	15
Nicaragua		(1963)	(1971)		(1963)	(1971)
< .7	–	2.1	5.8	–	–	–
.7 < 3.5	–	33.7	25.9	–	1.6	1.0
3.5 < 7	–	15.6	12.1	–	2.0	1.2
7 < 35	–	28.1	31.7	–	12.0	11.1
35 < 77	–	10.2	12.3	–	12.5	11.7
77 < 350	–	8.9	10.3	–	30.8	28.1
350 < 777	–	0.9	1.1	–	11.3	11.0
777+	–	0.6	0.7	–	29.7	35.8

SOURCES: For Costa Rica, Carvajal 1979b:2; for El Salvador, OAS 1975:53; for Guatemala, Hough et al. 1983:71; for Honduras, Ruhl 1984:50; for Nicaragua, Warnken 1975:47, 49.

TABLE 4.2   Coefficients of Inequality in the Distribution of Land, 1950s/1960s and 1970

	Smallest Farms		Largest Farms	
	1950s/1960s	*1970s*	*1950s/1960s*	*1970s*
Costa Rica	.1	.079	74.3	50.4
El Salvador	.08	.098	75.4	94.6
Guatemala	.037	.041	167.7	114.7
Honduras	.04	.047	93.3	110.0
Nicaragua	.04	.032	49.5	51.1

NOTE: Coefficients were obtained by dividing percent of all land by percent of all farms in both the smallest and largest farm categories from Table 4.1 (to provide closer equivalence, the two smallest Nicaraguan categories are used and the two largest for Guatemala and Honduras). A coefficient of 1.0 for all size categories would represent an equal distribution of land. A figure less than 1.0 indicates underdistribution; over 1.0 means overdistribution. For example, Costa Rica's ".1" in 1950s/1960s means the smallest farms had one-tenth of an equal share of the land, and the "74.3" in the third column means the largest farms had 74.3 times an equal share.

which thus had the worst underdistribution of land in the 1970s. Costa Rica also registered a decline sufficient to place it behind El Salvador in the 1970s. The latter had the biggest increase in the share of land in the smallest category, a still very small 9.8 percent of an equal share. In each country new land had been brought into cultivation by small farmers in the period covered here, land either previously too marginal to be attractive or in frontier regions. Nonetheless, most of these gains by smallholders are not registered in these data, as they were offset by population growth and dispossession.

Limited access to land combined with rapid population growth has meant a declining person-to-land ratio and a growing landless population. In Guatemala, for example, arable land per capita was 4.2 acres in 1950, 2.3 in 1973, and 2.0 in 1980 (Hough et al. 1983:73). The problem has been regionwide; the percentages of rural families with 10 acres of land or less in 1970 were as follows: El Salvador, 86.7; Guatemala, 83.9; Costa Rica, 72.6; Honduras, 65.8; and Nicaragua, 59.5 (Weeks 1985:112). Such figures are not fully comparable because of productivity differences among the countries; generally, subsistence requires more land in the last two countries and less in Costa Rica. Furthermore, complete landlessness has developed during recent decades as a particularly severe problem for the rural population. Rates for the region in 1970 varied from around one-quarter to one-third of rural families without any land (Weeks 1985:112; also see Lassen 1980:125–157). Landlessness then continued to climb during the decade, reaching the highest levels in El Salvador at perhaps around 40 percent (Burke 1976:476; Seligson 1995).

For the largest farms summarized in Table 4.2, the country groupings change somewhat: Guatemala and Honduras remain the most unequal group, but Nicaragua and El Salvador shift places from the comparison of the smallest holdings. For the three countries with the worst overdistribution of land in the largest farms, the disproportionate share of these estates by the 1970s was around 100 times that of an equal distribution. Even in Costa Rica and Nicaragua, the shares were more than fifty times that of an equal distribution. The most substantial trend toward decrease in overdistribution occurred in Guatemala (though it still had the greatest inequality), followed by Costa Rica. However, increases in this measure of land concentration occurred in El Salvador and Honduras and marginally in Nicaragua. What is remarkable here is that in three of the countries the share of land in the largest farms actually increased, as measured by official censuses. Observers in each country have pointed out that in recent years owners have subdivided large holdings and registered them in the names of various family members as a precaution in the face of threatened land reform (especially the expropriation of underused land on large estates). It should also be noted that the underreporting of large estates is a recurrent problem (Hough et al. 1983:19).

Access to land also has a qualitative dimension. A peasant family that has been forced off of 10 acres of fertile land and has moved to 15 acres of eroded hillside with little fertility has improved its position in the data discussed above; in reality, of course, its living standard will deteriorate with its ability to produce. Numerous reports point out that the most fertile land is controlled by the largest holdings, the farmers with the smallest holdings being left with the less valuable land. Yet the small farmers use their land intensively, usually for food crops, whereas many of the large holdings are still underutilized and devoted primarily to export crop production and cattle grazing. Data from El Salvador in the 1970s make the point well. Farms with under 2.5 acres cultivated 80.9 percent of the land; farms over 500 acres were on the average only 26.8 percent cultivated (Durham 1979:52).

In summary, Central America entered the contemporary period with gross inequalities in access to land because of the agrarian transformations of the conquest, the colonial period, and the Liberal reform era. In the decades following World War II, this already serious inequality was worsened by both rapid population growth and further land concentration, as the powerful outbid the poor or dispossessed the weak of land in order to take advantage of new commercial opportunities, especially for export commodities.

Increasing numbers of rural families have found themselves with a diminishing land supply or, most seriously, with no land at all. Their loss is both psychological and material. The continuation of a land-based lifestyle is a strong value for farming families, not only in peasant communities in later developing countries but also among commercial family farmers in other countries such as the United States. When pushed off of the land, the farming family has lost a lifestyle that is usually intensely preferred, from which a meaningful and stable identity and worldview were derived, and that connected it to earlier generations. The loss is also material, of course. Land provides security: Even the smallest holding has room for a home, for some subsistence crops, and perhaps for growing firewood. As the size of that holding shrinks, its ability to produce subsistence diminishes as well. The great majority of the region's rural people no longer have enough land to sustain a family.

Access to Food

The damaging impact of the conversion of land to coffee growing in the past century was noted by many observers. In Guatemala, for example, the first report of the newly organized Department of Agriculture pointed out in 1899 that "Guatemala has found it necessary to import corn and other foodstuffs, whereas before coffee production became so extensive articles of prime necessity were produced in adequate amounts, and at low prices, within the country itself" (quoted in Mosk 1955:17). As coffee cultivation continued to spread during the next decades, food production suffered; annual corn production from 1919 to 1929 was no better than it had been in 1899 (Jones 1966:189). Similarly, in El Salvador in the 1920s a new wave in the conversion of food crop land to coffee drove food prices up rapidly; between 1922 and 1926 corn prices doubled and bean prices escalated 225 percent (Durham 1979:36).

The expansion of export crop production is directly related to food scarcity, and therefore to malnutrition, in at least four ways. First, land was often converted from food to export production. Sometimes small farmers undertook this conversion, but generally it was the work of larger landowners, who might dispossess peasants in the process. Second, during the postwar period new land was opened up for cultivation—67 percent more land up to 1976–1978 for the crops examined in this study. Much of this land could have been devoted to the production of food for the growing population, but instead 63 percent of it went to export crops, and a substantial amount of additional land (not included in the present data) was converted to cattle grazing. Third, peasants desiring to buy their own land have had to face not just a decreasing supply but also its inevitable, concomitant, higher prices, which they often cannot pay. Finally, there are the vast holdings the banana companies obtained earlier in the twentieth century, largely without disturbing landholding patterns. As good land became scarce in the past several decades, these holdings were needed by but inaccessible to a rapidly growing rural population. United Fruit's Costa Rican holdings in 1950, for example, constituted not only 4 percent of the country's entire territory but also almost double the amount of land planted in the three basic food crops. Banana company holdings in Honduras in 1971 were estimated still to be around 494,000 acres, which was about one-half of the total area planted at that time in the three basic food crops. Furthermore, the land controlled by the banana companies is usually among the most fertile in the region, yet over the years much of it has been left uncultivated; in Honduras in 1960 only 17.7 percent of that land was under cultivation and another 11.1 percent was devoted to cattle pasture (Carias and Slutzky 1971:275).

Food Supply Trends

The data provided below indicate that Central American food production has been harmed, in some cases significantly, by the expansion of export agriculture. Figure 4.1 gives the per capita domestic production of the basic food crops (beans, corn, and rice, plus wheat for Guatemala) for each country indexed to 1961–1963. What stands out from this data is that per capita basic food production is lower in every case at the end than it was at the beginning of the postwar period, in some cases notably so. Most of this decline occurred in the first decades up to the early 1960s, with the sole exception of Honduras. In the latter country, food supply has shrunk consistently across the years, as it virtually has in Guatemala up to the present and in Nicaragua up to the early 1990s. Patterns for the other two countries are more complex.[5]

In Costa Rica and El Salvador, basic food production rose on a per capita basis from the early 1960s to the late 1970s, but then their patterns diverged. In the most recent years, grain production in Costa Rica has dropped sharply, corresponding to a decline in land devoted to these crops, especially rice. Although there has not been a corresponding increase in land planted in the traditional export crops, this decline does correlate with a significant boom in the production of the new nontraditional crops.[6]

El Salvador is the only country of the five with a strong record in basic food production in recent decades, the only one where per capita production in the mid-1990s was greater (and considerably greater) than it was in the early 1960s. Land planted in corn increased in both the 1960s and the 1970s, but much of this was of marginal quality. More important was a significant effort undertaken to increase corn yields with the technical and financial assistance of international advisers (Davis 1973; Davis and Weisenborn 1981; T. S. Walker 1981). As a consequence, corn yields rose in El Salvador from 1961–1965 to 1978–1979 by 70 percent, almost double the rate for Central America as a whole. Corn yields by 1979 were almost double those of Honduras and Nicaragua. They then climbed by close to

Food Supply
Index

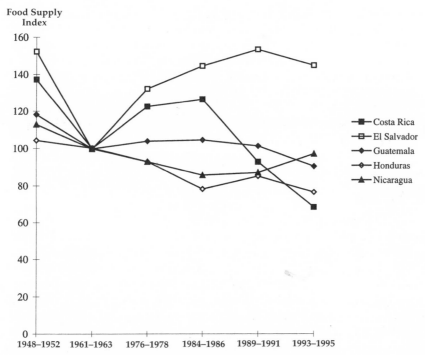

FIGURE 4.1   Change in per Capita Domestically Produced Food Supply,
1948–1952 to 1993–1995

NOTES: Index of per capita domestic production of basic food crops (beans, corn, and
rice, plus wheat for Guatemala). Annual averages. Indexed with 1961–1963 = 100.

SOURCE: UNFAO at <http://www.fao.org> except for 1948–1952, which is from
Production Yearbook.

another 20 percent, explaining the per capita production increase to the
mid-1980s, but essentially have leveled off since, with the production increase to the end of the decade more a function of about a 15 percent expansion of land planted in corn. Meanwhile, the gap in corn yields with
the rest of the region has been closing, with Guatemalan yields now virtually at the same level—indeed, increase in yields for the entire period
since 1961 has been the greatest in Guatemala.

As domestic food production has dropped behind population growth
rates, the countries of the region have been forced to import greater quantities of food to meet expanding needs. All of the countries now import a
substantial percentage of their basic grains and beans: from 14 percent of
total supply in Guatemala in the late 1970s to 41 percent in Costa Rica
(Brockett 1990:80). Imports are an important addition to the food supply
for the urban population, but the impact they have on the lives of rural
people, especially those living in isolated areas, is unclear. It might be

economically rational at the aggregate level to convert land to export crops commanding higher prices than basic food crops, which are then imported to cover the resulting food deficit, but it would be rational at the individual level only if everyone were reached by those imports and only if the balance held true for each person. The unfortunate reality is that what a rural family would be able to produce for itself if it had access to land, it might not have the income to purchase in the marketplace, especially if it has been displaced from land then converted to export crops.

A good illustration of this point is provided by Boyer's (1982:226–234) field research in the southern highlands of Honduras. Among the families he studied, two-thirds commonly could not produce enough food to meet their needs. Boyer estimates the minimal amount of land (with a three-year fallow cycle) needed to provide a family with an adequate diet to be about 17.8 acres in that area; but the mean land access of his subjects was only about 6.4 acres. Later research found these trends continuing in the same area (Stonich 1993), as indeed they are throughout all of Honduras.

However, it does not follow that government policies promoting national food self-sufficiency would necessarily benefit the poor either. Data from Honduras in the late 1980s, for example, indicate that large farmers were sixty-five times more likely to sell their grains at subsidized prices than small farmers, six times less likely to report lack of access to subsidized credit, and three times more likely to receive adequate and timely support from the extension service (Norton 1992:47). As amplified in this chapter's conclusion, the crucial variable is the social context within which policies are implemented. The more unequal the society, the greater the importance that policies be carefully targeted to the interests of the poor (but the less likely that this will occur).

Meat Supply Trends

Food crop land has been lost during recent decades not only to export crops but also to cattle raising. If this conversion resulted in enhanced domestic meat supply, then its impact on food supply in the countryside might be neutral or even positive. This has not been the case, however, as Table 4.3 clearly demonstrates for 1961 to 1995. Across the entire period, beef production expanded, but not enough to keep up with a growing population, except in Costa Rica.

Actually, it is important to divide the period into two stages. Up to the late 1970s, production in the region grew rapidly, more than enough to exceed population growth, with the narrow exception of El Salvador. However, much of this production was targeted for the expanding export market discussed in the prior chapter. Consequently, when exports are taken into account, the beef supply available domestically shrank in all but Costa Rica

TABLE 4.3   Changes in Meat Production and Supply, 1961–1963 to 1993–1995 (% change in annual averages)

		Beef and Veal		Chicken
	Production	Production per Capita	Supply[a] per Capita	Supply[a] per Capita
Costa Rica	194	17	4	1,131
El Salvador	35	−35	−35	708
Guatemala	36	−45	−48	526
Honduras	109	−22	−38	519
Nicaragua	68	−37	−61	256
Central America	87	−24	−35	586

[a]Supply equals production minus exports.
SOURCE: Calculated from UNFAO database at <http://www.fao.org>.

and Nicaragua (and with the latter undoubtedly because of herd reduction due to the civil chaos). Because much of the cattle grazing occurs on land previously devoted to food crops, the impact of these developments on domestic food supply has been severe. Compounding the problem for many peasants is that they did not themselves make this switch in production; instead, they were dispossessed by cattle ranchers. Beef exporting had a further deleterious effect as domestic beef prices were internationalized: In 1949 beef prices in Costa Rica were about 25 percent of those in New York City, but by 1978 they had climbed to 77 percent (Place 1981:147–148).

As discussed in Chapter 3, beef exporting in recent years has encountered serious difficulties, from quota ceilings and price problems in the United States to pesticide contamination at home; accordingly, export pressures have diminished. However, beef production itself has grown at slower rates since the late 1970s, so the decline in per capita production has grown more severe since that time. When combined with exports, the drop in supply per capita across the entire period has been serious in each country except Costa Rica, which registered just a small increase.

The data thus far, then, indicate a serious decline in this significant aspect of food supply; however, there has been an important offsetting development: the greater role of chicken in Central American diets. The final column of Table 4.3 shows the dramatic increase in chicken meat supply for the region. When chicken meat supply is combined with beef supply, it is clear that growth in the former has more than compensated for the decline in the latter. Figure 4.2 indicates that coming into the 1980s the per capita meat supplies of the five countries (i.e., both beef and chicken) were essentially the same as in 1961, but since then three very different patterns have emerged. Already with the largest supply, Costa Rica also has enjoyed the greatest increase, opening a pronounced gap in domestic meat supply between it and the other four countries. Con-

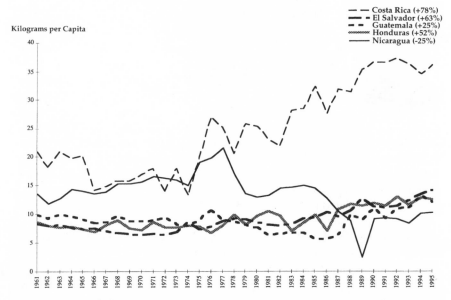

FIGURE 4.2   Meat Supplies, 1961–1995

NOTE: Per capita domestically produced bovine and chicken meat, minus exports. Percentage next to country name is change, 1961 to 1995.

SOURCE: Calculated from UNFAO at <http://www.fao.org>.

versely, the drop in meat supply in Nicaragua that began in the late 1970s continued through the 1980s, almost reaching the point of exhaustion in the economically calamitous year of 1989, and then subsequently climbed back up, but still not enough to reach 1961 levels. Compared to the contrasting Costa Rican and Nicaraguan patterns, the remaining three track fairly closely, with relatively minor fluctuations across the years and with most of their gains occurring since about 1986–1987. Perhaps most notable is that of the three, Guatemala began at a higher level and El Salvador at the lowest, but by 1995 these relative positions had reversed, with El Salvador having the largest increase in domestic meat supply across the period after Costa Rica.

The Scope of Malnutrition

If the people of Central America had access to sufficient food to provide adequate diets, then the harmful effects of agricultural export expansion on food supply would be of little concern. Costa Rica makes the point well. In 1972 it produced three times its protein requirements and almost twice its caloric requirements, yet about one-fifth of the population around that time consumed less than 90 percent of the recommended calories and in some areas this was true for the majority (Carvajal 1979b:71–73). As Carvajal (1979b:74) points out, "the constraints on these nutrients getting to the people lie in their distribution system."[7] Unfortunately, malnutrition is one of the most prominent manifestations of the region's poverty; the nutritional impact of major socioeconomic changes must accordingly be a primary criterion in their evaluation. The best data still come from the 1970s. If anything, the situation outside of Costa Rica can be expected to be worse today since these data predate the full impact of the agricultural commercialization of that decade and the violence and economic crisis of the next. This can be inferred, for example, from rural poverty rates, which escalated for the region as a whole by 10 percent to 80 percent of rural inhabitants from 1980 to 1990 (Vilas 1995:148).

In three of the countries (El Salvador, Guatemala, and Honduras), 48 to 61 percent of the population consumed less than 90 percent of the recommended daily calories in the early 1970s (IDB 1978:138–141). And many people received much less. An FAO study of Guatemala in 1970 estimated that average daily calorie consumption for the poorest half of the population was only 61 percent of the recommended amount. In contrast, the consumption of the highest income groups was excessive: Those with the highest incomes (the top 5 percent) consumed 193 percent of the recommended calories; the next 15 percent consumed 133 percent (USDA 1981).[8]

Although the malnourished of all ages are more susceptible to diseases than others and less capable of recovery, this vulnerability is the greatest among small children, and malnutrition is associated with high rates of mortality among the young. Furthermore, protein deficiency is of greater consequence for the young: If deprivation is severe in the first years, it can result in diminished brain development. The percentages of protein-calorie deficiency for children under five in Central America in the early 1970s were very high, ranging from the high 50s for Costa Rica and Nicaragua to the low 70s for Honduras and El Salvador to 81.4 percent in Guatemala. When the children with mild malnutrition are removed, almost one-third of all children under the age of five suffered from moderate to severe rates (mainly the former) in Guatemala and Honduras, about one-quarter in El Salvador, and around 15 percent in the other two countries. Tragically, the occurrence of malnutrition among Central American children increased during 1965–1975 (outside of Costa Rica), a decade in which the region's GNP increased annually by a rate of 4.9 percent (Reutlinger and Alderman 1980:407–409).

The obvious connection between childhood malnutrition in rural areas and the family's lack of sufficient land has been documented by several studies (Brown 1983:18; Carvajal 1979a:227; Valverde et al. 1977:6). Children's nutritional status also can be a function of the type of agricultural system in which families live. The worst instances of moderate to severe malnutrition in El Salvador in 1976 were found in the coffee and the sub-sistence regions, but for different reasons (Valverde et al. 1980). In the subsistence regions, inadequate fertile land and the lack of other income-generating opportunities accounted for diets unable to meet basic needs. In the coffee-growing regions, however, land is fertile, and the cash crop produces substantial incomes for the landowners. The inadequate diets of the 13 percent of the Salvadoran population that lived on this land and produced the crop, then, were a function of the form of social organiza-tion within the region and the resulting maldistribution of the income that was largely generated by the poorly paid coffee workers.

The continuing high rates of malnutrition in Central America are in part a result of the region's rapidly increasing population. But the deterio-ration of the per capita domestic food supply documented in this chapter has occurred simultaneously with a major transformation in agrarian so-ciety. The spread of commercial agriculture and the rapid expansion of the share of land devoted to agricultural commodities aimed at foreign markets are fundamental causes of the continuing misery of many of the rural people in Central America. Now they must find new means of pro-viding for their needs. Under existing socioeconomic structures, however, alternatives have been difficult to discover.

Access to Employment and Income

Public officials and technical advisers have urged peasants to diversify their production into cash crops both to enhance their living standards and to contribute to the economic development of their countries. Generally, this is good advice for farmers with enough land to follow it, and they have tended to follow it. But this strategy is relevant only to a small and dimin-ishing percentage of the rural population. With the rates of landlessness and near landlessness escalating, the goal of improving rural incomes must be discussed in the context of access to more land and/or to other income-producing opportunities. Pending a redirection of the trend toward re-duced land access (a subject of Part 2), the availability of other income-producing opportunities is the major hope for many rural people.

One option, of course, is to leave the countryside altogether and migrate to the cities. Increasing numbers of peasants have made just this choice. The percentage of the total population living in urban areas has grown in each country; in Guatemala, for example, it went from 25 in 1950 to 40 in 1980. Indeed, Guatemala City is expected to hold about 30 percent of the country's entire population by the year 2000. For many migrants, however, migration alters the context of the problem but does not solve it. Between 1964 and 1973, the number of urban jobs in Guatemala grew at only one-half the rate of the urban population (USAID, Office of Housing 1980:4).[9]

For the landless and near landless who have remained in rural areas, the situation has generally deteriorated; for many, it has become desperate. Relative to need, few significant employment opportunities have been created in rural Central America in recent decades, with the exception of jobs on the large, commercial, export-oriented farms. These have done more to worsen the unemployment problem than to ameliorate it, however, because the conversion to export crops created much of the landlessness in the first place. Furthermore, the major export crops of the postwar period require less labor than others. This is particularly true of cotton growing, which is heavily mechanized and which at its peak covered about 10 percent of the region's cropland but provided permanent employment to less than .6 percent of the agricultural labor force (Quiros Guardia 1973:102). Similarly, cattle raising is seven to twenty times less labor intensive than are other forms of agriculture (Ashe 1978:15). It is the small farm that makes the best use of Central America's abundant labor supply, yet the great bulk of the region's land is owned by a small percentage of large holders. In Costa Rica, for example, small farms generate three to four times more employment than do large ones and are usually just as productive (Ashe 1978:13).

This system of export production in concentrated landholdings is incapable of utilizing the existing labor supply effectively, especially in Guatemala and El Salvador. Consequently, rural unemployment and underemployment have climbed in recent years. In Guatemala in the early 1970s, the World Bank (1978:15) estimated, rural unemployment reached 42 percent. In the early 1980s three-quarters of the landless had no permanent employment (Hough et al. 1983:77). Studies of Guatemala during this period accordingly found "a general deterioration of the social and economic conditions of its peasant population," especially the Indians (Davis and Hodson 1982:46).

Even before the 1970s, full-time employment potential was estimated to exist for only 43 percent of El Salvador's rural population (Nathan Associates 1969:59s). A 1976 International Labor Organization study found El Salvador's underutilization of its agricultural population (47 percent underemployed) to be the greatest in all of Latin America (Daines 1977:30; also see OAS 1975). Rural unemployment in each of the countries has been cyclical. In Nicaragua in the mid-1970s, for example, the rural workforce was fully employed for four months of the year; unemployment rates for the rest of the year varied from a monthly low of 13 percent to a high of 42 percent, with an average rate of 24 percent for those eight months (Peek 1983:284; also see Núñez Soto 1981:70–73).

The major income-earning opportunity for this growing surplus of unemployed and underemployed peasants is seasonal work on the large export-producing estates. Some live close enough to do this work with minimal disruption to their family lives, but many others, especially in Guatemala, must leave their homes and migrate to the estates temporarily. The most substantial migratory pattern in the region is the flow of Indians from the western highlands to the large farms in the Pacific lowlands. This pattern, it will be recalled, goes back centuries. Labor was coerced from highland Indians by the conquerors in the sixteenth century for the cacao and indigo plantations. Continuing labor scarcities led the political system to sanction the coercion of the labor necessary to develop the coffee sector in the nineteenth and twentieth centuries. Such laws were repealed in the 1940s; now the coercion comes from the impersonal workings of the economic system.

Deteriorating living standards in the western highlands (from declining person-to-land ratios, soil exhaustion and erosion from overuse, and few opportunities for migration to new lands) have created a surplus labor pool that provides the necessary labor for the coastal plantations. By 1975 some 60 percent of the economically active rural population of the highlands migrated to work on the plantations (Cardona 1978:36–37),[10] making it the world's largest migratory labor force as a percentage of total population (Paige 1975:361). By the end of the decade, some estimated that around 600,000 peasants were part of this seasonal migration (WOLA 1983:3). Yet the income earned in this work is meager, and the transportation, living, and working conditions are often subhuman, according to an International Labor Organization report (Plant 1978:85; also see Burgos-Debray 1984:21–22). Prescient Indians displaced by the expropriation of communal lands by coffee growers over a century ago sent the following message to the president of Guatemala in 1864:

> Everyone is well aware of the ploys used by the coffee growers to seize almost all our land. . . . We cannot help but deplore the fact that these coffee growing gentlemen want to treat us like the European colonists treated the Indians or natives in the country we know today as the great Republic of North America. . . . Could it be that they want to use this factor and historic precedent against us . . . that they want to take our only element of vitality from us, throw us out of our homes and off our land and turn us and future generations into a nomadic and wandering people . . . ? (quoted in Cambranes 1985:74–75)

Income distribution figures for each of the Central American countries make it clear that there is a direct relationship between access to land and rural families' incomes. In 1973 in El Salvador, for example, rural families with landholdings of over 124 acres constituted only 1 percent of the population but received 30 percent of all rural income. Meanwhile, the 9 percent of the families with adequate farm holdings (between 12 and 124 acres) received 16.6 times the income of those with less than 2.5 acres of land, and 20.6 times the income of the landless. Income inequality for

Guatemala during this period was similar,[11] but it was less in Costa Rica (Fields 1980:241; Seligson 1980a:90) and Honduras (Molina Chocano and Reina 1983:77; Torres 1979:16–17), with prerevolutionary Nicaragua somewhere between the two sets of countries (Núñez Soto 1981:50). In recent years, though, the situation has improved in El Salvador but deteriorated in Honduras to closer the level of Guatemala. In 1990 rural poverty was about 30 percent of the total population in Costa Rica but about 80 percent in Guatemala and Honduras (UNDP 1995:178). The income share of the top 10 percent of the rural population in 1989 was 41 percent in Guatemala and 39 percent in Honduras but 30 percent in Costa Rica; in 1995 it was 32 percent in El Salvador. Similarly, when the median income of the bottom 20 percent of the rural population is compared to the median share taken by the top 20 percent, the rural rich received 10.4 times more in Costa Rica, 12.4 more in El Salvador, 13.7 more in Honduras, and 21.4 times more in Guatemala.[12]

To assess more accurately the relationship between rural stratification and income, we must also differentiate categories among both the landless and the landed. Seligson (1980a:90–99), for example, divides the Costa Rican landless into four types. The first two have steady employment but substantial differences in incomes and living conditions. Plantation workers (mainly banana workers) are the envy of the rest of the landless, who rank these unionized laborers in status just after titled landowners. Employees of haciendas (mainly coffee workers), however, make only one-third the income of the plantation workers and usually suffer terrible living conditions as well. But they do have security, unlike the remaining two types of landless peasants, day laborers and migrants.

Modern cotton farms are not important in Costa Rica and are not included in Seligson's study. Other evidence (Valverde et al. 1980) would suggest that life for permanent workers on such farms is better than it is for coffee workers, although certainly less desirable than that of the banana workers. Temporary workers (day laborers and migrants) not only lack employment security but also often toil under inhumane conditions. The plight of the worker in the cotton fields of prerevolutionary Nicaragua, for example, has been summarized this way:

> Harvest workers were stuffed into barracks shelves with roughly the room per person of an Atlantic slave ship; fed rice and beans only if they picked 100 pounds or more of cotton per day; deprived of any semblance of privacy or sanitary facilities; exposed to the unrestricted use of pesticides; and driven to backbreaking labor in the 110 [degree] heat of the Pacific coast by man-killing piece rates. Malaria, dysentery, and diarrheal disease were endemic; intestinal parasites, almost universal. (Paige 1985:106)

Important distinctions can be made among rural people with landholdings not just in terms of the quantity of land they possess but also in the relative security of their access. The most secure but least numerous are owners with legal titles. They are followed by landholders without such titles (who constitute the majority in Honduras, for example, though not in Costa Rica), tenants, and then squatters.

The impact of the spread of commercial agriculture on rural incomes, then, varies among social groups. Those who have managed to hold on to sufficient land have undoubtedly benefited from new income-producing opportunities (for example, see Brintnall 1979:111–114). Others who have been able to obtain permanent employment on modern commercial farms may have improved their position as well, but peasants who have been pushed into the growing pool of the landless and near landless and who survive as day laborers or migrant laborers or as peddlers in urban slums are more likely to have experienced a decline in living standard as well as a loss of economic and psychological security. Consequently, many studies conclude that living standards deteriorated for much of the rural population in Guatemala and El Salvador, followed by Nicaragua, leading to the political conflicts of the late 1970s and 1980s. In contrast, there are data indicating a lessening of both rural poverty and income inequality in Costa Rica continuing up to the present. The implications of these contrasting trends are discussed in the concluding section of this chapter.

Social Impact of Nontraditional Exports

In comparison to the well-established negative social consequences of the prior rounds of export crop expansion, the nontraditional agricultural exports of recent years have been promoted not just for their potential contribution to economic growth and foreign exchange earnings but also for purported positive social impacts. NTAE crops are praised as especially suited for cultivation on smallholdings. Furthermore, they are more labor intensive than the traditional crops, in some cases substantially so: The labor requirements of snow peas are eleven times greater than those for corn and beans (Thrupp 1995:85). Examples of positive social effects have been publicized, but the preponderance of recent evidence indicates that this latest stage of export crop development has once again favored those with greater resources.

One of the most frequently cited cases by both advocates and critics of NTAEs has been the ALCOSA project in Guatemala, discussed in the previous chapter. Critics of multinational agribusiness have used the USAID-sponsored evaluations of ALCOSA as supporting evidence for their viewpoint (e.g., Lappé and Collins 1978:425–426); however, it should be noted that the most complete evaluation (Kusterer et al. 1981) found that the ALCOSA projects had a number of beneficial results, psychological as well as economic and social. As in many NTAE operations, the ALCOSA crops are grown by small to medium-sized landholders producing under contract to U.S.-based multinational agribusiness. It is clear that peasants welcomed the new marketing opportunities and that peasant women benefited from the employment opportunities at the processing plant (Kusterer et al. 1981:2–11). But though ALCOSA clearly responded to very real needs, there were significant costs as well. Contracting peasants became dependent on the company for increasingly expensive seeds and fertilizer and for credit. As production rose, so did the company's quality standards. Finally, in 1980, supply overwhelmed the company's processing capacity, so it temporarily suspended purchases, reneging on many contracts. Some 300–400 of the 2,000 contracting peasants took losses for the year, including a majority in two of the four towns studied. They were left with an abundance of cauliflower in place of the corn and beans they had previously planted (Kusterer et al. 1981:17–24). Similar stories are related throughout the region (e.g., Conroy et al. 1996:49–52).

The example that receives perhaps the highest praise is Guatemala's most successful agricultural cooperative: Cuatro Pinos. Its members (about 1,600 in 1989) had about 740 acres in export vegetables in the mid-1980s, up fourfold from the decade's start. While raising export vegetables, members continued to grow their food crops (and with higher yields than before), but their net return per unit of land was fifteen times higher for snow peas than for corn. Their incomes were rising in the late 1980s, as were those of other area residents who found employment on the members' farms or at the co-op's packing facility. Consequently, both the landowners and the laborers were able to reduce their seasonal migration to export estates outside of the highlands (Barham et al. 1992:72; von Braun and Immink 1994). It might be difficult to generalize from this particular model, however, since the farmers' successes were linked to that of the cooperative itself. There are few examples of successful cooperatives in Central America that were built without significant outside assistance; certainly this one enjoyed such support. And international assistance for rural cooperatives has been declining in recent years.

Furthermore, Cuatro Pinos's successes might be short-lived. For reasons of both risk and capital, the smallest farmers place a smaller portion of their land in export production than do those with more land. Consequently, the smallest farmers capture disproportionately less of the return from NTAEs than the larger farmers, who then use their greater gains to expand their landholdings.

Compounding this dynamic are recent problems with pesticide contamination, which has been working against the smallest producers throughout the region (Carter et al. 1996:51–54). The new nontraditional crops invariably require expensive inputs, especially pesticides. Not only is the cost a problem for smaller growers but because they do not have the expertise for correct use, they tend to use pesticides indiscriminately. Pests then develop resistance, and farmers increase their use of the pesticides, leading to pesticide contamination of the crop and more frequent rejections by U.S. inspectors. Larger growers tend to monitor pesticide use more carefully. When marketers need to test each producer for contamination, it makes sense to purchase from fewer, larger producers, which is the current trend (Murray 1994:65–97; Conroy et al. 1996:11–133). Snow pea growers, who supply a little over half of the fresh snow peas consumed in the United States, are trying a different approach: lobbying the U.S. government to lighten its fungicide restrictions (*Tico Times,* January 27, 1995).

This technical advantage of the larger producers is reinforced in other areas as well. NTAEs are new crops for small producers and often not native to the area (e.g., snow peas). Smallholders lack knowledge about raising the crop, just as they do about marketing it. In these areas the larger producers enjoy substantial informational advantages, as well as the ability to weather fluctuating production levels and foreign market demand. Aggressive technical assistance targeted to smallholders could compensate for some of these disadvantages, but in recent years governments have tended instead to concede the natural advantage of larger producers and have aligned assistance toward them (Barham et al. 1992:68–70; Conroy et al. 1996:43–48).

For such reasons, the larger producers disproportionately benefit from NTAEs. One study of Costa Rica and Honduras in the mid-1980s, for example, found that the largest three enterprises controlled on average 60 to 70 percent of the production of about a dozen different export crops (Thrupp 1995:69). Many of these producers are multinational agribusinesses or nonnative individual entrepreneurs. Furthermore, as with bananas, much of the economic gain of NTAEs appears to go to shippers and brokers rather than growers (Conroy et al. 1996:92–106). In contrast, smallholders often venture only a few years of raising NTAEs, efforts then judged not worth continuing. Yet the apparently never-ending numbers of new farmers willing to try provides contract buyers with a continuing supply for their exporting activities (Conroy et al. 1996:53).

Environmental Degradation

Rapid population growth and the expansion of export agriculture have accounted for substantial damage to the natural environment in Central America. Both forces have caused deforestation and soil erosion and exhaustion, diminishing the land's ability to support the future's even larger population.[13]

Because of population growth and commercial growers' encroachments on peasants' land, land scarcity has been a major contributor to erosion and to the depletion of soil fertility. Peasants have been forced to overwork their land, for example, reducing or eliminating the crucial fallow cycle of traditional growing practices. They have also been pushed onto steeper hillsides, which, once cultivated, are soon eroded by torrential rainfalls. The rains carry the soil into reservoirs, silting them up and ending their usefulness earlier than projected (Hoy 1984).

Commercialization, especially the rapid conversion of land to cotton growing, has also had a direct impact on soil exhaustion and erosion. Browning's (1971) comparison of coffee and cotton growers is most telling in this respect. As he points out, "Whereas coffee farmers realized that sound techniques of cultivation based on applied research were a necessity for the long-term future of the crop, the cotton farmers cleared and cultivated the coastal plain in an attempt to gain maximum and immediate profits with little thought of the long-term effects of their activities" (pp. 240–241).

The conversion of land to cotton growing in Guatemala is discussed by Adams (1970:375–378) in the same terms; he found "short-term investment for quick profits" leading to the "systematic destruction of the land." An international study mission in the first years of the cotton boom described similar damage to the soil of the Nicaraguan Pacific lowlands (IBRD 1953:29). The later introduction of nontraditional export crops has been associated with the same results. Growing NTAEs leads to greater deterioration of soil quality (e.g., depletion of organic material) and erosion than does the farming of traditional crops (Murray 1994:67).

A major victim of the expansion of agricultural land has been the region's forests and woodlands. Much of the forest cover had already been eliminated in the highlands before the contemporary period and in the Pacific coastal region before the 1960s. Since 1960 deforestation has accelerated. Between 1961 and 1978, almost 40 percent of the remaining forests were cleared (Myers 1981:5). This destruction has been the greatest, in both percentage and absolute area, in Guatemala, which lost almost one-half of its remaining forests in less than two decades, leaving only about one-third of the country covered by forest in 1992. The same is true for Costa Rica, and only about a quarter of Honduras and Nicaragua remain in forest. In one sense, though, the most serious impact has occurred in El Salvador, which has been stripped of virtually all of its little remaining forest (UNDP 1995:185).

Some of the forests lost have been those on mountain slopes cleared by peasants in their search for land. Probably the major cause of denudation since 1960, however, has been the expansion of beef raising for export markets. Forests have been felled in formerly frontier regions to make way for cattle, with much of the timber left to rot on the ground; up to 86 percent of it was wasted in this manner in Costa Rica between 1955 and

1973 (Ashe 1978:37; also see Guess 1979 and Place 1981). More recently, the region's largest remaining frontier has been under attack: El Petén in northeastern Guatemala. Responding to government incentives, farmers (particularly large absentee owners) have deforested the region so thoughtlessly that by one estimate half of the converted area is not even suitable for agriculture (Kaimowitz 1995:1–4). Since the mid-1970s, though, Costa Rica at least has begun to give attention to this destruction, consider conservation measures, and develop national parks, as discussed more thoroughly in Chapter 9.

An additional dimension of deforestation is its effect on the region's energy supply. Wood fuel is the major source of energy for rural Honduras, El Salvador, and Guatemala, and in 1979 wood provided about 47 percent of all energy consumed in the isthmus as a whole, especially in cooking. Diminishing forests, then, also mean a shrinking supply of this major energy source and, consequently, higher firewood prices in both rural and urban areas. Forestry by small farmers is the most important source of fuelwood, though it is not the major cause of deforestation (Jones 1984:8). As peasants lose access to land, they are probably losing access to their major source of fuel as well. Despite the central importance of small farmers' forestry to the well-being of much of the region's population, until recently virtually all forestry research was concerned with construction-quality timber, most of which comes from larger farms.

A final environmental problem has been the indiscriminate use of pesticides, especially by cotton growers and more recently by growers of the new fruit and vegetable exports. One report (cited by Weir and Schapiro 1981:12) documents more than 14,000 poisonings and forty deaths from pesticides in the Pacific lowlands between 1972 and 1975 alone. Because of excessive use of pesticides, people in Guatemala and Nicaragua during this period were thirty-one times as likely to have DDT in their blood as people in the United States (Weir and Schapiro 1981:12–13; Collins 1986:161–166). Recent studies are finding heavy levels of pesticide poisoning among workers dealing with nontraditional crops; in some studies over 50 percent of producers had in their lifetimes undergone at least one acute poisoning event. Many of the pesticides used are highly toxic, associated with cancer, birth defects, and permanent neurological damage (Murray 1994:68–71). Yet often workers do not take even the most minimal precautions, such as hand-washing, not to mention the recommended bathing (though of course in many fields water is not available). Careless pesticide use has also led to the evolution of pesticide-resistant species of malaria-carrying mosquitoes. Once largely eliminated from the region as a health threat, malaria has now returned as a serious concern (Murray 1994:129, 53–54).

Conclusion: Agro-Export Development in Unequal Rural Societies

Implementation of the agro-export development model in Central America in the postwar period has eroded the economic security of many of the region's rural people. The quantitative evidence provided in this chapter supports the numerous descriptive accounts that portray the conversion of land to export crops as enriching the few as a much more sizable proportion of the population suffers from diminishing land access, food supply, and employment opportunities. The harmful effects of the expansion of agricultural export production under conditions of gross inequality have occurred throughout the region and in each of the individual countries, though with meaningful variations.

The postwar agrarian transformation in Central America carries an impact strikingly similar to that of earlier eras. Like the cacao, indigo, and coffee booms of the past, the rise in agricultural exports in the contemporary period was ignited by elites who were able to use foreign markets to enrich themselves and to bring in badly needed revenues to underwrite the region's development. In each case some prosperity and progress were created, but primarily in urban centers. In rural areas the implementation of the agro-export development model has often diminished the quality of life for peasants. For example, Place (1981) concludes on the basis of her field research in Costa Rica's Guanacaste Province that

> rapid economic growth in Guanacaste during the past several decades has apparently not improved the quality of life of many *campesinos.* Every "old-timer" that I interviewed told the same story: each claimed that 20 or 30 years ago people used to live better, although they had little money. There was plenty of land available on which to grow crops, there was abundant game to hunt and more domestic animal products were available. Diet was apparently more varied and food was more abundant. *Campesinos* were basically self-sufficient and could support a family with relatively little effort. Today, they have no access to land because affluent investors have moved in and taken over, and . . . [public lands] have disappeared. They have to buy food now, but wages are insufficient to cover a family's needs. (p. 177)

The response of rural people to the disruption in their lives and the deterioration of their living standard is crucial to an understanding of recent political dynamics in the region. Before we take up that discussion in Part 2, we must examine the implications of Part 1 for the agro-export development model itself.

Agriculture can support a large percentage of a country's population at a subsistence level. But nowhere has production for only the domestic market been able to support many above that level. Export agriculture, then, is imperative for generating additional income to meet rising mater- ial aspirations of people who would prefer to maintain an agricultural livelihood. The conclusion here is not that export agriculture in itself has been destructive but rather that its consequences, as with any develop- ment model, are dependent upon the social structures within which it is pursued.[14] Similarly, recall that agricultural modernization in later-devel- oping countries has tended to reinforce social inequalities, as noted in Chapter 1, especially and most seriously in those with social structures al- ready significantly unequal. More generally, initial social conditions are a major determinant of the consequences of any set of public policies (Weaver et al. 1997:53, 67).

The experiences of countries that have combined rapid economic growth with income distributions more equitable than those in most na- tions, such as South Korea and Taiwan, demonstrate that the social con- text is at least as important as the model itself. On the basis of her exten- sive research, Adelman (1980) makes the point well:

> The successful countries all followed a process in which the asset that was going to be the major asset of production at each stage of development was redistributed before rather than after its productivity was improved. This as- set was redistributed either in terms of direct ownership or in terms of insti- tutional access to its productive utilization. Only after redistribution were policies undertaken to improve the productivity of the major asset. (pp. 442–443)

More specifically, the agricultural commodities stage of these countries' export-led development experience *followed* a substantial redistribution of the key resource at that stage: land. This prior structural change provided the foundation for rapid economic growth with relative equity through agricultural diversification and exports (and then later industrial ex- ports), a direct contrast to the recent Central American experience. These Asian successes, then, no more vindicate a general export-led develop- ment model as viable for all societies than the failure of the Honduran ba- nana enclave to ignite the development of that country can be taken to teach the opposite lesson.

Neither do the successes of countries such as South Korea and Taiwan establish land reform as sufficient for sustained growth with equity, any more than the failures of Mexico demonstrate the unimportance of land reform to sustained rural development. The redistributional measures in Asia were congruent with long-term forces working toward broad-based development, whereas land reform in Mexico worked against deeply en- trenched structures of inequality and was eventually overwhelmed by the reassertion of those structures (Tomich et al. 1995:315–365). In contrast, the redistribution of land in the Asian success stories was reinforced by subsequent policies that promoted broad-based rural development. What stands out from the Asian cases as instructive for Central America, in addition to land redistribution, are the following.[15] First, the Asian countries created a rural infrastructure and provided services that included the rural majority as their target. Second, they effectively spread educational opportunities throughout the countryside. In both of these sets of policies, there has been greater equity in the investment of resources between rural and urban areas than found in other regions. Third, the Asians showed a healthy distrust of the state's ability to replace market forces in establishing prices and exchange rates. Speaking comparatively, Asian "market-friendly" policies have been less prejudicial to rural development than those often found in Latin America, which instead have tended to squeeze agriculture to the benefit of urban consumers and industrial development. And fourth, the Asian countries demonstrated a commitment to labor-intensive industrialization, in rural as well as urban areas.

This commitment to rural industrialization has been especially important. In order to meet rising material aspirations without migrating to urban areas, rural people must have off-farm employment opportunities. Even a highly successful strategy of promoting new agricultural exports will be insufficient to meet rural income needs. As the Asian countries moved from agricultural to industrial exports, they did so through a strategy of small and medium labor-intensive enterprises often located where they could provide accessible employment to farm families. Rural living standards then improved as families earned a growing proportion of their income outside of agriculture. By the mid-1960s, for example, about one-third of the total income of South Korean farm families came from nonagricultural sources; by the mid-1970s this had increased to over 50 percent overall and to over 60 percent for the poorest three deciles of the population (Campos and Root 1996:55).

Central America, in contrast to Asia, serves as a negative example of the socially conditioned impact of the agro-export development model, with Costa Rica largely an exception. Costa Rica currently has the highest ratio of export land to food land in the region, and by a good margin (see Figure 3.4). But its social context is also different. In comparison to its neighbors, Costa Rica developed over its history a strong rural middle class, which, together with the relative absence of a neofeudal class of elite landowners supported by coercive labor systems, allowed it to develop a vibrant political democracy after World War II. Consequently, Costa Rican development policy has been implemented with a more explicit welfare component in a less stratified society than those of neighboring countries. This has been especially true for education.

In 1970 Costa Rica's public education expenditure was more than double that of the average for the other four countries, and in 1979 it was more than triple (Bulmer-Thomas 1987:215). Conversely, its military expenditures as a percentage of combined education and health expenditures at the start of the 1990s was only 5 percent, compared to 31 percent in Guatemala, 66 percent in El Salvador, 92 percent in Honduras, and 97 percent in Nicaragua (UNDP 1995:182). These trends are reinforcing: The softer social stratification in Costa Rica facilitated more equitable social policy, accentuating the differences with its neighbors. Whereas the income share grabbed by the top 20 percent of society in Guatemala in recent years has been about thirty times that of the bottom 20 percent of society, in Costa Rica the disparity is 12.7 times (and in Honduras about 23.5) (UNDP 1995:178). Similarly, Costa Rica's global ranking on the human development index is far higher than its economic development ranking; Guatemala's performance is the reverse (UNDP 1995:20).

A six-nation study of a diverse set of Third World countries published in 1980 found Costa Rica and Taiwan unique in having successfully combined rapid economic growth with declining inequality. The author concluded that perhaps "a distributionally oriented development program that integrates the poor into the mainstream of the economy may cause a higher growth rate, other things being equal" (Fields 1980:241). Costa Rica has maintained the best performing economy in Central America since that time, validating the critical point, as have the Asian success stories, that not only do equitable growth strategies do less harm to the poor but they also produce better for the whole of society.

These issues of equity and stratification were at the heart of political conflicts, including prolonged civil wars, that dominated the region in the 1970s and 1980s. In Part 2 the unique features of each country's experience are analyzed in individual chapters, with a primary question for each the extent to which this turmoil might have succeeded in liberating each society from the shackles of the rigid stratification systems inherited from the past.

Notes

1. For similar analyses, see, for Central America, Bulmer-Thomas (1987) and Williams (1986); for Latin America, Grindle (1986:111–131); and for the Third World, Barkin et al. (1990).

2. One good description of this process is Posas (1981a), which discusses the Honduran north coast region.

3. Although Kaimowitz (1995:22) concurs concerning the large holdings of Lucas García, his research found little evidence of government titling of holdings in the area larger than 90 hectares.

4. A Gini index for land concentration was not used here because it misses the different patterns that exist for inequality among smallest and largest holdings, since it provides only a single score for the overall level of inequality.

5. These findings are validated by a more accurate estimate of the region's supply of basic food in the late 1970s (for two to five years, depending on the country), using data supplied to the U.S. Department of Agriculture by its regional attachés (see Brockett 1990:80). These data include not only domestic production but also exports, livestock feed use, and stocks on hand at the beginning of the year for the same food crops as well as for sorghum. With the exception of Nicaragua, the more complete measure is either less than or only marginally greater than the domestic production figure used here for the longer time period. Nicaragua is indeed exceptional because these data are only for the tumultuous years of 1979 and 1980.

6. Data on land planted in specific crops, as well as yields, can be obtained from the UNFAO database at <http://www.fao.org>.

7. For the reasons stated in the text, national-level trends on average daily caloric and protein consumption cannot be used to assess levels or trends in malnutrition. See the related discussion in Wilkie and Moreno-Ibáñez (1984).

8. The complete citation is USDA Foreign Agricultural Service, "Guatemala— Agricultural Situation." Guatemala:USDA, 1981.

9. Some see this situation as a blessing. The following appeared in a 1963 guide for U.S. businesspeople under the heading "LABOR POOL WITHOUT BOTTOM!": "To the prospective plant operator, the availability of labor in El Salvador is one of the most favorable factors to be found. The industrialist is assured of one of the most plentiful labor supplies in the Hemisphere. . . . It is evident that there will be many applicants for every industrial job created here" (quoted in Conway 1963:19–20).

10. Migration is the greatest from the most remote of the highland provinces. Smith (1978, 1984a, 1984b) suggests that this is because land scarcity problems are more recent in those areas and therefore economic alternatives have not been developed there. In the more central areas, by contrast, such problems are longstanding and adaptation has been possible over time.

11. A 1974 survey of metropolitan San Salvador found that the top 10 percent of the population received more of the total income than did the remaining 90 percent (Karush 1978:72). A similar feat was almost accomplished in 1968 by the top tenth of all Guatemalans; their share of the national income was 47.5 percent. Just the top 5 percent received 35.2 percent of all income (Graber 1980:15).

12. InterAmerican Development Bank data at <http://www.iadb.org/IDB/data/debt.htm>.

13. In addition to the sources cited in the text here and in Chapter 9, see Faber (1993) and Stonich (1993). For a discussion of well-developed conservation methods among Guatemalan Indians in an area of high population density, see Veblen (1978).

14. For related arguments, see Adams and Behrman (1982), Bulmer-Thomas (1987:267–294; 1994:410–429), Johnston and Clark (1982:254–256), Timmer (1982:37–39), and Weaver (1994:67–106). This is the critical point too often overlooked by proponents of the model, such as Goldberg (1981), Hillman (1981), and USAID (1984).

15. For further discussion of these points, see Campos and Root (1996); Corbo, Krueger, and Ossa (1986); Koo (1987); Oshima (1993); Tomich et al. (1995); World Bank (1993b); as well as the following country-specific works: on South Korea, Adelman and Robinson (1978); on Taiwan, Fei et al. (1979) and Puchala and Stavely (1979). Some of these authors also provide provocative discussions of the role of values in promoting (or impeding) equitable growth among the general population, within state bureaucracies, and among political and economic leaders. A thorough examination of these issues would include the intersection of culture, class structure, political institutions, and the global economy.

Part Two

Political Conflict

Chapter Five

Guatemala: Between Reform and Terror

The postwar period began with much promise in Guatemala. Through large popular demonstrations in 1944, the country cast off the tyranny of right-wing dictatorship with the overthrow of Jorge Ubico. Relatively fair and free elections were held for the first times in 1944 and 1950.[1] In contrast to the traditional system, which served and protected narrow, elite interests, the popular governments initiated reform programs, including an ambitious agrarian reform. The reform period was aborted in 1954, however, through a destabilization campaign and an armed invasion by a small exile army, both sponsored by the United States.

The military has been the dominate power in Guatemala since 1954, with a military officer invariably serving as president through the mid-1980s. For a variety of reasons, ranging from personal, institutional, and class interests to ideological orientations, many in the military have perceived popular mobilization as a threat. When provoked, the military has relied on repression, with each round more widespread and indiscriminate than the one before. The repression after the "liberation" of 1954 was followed by a regional reign of terror in the late 1960s and early 1970s. By the end of the 1970s, the entire country was engulfed in state terrorism that continued in the countryside through the 1980s. The death toll under military domination climbed to perhaps 120,000 killed and another 42,000 disappeared since the early 1960s; 1 million more fled from their homes (Perera 1993:9, 17)—this in a country whose population is still less than 10 million people.

Although all sectors of society suffered from this terror, most victims have been peasants, especially from the country's Mayan majority. As this chapter demonstrates, the system of control established in rural areas during the colonial period and reinforced by the Liberal reforms of the nineteenth century has been threatened in the postwar period by the mobilization of the peasantry and by the appearance of guerrilla movements committed to radical change. The immediate object of the military's wrath, the revolutionary forces commanded considerable support in the early 1980s in the Indian-populated highlands of the west.

Despite the ferocity of the government's repression, nonviolent opposition continues to rise to challenge the military's dominance. Combined with international influences, these pressures led to a transition to civilian government initiated with the election of 1985. Guatemala now has had four successive civilian presidents. And in 1996 considerable progress was made to end formally the civil war and proceed with the difficult work of creating a more peaceful and more just society.

The Reform Years: 1944–1954

The most important public policy of the progressive administrations of 1944–1954 was the agrarian reform program initiated in 1952. The constitution adopted in 1945 prohibited the latifundia (neofeudal estates with much unused land) and the extension of those already in existence, but land redistribution did not reach the top of the political agenda until the election of Jacobo Arbenz, who assumed office in March 1951. The agrarian reform law, which passed the Guatemalan congress by an overwhelming margin in 1952, was intended, as it stated, to "eradicate feudal property in the rural areas" and to "develop capitalist methods of agricultural production." At the time the twenty-two biggest *latifundistas* owned more land than did 249,169 peasant families.[2] The new law and its implementation generated much controversy within Guatemala, especially concerning the issues of the lack of judicial oversight and autonomy, the concentration of power in the hands of the president, the amount to be paid in compensation, the impartiality of the reform bureaucracy, and the role of communists and other radicals in encouraging peasants to initiate expropriation proceedings. Nonetheless, in its brief lifetime the program had major success. About 17 percent of privately owned land was expropriated by the reform (although some was still in process when the reform was halted), with close to 20 percent of the eligible population receiving land. Among those who lost land were the president himself and a number of his top advisers. Furthermore, production of basic food staples rose, allowing imports to be reduced, and the value of agricultural exports increased (Handy 1994:94–95).

The approximately 1.8 million acres distributed under the program represented three types of holdings: public lands, domestically owned latifundia, and United Fruit Company lands. Guatemala had a substantial amount of public land that could be distributed because of the confiscation during World War II of farms owned by German nationals, who held many of the most productive of the large coffee estates. These lands constituted a little over 18 percent of those distributed under the program.[3]

Of the 1.5 million acres of private land both expropriated and distributed by the program, most were unused land on large, domestically owned estates. The law exempted from expropriation farms under 223 acres as well as those between 233 and 670 acres that had at least two-thirds of their area under cultivation. Clearly, the purposes of the law were simultaneously to bring into production the vast expanses of unused fertile land and to provide individual plots to landless peasants. This was frustrating for many among Guatemala's large Indian community who would have preferred a communal reform to restore lands lost to ladinos in earlier periods. Furthermore, few of the lands eligible for expropriation under the reform were located in the western highlands where most Maya lived; instead, reforms were concentrated in less densely populated piedmont and lowland areas. Still, some enterprising Indians were able to turn the reform to their advantage by using its provisions to gain access to communal municipal lands, the control of which often had been long dominated by local elites.

Some of the most glaring examples of idle land belonged to the United Fruit Company, long a dominating and controversial presence in Guatemala. In 1953 and 1954, a total of about 70 percent of the company's 550,000 acres of holdings were expropriated. Despite the massive loss this seizure represented to the company, its production activities were not directly threatened. Most of its land—between 74 (Aybar de Soto 1978:200) and 85 percent (Schlesinger and Kinzer 1983:75)—lay fallow. Only about 4 percent of its holdings were at the time used for growing bananas, so even granted that the company required reserves of four times that amount to rotate cultivation in the event of disease, clearly it was left after the expropriations with adequate holdings for its banana-growing activities. But even though its productive potential was not directly jeopardized, the dominant position that United Fruit had enjoyed over both its workforce and the government of Guatemala certainly were.

The fruit company was also distressed over the form and amount of compensation that it was offered. The law provided for compensation in twenty-five-year bonds based on property values as declared for tax purposes (always understated). The government offered about $1.2 million in compensation; the company demanded $16.5 million as the land's fair value. In response to these various challenges to its hegemony, United Fruit expanded its already considerable efforts to convince the U.S. government and public that vital U.S. interests were seriously endangered in Guatemala.

United Fruit had felt threatened at least since 1947, when a labor code favorable to workers was passed in order to actualize the promises of the 1945 constitution. The code initially limited the right to organize rural unions to agricultural enterprises that employed at least 500 people. Not only did United Fruit now have to contend with lawful labor unions, but it also was bitter about what it perceived to be the discriminatory scope of the code. The size restriction was removed the following year, however, generating more domestic opposition to the reform program. There were other reforms, too, that addressed the historic imbalance of power in rural areas. The vagrancy law was abolished in 1945, and a ceiling on land rents was established by the law of forced rental in 1949 at 10 percent of yield, reduced in 1951 to 5 percent.

Ladino landowners were vociferous in their opposition—and with good reason. Without the coercive laws of the past, labor shortages started to occur. More generally and more fundamentally, the established powers were threatened by the spreading politicization and mobilization of the rural population. This social change was the result of three major factors, though there were substantial variations from village to village.[4] First, beginning in 1945 local officials were to be elected, an important move given the broad power enjoyed by municipal officials in Guatemala. Many villages and towns soon were led by elected Mayas rather than appointed ladinos, bringing "dignity and responsibility to the Indians in place of the traditional subservience and dependency" (Siegal, quoted in Davis 1983a:8). These elections encouraged the penetration of the countryside by the major national political parties, catalyzed political activity in many localities, and often heightened ethnic tensions.

Second, the reforms themselves mobilized rural people. Through the rights guaranteed by the constitution and the new labor code, peasants began to organize leagues and unions. The National Confederation of Peasants of Guatemala (CNCG) was formed in 1950 and held its first national meeting the next year; by 1954 it claimed some 400,000 members and reached all but the most isolated villages.[5] The formation of unions eventually led to strikes, such as the successful campaign for a minimum wage hike that started on the national coffee estates in 1950 and then spread to large private estates. A new round of strikes during the 1952 harvest won fuller compliance with the 1950 agreement. Most important, the reform law called for the creation of local agrarian committees that were to initiate expropriation proceedings, when appropriate, in response to peasants' requests. The committees consisted of two representatives appointed by government officials and three from local peasant leagues or unions. The grassroots nature of the program encouraged the mobilization of rural people, both to initiate expropriations and to form peasant organizations. By late 1953 up to 3,000 of these committees had formed.

Finally, for the first time outside forces penetrated rural society with the intention of assisting peasants to organize on behalf of their own interests. These organizers were especially important in explaining the agrarian reform, assisting in the formation of agrarian committees, and stimulating expropriation proceedings. Because these organizers were often radicals, and sometimes communists, they and their activities represented a major threat to established interests. Although Arbenz envisioned an agrarian reform that would modernize agricultural production without alienating middle-sector groups, some leftist politicians and labor organizers hoped to radicalize the reform in order to transform the agrarian class structure (Wasserstrom 1975:454–457). In particular, they encouraged—and sometimes led—illegal land seizures, especially in Escuintla, where peasants were well organized. Rural tensions were aggravated not just by class and ethnic differences but also by organizational, personal, clan, and municipal rivalries. As the number of seizures increased into 1954 (sometimes with violence, such as the lynching in January of two landowners), opponents of Arbenz believed that his administration lacked both the will and capability to maintain rural order.

Although the various agrarian policies of the reform period were relatively moderate by today's standards and did not directly threaten fundamental economic interests of the elite, the system of domination from which elites profited was endangered as peasants began to claim some of their potential power. It was this empowerment that was the most serious menace, not just politically and economically but, more basically, psychologically. Ladino elites were a small minority surrounded by the majority indigenous population that these elites had dominated and exploited. Elites feared violence from below, a fear heightened by the growing agitation in the countryside. Still, most violence continued to be committed by those with power directed against their challengers: "Peasant leaders were shot, hung, beaten, burned, and run over throughout the country" (Handy 1994:102).

The change in the countryside during this period was substantial. As pointed out in Chapter 1, patronage relationships are a primary embodiment of peasant subordination in the traditional social structure. Outside organizers often help to break down this domination by offering alternative sources of economic assistance and protection as well as advocating competing value systems. This transformation in Guatemala from 1944 to 1954 has been well described by anthropologist Richard Adams (1970):

> Indians and Ladinos found that it was possible to seek out other authorities and sources of power than those familiar in the unitary patronal system.

Whereas before, the *patrón* or the elders had the last word, it was increasingly assumed that not only were they no longer the final authority, but they also could be ignored almost at will. The operation of these new organizations demonstrated that *campesinos* could expect some satisfaction without retribution from the local landowner or the local council of elders. (p. 191; see also p. 205)

The growing numbers of peasant organizations illustrate this change: In 1948 twenty-three peasant *sindicatos* (unions) and five peasant *uniones* (leagues) had been legally recognized; in 1954 the respective numbers were 345 and 320 (Murphy 1970:445–447).

The Arbenz government was overthrown in June 1954 by a destabilization campaign and an armed invasion, both organized and financed by the United States (Immerman 1982; Schlesinger and Kinzer 1983). Central to the animosity of the Eisenhower administration toward the Guatemalan government was the impact of the agrarian reform program on the United Fruit Company. Nonetheless, it is well established (e.g., Blasier 1976; Bowen 1983; Gleijeses 1991; Krasner 1978) that the U.S. intervention was motivated not so much by a desire to protect the economic interests of United Fruit as by Washington's unwarranted concern that "international communism" (as evidenced in Guatemala's attack on United Fruit) was successfully establishing a beachhead in the Western Hemisphere—a perception that United Fruit invested considerable efforts in promoting (Schlesinger and Kinzer 1983).[6]

Rural Contradictions Sharpen: 1954–1980

Following Guatemala's "liberation," as it was called by its supporters, urban and rural masses were demobilized through repression. Within a month over 5,000 suspects were jailed; according to the U.S. embassy, they were "mostly farm workers from the local Agrarian Committees" (U.S. State Department 1954). Labor leaders and peasants also were murdered but in numbers that are impossible to specify; a *New York Times* correspondent estimated a minimum of 200 (June 29, 1956:5). The leading union confederations, such as the National Confederation of Peasants of Guatemala, were abolished, many local unions were declared illegal, and the remainder were sharply restricted in their activities. The right to vote was limited, disenfranchising over one-half of the electorate. However, this demobilization of the peasantry proved to be successful only temporarily.

Counterrevolutionary Agrarian Reform

The "liberation" program reversed the accomplishments of the agrarian reform. Virtually all recipients of expropriated land were removed, by force if necessary, and the land was returned to its original owners. The primary beneficiary of this campaign was the United Fruit Company, which won back all of its expropriated lands. Furthermore, a number of the national farms were privatized; thirty-nine were distributed to private owners in holdings averaging over 7,700 acres each (Hough et al. 1983:29). Then in 1960 President Miguel Ydígoras announced that two of the remaining national estates would be divided among deserving members of the military—probably meaning officers who had sided with him against a coup attempt eleven days earlier (Adams 1968–1969:109, n. 3).

In the context of counterreform in 1954, both the new president of Guatemala, Carlos Castillo Armas, and the U.S. government needed to develop an alternative solution to the country's agrarian problems.[7] But neither responded with any degree of effectiveness. The Eisenhower administration spoke of making Guatemala a "showcase for democracy," but lack of interest at the highest levels of the administration once Arbenz was overthrown continually frustrated Guatemalan officials and U.S. embassy personnel. For example, the amount of U.S. funds actually expended in Guatemala by the end of the first year of Castillo Armas's rule was probably less than $2.3 million, according to U.S. embassy estimates (U.S. State Department 1955). Finally, under the prodding of Congress, U.S. financial support increased for a few years, including about $14 million for rural development through 1959, primarily for the resettlement of peasants in nineteen colonization projects located mainly along the Pacific slope.

Much of the land for the colonization projects (over 100,000 acres) was donated by the United Fruit Company. When its lands were returned after the overthrow of Arbenz, they came back with many poor peasants living on them. The understanding was that in return for United Fruit's donation of land, the government would clear out the squatters on the company's remaining holdings.[8] By 1963 the U.S.-backed project had resettled 4,887 families, and a separate effort distributed 16,722 small plots to landless peasants. Meanwhile, between 1950 and 1962 the number of landless farm families had increased to 140,000 (Hildebrand 1969:59).

The model employed in the development projects was imported from the United States; its objective was "to create independent middle class farm owners and operators" (Hildebrand 1969:36). A 1970 USAID evaluation concluded, not surprisingly, that the impact of such colonization projects on the "land tenure structure has been negligible, if any" (Gayoso 1970:5). Nonetheless, in the late 1970s the United States once again became involved in a resettlement program, this time in the western corner of the Northern Transversal Strip, which runs across the neck of the country. USAID provided $5.6 million to finance a pilot resettlement project involving 4,000 families. Because of land grabbing by elites in the region, however, one foreign analyst was quoted in 1979 as claiming that "by the time the experiment is completed, there'll be no land left to distribute." Indeed, it was reported that "much of the best land ha[d] already fallen into the hands of wealthy farmers and army officers" (*NY Times*, April 5, 1979:A2).

Overall, very few of the landless or land-poor peasants of Guatemala have been served by the land distribution programs of the post-1954 governments. Even when permanently employed plantation workers are excluded from analysis, a study prepared for the USAID mission to Guatemala found that only 8.9 percent of the needy benefited in 1955–1964, 3.5 percent in 1965–1973, and 5.7 percent in 1974–1981 (Hough et al. 1983:32–35). However, half of the parcels distributed have been larger than 62 acres, the bulk of them over 250 acres, especially under the 1970–1974 administration of Arana Osorio (Hough et al. 1983:98; Gayoso 1970).

Rural Repression

Given the deterioration of the position of much of the peasantry (detailed in Part 1), it is not surprising that guerrilla organizations appeared, hoping to mobilize the peasantry in behalf of a radical restructuring of Guatemalan society. The first such organizations, led by military officers who had failed in an attempted coup in November 1960, centered their activities in the eastern mountains. Regrouping, they never numbered more than several hundred fighters and eventually divided into two different organizations. Although they tried to mobilize Indians, the group remained almost totally ladino in composition. Their efforts were frustrated both by the legacy of centuries of well-grounded Indian distrust of ladinos and by the intensification of ethnic tension in the east because of the politics of the reform period.

The military allowed civilians to take control of the government with the elections of 1966, in which Julio Méndez Montenegro was the victor. It is widely acknowledged that in return the civilian government consented to give the military a free hand to conduct its counterinsurgency campaign. The military, and the paramilitary death squads allied with it, eliminated not only the guerrillas but also thousands of innocent peasants, especially in the department of Zacapa, apparently believing in the deterrent effect of widespread, systematic terror. Between 3,000 and 8,000 noncombatants are estimated to have been killed between 1966 and 1968.[9] U.S. military assistance was important to the counterinsurgency effort, supplying training, advice, and helicopters and other equipment. The attitude of the U.S. military mission was clear:

> To aid in the drive, the army also hired and armed local bands of "civilian collaborators" licensed to kill peasants whom they considered guerrillas or "potential" guerrillas. There were those who doubted the wisdom of encouraging such measures in violence-prone Guatemala, but ... the head of the U.S. military mission was not among them. "That's the way this country is," he said. "The Communists are using everything they have, including terror. And it must be met." (*Time* 1968:23)[10]

From 1950 to 1979, the United States supplied Guatemala with over $60 million in military assistance and trained over 3,300 Guatemalan military officers at U.S. military facilities (Trudeau 1984:61; McClintock 1985b).

Violence by both leftists and especially right-wing death squads escalated in urban areas during 1966–1968 as well. The paramilitary groups were not independent organizations but were rather, according to Amnesty International (1981a:24–25), "providing cover for military and police activities" and "preserv[ing] some semblance of democratic government." The violence diminished somewhat in 1968 when, in the wake of the daylight kidnapping of the archbishop of Guatemala City, the defense minister and Colonel Carlos Arana Osorio, the head of the military's counterinsurgency campaign, were sent to diplomatic posts overseas. However, in 1970 Arana, "the butcher of Zacapa," was elected president. The repression intensified once again, primarily in the eastern mountains and Guatemala City. With Arana in control of state power, a "regime of terror and violence may be said to have been institutionalized" (Johnson 1972:17). Popular mobilization was checked, this time ferociously; "official violence was now used to stamp out any form of peasant or labor protest" (AI 1981a:26). The Committee of Relatives of Disappeared Persons estimated that there were some 15,000 cases of disappearance between 1970 and 1975, at least 75 percent of them attributable directly to government security forces (AI 1981a:26).

Despite considerable violence committed against its leaders and membership, the Christian Democratic Party was able to run such an effective campaign for the presidency in 1974 that the military's candidate was able to "win" only through fraud. During the first year of General Kjell Laugerud's administration, official violence declined, but following the earthquake that devastated the western part of the country in February 1976, rural repression mounted. Its scope expanded yearly until a reign of state terrorism pervaded the country, especially the western highlands. As in the earlier operations in the eastern mountains, the immediate target was leftist guerrillas. The military's indiscriminate counterinsurgency campaign, however, was directed not just at denying the revolutionaries a supportive popular base but also at destroying any autonomous popular organizations in the countryside, especially among the indigenous population. In contrast to the previous decade, by the late 1970s a substantial degree of popular mobilization had occurred; accordingly, the military engaged in much more widespread violence in order to secure its objectives.

Peasant Mobilization

The sources of peasant mobilization and organization in the 1970s were many. Among the most important were the activities of church workers, especially those involved with Catholic Action; the efforts of progressive political parties; development efforts initiated by agents entering from outside the community; the continuing deterioration of the peasantry's economic condition; government repression; and the resurgence of radical guerrilla movements.

Life in Indian villages had been grounded in religious beliefs and practices that combined Catholicism with pre-Columbian religion. As this synthesis evolved, the authority of Indian religious leaders was reinforced, partly as a defensive reaction against the waves of ladino attacks on Indian communities over the centuries and partly because ladinos countenanced it, since Indian deference to the religious hierarchies reinforced the overall system of social control (Carmack 1983:244; Warren 1978:89). Ironically, one of the primary forces that undermined this system was a movement intended to bolster conservatism.

Archbishop Mariano Rossell y Arellano initiated Catholic Action in 1946 as a conservative reaction to the social change of the reform period. As the archbishop stated, "Our small Catholic Action was one of the greatest comforts in those hours of enormous distress in the presence of Marxist advance that invaded everything" (quoted in Warren 1978:89). A major purpose of Catholic Action was to further the Christian conversion of Indians by attacking and undermining indigenous "superstitions." But as Indians rejected some traditional religious beliefs, they also freed themselves from the conservative authority of traditional religious leaders and societies (i.e., the *cofradías*). This process of conversion was often experienced as one of "liberation" (Falla 1978:519–525), which made participants available for later mobilization by change-oriented outside forces. Freed from beliefs that gave supernatural and individualistic explanations for suffering, the new converts became more open to the attribution of material and collective causes to suffering and to the acceptance of material and collective solutions to problems. In many communities the cleavage between traditionalists and the new converts (catechists) became one of the most important lines of conflict.[11]

If the catechists rejected some of their traditional customs, they did not repudiate their Mayan heritage; instead, they "affirm[ed] Indian ethnic pride in the face of *Ladino* racism, economic exploitation, and political control" (Davis 1983b:8; see also Brintnall 1979; Burgos-Debray 1984; and Warren 1978). Studies found that Catholic Action fostered in the new converts, usually younger Indians, a group consciousness that connected them to neighboring villages (Handy 1984:241) and that encouraged them to see "themselves as 'apostles' carrying the new 'social gospel' of the Catholic Church to their less fortunate Indian brothers and sisters" (Davis 1983b:8). Consequently, the conversion process promoted by Catholic Action attacked not only the traditional Indian hierarchy but also the system of social control benefiting ladinos.

This point is well illustrated in a highland Indian's answer to a ladino's comment that the fading of native customs was "very sad": "Yes, it is sad ... *for you!*" (Brintnall 1979:141). If traditionalists worried about maintaining good ties with their ladino *patrones*, the catechists tended "to see such relationships as repressive and exploitive, blocking the progress of Indians and the leveling of the two ethnic groups"(Warren 1978:135). They also rejected deferential, submissive behavior toward ladinos, even openly expressing hostility toward them (Brintnall 1979:175). These converts were often leaders of new peasant organizations. The first fifty members of a peasant league in El Quiché discussed by Falla (1978: 485–489), for example, all were Catholic Action converts.

Historically, few Mayan communities have been served by priests; in the early 1950s there were only three priests in all of the department of El Quiché and only 194 active priests in the entire country (Falla 1978:440). In order to promote Catholic Action and to meet the challenge of Protestant missionaries, foreign priests were welcomed to Guatemala. By 1963 El Quiché had twenty-five priests, and the country had 415 by the late 1960s, only 15 percent of them native born (Falla 1978:451; Handy 1984:239).

The concerns of many of these priests went beyond religious conversion, however. In the northern portion of the Indian department of Huehuetenango, Maryknolls from North America had established a presence in most villages by the early 1960s and had converted thousands of Indians. But their efforts were also addressed to rural development and included founding schools, clinics, and credit cooperatives. In response to government inaction in face of the serious land pressures in the highlands, the religious workers initiated their own colonization project in the late 1960s in the underpopulated Ixcán region of the far north of the department (and the country). Encouraging Indians to become colonists rather than continue to migrate seasonally to the Pacific plantations, they helped with infrastructure construction and the creation of a broad rural development movement across northern Guatemala. Most significant, the foreign church workers gave serious attention to the development of indigenous leadership, not only to carry out these projects but also to take the reformist social message into the most remote Mayan villages (Chernow 1979; Davis 1983a:3–5).

The missionaries were not alone in their efforts. Among the outside organizing forces were new, progressive political parties. The most important of these was the Christian Democratic Party, which had close ties to Catholic Action. Organizers established local affiliates of the national party, encouraged supporters to run for local offices, and helped to establish peasant leagues and cooperatives. Furthermore, the Christian Democrats were critical in some areas to Indians' achievement of political power on the local level (see, for example, Brintnall 1979:158–160).

These efforts were reinforced by the activities of rural labor organizers, many in the beginning also inspired by Christian Democratic thought. The work of the Campesino Federation of Guatemala (FCG) can be traced back to the early 1960s, with its endeavors focused first on agrarian reform in the highlands and then labor relations for migrant workers on the coastal plantations. Coming into the 1970s, though, the FCG split, further fragmenting what was already a splintered sector. Although they enjoyed some organizing successes, the peasant organizations reached none of their larger goals, such as written contracts with employers, before the late 1970s (May 1993:157–170).

Rural development projects were also initiated by foreign governments and private organizations. Beginning in the late 1960s, the USAID mission to Guatemala began "placing high priority" (Davidson 1976a:1) on rural development; a $23 million rural development sector loan approved in 1970 for cooperative development and basic food crop production was seen as marking "the first time substantial resources were being directed at the Highlands" (Davidson 1976a:1). The Arana administration was skeptical of the value of such "socialist" institutions as cooperatives, but it was willing to allow USAID to undertake the project as long as the cooperatives did not lead to "the development of a potential 'pressure group' that would become 'broadly representational' in nature and begin to apply political pressure on the government" (Davidson 1976b:14). Although the USAID contractor consciously tried to keep the cooperatives nonpolitical, the project generated conflict with the existing cooperative movement, which consisted largely of Christian Democrats who opposed the Arana regime. Many of them "bitterly criticized" the cooperatives as an imposed foreign model; some even viewed the USAID project as an attempt to destroy the cooperatives already in place (Davidson 1976b:15, 23–24).

Within a few years, many of these tensions were reduced. The USAID project grew more sensitive about competing with existing cooperatives, more Guatemalans were moved into leadership positions, and the Christian Democratic cooperative federation began receiving some USAID funding. Furthermore, during the early years of General Laugerud's administration (1974–1978), the government's attitude toward cooperatives changed to one of cautious encouragement. By fall 1975 about 20 percent of highland Indians participated in some form of cooperatives (Handy 1984:240). Following the earthquake of February 1976, which killed over 23,000 people, especially in the highlands, another 200 private and public foreign organizations initiated activities in the country (Gondolf 1981). Shortly thereafter, Guatemala had 510 cooperatives, 57 percent of them in the highlands, with a combined membership of more than 132,000 people (Davis 1983c:162).

These rural development efforts brought new credit opportunities, technical assistance, marketing possibilities, schools, literacy projects, and health clinics. Some Indians were able to take advantage of these opportunities to improve their economic situation. They became leaders in their communities, some of them joining the new developmental organizations (Brintnall 1979:111–115; Ebel 1988). However, for many other Mayas their economic situation continued to deteriorate. As detailed in Part 1, the eviction of peasants from their land, together with the steady increase in population, intensified already serious pressures on the land. Arable land per capita declined from 4.2 acres in 1950 to 2.3 acres in 1973 to just under 2 acres in 1980. Consistently since the 1950 census, 88 percent of the farms in Guatemala have been under 17.3 acres, the estimated size necessary to support a family adequately. Landlessness among rural families was estimated in 1970 at 26.6 percent. By 1975 about 60 percent of the economically active rural population of the highlands had to migrate to plantations to find work, making this the most migratory labor force in the world (Paige 1975:361).

During the 1970s, competition developed for land in underpopulated northern lowland regions, which became increasingly important as an alternative to the ever more densely populated highlands. Across the northern neck of the country, Indians were dispossessed of land by military officers and domestic and foreign economic elites, who coveted the region for its cattle ranching and mineral possibilities. Peasants were repressed as well. A counterinsurgency campaign began in northern El Quiché a month after the earthquake. Provoked by a small guerrilla band, the repression was soon targeted against the cooperative movement; within the next year and a half, close to 200 cooperative members in the region disappeared. Similar repression occurred in northern Huehuetenango. It was during this period that one of the most activist of the Maryknoll priests died in a mysterious plane crash (Chernow 1979; Davis 1983a:5–6; Falla 1994). It will be recalled that the infamous massacre at Panzós, discussed in Chapter 4, was directed against Indians who were protesting the appropriation of their lands in the northeastern part of the country.

Freed from deference to traditional conservative authority structures, encouraged by outside social change advocates, confronting a deteriorating economic situation, and faced with renewed government repression, growing numbers of Mayas began to organize for economic and political action. Indian candidates were again winning municipal elections, and in the mid-1970s two were elected to the national congress. In 1978 the Committee for Peasant Unity (CUC) was founded as the first organization to bring together indigenous subsistence and migrant farmers with poor ladino farmworkers. Many of its Mayan leaders had been involved earlier with Catholic Action programs and with community reconstruction following the 1976 earthquake. CUC quickly affiliated with the two-year-old, urban-based National Committee of Trade Union Unity (CNUS), which the previous November had engineered the biggest labor demonstration since 1954, turning out some 100,000 urban and rural workers in front of the presidential palace. In its first public appearance, at the May 1, 1978, Labor Day parade, CUC mobilized the largest public demonstration of Indians the country had seen.

The strength of the CUC and its threat to elite interests were demonstrated by a series of strikes in 1980. A strike of up to 80,000 sugarcane workers and 40,000 cotton pickers was called in February to protest working conditions and the abysmally low minimum wage.[12] Although it did not meet their demand for a $5 daily minimum wage, the government was forced to raise the daily minimum from $1.12 to $3.20. Another CUC strike in September took 10,000 coffee pickers off the job during the crucial days of the harvest period. Further organizing successes were precluded, however, by the government's stepped-up use of violence against union leaders and members. During 1980 alone, about 110 union leaders as well as over 300 peasant leaders were killed (Bowen 1985:104).

What was most notable about Indian political activities, though, was the support many gave to the new guerrilla movements and the high proportion of active involvement in the revolutionary struggle.[13] There was much diversity in material conditions between and within Indian communities, and different levels of exposure to regime violence and guerrilla activities; accordingly, the degree of receptivity to the guerrilla armies varied as well. Nonetheless, involvement was sufficiently widespread by the early 1980s to place Guatemala in the initial stages of a "modern 'peasant war'" (Davis 1983c:159).

A remnant of the guerrilla organizations of the 1960s made its first appearance in the western highlands in January 1972 as the Guerrilla Army of the Poor (EGP). Dedicated to winning the support and involvement of the Indian peasantry, it undertook the slow process of education and mobilization. Its first military action was the public murder in 1975 of a local landlord notorious for oppressing his labor force. It was in response to this killing that the army initiated its counterinsurgency campaign in northern El Quiché. The number of indiscriminate killings associated with this campaign exploded in 1979 when another of the area's most powerful ladino landlords was executed by the EGP (purportedly by a female combatant who had been abused when serving as a servant in the man's household). As the state violence increased, so did Mayan support for and involvement in both the EGP and a second guerrilla group, the Organization of People in Arms (ORPA). Begun in 1971, ORPA emerged publicly in 1979 in the southern portion of the highlands. Support was so substantial that by 1982 it could operate freely throughout the area. At their peak in the early 1980s, the combined guerrilla forces might have numbered about 7,500 trained militants with support from about .5 million peasants (Perera 1993:10).

The system of control over the indigenous population established in the colonial period and tightened through the centuries was coming apart. The history of many Mayan communities featured periods of rebellion (Carmack 1983), but the mobilization had become regionwide. Although it began as Indians' peaceful effort to assert and defend their interests through both the cooperative movements and the political process, as these efforts were repressed, increasing numbers of Mayans gave their support to the guerrilla armies. Undoubtedly greatest of all threats to elites was the active involvement of numerous Indians themselves in the revolutionary struggle. In response to these various forms of mass politicization and mobilization and in order to reinstitute control, the Guatemalan military undertook a systematic campaign of state terrorism that exceeded even its own past levels of barbarity.

Systematic State Terrorism: 1980–1984

On January 16, 1980, 100 peasants from the northern region of El Quiché completed their long journey to Guatemala City to request the appointment of a special commission to investigate military repression in their area. They were from the communities where the counterinsurgency had begun in 1976, and in recent months the harassment, torture, rape, and murder of noncombatant Indians had intensified. Some of the Indians, along with a few supporters, occupied the Spanish embassy on January 31 to publicize their grievances. They selected this embassy because most of the priests active in their area, some of whom had recently been deported by the government, were from Spain. Against the wishes of the ambassador, the police attacked, killing all but one of the demonstrators and two former Guatemalan officials who were in the embassy talking with the peasants. A letter that the protesters had given to the ambassador explained that they had undertaken the long journey to the capital and faced the risks of the occupation in order to enlist the support of "honorable people," who would, they hoped,

> tell the truth about the criminal repression suffered by the peasants of Guatemala. . . . To a long history of kidnapings, torture, assassinations, theft, rapes and burnings of buildings and crops, the National Army has added the massacre at Chajúl [one of the villages in their region]. . . . We have come to the capital to denounce this injustice, this evil, this cowardice of the National Army, but we also come because we are persecuted and threatened by forces of repression. (quoted in Handy 1984:247)

Tragically, their efforts were futile. The scope of the rural violence increased until it surpassed that in urban areas, which had escalated since the controlled election of General Romeo Lucas García in 1978 (AWC 1982). Opponents and possible opponents of the regime disappeared by the hundreds—politicians, labor leaders, journalists, professors, students, and church workers. A fiction was maintained that this was the work of autonomous paramilitary groups, but an Amnesty International report (1981b:3) established that the selection of victims and the deployment of the murderers "can be pin-pointed to secret offices in an annex of Guatemala's National Palace, under the direct control of the President of the Republic."[14]

General Lucas had at one time been the commander of the counterinsurgency effort in El Quiché, and under his presidency the rural violence intensified. At first, leaders were assassinated or disappeared in small numbers. Increasingly through 1980 and 1981, key villages were attacked, often with dozens of casualties, in an effort to deprive the guerrillas of a supportive population. Instead, this intermittent but brutal repression often strengthened Indian support for the revolutionaries, if for no other reasons than self-protection. A scorched-earth policy was instituted in late 1981; "thousands of troops swept across an area, killing suspected leaders, burning fields, and attempting to drive a wedge between the peasantry and the guerrillas" (Davis 1983c:167). Forced out of the old villages, the surviving population had to flee to the mountains or relocate in new ones controlled by the military. This change in military strategy coincided with the president's brother's assumption of the role of defense minister. Trained by the French, Benedicto Lucas employed a strategy apparently inspired by the French experiences in Vietnam and Algeria.

The scope of the violence directed against the Mayas and those who worked with them is indicated by the following small sample of the incidents Davis and Hodson (1982) compiled and verified by cross-checking with other independent sources.

December 7 [1979] Soldiers stationed at the army base in Jaboncillo, Chajul, make daily incursions into the town, ransacking houses, raping women and stealing money. They kidnap, torture and interrogate 12 persons at the army base. Residents flee to the hills to escape from the soldiers. . . .

February 1 [1980] Men in civilian dress kidnap Gregorio Yuja Xona, the only Indian survivor of the Spanish Embassy massacre, from a Guatemalan City hospital where he was being guarded by government forces. He is later found tortured and assassinated. . . .

September 6 [1980] The army attacks the village of Chajul. Early in the day, Father Tomás Ramírez is taken to a cornfield and shot in the head.[15] At noon, helicopters drop four bombs on the convent, killing eight people. Soldiers go into the streets and kill everyone they meet. They enter a house and kill an 11-year-old boy. In the evening, they round up 65 peasants, interrogate and beat them, and kill 36. Many villagers flee to the mountains. Those who remain, mostly widows and children, have little to eat and no firewood to keep them warm. . . .

February [1981] Soldiers invade several villages in San Juan Comalapa, Chimaltenango. Residents initially resist the soldiers after they grab an infant from its mother and kick it to death. Their resistance is broken, and the soldiers kill 168 peasants in the villages of Patzaj and Panimacac. . . .

September 19–20 [1981] The army launches a major offensive against the villages of Xeococ, Buena Vista, Pascaal, Vegas Santo Domingo, Pachicá, and Pichec in Baja Verapaz. Villages are bombed and people are machine gunned as they try to escape. In Vegas Santo Domingo, the soldiers line the people up in a row, cut off their arms and legs and kick them into a grave. Residents claim that 200 people, including entire families, are killed. (pp. 47–52)

In March 1982 the official candidate, General Angel Aníbal Guevara, won the presidency in a clearly fraudulent election. He was denied the opportunity to assume office, though, by a coup undertaken the following month by junior military officers. By this point the Lucas regime commanded little support at home or abroad. Corruption was rampant, the economy collapsing; the war against the rural guerrillas was going poorly; the urban violence was too excessive even for most opponents of the left. As Lucas's candidate and as the former defense minister and architect of the failing counterinsurgency campaign, Guevara was unacceptable to too many influential people.

The United States had pressured Lucas to hold fair elections: The administration of Ronald Reagan wanted to assist the Guatemalan military in its "fight against communism" but was restrained by Congress from doing so because of the Lucas government's atrocities. The Reagan administration believed that elections could lead to a legitimate, moderate government, which it would then be allowed to provide with military assistance.[16] As acting assistant secretary of state, John A. Bushnell testified before the Senate in May 1981: "I think given the extent of the insurgency and the strong communist worldwide support for it, the administration is disposed to support Guatemala" (AP 1981). In congressional testimony two months later, the administration ignored the Guatemalan government's responsibility for the killings, blaming the violence on "the willful efforts by both right and left to polarize the country" (U.S. House 1981c:5).[17]

Placed at the head of the new junta in 1982 was retired General José Efraín Ríos Montt, brought out of obscurity to serve. The defrauded candidate of the Christian Democratic victory in 1974, a committed evangelical Christian, and a man with a reputation for personal integrity, he had also served as Arana's chief of staff in 1973 and had left Guatemala in 1974, a rich man with large estates in the northern regions of the country

(Black 1983b:16–17). Under Ríos Montt, the violence did largely end in the cities. The Reagan administration hoped that this change would be sufficient to win the grant of military aid, but Congress continued to balk.

Following his visit to Guatemala in December 1982, Reagan declared that Ríos Montt had been getting "a bum rap" and was "totally dedicated to democracy in Guatemala" (*Post,* December 8, 1982:A17). Reagan did provide Ríos Montt with some support through executive action: The State Department announced in October 1982 that the United States would no longer block international development bank loans to Guatemala. Even during Reagan's first year in office, Guatemala had been able to purchase jeeps and helicopter parts because such equipment had been removed from a control list that restricted their sale to gross violators of human rights. The administration went further in 1983, removing the five-year-old embargo on arms sales to Guatemala (Black 1983b:27–32; Trudeau and Schoultz 1986:44–45).

Some semblance of order had been returned to urban areas, and the Reagan administration also claimed that the rural campaign had been cleaned up (Black 1983b:28). In fact, the reign of terror in the countryside intensified under Ríos Montt and under his successor following Ríos Montt's overthrow in 1983. An Americas Watch Committee (1983) mission to the Guatemalan refugee camps in southern Mexico reported:

1. The Guatemalan government's counterinsurgency program, begun in early 1982, has been continued and expanded by the Ríos Montt government and remains in effect at this time.
2. A principal feature of this campaign is the systematic murder of Indian non-combatants (men, women and children) of any village, farm or cooperative, that the army regards as possibly supportive of the guerrilla insurgents or that otherwise resists army directives.
3. Although civilian men of all ages have been shot in large numbers by the Guatemalan army, women and children are particular victims; women are routinely raped before being killed; children are smashed against walls, choked, burned alive or murdered by machete or bayonet. . . .
5. Incidental to its murder of civilians, the army frequently destroys churches, schools, livestock, crops, food supplies and seeds belonging to suspect villages, cooperatives or private farms. An apparent purpose, and clear effect, is to deprive entire villages and farm communities of the food necessary for survival. . . .
8. The Guatemalan armed forces make extensive and conspicuous use of helicopters, mortars and incendiary bombs in attacking rural villages, in destroying and burning crops, and in harassing

refugees seeking to escape and routinely use helicopters for sur-
veillance of refugee camps in Mexico. . . .

10. It is widely known within the refugee community, and among
displaced Indians in Guatemala, that the principal supplier of
such helicopters—and the principal supporter of the Ríos Montt
government—is the United States. (pp. 6–7)

As the Americas Watch Committee (1983) report *Creating a Desolation
and Calling It Peace* notes, "The enormity of the horrors being perpetrated
by the Guatemalan Army may make it difficult to grasp the cruelty and
impact of the Army's actions" (p. 21). The authors go on to relate the following vignette:

> Late in the heat-choked smoky evening that we spent in the Chajul refugee
> camp, we sat on a wooden bench with three refugee farmers, all middle-
> aged, who had heard about our visit earlier in the day. One man turned to us
> in the darkness and said, "You know, I had heard stories from others in my
> village that the army was murdering women and children in other towns,
> but frankly I did not believe those accounts since the murders seemed so
> brutal and without reason. But then the army killed my son and his children
> and my daughter and her children, and now I believe all of these stories."[18]

Reconstructing Rural Society: 1984 to the Present

Following the decimation of the indigenous population in the first
decades after the conquest, the remaining Indians were resettled in centralized villages in the 1540s. Sometimes they were brought from outlying
areas to more central locations; in other cases new villages were created.
This resettlement facilitated the Europeans' creation of a system of social
control that was to their benefit, allowing them better to manage the
threat of rebellion, utilize Indian labor, and alter indigenous religious
practices. Over four centuries later, in the early 1980s, the Mayas of
Guatemala were again violently subjugated, and again the conquest was
accompanied by the reconstruction of rural society, this time in order to
ensure the long-term elimination of the threat of radical insurgencies. The
major components of this reconstruction were the penetration of the
countryside by the military apparatus, the resettlement of the population
in model villages located within new development zones, and the implementation of reeducation programs. But the contemporary military has
faced more constraints than the conquistadores, leaving the Mayas of the
highlands today with more opportunities to exercise some control over
their lives than had their ancestors.[19]

The military did not have the resources or personnel to control directly
most of the countryside, especially remote mountain areas. Crucial to this

task was the creation of civil defense patrols in the highlands. Initiated on a small scale in 1981, the patrols grew rapidly. By 1986 there were 1 million participants, usually coerced conscripts, and in 1992 the patrols still enlisted half that number, making it one of the largest civilian militias in the world (Perera 1993:92) until their formal end as part of the 1996 peace agreements. The patrols nominally existed to protect villagers from "subversives," but it was their other functions that proved most valuable to the military. The civil patrols served as paramilitary surrogates by maintaining a military presence (important tangibly as well as symbolically) and collecting information. They also augmented the regular military units in action and searched for and returned those who fled the violence into the mountains. Finally, the patrols were used as a socialization instrument. Participants were not only involved in various activities aimed at instilling patriotism and identification with the military but also implicated in the military's atrocities, such as torturing and killing suspected insurgent sympathizers (White 1984:111–112; also see Perera 1993:118–119 and Stoll 1993:106–107).

At times, though, the civil patrols could be of some use to local communities. Much of the Indian support for the revolutionary forces was a defensive reaction to the military repression. But the guerrillas could not protect them from the military; indeed, revolutionary activities often brought in further military violence. The following story would not be atypical: An inhabitant of the Ixil region, a northern area hit especially hard by the violence, acknowledged that he originally supported the guerrillas, as did most of the people of his area. But he had come to blame the revolutionaries for provoking the death of his father, who had tried to stay out of the way of both sides. The father was murdered by the military in retribution for an ambush against them that had taken place close to his home. The guerrillas, this Ixil man said, "were like the boy who cried wolf. When the real wolf came, he was much bigger and more powerful than any of them ever imagined" (quoted in Perera 1993:86). Stoll (1993) makes the point that in addition to placating the military, the civil patrols kept the guerrillas away from Indian settlements, thereby avoiding the indiscriminate military violence that guerrilla activities provoked.

The military acknowledges that 440 villages were destroyed during the counterinsurgency of the early 1980s (Black 1985:16). During recent years over 1 million Guatemalans—close to one-seventh of the population—have been displaced from their homes. Their resettlement gave the military a further opportunity to extend its control of the countryside. Seven "development poles" (zones) were created in the northern areas that provided the greatest support to the guerrillas. Within each pole, model villages were built for the resettlement of Indians, including those rounded up by military and civil patrols in the mountains to which they had fled or after they had given themselves up. The villagers have done the construction work under the supervision of the military and its civilian technicians; in return, they receive food and eventually a home. In the early years these efforts were facilitated by a substantial international relief effort directed toward the highlands. Although the infrastructure plans were ambitious in the beginning, year by year they were scaled back, and in a number of cases the inhabitants received virtually no assistance. Twelve model villages as well as eight more minor sites had been completed by the end of 1985, another sixty were completed by the end of 1990, and about a dozen more by mid-1992, but seldom with the infrastructure imagined by some of the original architects (Stoll 1993:334, n. 20). As Anderson and Simon (1987:15) point out, "The Army is well aware that the oligarchy prefers it shed its own blood rather than spend the oligarchs' money on long term security projects which would promote longer term social order."

Pacification of the highlands was to be accomplished by indoctrination as well. Indians are constantly reminded that the guerrillas were unable to deliver on their promise of a better life and are told repeatedly that the attacks on their communities were actually carried out by the guerrillas. Indigenous religious beliefs are also manipulated in order to instill guilt among the Indians for their own suffering (Wilson 1991:47–48). Within the model villages, much attention has been given to patriotic symbols and activities, such as the raising and lowering of the flag and the singing of patriotic songs. At school, children learn "respect for the flag, respect for the authorities, and how not to be deceived by the communist delinquents" (quoted in Barry 1986:35). That "hearts and minds" have been won, however, is unlikely. Rather, what the military has gained is an acquiescence to the realities of power. Probably most crucial to the pacification of the countryside has been the military's willingness to allow Indians to resume cultivation on their lands and seasonal migration to the lowland plantations (Stoll 1993).

There also have been some surprising gains for Indians in the highlands. At least in some communities much of the local ladino power structure fled with the escalation of violence and has not returned. Lands have been sold to Indians and others divided and distributed by the government. The ladino absence has made it easier for ambitious Indians to expand their commercial activities, including as labor contractors. The proliferation of labor contractors has in turn placed the seller of labor in a somewhat better competitive situation, as has dealing with a fellow Indian as opposed to a ladino. Finally, local chapters of political parties, as well as local governments, have been taken over by Mayas (Stoll 1993:197–220).

However, living conditions remain dismal for the country's population, especially the peasantry. The poverty rate rose from 79 percent of the population in 1980 to 87 percent in 1991 as real median wages declined across all major sectors of society from 1980 to 1988 (Trudeau 1993:95, 104, 167). The percentage of Guatemalans unable to afford the "minimum diet" climbed from 52 percent in 1980 to 72 percent in 1990. It is not surprising that income distribution worsened, the share of the top 20 percent of Guatemalans increasing from 47 to 57 percent from 1970 to 1984 (Jonas 1991:178–179). The rural population continues to grow, leading to further fragmentation of holdings already too tiny and further overuse of soils already depleted. Worsening economic insecurity is especially prominent in the Indian areas hit hardest by the counterinsurgency: Access to land and commerce are down, and rural incomes have declined (Smith 1990).

These are conditions that lead to popular organizing and agitation when repression is relaxed. No sooner had the military eliminated the threat of the guerrillas (if not the guerrillas themselves) than it confronted a new situation that over time has served to undercut its domination. In a relatively fair and free election in 1985, Vinicio Cerezo, the civilian candidate of the Christian Democratic Party and a well-known reformer, won the presidency. The military was compelled to allow this "democratization," especially because of the continuing economic crisis. The real GDP declined by almost 5 percent from 1980 to 1984 and did again the next two years (IDB 1986:394). The nation's economic problems made elites vulnerable to international pressures as external assistance was conditioned upon an improvement in the country's human rights performance. As the transition to civilian government proceeded, assistance resumed, including military aid.[20] Cerezo hoped to utilize this opening to consolidate a democratic system in Guatemala, but he had to move cautiously, acknowledging that he actually held little power. Consequently, he refused to propose land reform or to investigate past military human rights abuses, particularly in the face of significant coup plotting

Popular groups bravely took advantage of this democratic opening to organize and to assert their demands, even though violence against them continued. In the first three years of civilian government, it was reported that there were more strikes and protests (including land invasions) than in the previous thirty years (*Monitor*, March 14, 1989:2). What was perhaps most notable, given the tragic history of the prior decade, was the development of rural organizations, including the reappearance of the Committee for Peasant Unity, which publicly resurfaced in 1988. The greatest attention, though, was given to the activities of Father Andrés Girón starting in early 1986. His National Peasant Association (ANC), which claimed a membership of 115,000 by the end of 1988, organized marches, protests, and hunger strikes in behalf of the continuing desperate plight of the country's peasantry but at the same time took care to stress its commitment to nonviolence and to the market economy (*NY*

Times, December 27, 1988:3; Trudeau 1993:96–100). Rather than redistributive land reform, Girón and the ANC called upon the government to purchase available farms and then turn them over to peasant cooperatives. This did become the Cerezo agrarian policy. President Cerezo claimed in his report to the Guatemalan congress in January 1988 that his government had distributed nine parcels benefiting over 2,000 families.

The activities and demands of these groups then led to a counterresponse from the right. Although the tactics of the popular forces were assemblies, demonstrations, and strikes, elements on the right continued to rely on terror. In just the one month of September 1988, seventy-five people were assassinated (*NY Times,* November 19, 1988). In fact, the violence would get even worse: A leading human rights organization reported 1,513 political murders and 238 disappearances during 1990 (Berger 1992:209). Finally, the violence started declining. Reported political assassinations for 1993 were 348, with thirty disappearances, and for 1994 were 287, with forty-five disappearances (*NotiSur,* August 12, 1994; February 17, 1995).

As part of Central American peace accords (discussed in Chapter 7), the Guatemalan government committed itself to meet with the revolutionary opposition.[21] Preliminary discussions that began with the National Guatemalan Revolutionary Unity (URNG) in 1988 produced no results. More serious talks resumed in 1990, eventually with United Nations observers, but still with minimal results. Part of the difficulty was that the victor in the 1990 presidential elections, Jorge Serrano Elías, was a wealthy conservative who showed little inclination to take on the hardliners within the military. In May 1993 he overreached, attempting a move toward dictatorial government that failed. He and his vice president were removed from power, the more moderate faction gained an upper hand in the military, and the congress elected the human rights ombudsman Ramiro de León Carpio to serve out the president's term. In spring 1994 the negotiations got back on track, and over the next two and a half years the two parties reached agreements on a number of critical items, especially after the inauguration of the winner of the December 1995 elections, Alvaro Arzú. These agreements included a United Nations on-site verification commission, a truth commission to report on past abuses (although with less authority than in most other countries), a right to repatriation, socioeconomic reform, and restrictions on the size and role of the military.

The de León–Arzú period witnessed several events significant for popular mobilization. There is no question that military abuse remains a serious problem in Guatemala, as the UN verification team reported in July 1995, but strides have been made that would have been unimaginable just a few years earlier. Although massacres are largely a horror of the past, on

October 5, 1995, soldiers opened fire on some 200 unarmed villagers in Xamán, killing eleven and leaving more than thirty others wounded. This time, though, United Nations observers arrived on the scene within hours; the responsible regional commander was dismissed, and the defense minister eventually resigned his position. President de León visited the site, promised to bring the guilty to trial, and pledged compensation to the victims and their families. When Arzú came to the presidency a few months later, he discharged some 200 police officers suspected of corruption and human rights abuses and removed eight generals and a number of colonels. Then in September 1996 the government ordered the arrest of nine military officers, five police chiefs, and four customs officials just two days before agreeing to an accord with the URNG that called for a 33 percent cut in the size of the military.

The other peace agreement of greatest relevance to rural society was signed earlier in 1996. As part of a larger socioeconomic package, in the May accord the government promised to address the needs of the landless through a land bank and adequate credit. The land is apparently to be obtained through methods such as open market purchases, confiscation of lands distributed in the past through corrupt means, distribution of public lands, and expropriation of fallow lands. Even assuming adequate will on the part of the government, it is not clear how there could be anywhere near adequate funds to cover this market approach to acute landlessness (*NotiSur*, June 7, 1996).

What is perhaps most significant about this accord is that it symbolizes that land reform is now back on the political agenda in Guatemala. Crucial to this accomplishment have been the efforts of CUC and the other leading campesino organization, the National Coordinator of Indigenous and Peasants (CONIC). Since early 1995 the two have pursued a campaign of land invasions to dramatize the land issue and to force elites to respond to their demands. The first half of 1995 saw over 100 land invasions; some 15,000 campesinos were involved in twenty more in the first five months of 1996. In one case events took a particularly ugly turn: When national police were sent to evict the squatters, violence ensued, leaving ten from both sides seriously injured and the head of the riot squad hacked to death by peasant machetes. CONIC leaders blamed the outcome on police brutality, but the United Nations observer mission at the scene disagreed. It is clear that tensions in rural Guatemala remain high (*Chronicle*, May 2, 1996).

Conclusion

Guatemala exemplifies the essence of the causes and the extreme of the consequences of the crisis in contemporary rural Central America. The system of elite domination established in Guatemala over the centuries to coerce land and labor from the peasantry is rivaled only by El Salvador's famed oligarchy. The first effort to reform this system ended with the overthrow of Arbenz in 1954. The reforms were overthrown as well, and the newly mobilized popular forces were repressed into passivity. Before the democratic period, Guatemala had been ruled by personal dictatorships; after 1954 the power was in the hands of the military. Its coercive capacity expanded in the following decades with substantial assistance from the United States, which remained vigilant about a "communist" threat to Guatemala. When small guerrilla forces appeared in the 1960s, the military demonstrated its willingness to kill indiscriminately and on a massive scale.

Nevertheless, the domination of Guatemala by the military and by prospering economic elites did not remain unchallenged. Popular mobilization continued through the 1970s at ever increasing levels. Some of the popular groups had shared in the benefits of the country's economic growth and were seeking reforms characteristic of the aspirations of emerging middle sectors worldwide. Many others, especially Mayan peasants, were motivated by deteriorating economic security as they lost their access to land, in short supply because of population growth and the landgrabbing of elites. The mobilization of both middle-sector and peasant groups was facilitated by the efforts of other political actors, who entered rural areas in new numbers during the 1970s. Priests, development workers, political party organizers, labor activists, and revolutionary guerrillas offered their encouragement and their assistance to help peasants build better lives for themselves.

In order to combat the new round of guerrilla activities, the military applied its strategy from the 1960s: Eliminate not just suspected guerrillas but also potentially supportive populations. The first years of this repression only intensified and widened opposition to the military and the system. The structures of domination were coming apart. To hold them together and to reinstitute control where it had eroded would require tremendous coercion—a step that the military was willing to take.[22] By the early 1980s, state terrorism was instituted on a systematic level. Tens of thousands of Guatemalans, especially Indian peasants, were murdered. At least for the time being, the system was maintained.

But although the military's defeat of the revolutionary forces elevated it to new heights of domination of Guatemalan society, it appears now that this power might prove to be short-lived, opening more space for true democratic politics. The enormous price of the military victory aggravated tensions between the military and civilians, not just the lower and middle sectors but also the economic elite. These tensions in turn spurred conflicts between factions within the military. With changed domestic and international circumstances, a new civilian president was able to move assertively against the military in 1996, forcing corrupt and abusive officers out of the services and then concluding an agreement with the URNG that called for substantial cuts in the budget and size of the military. Certainly the military will remain a dominant force within the country but perhaps under tighter constraints.

As the century closes in Guatemala, most of its rural citizens remain desperately poor. Their chances for a more decent life depend on many factors. At the top of the list is the absence of violence. Revolutionary violence seldom succeeds in its objectives; instead, the usual result is, as in Guatemala, to provoke state terror against the poor. With the end of the civil war, at long last, Guatemalans have the opportunity to restrict further the role of the military and to ensure that it respects their basic rights. This would allow the poor and their advocates to work for justice without worry of death as a possible cost of asserting their dignity. Given the magnitude of the obstacles that they face, they should be able to have at least that.

Notes

1. More controversial is what happened to the leading conservative candidate prior to the 1950 elections. With the country polarizing, the primary candidates were General Francisco Arana, the champion of conservatives and the chief of the armed forces, and Colonel Jacobo Arbenz, the defense minister who was moving further to the left. After having given an ultimatum to President Juan José Arévalo, Arana was killed in a gun battle apparently resulting from Arévalo's effort to have him arrested and sent into exile (Gleijeses 1991:50–71).

2. Handy (1994:88). This is the most complete source on agrarian issues during the reform period. Other sources for this section include: Aybar de Soto (1978), Blasier (1976), Forster (1994), Handy (1984), Martz (1956), Monteforte Toledo (1972), Schlesinger and Kinzer (1983), Wasserstrom (1975), and Whetten (1961).

3. For further background on these farms and the controversy over what to do with them, see Monteforte Toledo (1972:219–222). At least one scholar maintains that their confiscation was forced by the U.S. government (Schmid n.d.).

4. Handy (1984:125–126) gives a good summary of these variations. Also see Wasserstrom (1975).

5. Pearson (1969:350–373) cites a CNCG membership in 1954 of 256,000—a figure he still sees as inflated. The CNCG was organized by noncommunist progressives, originally in the face of hostility from the Communist Party, which was largely unsuccessful in similar organizational attempts. The extent to which it eventually came under communist influence is the subject of some dispute; compare, for example, Blasier (1976:155) and Handy (1994:115–120).

6. Probably the most compelling evidence of the greater concern for international communism as opposed to the plight of United Fruit is the extensive set of declassified State Department documents from the period available for review at the U.S.

National Archives. See, for example, the letter of May 14, 1954, to the secretary of state from Assistant Secretary Henry Holland (decimal file 714.00/5–1454).

7. For further information on agrarian reform in the post-1954 period, see Adams (1970), Berger (1992), Handy (1984), Hildebrand (1969), Minkel (1967), Pearson (1963a, 1963b), and Whetten (1961).

8. Despite the counterrevolution, United Fruit was never able to return to its previous dominant position in Guatemala. An antitrust suit filed by the U.S. Justice Department within a week of Arbenz's overthrow eventually led to judgments that forced the company to divest some of its banana-producing and -marketing operations and that forbade it to expand its banana operations. Later Del Monte cleverly preempted a United Fruit Company takeover attempt by entering the banana business itself. In 1972, ironically, it purchased United Fruit's Guatemala operations. (On Del Monte's operations in Guatemala, see Burbach and Flynn 1980:207–210.)

9. For discussions of this period, see Amnesty International (1981a), Berger (1992), Booth (1980), Bowen (1985), Collazo-Davila (1980), Gott (1971), Johnson (1972, 1973), Jonas (1991), and McClintock (1985b).

10. The quotation is from Colonel John D. Webber; his assassination is the subject of the story.

11. For further information, see Adams (1970:278–317), Brintnall (1979:117–169), Colby and vanden Berghe (1969:102–103), Ebel (1964:100), Falla (1978:446–459), Warren (1978:87–169), and Watanabe (1992). As Scott (1990) warns, though, it is possible that researchers from outside of subordinated communities overstate the difference in beliefs between "traditionalists" and more "modern" members of that community because of a greater reluctance on the part of the former to reveal their beliefs to outsiders.

12. For contrasting Indian peasant views of the strike (and broader issues), see Burgos-Debray (1984:227–235) and Sexton (1985:148–151); the first is the testimony of Nobel laureate Rigoberta Menchú, a radical organizer; the second, that of a labor contractor. The strike was illegal since the labor code prohibited agricultural strikes during the harvest season. For discussions of both the Committee for Peasant Unity and more generally the indigenous mobilization of the late 1970s and early 1980s, see Arias (1985), Black (1983b), Burgos-Debray (1984), Davis (1983c), Jiménez (1985), and May (1993).

13. For discussions of the guerrilla movements of the 1970s and 1980s, see Black (1983a, 1983b), Handy (1984:244–250), Jonas (1991), Paige (1983), and Payeras (1983). In addition to the two organizations discussed in the text, there were three other, less important guerrilla organizations: the Rebel Armed Forces (FAR), the Guatemalan Workers' Party (PGT), and the Revolutionary Movement of the People (MRP-Ixim). In 1982 the five grouped together as the National Guatemalan Revolutionary Unity.

14. President Lucas's brother, General Benedicto Lucas García, is reported to have admitted that the government was responsible for at least 70 percent of the murders and disappearances during that administration (Nairn and Simon 1986:14).

15. Sixteen Catholic priests were murdered in Guatemala from 1976 through 1984 (U.S. House 1985a:78).

16. In the face of the human rights legislation of the mid-1970s and the commitment of the Carter administration to the promotion of human rights, a split developed between the United States and Guatemala from 1978 to 1980. It should be noted, however, that economic assistance to Guatemala continued during this period, as did the delivery of military aid already in the pipeline (Schoultz 1983:188–189). Guatemalan officials rejoiced when Ronald Reagan defeated Jimmy Carter in 1980 because it was widely expected that the new president would sharply alter policy toward their country.

17. The Reagan administration spoke in 1981 of a new approach directed toward establishing communications with the Guatemalan government to bring it out of its "siege or . . . bunker mentality." It was hoped that this stance would give the Guatemalans the "self confidence [they] needed" to end "terrorism and violence" without violating human rights (U.S. House 1981c:10–13).

18. Especially important sources for this period are Carmack (1988), Falla (1994), and Manz (1988). An estimated 200,000 Guatemalans fled into Mexico, many in the region across the border where they were grouped in almost 100 camps, some reaching 7,000 people in size (Manz 1988:147–156).

19. Major sources for this section were Barry (1986), Black (1985), Handy (1984), Manz (1988), Smith (1990), Stoll (1993), and White (1984).

20. The U.S. Congress agreed to appropriate the following sums for fiscal year 1985: for development aid, $40.1 million; for cash transfers, $12.5 million; and for military training, $300,000. For the next fiscal year, the Reagan administration requested $10.3 million for military aid but $7 million less for development aid (Trudeau and Schoultz 1986:45).

21. This section is based on the following: Human Rights Watch (1996), *NotiSur* (May 13, 1994; September 23, 1994; January 20, 1995; February 23, 1996; April 12, 1996; June 7, 1996; August 11, 1996; September 27, 1996), and Trudeau (1993: 135–141).

22. The military's scorched-earth policies were opposed by some field commanders. The Central American militaries are not unified institutions but are permeated by divisions based on service, generational, personalistic, and ideological lines.

Chapter Six

El Salvador: From Obstruction to Civil War and Toward Reconciliation

El Salvador ends the twentieth century with hopes of having broken down patterns of domination that oppressed its peasantry for centuries. But this hope emerges out of a tragic process that took the lives of some 75,000 Salvadorans during the 1980s. The great majority of those killed were civilian bystanders to a civil war between the left and a militarized government, the latter of which bears the responsibility for most of these deaths.[1]

Peasant mobilization in El Salvador in the 1970s challenged the system of domination that had allowed a small elite to control most of the land and the profits from its cultivation. This threat was reminiscent of events of half a century earlier. In the 1920s many peasants lost land to coffee growers, who expanded their holdings in tandem with growing markets. The ranks of the landless and unemployed increased further when the Great Depression caused growers to cut back operations. Encouraged by leftist organizers from the cities, peasants mounted demonstrations and joined unions. Finally, thousands staged an uprising in 1932. After the rebellion was smashed, close to 1 percent of the country's entire population was massacred. Rural peace was thus restored.

Similar forces were at the core of the contemporary Salvadoran tragedy, as this chapter documents. Living conditions for many rural people deteriorated in the postwar period as the impact of high population growth rates was aggravated by the loss of land to larger farmers motivated by new commercial opportunities. Breaking out of the "culture of repression"[2] reinforced by the 1932 massacre, many peasants in the 1970s risked joining new organizations that advocated their interests. The elite re-

sponse was once again obstructionist. A minimal agrarian reform proposal in the mid-1970s was aborted; instead, the powerful relied on repression. Hundreds of people were killed annually through the rest of the
decade; rather than a successful means of intimidation, this terrorism in-
cited further popular mobilization, in urban areas as well as the countryside. By the time of the Sandinista victory in Nicaragua in July 1979, El
Salvador was on the verge of a popular revolution.

A coup by junior military officers in October 1979 initiated a process
that instead led the country into prolonged civil war. A series of rapid
changes in government brought a U.S.-sponsored "centrist" regime to
power in early 1980. Vital to the purposes of both this regime and the
United States was an agrarian reform that is examined closely in this
chapter. Whatever the gains won by the peasantry, they came at tremendous cost. As in 1932, beneficiaries of the traditional system were willing
to employ mass murder as an instrument to protect their fundamental interests. This time, however, they were not able to prevail. A leftist insur-
gence propelled by revulsion against pervasive injustice and the growing
repression fought the military to a stalemate. After a dozen years of fighting, negotiations finally led to the signing in early 1992 of a peace agreement that is historic in the scope of the social change it institutionalized.
Poverty and injustice are still rampant in El Salvador, but the possibilities
for public policy responsive to the needs of the poor now exist on a scale
unimaginable but a few years ago.

The Obstruction of Change

On May Day 1930, up to 80,000 peasants paraded through the streets of San
Salvador.[3] Around the same time, the Marxist Regional Federation of
Workers of El Salvador claimed to have organized a similar number of agricultural workers. The situation in the country was desperate; male rural
unemployment in 1929 was estimated at 40 percent, and it was still climbing the following year (North 1985:35). Thousands of people were attend-
ing "popular universities" presented in the countryside by radical students
to encourage peasant organization. The administration of Pío Romero
Bosque (1927–1931) alternated between permissive and repressive responses to this unprecedented mass mobilization. Perhaps most significant,
Romero allowed the country to hold its first fair and free presidential election in 1930. The victor, Arturo Araujo, was an upper-class maverick inspired by the British Labour Party. Any promise of reform was doomed,
however. Politically inept, Araujo could not satisfy his multiclass coalition,
especially not during the difficult days of the Depression and under the
tightest of political constraints. After he had been in office nine months, a
coup replaced him with General Maximiliano Hernández Martínez.

Disappointed with the failures and repression of the Araujo administration and faced with indefinite military rule, radicals decided on a mass uprising as their best alternative. Led by the effective communist organizer Augustín Farabundo Martí, the conspirators enjoyed substantial success working in Indian communities in the western part of the country, even gaining the support of a number of village chiefs. Unfortunately for their cause, authorities discovered the plot three days before the uprising was to take place and soon had Martí and other leaders under arrest. Nonetheless, the rebellion went on as planned in January 1932 in the western region, where the scope of the uprising was impressive. Bands of up to 500 people each stormed the towns of Juayuá, Nahuizalco, and Sonsonate; up to 1,400 attacked Ahuachapán, and 1,800 attacked Tacupa. As the counterattack mounted, some 5,000 rebels regrouped at Tacupa and a like number at Sonzacate.

Later the upper sectors of society would justify their system of domination in El Salvador with their "memory" of the unrestrained barbarity of the communist-Indian uprising. In reality, though the scare must have been substantial and looting was common, Anderson's (1971:136) careful reconstruction estimates about thirty-five civilians killed by the rebels, with other violations of personal integrity minimal. In contrast, the state and private elite forces slaughtered on a massive scale, mostly in revenge after the rebellion had been crushed. A figure of 30,000 deaths is often cited, but Anderson (1971:135) considers 8,000–10,000 more realistic; this number would still constitute close to 1 percent of the population at that time. Especially targeted for death were people who looked Indian in feature or dress and those known or thought to be communists.[4]

La Matanza (the Massacre), as the event is known, fulfilled its purpose: For the next four decades neither the peasantry nor the left was a force in Salvadoran political life. The military governed the country directly from 1932 until 1979. Along with other security forces, it provided the coercion necessary to keep the agrarian structure intact. Over the following decades, the small agro-export oligarchy continued to enjoy the fruits from their possession of the majority of the land, even as landlessness and unemployment reached serious heights. Fundamental to this system was the continued demobilization of the rural population. The 1907 agrarian code's ban on rural unions and strikes was enforced by a national guard formed in 1912, which large landholders customarily employed to maintain order and prevent protest on their estates. As White (1973:120) observed, "Any 'agitator' among coffee-workers [was] of course dismissed and if necessary imprisoned or otherwise dealt with."[5]

Maintenance of this culture of repression had become more difficult, however, by the 1960s. The regime's response was the creation of the Nationalist Democratic Organization (ORDEN; i.e., "order"), formed secretly at middecade by President Julio Rivera and General José Medrano, chief of the national guard. This paramilitary organization grew rapidly, eventually "enlisting" up to 100,000 peasants and residents of small towns. Assisted by U.S. Green Beret trainers, it linked its members to the military regime through both patronage and socialization into its national security ideology. ORDEN functioned as an auxiliary to the national guard for maintaining rural order and as an instrument of repression with which the regime could—hypocritically—deny complicity.

The military regime made few efforts to address agrarian problems. The government did purchase some estates through a colonization program initiated in 1932 to make land available to landless peasants. But little technical or credit support was provided to the settlers, and some of the land was of poor quality. Subsequent reconcentration of holdings was not uncommon. Government land purchases largely ended in 1951. As of 1966 thirty colonies covered 124,000 acres and held a population of around 60,000. By this point, though, the issue of land reform could not be kept off of the policy agenda.

Responding to the economic growth and prosperity of the 1960s, the domestic unity that followed the 1969 war with Honduras, and pressures from the growing urban middle sectors, the presidential term of Fidel Sánchez Hernández (1967–1972) was marked by a more tolerant attitude toward discussions of the need for reform and efforts at organizing. Although the government's specific intentions were never made clear, its rhetoric helped to legitimate the opposition's discussion of the subject.

The Christian Democratic Party (PDC), the most dynamic popular force during this period, soon proposed an agrarian reform program that sought to create a rural middle class through the elimination of both latifundia and *minifundia* (minifarms). After gaining control of the legislative assembly, lawmakers favoring reform convened a National Agrarian Reform Congress in early 1970. Although it failed to include peasant interests, the assembly was otherwise broadly representative. After conservative forces walked out on its deliberations, the assembly called for an agrarian reform that would include both the "massive expropriation in favor of the common good" of lands not fulfilling their social function and the active participation of the peasantry in the reform process (quoted in Webre 1979:128). Significant legislative action was precluded, however, by the victory of the government party, the National Conciliation Party (PCN), in the legislative elections of March 1970, most likely the result of renewed tensions with Honduras.

As the 1972 presidential election approached, the Christian Democrats entered into a coalition with several smaller social democratic parties. They united behind the PDC's most popular leader, José Napoleón Duarte, who had been elected mayor of San Salvador three times. His running mate was Guillermo Ungo of the National Revolutionary Movement (MNR), a close personal friend and the son of one of the founding leaders of the PDC. A major plank in the platform of their National Opposition Union (UNO) was agrarian reform; it called for a legal ceiling on the size of landholdings and the expropriation and redistribution of lands over this limit. The election campaign followed several years of increasing popular organizing. To conservatives it appeared "that leftist agitation was rampant in the country" (Webre 1979:152)—an especially frightening spectacle given events in Chile, where Salvador Allende's Marxist government had just followed that country's first Christian Democratic government into power. Consequently, the landed elite and its rightist allies decided to field their own candidate, General Medrano, who had recently been dismissed as commander of the national guard for allegedly planning a coup.

The military was prepared to protect the system from the threats of reformism and popular mobilization. When Duarte's share of the vote started to gain on that of the government's candidate, radio announcement of the returns was discontinued; when it resumed, the government's candidate, Colonel Arturo Molina, had won. In response to this obvious fraud, a coup was attempted, but it was put down and Duarte was arrested, physically abused, and exiled. The consequences of the fraud were tremendous; in particular, many UNO supporters decided that the electoral process was not a viable instrument for social change under present circumstances in their country. Instead, other strategies would have to be developed.

The desperate need for agrarian reform intensified during the 1970s, but the regime's only response was minor, and even that was aborted.[6] The government created the Salvadoran Institute of Agrarian Transformation (ISTA) in 1975, and the following year it proposed a reform program in the eastern coastal departments of San Miguel and Usulután. Landowners were given a deadline by which to sell their property, after which it would be expropriated; either way, the land was to be distributed to landless families. The owners were to be fully compensated by funds provided by USAID, support that apparently was critical to the formulation of the proposal. Although a major purpose of the reform was to bolster falling popular support for the regime with the 1977 elections approaching, in the end the government was more responsive to the vested interests.

The dispute quickly grew into an intense confrontation between different factions of the elite over the future course of Salvadoran agrarian policy. Cutting across military-civilian lines, the debate was essentially between the landed oligarchy and its rightist allies—which adamantly opposed any changes in the agrarian system—and other, more moderate groups, which supported mild reform for developmental or political reasons. The government was able to bring 70,000–100,000 rural people (largely ORDEN members) to the capital to support its proposal, but the oligarchy mobilized its many trade associations and utilized its power over the press to force the government to back down amid a campaign of "hysterical anti-communism" (Baloyra 1982:59). A compromise with the landowners was announced, which in effect negated the program. The inability of the Salvadoran elite to accommodate even mild reform had been demonstrated once again.

Popular Mobilization

This continuing obstruction of reform by Salvadoran elites was confronted in the 1970s by an unprecedented challenge from popular forces in both urban and rural areas.[7] The economic growth of the 1960s and 1970s increased the size and the aspirations of the urban middle and working classes. Following their politicization and radicalization, these urban forces played a critical role in promoting peasant mobilization. Meanwhile in the countryside, the rapid spread of commercial agriculture undermined the economic security of much of the peasantry, as elaborated in Part 1. Reinforcing this loss of land and employment were the impacts of both a continuing high rate of population growth and the 1969 war with Honduras, which eliminated the neighboring country as a frontier safety valve and returned tens of thousands of settlers to El Salvador.

Some observers have denied that deteriorating economic conditions contributed to popular frustrations in El Salvador in the 1970s and therefore to the civil war that followed. It is true that the Salvadoran GDP grew by 5 percent annually from 1968 to 1978, for an annual per capita increase of 1.4 percent, and that per capita production of basic grains increased during this period as well (Mooney 1984:61–63).[8] However, these aggregate figures hide the mounting economic insecurity of significant elements of the rural population. Landlessness among agricultural families climbed from approximately 28 percent in 1961 to 38 percent in 1971 and then higher as the decade progressed.[9] While the ranks of the landless grew, their incomes declined by 19 percent (more when adjusted for inflation) from 1971 to 1975. When their incomes are measured against the average for all rural groups, they declined by 24 percent for the same years, whereas the relative share of the largest landowners increased by 23 percent (Montes 1980:132). Meanwhile, rural salaries declined in both absolute and relative terms. Measured in constant units, agricultural wages fluctuated from 1967 to 1973 and then fell by 25 percent to 1976 and by 30 percent to 1978. During the same period, agricultural salaries lost 23 percent of their value compared to industrial salaries (Montes 1980:115).

The objective conditions for popular mobilization were clearly present by 1973, and they became even more urgent as the decade progressed. But as Montes (1980) points out, there was little subjective readiness by peasants to organize early in the decade. Soon, though, the emergence of a grassroots reform movement was facilitated by agents from the outside, especially church workers as well as urban students and politicians.

Even though rural unions continued to be illegal, new organizations that appeared in the countryside in the 1960s began to address the needs of the peasantry. The two most important were the Salvadoran Communal Union (UCS) and the Christian Federation of Salvadoran Peasants (FECCAS). The American Institute for Free Labor Development (AIFLD, an affiliate of the AFL-CIO) initiated training of peasant leaders in El Salvador in 1962 through its Alliance for Progress program. With assistance from USAID, the Christian Democratic Party, and the Salvadoran government, this project eventually led to the development of cooperatives and then, in 1968, to the founding of UCS. The formation of FECCAS was catalyzed in 1964 by Christian Democrats. At first primarily a self-help organization, it had grown more assertive by the end of the decade as both peasants and priests deepened their understanding of the challenges they faced.

Elements of the Catholic Church played a critical role in the mobilization of peasants as they did elsewhere in the region. The process often began with the formation of Christian base communities, small Bible-study groups in which peasants were encouraged to apply religious lessons about dignity and justice to their own lives. Participants elected their own leaders, both lay teachers and preachers; between 1970 and 1976 about 15,000 were trained. An early indication of what the base communities portended for the landed elite came in 1969 in Suchitoto, a town about 30 miles northeast of San Salvador. Shortly after base communities started in this area of land scarcity, two of the country's wealthiest landowners bought a local hacienda and subdivided it, selling the new units at prices ranging from three to seven times their original cost. Up to 3,000 local people demonstrated their outrage in front of the hacienda, demanding lower prices. When this action proved futile, 400 of them demonstrated in the capital, the first such showing since 1932 not organized by the government.

Rural organizing in the 1960s and early 1970s was outpaced by similar efforts in urban areas, especially by teachers, students, and industrial workers. Following the disenchantment that resulted from the fraud of the 1972 presidential election and similar duplicity in the 1974 elections, a new type of political organization was created in June 1974, the United Popular Action Front (FAPU). Representing rural interests in this coalition of popular groups were FECCAS and peasants from around Suchitoto. Soon other popular organizations would develop, and by the end of the 1970s they were the most dynamic political force in the country.

By the mid-1970s, then, there were three different kinds of peasant organizations in El Salvador. First, there was ORDEN, a paramilitary force organized by the state to control the countryside. Although its membership was estimated at around 100,000, it is usually claimed that only about 5 to 10 percent actively provided services for the government (Montgomery 1995:56). Second, there was UCS, which claimed a membership of about 60,000 by 1980. Given its origins and continuing ties to AIFLD (which provided most of its financial support, the bulk of which came in turn from USAID),[10] it is not surprising that critics of the UCS from the left perceived it "as a means of controlling the peasantry by giving its members a piece of the pie" (Montgomery 1995:106; also see Dunkerley 1982:98).[11] Third, increasing numbers of peasants were mobilized as the 1970s progressed by more radical groups such as FECCAS and the popular organizations.

The right's victory over the moderate reformers in the conflict about the 1976 agrarian reform proposal was relatively easy within the reigning policymaking system, but the rightists' determination to maintain the rural status quo faced an equally insistent challenge from newly mobilized popular forces. The right relied on violence to protect its position. Coming at a time of rapidly deteriorating economic conditions for many rural people, however, the repression of the 1970s had largely the opposite effect, generating even more widespread popular opposition.

What had been isolated instances of violence in the early 1970s became more frequent by the middle of the decade. Peasants from a local base community were attacked in November 1974 when they occupied idle private land in La Cayetana; six of them were killed, thirteen disappeared, and twenty-six were arrested. Soon afterward peasants of the area formed the Union of Rural Workers (UTC), which then allied with FECCAS. At about this time, student activism at the University of El Salvador reached a new peak. A student march in July 1975, protesting the breaking up of an earlier campus demonstration against the extravagant holding of the Miss Universe pageant, was fired on by the national guard. As many as thirty-seven marchers were killed (Berryman 1984:109–111; Webre 1979:188–189). One study of the Molina years suggests that 106 people were murdered or disappeared at government initiative from 1972 to 1977, and the increasingly assertive armed movements of the left killed forty-two security or paramilitary personnel (cited in Baloyra 1982:190). Leftists also kidnapped members of the elite for ransom and in 1977 executed two of their victims. Since both were from the more modernizing elite faction, their murders—along with the other kidnappings—certainly contributed to the growing polarization in the country.

Two other sets of events in early 1977 indicated what the next two and a half years would be like. First, the regime maintained itself in power by once again committing massive fraud in the presidential election of February 20. Outside observers generally agreed that the slate put forth by the democratic opposition would have won the election had legality prevailed. A week later, a continuing vigil by the democratic forces was attacked by the security forces; up to 100 people were killed, 200 wounded, and 500 arrested (Berryman 1984:121–122). In this fashion the regime was perpetuated. Molina's reformist façade was shed, however, as the new president, General Carlos Romero, was a man of the far right.

The second foreboding event occurred in March 1977, when Father Rutilio Grande, along with two peasants accompanying him, was assassinated. Although five other priests were killed during the 1970s, Grande's murder was especially significant. Grande began his pastoral work in 1972 in Augilares, a sugar-growing area close to his birthplace. With a team of co-workers, he sought to facilitate a deepening of the peasants' religious understanding so that they would become active participants in creating, in his words, "a community of brothers and sisters committed to building a new world, with no oppressors or oppressed, according to God's plan" (quoted in Berryman 1984:108). Soon the team had established twenty-seven rural base communities and ten urban ones, with about 300 leaders selected by the participants themselves. Grande tried to maintain a separation between his religious work and political activities, but many of those affected by the teachings of his team became active in political organizations, especially FECCAS. As popular mobilization grew, the right blamed the transformation on church people who espoused liberationist messages.

During the three months following the electoral fraud of February 1977, another priest in addition to Grande was murdered, ten priests were exiled, eight were expelled (five were tortured first), two were arrested, one was beaten, and another was seized and tortured on two separate occasions. This was the context of Oscar Romero's selection as archbishop of San Salvador, the country's key religious leader. Misperceived by many as a "safe" choice, he had been undergoing his own process of consciousness-raising for several years, a transformation accelerated by the murder of his friend Father Grande. Archbishop Romero met a similar fate in March 1980, his assassination eliminating the most powerful voice for peace, justice, and reconciliation in El Salvador.

For the regime to maintain itself and to protect the oligarchy, however, repression would have to increase, because popular mobilization continued to grow in both urban and rural areas. Key examples in the countryside in 1977 included two important land invasions organized by the Popular Revolutionary Bloc (BPR), the largest of the popular organizations; a demand for an increase in the minimum daily wage presented in mid-October by radical peasant unions such as FECCAS-UTC; and rural workers' occupation of the Ministry of Labor in November. For the next two years, popular forces kept up a steady pace of such activities, especially strikes, occupations, and demonstrations. Actions by the revolutionary organizations occurred more often as well. But government repression increased even more rapidly: During Romero's twenty-seven months in office, over 600 Salvadorans were assassinated or disappeared. The most frequent victims of this state terrorism were activists in the popular organizations. Meanwhile, about 132 security and paramilitary personnel were killed by the armed left, and another sixteen were kidnapped (cited in Baloyra 1982:190).

The growing movement against the Somoza dictatorship in Nicaragua in 1979 intensified the conflict in El Salvador by emboldening the left and scaring the right. Romero made his situation even more precarious by alienating his rightist support when he eased the repression in an attempt to reduce tensions with the Carter administration. When Somoza fell in July, Romero's days were clearly numbered. Indeed, three different factions within the military were plotting against him: reformers, the U.S.-oriented center-right, and the rightists. The reformers acted first, deposing Romero in October 1979 and setting up a progressive government with many of the civilian interests that had opposed the regime's candidates in 1972 and 1977.

A "Centrist" Model for Change

The new government was based on an alliance of the reformers with forces to their right rather than with popular interests represented by the mass organizations.[12] Neither did the new junta control the military and security forces, whose repression actually intensified in the last months of 1979. Since the October junta was unable to end the repression, initiate meaningful reforms, or placate the increasingly restive left, it soon fell, to be replaced by new governments in both January and March 1980. The October government did formulate an agrarian reform under the leadership of the minister of agriculture, Enrique Alvarez (who had held the same position in the Sánchez cabinet almost a decade earlier). The inability of reformers to overcome strong military opposition to this proposal was a major factor leading to the departure from the government of the civilian reformers, a number of whom became leaders of opposition forces.[13]

In March 1980 an agrarian reform was initiated under a less progressive government. The involvement of the United States was critical to this turnabout. It took Washington some time to decide how to respond to the changed situation after the October coup. By the beginning of 1980, the United States faced in El Salvador governmental instability on the one hand and growing mass mobilization and radicalization on the other. Determined to avoid "another Nicaragua," the Carter administration dispatched a new ambassador to El Salvador to engineer a viable reformist government of the center. At the heart of what Ambassador Robert White later called "a new model for profound . . . economic and social change" (U.S. House 1981a:6) was agrarian reform, accompanied by the nationalization of the banking and export marketing sectors.[14]

The purposes and the evolution of the reform need to be understood as the outcome of a political process involving the U.S. government and three major sets of actors in El Salvador—the military, the economic elite, and the frequently changing civilian government. Less powerful actors had an impact at times as well, such as the UCS with the formulation of the agrarian reform. Different factions in turn struggled within each of these arenas to control their role in the fight over the Salvadoran reform. As political fortunes and alliances changed, so did the fate of the reform. Particularly critical was the struggle within the military. At the time, reformists dominated among the junior officers, but they proved to be no match for their conservative superiors. Of all groups involved, it was the hard-liners within the Salvadoran military who were the most adept (and ruthless) at realizing their objectives (Stanley 1996).

Promulgation of a reform program required a change in the attitude not only of the U.S. government but also of the Salvadoran military. The increasing threat from the popular-leftist forces softened resistance within the military to reform, giving credibility to the argument that such changes were necessary to preempt the program of the left and to give the government some measure of legitimacy. U.S. officials accompanied such arguments with considerable pressure, making it clear that reform was the price for U.S. support. Finally, the military was given a central role in the implementation of the reform, which meant that the program could be used as an instrument of repression to combat the growing leftist insurgency.

Repression

Because it was improbable that the reform program would have been adopted without the pressure from the United States, the domestic distribution of power in El Salvador was insufficient to ensure its faithful implementation.[15] In this situation it was probably inevitable that the reform process would be used by those with power to pursue other objectives, such as counterinsurgency and intimidation. This became all the more likely as U.S. security concerns grew, especially when the Reagan administration entered office in January 1981.

The promulgation of the reform was followed by the announcement of a state of siege. Teams from the agrarian reform agency (ISTA) traveled to the targeted large estates, accompanied by the military, to announce their expropriation. But hard-liners in the military had other purposes for their new presence in the countryside. Reports of large numbers of murdered peasants soon reached the capital. It was in these areas that the flow of refugees and the numbers of peasants killed by armed forces in 1980 were the highest (LeoGrande 1981). Over the next few years, the peasant death toll mounted rapidly. Tens of thousands of peasants died, either as the objects of direct attack or as a consequence of military counterinsurgency tactics.[16]

The rural victims of the Salvadoran violence were usually identified with three groups: agrarian reform workers, peasant leaders, and members of peasant communities suspected of being sympathetic to the guerrillas. Forty employees of the agrarian reform agency were murdered in the first year and a half (AWC and ACLU 1982:63). Indeed, the agency's director, José Rodolfo Viera, and two AIFLD advisers were assassinated in January 1981 while dining at the San Salvador Sheraton Hotel. Viera had been the head of the UCS and played a critical role in pushing for the reform, influencing its formulation, and fighting for its full implementation. The identities of the powerful figures behind the gunman have long been known, but they have never been brought to justice.

Peasant leaders, including those who emerged during the reform process, also were murdered in large numbers. Some estimate that in the first year of the agrarian reform more than 500 peasant leaders were killed by security forces or allied right-wing paramilitary groups (CAMINO 1982:73). There were various reports of security forces' occupying newly expropriated estates asking peasants to elect leaders, whom they executed in subsequent days. Many of the victims were members of UCS. Also targeted were the progressive organizations such as FECCAS, which was destroyed along with the larger popular organizations in the early 1980s. Many of the survivors joined the revolutionary forces, which grew significantly in strength and support in 1980 and 1981.

Finally, there were the tens of thousands of victims of the rural pacification prong of the war against the guerrillas. According to a 1981 report of the legal aid office of the archbishop of El Salvador, "The assassinations, the massacres, the robberies and burning of ranches are frequent, especially in the northern and eastern zones. The testimonies heard and read, most coming from persons not affiliated to organizations, have shown that to be a victim of the repression it is enough to be a relative of a militant or to be suspected of having collaborated with the insurgents" (quoted in CAMINO 1982:74). Although efforts were made in later years to clean up military practices, the increasing reliance on airpower after 1983 to pursue the counterinsurgency campaign introduced a new source of noncombatant casualties and loss of homes.[17]

Rural people suffered from actions by the revolutionaries as well, although at a level far less than from the government. Economic sabotage was a major tactic of the Farabundo Martí National Liberation Front (FMLN), but destroyed bridges and power lines hurt neutral parties and even friends as well as foes. Sabotage campaigns against export crops hurt not only the agro-export elite but also agrarian reform cooperatives. Many peasants supported the FMLN and freely gave from their limited supplies to help support the revolutionary effort. Others, however, felt their produce was extorted by the armed groups (Strasma 1989:414–415). FMLN violence against civilians became more frequent in the late 1980s. One of their most controversial tactics was the assassination of mayors, whom the rebels portrayed as key units of the government's counterinsurgency strategy. The use of land mines also led to a number of unintended civilian casualties (Americas Watch 1988b).

The Reform Program

The agrarian reform was announced on March 6, 1980, with the first two of its three phases largely taken from the unsuccessful proposal of the previous fall. Implementation of phase one was authorized the same day; in the end it expropriated the 472 properties that were in excess of 1,235 acres and converted them into 317 cooperatives with over 31,000 members (about 8 percent of all peasant families). Covering more than 548,800 acres, the reform affected about 15 percent of the country's farmland, much of which had been devoted to the cultivation of export crops, especially cotton and sugar (U.S. House 1984:271).[18] Phase two, which applied to farms of between 247 and 1,235 acres, was never implemented because of intense opposition.

The implementing decree for phase three was issued on April 28, 1980. Often referred to as "land to the tiller" (or "tenant"), phase three allowed those farming all rented or sharecropped land under 17.3 acres to claim title to it. At the time of its legal expiration (June 1984), about 63,660 of the estimated 150,000 eligible peasants had registered for title to some 240,000 acres—about 6.6 percent of the country's farmland, although later figures lowered the beneficiaries to about 42,500 with about 172,000 acres (Thiesenhusen 1995:154). Altogether the U.S. State Department estimated that the reform benefited more than one-quarter of El Salvador's rural poor (about 12 percent of the total population) and affected around 22 percent of the agricultural land (U.S. State Department 1985a).

There is some evidence that the United States was less than happy at the time with the cooperative nature of phase one of the reform (Buckley 1984:116); certainly the Reagan administration was dissatisfied. Major peasant leaders like Viera apparently wanted alternatives to cooperatives as

well (Prosterman and Riedinger 1987:150). However, communal organization was central to the Christian Democratic ideology of leaders such as
Duarte, who were brought into the government at that time.[19] This situation was reversed with "land to the tiller." Duarte claimed that he reluc-
tantly accepted the program under heavy U.S. pressure and after having
been promised substantial financial assistance to pay for the requisite compensation (Buckley 1984:118). In contrast, Viera and the United States were
pleased with the individualist nature of this third phase. A key architect of
the program was Roy Prosterman, who was brought to El Salvador by
AIFLD, the "foreign office" of the AFL-CIO.[20] Prosterman had long been an
enthusiastic supporter of programs that turned tenants into small farmers,
for example, as a primary formulator of a similar land reform program in
South Vietnam in the late 1960s. In addition to their merits as social and
economic reforms, such programs were seen as invaluable in the "fight
against communism" because they robbed radicals of their major appeal to
the peasantry. Given the concerns of the United States in El Salvador at the
time, "land to the tiller" was a most attractive concept.

Phase three eventually benefited tens of thousands of peasant families
but far fewer than planned.[21] The transformation of smallholder tenants
into property owners would work most smoothly if their land belonged
to absentee owners with large holdings and if the state security forces enforced the reform faithfully. To the contrary, in El Salvador many of the affected plots were owned by local residents with only minor holdings,
many of whom were very bitter over the possible expropriation of their
property. Many owners resisted implementation of this reform, often
evicting their tenants, sometimes assisted by local security forces and
paramilitary groups. A cumbersome implementation process further hindered the reform, as did the halfhearted support for the program from
both the Salvadoran and U.S. governments as time went on (Diskin 1982;
Prosterman and Riedinger 1987; Strasma et al. 1983).

Still, implementation of the Salvadoran agrarian reform was greatly assisted by financial support from the United States. Total development assistance from 1980 through 1990 was around $718.2 million.[22] Most of this
amount was for agricultural credit, though the United States provided
funds for technical assistance and the implementing institutions as well.
U.S. monies did not go to help the government of El Salvador with the
burden of compensation, however, because of legislative restrictions promoted by Senator Jesse Helms in both 1980 and 1981. Funds for compensation have been difficult for the Salvadoran government to raise. By November 1982 it had paid for only 29 percent of expropriated phase one
land and by early 1985 for 54 percent of the properties, but almost all of it
in bonds (Browning 1983:414; Strasma et al. 1983:80–86; U.S. House
1985b:282). Even more financially strapped have been the cooperatives;

the phase one beneficiaries are required to repay to the government over a twenty- to thirty-year period the total cost of the expropriation (land, improvements, livestock, machinery, and so on) and of any government-funded improvements. One report found that as of November 1984 three-quarters of them lacked the resources just to keep up with the service payments (U.S. House 1985b:284). These problems have continued, as discussed later in this chapter.

Implementation of the Reform

Implementation of the various phases of the reform was complicated by shifting political fortunes in both Washington and San Salvador. The second phase, which would have affected about 18.5 percent of the farm-land, including many of the elite's coffee estates, was postponed virtually as soon as it was announced.[23] The right-of-center coalition that dominated the Salvadoran constituent assembly elected in March 1982 in the country's first relatively democratic elections then annulled phase two in its first legislative session. Not only did the owners of the targeted land possess considerable political power, but the Carter administration was divided about the merits of phase two, and the Reagan administration was solidly opposed to it (Bonner 1984:197, 239). Officials in both Washington and San Salvador were receptive to landowners' argument that redistribution of these lands would seriously reduce the country's foreign exchange earnings. They also argued that the first phase alone had overtaxed the capabilities of the Salvadoran government, which therefore lacked the financial, administrative, and technical capacity to undertake further expropriations. The issue was settled by a provision in the 1983 constitution establishing a ceiling of 605 acres on the amount of land that an individual could own. Owners were given up to three years to sell property in excess of this limit (with sale to close relatives prohibited), after which time the excess would be subject to expropriation. Evidence suggests that landowners have largely complied with this provision. The end result has been the elimination of large estates from El Salvador.

The history of phase three has been more complicated, given the support it received from the United States on the one hand and the struggle over its implementation in El Salvador on the other. The conflict within the country involved a multiplicity of actors, with many landowners, local security force officers, and rightist politicians who were seeking to frustrate its implementation pitted against peasants, rural organizations, agrarian reform workers, and centrist politicians who were attempting to maximize the reform potential of the program.

"Land to the tiller" was intended to be virtually self-executing. All tenanted and sharecropped land under the ceiling of 17.3 acres was expropriated and transferred to the families working it. They had until April 1981 to register their claims, but because of insufficient response by beneficiaries and government alike, the program was extended three times until it finally expired at the end of June 1984.

Considering that the program was begun in the middle of a civil war marked by a tremendous level of state terrorism in a country with a long history of peasant repression by both the state and landowners, it was not surprising that individual peasants were hesitant to undertake what was in effect their own expropriation process. A December 1981 UCS report to President Duarte, for example, claimed that the entire reform effort was near collapse because of repression backed by the military, illegal evictions, and a "frequently hostile" bureaucracy (*Post*, January 25, 1982:A1). Evictions continued through the first half of the decade, but few were reported after that point. In 1983 UCS charged that about 10,000 of the beneficiaries had been turned out since the beginning of the program, and even the agency responsible for phase three, the National Financial Institution for Agricultural Lands (FINATA), counted about 8,000 through early 1985. FINATA claimed, though, that most had their new land restored to them (Prosterman and Riedinger 1987:167). More generally, an internal USAID audit of the program in January 1984 found that as many as one-third of its "beneficiaries" were not farming the land they had filed for "because they had been threatened, evicted or had disappeared" (*NY Times*, February 15, 1984:A3). The State Department concurred in its 1984 certification report to Congress, noting that "landowners affected by Phase III have resisted strongly, often with violence and forced eviction of campesinos" (U.S. House 1984:284).

Attempts to frustrate phase three occurred not only on the individual level but also through the political system. The democratic forces of El Salvador received little international support (or attention) when their victories in 1972 and 1977 were stolen by the military. In the 1980s, however, the institutionalization of the electoral process was at the heart of U.S. objectives in Central America. Consequently, the forces of the oligarchy and other rightists in El Salvador organized their own political party, the Nationalist Republican Alliance (ARENA), to compete in the electoral arena. At the middle of this effort was Roberto D'Aubuisson, a charismatic figure from a military background repeatedly tied to death squad killings, including the assassination of Archbishop Romero (see Betancur et al. 1993:131). His close ties with ORDEN gave the party an immediate "grassroots" presence throughout the country.[24]

ARENA controlled the constituent assembly elected in March 1982 and quickly moved to undermine phase three; one of its first acts was to suspend the law for one crop year. This setback occurred just before the July 1982 date when the Reagan administration needed to certify to Congress that the Salvadoran government was "making continued progress in implementing essential economic and political reforms, including the land reform program," as legislation passed the previous year required.[25] When the provisional president voided the assembly's action and reaffirmed the program by decree, it was assumed that he was acting at least partly in response to pressure from the Reagan administration. Not only was the reform important to the U.S. "centrist" solution for El Salvador, but the administration also believed that it was vital for avoiding further constraints mandated by legislators wary of the administration's policy.

Responsibility for phase three had been placed not in ISTA but in a separate agency, FINATA. For some time it was headed by an active-duty military officer, Colonel José Torres, praised by observers for his dedication, honesty, and commitment to the beneficiaries (Strasma 1989:410; U.S. House 1984:162).A countervailing presence was maintained by the Salvadoran right, however, through control of the ministry of agriculture and its agencies responsible for the land reform programs. The right lost these positions to Christian Democrats following Duarte's presidential victory in May 1984, but the next month it was able to end further land distribution through phase three when the legislature refused to extend the program's life once again.

D'Aubuisson was an effective organizer and campaigner but also a great liability to ARENA as its leader because of his infamy. If he were to have won the presidency, the U.S. Congress clearly would have cut off the funds vital to the operation of the Salvadoran government. Pressure from the Reagan administration in 1982 prevented the selection of D'Aubuisson as provisional president. When he ran for that office in 1984, substantial U.S. financial support went to the victorious campaign of Duarte. The following year the Christian Democrats also took control of the legislature. Acknowledging this political reality, ARENA's leadership moved to moderate the party's image and to broaden its base of support. Crucial to its efforts was the selection in 1986 of Alfredo Cristiani as the party's president. A wealthy businessman, coffee cultivator, and graduate of Georgetown University in Washington, D.C., Cristiani had no known connection to the death squads. With its new leader and expanded constituency, ARENA took control of the congress in 1988 and the presidency in the elections the next year.

ARENA's victories, however, were due to more than a moderating image. At least as important was the collapse of support for Duarte and the Christian Democrats. They had been elected on the twin promises of peace and reform. They failed miserably on both counts. Popular support for the Duarte government could be maintained only by implementing a reform program that would improve the material conditions of the desperately poor majority. His freedom was limited, though, by policy restrictions placed on him by his coalition partners, the Salvadoran military, and the Reagan administration.[26] From the other direction, Duarte faced a courageous resurgence of popular political activity in major urban areas when death squad killings declined following belated pressure from the Reagan administration (which in turn was responding to pressure from the U.S. Congress). When these factors combined with the economic sabotage of the FMLN, capital flight, the devastating earthquake of 1986, a drought in 1987, a decline in world coffee prices, and widespread charges of rampant corruption, Duarte was unable to deliver on his promises, and his support fell. Furthermore, his party split when rival factions could not compromise on its 1989 presidential nominee.

Following ARENA's electoral victories, reports increased of the harassment and eviction of land reform beneficiaries (Blachman and Sharpe 1988–1989:124). Death squad killings also "intensified dramatically" during 1988 (Americas Watch 1988b:1). The violence culminated the following year when the top command of the military ordered the murders (Betancur et al. 1993:53) of six Jesuit priests well known for their work for reconciliation (their housekeeper and her daughter also were slain). These executions occurred in the midst of an FMLN offensive in November 1989 that brought the war for the first time into the streets of the capital, including some of its most affluent suburbs. In the period prior to the offensive, the FMLN also had initiated an assassination campaign targeting leading government, military, and rightist figures. El Salvador ended the 1980s, then, with levels of violence and fear unparalleled since the first years of the decade. Unlike earlier, though, there was no basis upon which to construct a centrist solution. The country's best hope was that the forces of the far right and the far left, both still as strong as ever, would realize that neither could destroy the other without destroying the country in the process.

Toward Peace and Reconciliation

The November 1989 offensive proved to be the turning point. Peace negotiations began shortly thereafter, culminating two years later in a peace accord that is historic not just for the region but for the settlement of civil conflicts anywhere. The accord sought not only to end the violence but to provide a foundation for the reconciliation of the combatants. Given the ambitiousness of the accord, it should be no surprise that implementation quickly fell behind schedule and often short of the letter and spirit of the agreement. But it provided the basis for the situation today, in which ARENA and the FMLN have virtually an even share of seats in the national legislature, with the first controlling the executive of the country and the second the executive of its capital.

By the beginning of the 1990s, the rival forces had to acknowledge that neither possessed the ability to defeat the other and that neither had the support of the population; it was clear that the vast majority of Salvadorans wanted peace. At this point strong pressures for negotiations had developed in the grassroots sector, joined by younger, more moderate members of the elite, if for no other reason than the FMLN's continuing capacity to wreak economic havoc through its sabotage campaign, which by then totaled about $2 billion in damages (Stanley 1996:238).

Reinforcing these domestic pressures was the regionwide peace process initiated in 1987 by Costa Rican president Oscar Arias (discussed in Chapter 7). The larger global context also had changed in ways conducive to peace. The collapse of the Soviet bloc and the defeat of the Sandinistas in the February 1990 Nicaraguan elections deprived the FMLN of needed international support as well as reducing the threat level for the right in El Salvador and the United States. Meanwhile Reagan had left the presidency in the United States to a more moderate Republican. Perhaps more important, George Bush was constrained by a newly vigilant U.S. Congress following the Iran-Contra disclosures and the murders of the Jesuits. When Congress cut El Salvador's military funding in half in October 1990 and conditioned the rest on progress in solving the murders, the handwriting was on the wall. The peace negotiations were conducted under the auspices of UN secretary-general Javier Pérez de Cuéllar. With his term expiring at the end of 1991, pressures intensified from all quarters, especially the UN and the United States. As the year ended, the agreement was struck and then signed at Chapúltepec, Mexico, on January 16, 1992.

The scope of the agreement was broad. It established a cease-fire and schedule for the demobilization of the FMLN, the elimination of the state security forces (e.g., the treasury police and the national guard), and the reduction of the military by half. Commissions were created to investigate human rights abuses, with the worst offenders to be purged from the armed forces. The police force was to be restructured and retrained, with members from the FMLN integrated into the new force. The judicial and electoral systems were reformed and the FMLN legalized as a political party. A substantial program of national reconstruction was envisioned. Finally and most important for this study, efforts were made to settle the most pressing of the agrarian issues.[27]

Settling the Land Question

Struggles over control of the land have been central to Salvadoran politics for centuries and certainly to the civil war of the 1980s. Consequently, all sides recognized that any enduring settlement would have to address land distribution questions. The most important of these have concerned (1) the agrarian reform lands, (2) lands occupied during the war, and (3) land for the settlement of demobilized soldiers from the contending armies.[28]

The phase one cooperatives entered the 1990s with a number of serious problems. They had been created following existing estate lines; sometimes these were too big for effective management or grouped together disjointed properties. Although organized as collectives, they did not have the authority to pick their own managers, who instead were sent by the state, and some of them were incompetent or corrupt. Perhaps for such reasons some members still saw themselves as workers rather than collective owners. The difficulty of solidifying group identification manifested itself as well in problems with free riders—members who tried to maximize the benefits they received but minimize their contribution. Most important, the cooperatives were saddled with debts that most were unable to meet, following from the requirement at their formation that they pay back the expropriation price of the estate. Although the cooperatives were given thirty years at low interest, very few made the profits necessary to keep the payment schedule; instead, their debts climbed.

Landless peasants were able to occupy land that had been deserted or left unattended during the course of the war or was in zones controlled by the revolutionaries who carried out expropriations. During the peace negotiations the FMLN argued that the occupants should be granted title to the land, often small, relatively unfertile parcels in remote areas that many had by then worked for years. The other side, though, was firm that the rights of the formal owners be recognized. The compromise agreement acknowledged the rights of the formal owners but forbid them to evict the occupiers until the government could either buy the land for the occupiers or else find land elsewhere for their resettlement. The issue was not inconsequential; later the two sides jointly identified a total of about 25,000 occupants on 4,600 parcels constituting around 16 percent of the country's arable land (close to 600,000 acres). Implementation of this agreement grew even more complex as the government tried to handle the needs of the demobilized soldiers.

Both the government and FMLN forces were peasant armies. With demobilization, it was expected that many would want to return to the countryside. Providing them land would be not just a deserved reward for their service but also a prudent step toward rural stability. The original agreement provided for 15,000 recipients from the government's army and half that from the FMLN. Adding to these numbers the occupants of the contested land, this meant the government needed to settle around 47,500 families.[29] Later it was determined that only about half of the expected soldiers applied, part of the falloff undoubtedly due to the complexities and delays of the implementation process. Virtually all of these beneficiaries had received title by the end of 1996. However, because of administrative limitations the land was deeded to groups of recipients rather than to the individuals themselves, thereby deferring, delegating, and confusing issues of individual ownership.

Given that the land was to be distributed respecting private property rights, financial problems were thus created first for the government and then for the beneficiaries. The government had to find sufficient funds to buy the land from the titled owners. Money has come from international donors, especially USAID, but the government still has not had enough, dragging out the redistribution process. With receipt of the land, the beneficiaries in turn contracted debts to pay for it. In hopes of making this manageable, the bargaining parties agreed to reduce the amount of land in question to about 425,000 acres. In the end this provided an average of close to 7 acres for each recipient—certainly not much but more than most landholdings in the country.

Recipients, though, often were not grateful. Many occupiers believed that they deserved the land they had been working; they were unhappy when they were required to resettle, especially to other regions and climatic zones. Both they and the former combatants have suffered under the debts, which many considered inappropriate in the first place. With the mortgages, some observers claim these farms are not viable unless the farmers move from the traditional mix of peasant food crops to commercial nontraditional crops. This would require technical assistance that has not been forthcoming; even then, as argued in Chapter 4, the record of small farms in Central America with nontraditional crops is not a promising one.

Elimination of the agrarian debts (estimated at around $.33 billion) became a key demand of peasant organizations; in 1995 they petitioned the legislature to cancel them outright. Instead, those under $573 were canceled and the rest reduced by 50 percent. Still, most smallholders felt this was an inadequate response, in particular because credit for agriculture had been dropping (while increasing for other sectors). Peasant leaders initiated negotiations with President Armando Calderon Sol, ARENA's candidate elected in 1994 to succeed Cristiani. Calderon then proposed legislation that the ARENA-dominated legislature passed in May 1996 that would forgive 70 percent of the agrarian debts owed to the government if the remainder were paid within the year, with an additional $575 in relief for individual owners.

The law would wipe out virtually all debt remaining for phase three recipients (anywhere from 42,000 to 64,000 are estimated to be affected) as well as almost all of that of the resettled soldiers. However, the impact is more complex for both the rest of the postwar recipients (with the soldiers totaling 35,000) and the phase one members (anywhere from 32,000 to 40,000 affected) because of the collective nature of their titles.[30] Because groups might not have sufficient funds to pay the 30 percent of their remaining obligation and with the extra relief that individual owners receive, the program encourages breaking the collectives down into individual holdings. To further facilitate parcelization, a longtime ARENA objective, a second law was passed in May 1996 to create a legal structure for such a process. FMLN legislators opposed this law, unlike the debt program, which had their support.

Some peasant leaders, though, were against the debt relief measure, still pressing their position for complete cancellation. Despite ARENA's adamant opposition, their chances improved with the notable results of the 1997 legislative elections. The FMLN almost doubled its seats, leaving it just one short of ARENA's total of twenty-eight as ARENA lost eleven seats. Most opposition parties indicated that they would join the FMLN in new legislation to eliminate the agrarian debts, including the PCN, the party of the pre-1980 military regime, which surprised observers with a third-place showing of eleven seats (the PDC falling to fourth with seven).[31] However, when the legislature passed the measure in October 1997, it was vetoed by President Calderon, who declared it both unconstitutional and bad policy.

Complete cancellation of the debts would be a significant gain for the estimated 130,000 to 150,000 beneficiaries. But it would do nothing for the numerous remaining landless and land-poor peasants in the country. An important expression of their discontent in recent years has been controversy concerning estates larger than the constitutional limit of about 600 acres. Recall that even though phase two was never implemented through expropriations, farm size was limited in 1983 and owners given three years to comply. Most have, but peasants claim that many others have not and want the lands above the limit distributed to them. Beginning in 1995, peasants have invaded some of the farms in question to move the issue to the top of the policy agenda. Disagreement continues between them and the government over how many farms are in this category and therefore how much land is available for the needy. What is incontestable is the scale of the need. The best recent estimate places the number of landless agricultural workers at just about 200,000 and the number of land-poor peasants (plots of less than 1.7 acres) at half that amount (Seligson 1995:62–63).

Conclusion

The Salvadoran civil war had many causes, but among the most important were those pertaining to rural society. The agrarian transformations of the colonial period and the nineteenth century created a highly un-equal system that could be maintained only through repression—either directly, as occurred in 1932, or through the threats woven into the fabric of day-to-day life. In the 1970s the dislocations of the contemporary agrarian transformation, along with other factors, such as rapid popula-tion growth and the efforts of outside organizers, led many peasants to challenge the ground rules of the traditional agrarian structure. Peasants won a substantial agrarian reform but at extraordinary cost, as the right reacted with ferocious brutality.

It is important not to slight the accomplishments of the Salvadoran re-form, especially given the tragic circumstances of its implementation and the ultimate price paid by so many of its supporters. Phase one of the re-form was a major redistributive act; it expropriated the country's largest es-tates, constituting about 15 percent of its farmland, and benefited about 8 percent of peasant families. Over twice as many peasants gained from phase three, although since it was less redistributive in nature, it affected about half as much land. Finally, the farms distributed through the peace settlement have reached a number of families roughly equivalent to phase one, with the average size substantially larger than the country's norm.

Yet after all this effort and human and material cost, most of El Sal-vador's rural poor have not been reached by reform. Because of the tremendous scale of unattended need prior to the reform and continuing high population growth rates, about 300,000 peasants in the country still are landless or land-poor, only about 10 percent less than in 1971. Land grants for them the size of those distributed to the peace accord beneficia-ries would consume about 45 percent of all of the country's land (Seligson 1995:62–65). Consequently, El Salvador ends the twentieth century with a land distribution more equitable than a few decades before and a rural society far less repressive than before but a rural population still mired in poverty.

But agrarian society is less important to the country now. Although the size of the economically active population in agriculture continues to grow, as a percentage for the nation as a whole it has been shrinking: In the early 1990s it was only 33 percent, down from 43 percent in 1980 and 60 percent in 1961 (Seligson 1995:61). Similarly, agriculture's contribution to the overall economy also has been decreasing; in 1994 it provided only 14 percent of the GDP (UNDP 1997:178). Agriculture's most important contribution to the economy has been through export earnings, in 1980 providing 77 percent of the total. With the war, exports dropped signifi-cantly. By 1995 total earnings were still not quite back to their prewar level, but by this point agricultural exports only contributed about half of the total; similarly, coffee's share fell from just under two-thirds of total earnings to a little over one-third.[32]

Conservatives talk of turning El Salvador into another Taiwan through free market forces and aggressive export promotion. But as argued in Chapter 4, the "growth with equity" experienced in East Asia came after major structural reforms, including the transformation of the agrarian system. Unlike the 1960s, when similar ambitions were current, El Salvador has indeed experienced agrarian reform, but it did not reach the rural majority and did not come until the preponderance of the workforce had moved to urban areas. Furthermore, the war left the country's people, already very poor, even worse off. By one estimate the average Salvadoran in the early 1990s was at a living standard just half that of 1977, and urban income distribution was getting worse (Ramos and Adams 1993:39–41).

It is true that sustained economic development in today's world does require recognition of the realities of fiscal constraints at home and competition from abroad. However, experience teaches that the needs of the Salvadoran majority will not be met by such policies alone. Instead, public policies must continually address the structural causes of inequality, today at least as much an urban issue in El Salvador as it has been a rural one. Progress in the institutionalization of political democracy and recent election results offer some hope that policies that promote equitable economic development might now be possible.

Notes

1. Of the denunciation to the truth commission established under United Nations auspices to investigate this tragedy, 85 percent blamed government forces or the death squads allied with them; only 5 percent pointed to the FMLN (Betancur et al. 1993:43).

2. Huizer's (1972) formulation of this concept, which he applies generally to peasant societies, was undoubtedly influenced by his field experience in El Salvador.

3. This paragraph and the next two are based on Anderson's (1971) thorough account. Also see Kincaid (1987), as well as Dunkerley (1982), North (1985), Stanley (1996), and White (1973).

4. Anderson (1971) explains both the acceptance of this myth and the motivation behind the massacre in the following way: "[The army and the bourgeoisie] had sensed for a long time dark rumblings among the masses of the people, as the plantation owners of the Old South must have sensed them. In the rebellion of January, 1932, their worst fears had been realized. Indian and peasant discontent had been linked to the dread specter of International Communism. It is hardly surprising that their actions against the now doubly 'red' Indians were hysterical and violent" (p. 131).

5. Sources for the rest of this section include Dunkerley (1982), McClintock (1985a), Minkel (1967), Montgomery (1995), Stanley (1996), Webre (1979), and White (1973).

6. See Baloyra (1982), as well as Berryman (1984), Montes (1980), and Webre (1979).

7. Major sources for this section were the following: Alas (1982), Berryman (1984), Cabarrús (1983), Dunkerley (1982), Forché and Wheaton (1980), Montes (1980), Montgomery (1995), Morales Velado et al. (1988), Prisk (1991), Stanley (1996), and Webre (1979).

8. Mooney (1984) explains the popular mobilization of the 1970s as a consequence of aspirations rising faster than the rate of change. This explanation undoubtedly holds for many individuals, especially in urban areas.

9. See Seligson (1995:62–63) and Burke (1976:476). These figures are both approximate, because of limitations in data collection, and controversial, because of differences in how landlessness should be defined. See the critiques of Seligson (1995) by Diskin (1996) and Paige (1996), the response by Seligson (1996), and higher estimates by Prosterman and Riedinger (1987).

10. These ties were ruptured for a time during the late 1970s but were healed in June 1979. During 1978 and 1979, peasants with a more leftist orientation became increasingly active in the UCS (Forché and Wheaton 1980:14–l6).

11. It is true that compared to the more radical organizations, the UCS was more moderate, tied to U.S. interests, bureaucratic in structure with little grassroots participation in leadership selection, and quite corrupt, at least during the mid-1970s. An Organization of American States (OAS) study in 1977 estimated that almost half of the UCS's members also belonged to ORDEN and indicated that the UCS operated as the rural political arm of the government party (WOLA 1979:10). For a more positive view of the UCS as "one of the best developed peasant organizations in Latin America" in early 1980, see Prosterman and Riedinger (1987:148).

12. Because these events are crucial to the unfolding of the civil war and because interpretations vary, the reader should consult several sources, such as Baloyra (1982), Berryman (1984), Dunkerley (1982), LeoGrande and Robbins (1980), Montgomery (1995), Prosterman and Riedinger (1987), and Stanley (1996).

13. Most prominently, they included Alvarez, who became the secretary-general of the Democratic Revolutionary Front (FDR) upon its formation in April as an umbrella organization of nonviolent leftist opponents of the government; Guillermo Ungo, who replaced Alvarez after the latter was assassinated in November 1980 with five other leaders; and Rubén Zamora, who was a primary international spokesperson for the opposition and later a presidential candidate in 1994.

14. The coffee export trade had been nationalized in the fall by the first junta; the March decree affected the other major export commodities. The October junta also had frozen all transactions involving landholdings over 100 hectares (about 247 acres) pending passage of an agrarian reform law.

15. See AWC and ACLU (1982), Americas Watch (1991), Betancur et al. (1993), CAMINO (1982), and Morales Velado et al. (1988), as well as the sources listed in note 12.

16. There was a debate at the time over the extent to which the reform and the repression were distinct. Compare the criticisms by academic observers such as Deere (1982), LeoGrande (1981), and Montgomery (1995) to the positions of re-

form participants such as Gómez and Cameron (1981); Prosterman (1981); and Prosterman, Riedinger, and Temple (1981).

17. The intentions and consequences of the air war were the matter of some controversy; contrast, for example, Americas Watch Committee (1984:291–342), LCIHR and AWC (1984), and *Monitor* (February 6, 1986:1) with *Post* (July 19, 1985:A27). Duarte issued stricter regulations governing air force bombings in September 1984, in itself an indication of earlier civilian casualties (see *Post,* September 13, 1984:1).

18. Of the original properties, 194 were in excess of the limit; the rest were multiple holdings of the same owner that totaled over the limit. These properties made up about 23 percent of the country's cotton land, 36 percent of its sugar land, and 14 percent of its coffee land (Prosterman and Riedinger 1987:152). By 1982 twenty-eight of the cooperatives had been abandoned (Browning 1983:413). For discussions of phase one in addition to these authors and those mentioned in note 16, see Diskin (1984a, 1984b), Simon and Stephens (1982), Strasma (1989), Strasma et al. (1983), Thiesenhusen (1981, 1995), and U.S. State Department (1984).

19. Cooperatives are not always as progressive as promised. Long and Winder (1981) note that in practice in unequal societies "the beneficiaries are denied effective control over such organizations. In such situations the State will tend to take steps to prevent the emergence of independent organizations representing the interests of beneficiaries" (p. 86). Also see Dorner (1992:50–56).

20. Critics of U.S. policy emphasize both pressure by the United States in explaining the existence of phase three and the role of Prosterman in devising the program (see, for example, Diskin 1989:434–436 and Montgomery 1995:138). Prosterman, though, highlights the role of Viera and the similarity of the program to a proposal drafted under the first government after the October coup (Prosterman and Riedinger 1987:147–151). The latter view is shared by Strasma (1989:409), a close observer of Salvadoran agrarian policy.

21. For discussions of phase three, see Browning (1983), Diskin (1982, 1984a, 1984b, 1989), Simon and Stephens (1982), Strasma (1989), Strasma et al. (1983), U.S. State Department (1984), and the works by Prosterman (and associates) cited earlier.

22. Total U.S. assistance to El Salvador for 1980 through 1990 was $3.9 billion (Storrs 1990:11–12).

23. Although some early reports gave much higher figures, Prosterman (1983: 597) provides evidence suggesting that phase two would have affected about 31 percent of the coffee land, 30 to 41 percent of the cotton land, and 21 percent of the sugar land.

24. ORDEN's dissolution was one of the few accomplishments of the October 1979 government. But much of its repressive apparatus continued on under different guises, such as the Democratic National Front (FDN) organized soon thereafter by General Medrano. Presumably, there was substantial continuity between ORDEN and the paramilitary squads responsible for much of the rural repression of the early 1980s (Dunkerley 1982:143, 164; McClintock 1985a:253–254, 317–320). Some members of ORDEN suffered from reprisals in areas where they lost their dominance; see Dunkerley (1982:175) and Montgomery (1995:112).

25. The requirement that the administration certify progress by the Salvadoran government in six areas as a prerequisite for U.S. assistance was in effect for two

years until it was killed at the end of 1983, when President Reagan pocket vetoed its continuation.

26. As an example of the priorities of the Reagan administration, two-thirds of all of the funds that it gave to nongovernmental organizations in El Salvador between 1985 and 1987 went to a right-wing think tank, whereas only 9 percent went to groups involved in rural development *(Monitor,* August 28,1989:1). Sources on this period include Blachman and Sharpe (1988–1989), Miles and Ostertag (1989a, 1989b), Montgomery (1995), Smyth (1988–1989), and Lungo (1995).

27. For further information on the peace process and agreement, see Arnson (1993), Montgomery (1995), Spence et al. (1995), Stanley (1996), Tulchin (1992).

28. Crucial sources for the section are *Chronicle* (May 23, 1996), Spence et al. (1995, 1997). Also see Diskin (1989), *EcoCentral* (April 3, May 8, and November 20, 1997), GAO (1994), Montgomery (1997), *NotiSur* (October 7, 1994), Strasma (1989), and Thiesenhusen (1995).

29. The procedures by which this was to be done are very complex, thereby creating many new problems. For a good discussion, see Spence et al. (1995).

30. In addition to these smallholders, the program also affects some 1,500 larger landowners who benefited from earlier programs to assist farmers hurt by the war. The benefits of debt forgiveness for some of them is substantial.

31. The other most significant result was FMLN candidate Hector Silva's victory in the San Salvador mayor's race, the position that has been the stepping stone to the presidency for two of the three most recent heads of state (Duarte and Calderon).

32. See the UNFAO database at <http://www.fao.org>.

Chapter Seven

Nicaragua: From Obstruction to Revolution and Back Again

The elites of Nicaragua, along with those of El Salvador, were for many decades the most successful in the region at avoiding progressive changes in land tenure arrangements—perhaps one reason why their reforms of the 1980s were the most significant ever to be implemented in Central America. Despite notable differences in their agrarian structures, the essential pattern had been the same in both countries: minor colonization programs accompanied by the avoidance of any serious discussion of the need for land redistribution and by escalating rural repression as the major state response to deteriorating rural conditions.

But these similarities ended in July 1979 when revolutionary victory in Nicaragua initiated a sharp break with the patterns of the past. Agrarian reform was a central component of the revolutionary government's projects of national reconstruction and socialist transformation. The new regime brought substantial change to rural society, ranging from land distribution and tenancy arrangements to marketing structures and the provision of credit. However, the vision the new Sandinista leadership pursued was at odds with the desires of many of the intended beneficiaries. Although many peasants gained from Sandinista agrarian policy and supported the regime to the end, many others grew disenchanted, even to the point of taking up arms against the government.

A fundamental conclusion of the earlier chapters of this book is that agrarian structures prevailing in Central America have bound much of the rural population to lives of poverty and oppression. Consequently, these structures have generated social tension and political conflict, but they have proven highly resistant to reform. The case of Nicaragua indicates that popular victory is possible at times over the beneficiaries of the old order, permitting considerable changes in the socioeconomic system intended to create a more humane society. The Nicaraguan case also demonstrates, however, that intentions cannot be realized quickly or easily. There are always constraints on policymaking, especially in poor, vulnerable Third World countries. In Nicaragua, economic and political constraints operated at both the domestic and international levels to limit and frustrate the revolutionary government's objectives, especially a war orchestrated by the United States. But the Sandinista objectives themselves were controversial in Nicaragua, including among much of the peasantry. When the Sandinistas were voted out of power in February 1990, their peasant support in many areas was below what they won nationally. Although it is overstated, there was certainly truth in defeated President Daniel Ortega's comment that "we didn't lose the *campesinos*, simply because we never had them" (Ryan 1995:94). Because of the uniqueness of the Sandinista period for Central America, the causes, course, and consequences of its rule will be the primary focus of this chapter.

Nicaragua is now governed by its second post-Sandinista administration, both conservative governments that have attempted to implement policies dramatically opposed to those of the revolution. Both have been constrained, though, by many of the same forces that limited Sandinista accomplishments. In addition, their freedom to maneuver has been restricted by one of the most important results of the Sandinista period: the political mobilization of the Nicaraguan peasantry.

The Rural Roots of Revolution

The expansion of commercial and especially export agriculture greatly transformed rural life in Nicaragua, as documented in Part 1.[1] The coffee boom of the late nineteenth and early twentieth centuries, followed by those in cotton and cattle after World War II, strengthened and enriched a small elite and eroded the economic security of much of the rural population. During the years of the commercial boom, peasants lost land and their ability to compete in land markets; by 1975 the largest 1.8 percent of landowners held 47 percent of the land, whereas the largest 12 percent owned 75 percent (see Table 4.1). Only 13 percent of the economically active agricultural population had sufficient access to land by the late 1970s to meet subsistence requirements. Many rural people thus migrated to urban slums, and both the rural and urban poor attempted to make ends meet by joining the seasonal workforce on the large commercial estates. Close to 40 percent of that population consisted of landless wage earners—most of whom could obtain only seasonal work (Deere and Marchetti 1981:42). Still, rural polarization was not as severe as in Guatemala and El Salvador; a significant sector of small and medium farms remained, which would prove important for policy after the revolution.

Foremost among the beneficiaries of the agro-export development model in Nicaragua was the reigning Somoza family. The dynasty began in the mid-1930s after the United States withdrew from the country, ending (for the time being) its decades of military intervention. One legacy of U.S. interference was the national guard, which the United States had trained for the purpose of maintaining order. This the guard did most effectively, providing the crucial force that enabled Anastasio Somoza García and later his two sons to dominate Nicaraguan society until the revolutionary victory in 1979. The vast economic empire that the Somozas built was the result not of honest work but of "unchallenged conflict of interests, theft, embezzlement, and graft" based on autocratic political power (Booth 1985:69). The elder Somoza, for example, used his political position to acquire a number of the German-owned coffee plantations during World War II; by 1944 he was Nicaragua's top coffee producer and landowner.

Concentrating such economic and political power into their hands brought the Somozas into conflict with the traditional rural elite. These tensions were aggravated when the regime at times leaned too far in a progressive direction for the traditional forces, for example, when the elder Somoza gave some support to worker organization in the 1940s and when the first son (Luís) backed moderate agrarian reform during the 1960s as president and then under his successor. Implementation of the Alliance for Progress–stimulated agrarian reform law approved in 1963, however, was restricted to minor colonization and titling programs in the face of opposition from the rural elite and the second son and head of the national guard, Anastasio Somoza Debayle. Overall under the reform, 16,500 families did receive land titles, and sixty-three colonies were initiated with 2,651 families on 70,000 acres.[2]

When the latter Somoza became president in 1967 and his brother died the same year, any remnant of a reformist impulse disappeared. Still, tensions remained between the regime and the elite as Somoza's appetite for power and wealth seemed unrestrained. Two events were key. Hundreds were massacred in 1967 when demonstrators were attacked by the guard under Somoza's direction. Then in 1972 the capital of Managua was devastated by an earthquake. Rather than lead the reconstruction effort, Somoza used it as an opportunity for further enrichment. For such reasons, the coalition that overthrew the dynasty was broad, including even elements of the landed elite.

More crucial to the revolutionary victory was widespread popular opposition, in rural society as elsewhere. In response to their loss of economic security due to the spread of commercial agriculture, local leaders struggled to organize their communities. Although there were occasional successes, in the end peasants were no match for the national guard. But the configuration of power in rural society slowly began to change with the introduction of two new actors that challenged the system of domination pervading rural society: progressive church workers and the Sandinista National Liberation Front (FSLN).

As they did throughout Central America, Catholic clergy in Nicaragua began to organize Christian base communities in rural areas in the late 1960s and early 1970s, with consequences that were political as well as religious. Two groups were especially important: the Jesuit-created Evangelistic Committee for Agrarian Promotion (CEPA), which trained peasant leaders both to organize self-help projects and to make demands on political institutions in their own behalf, and the 900 Delegates of the Word trained by the Capuchins in the outlying department of Zelaya. With this support on the one hand and the attack on their economic security on the other, peasants began to take action; for the decade up to 1973, official records list 240 land invasions in just two departments, the major cotton-growing region of Chinandega and Leon (Collins 1986:22).

The FSLN was formed in 1961 but remained a relatively inconsequential and unsuccessful force until a decade later, when, with more experience and better ties to the peasantry, it became a greater threat to the regime.[3] In response, the national guard initiated attacks on the peasantry as part of its counterinsurgency campaign against the FSLN. Repression was already widespread in rural areas before the declaration of martial law at the end of December 1974. Following a successful Sandinista hostage-taking operation at a Christmas party honoring the U.S. ambassador, it became even more vicious.

In the rural areas where the FSLN operated, families and even villages were systematically eliminated. Amnesty International (1977:26) reported the northeast as under "virtual military occupation . . . with frequent, apparently arbitrary, killings, torture, massive detentions and disappearances, as well as the confiscation of goods, occupation of property, and the burning of crops, homes and farm buildings." Many more peasants were detained and tortured; girls were raped (Cardenal 1976). The purpose of this state terrorism was "to intimidate the *campesinos* who might, in the future, be impelled to collaborate with or conceal insurgents, to discover those *campesinos* who are already doing so and to locate the guerrillas" (AI 1977:26).

This repression did constrain the development of rural organizations, but at a more fundamental level its results were largely the opposite. The repression further eroded the legitimacy of the regime for both rural and urban groups. It radicalized church workers and peasants, many of whom then forged closer ties with the Sandinistas, if not out of ideological affinity, then out of a shared rage and a shared purpose. Indeed, "their mutual survival depended on a close alliance" (Gould 1990:287). For example, the Association of Rural Workers (ATC), which played an important role in the struggle against Somoza in the Pacific coastal area, received much organizational assistance from both CEPA and the FSLN from its creation in 1977.

Although the eventual overthrow of the Somoza dynasty was largely the result of its loss of support in all sectors of society (as well as throughout the Western Hemisphere) and a series of insurrections carried out by urban popular forces, rural society incubated the FSLN. The prolonged period of rural struggle served in the eyes of many Nicaraguans to legitimate the Sandinistas' claim to be the vanguard of the revolution. But any urban-rural distinction is misleading. Many of the urban participants in the struggle or their families were migrants recently driven to the cities by the commercialization of agriculture, and many still worked in the cotton fields during the harvest. "To a surprising extent," as Paige (1985:107) has pointed out, "Nicaragua's agricultural proletariat was urban."

Revolutionary Agrarian Policy

Agrarian policy was necessarily one of the primary concerns of the new revolutionary government; it also was one of its most difficult policy areas because of the numerous contradictory needs and interests involved.[4] About one-half of Nicaragua's people lived in the countryside in the late 1970s, and about the same proportion of the economically active population worked in agriculture. In the same period, agriculture accounted for about two-thirds of the country's foreign exchange earnings and one quarter of its GNP (Deere, Marchetti, and Reinhardt 1985:104, n. 2). The government faced strong pressures from the peasantry for land redistribution; however, it also confronted production imperatives to meet urban consumption requirements and foreign exchange needs. The government's policy response emerged gradually and in the end assumed a shape substantially at odds with the original objectives of at least some of the FSLN leadership. The evolution of this policy can be divided into three stages.

Stage One: 1979–1981

The most significant revolutionary redistribution of wealth occurred almost automatically. Because the Somoza family had concentrated so much of the land (as well as comparable assets in urban areas) into its own hands, with the defeat of the tyrant and his departure from Nicaragua these possessions were easily confiscated. With the addition of the property of his supporters, who also fled the country, about 23 percent

TABLE 7.1   Nicaragua: Changes in Landownership, 1978–1988 (percentage of total area of farmland)

Sector	1978	1981	1984	1988
Private				
Over 850 acres	36.2	14.8	12.7	9.5
86–850 acres	46.3	44.4	42.2	42.0
17–86 acres	15.4	15.3	6.9	7.2
Under 17 acres	2.1	2.1	1.6	1.6
Subtotal	100.0	76.6	63.4	60.3
Credit and Service co-ops		4.3	10.0	10.0
Production co-ops		1.4	7.8	13.3
State farms		17.7	18.8	13.3
Total	100.0	100.0	100.0	96.9[a]

[a]Remainder classified as abandoned.

SOURCE: Nicaraguan Ministry of Agricultural Development and Agrarian Reform as collected by Spoor 1995:55.

of the cultivable land passed from the private to the public sector, as shown by Table 7.1. The Somoza family's greed, then, allowed the new revolutionary government to undertake a major redistributive action without attacking the class of large and medium landholders, many of whom opposed Somoza at the end of his rule and whose cooperation was necessary in order to sustain agricultural production.

Consisting of about 1,500 estates, the confiscated lands were primarily large commercial operations devoted to export production. Most were reorganized into state farms, which, along with other nationalized properties, were collectively known as the area of people's property (APP). By 1984 there were over 1,000 state farms employing close to 65,000 workers. The decision to maintain these farms as large, collectively worked units under state control was partially a result of ideological commitments. Leaders such as agrarian reform minister Jaime Wheelock followed an orthodox Marxist belief in collective production over individual ownership and looked to the state farm model of the established socialist systems. But this decision was also a response to economic considerations, especially the need to maintain export earnings (discussed more fully in the next section). The creation of the state farms was facilitated by the fact that many of the confiscations had been conducted by the workers themselves. As wageworkers, they were more amenable to the decision for large state farms than land-hungry peasants would have been. Their acquiescence to this policy also demonstrated the legitimacy the Sandinistas had established with the large force of landless rural workers and their union, the ATC.

Despite the Sandinista commitment to socialist transformation, during this first period any further land redistribution was preempted by the need to reactivate production. Both industrial and agricultural production had dropped sharply during the civil war; their restoration depended in large measure on the willingness of individual producers to reinvigorate their activities. Reassurances by the Sandinistas of their commitment to a mixed economy were seen as a necessary incentive to restore private production. Most of agricultural production still came from medium and large farms; this was no time to scare their owners, the Sandinistas believed, as long as they were willing to produce. Indeed, the percentage of land in medium to medium-large farms (86 to 850 acres) remained almost constant across the decade of the Sandinista government (from 46.3 to 42 percent).

The revolution also had a significant impact on land usage, a result both of the destruction brought about by the civil war and of the new regime's policy. Land harvested in almost every crop fell during the last year of the civil war. The reactivation of production of all crops was a primary concern of the new government when it assumed power. The country desperately needed the foreign exchange earned by export crops, but several revolutionary objectives were dependent on the achievement of greater food crop production. By encouraging peasants to expand food production and by boosting the prices of food crops, the government could raise rural incomes. Increased production would also provide more adequate diets for urban consumers while reducing dependence on food imports, thereby freeing scarce foreign exchange earnings for other purposes.

The Sandinista government registered some important successes in bolstering the production of basic grains. Area under cultivation in corn, beans, and rice recovered in the early 1980s, then declined again at mid-decade before rising to historic highs in 1989–1990.[5] Nonetheless, expanded production was not sufficient to match population growth, and per capita consumption of grains declined at the end of the Sandinista period, as demonstrated later in this chapter.

The restoration of export production, however, was more problematic; in 1980 total area planted in cotton, coffee, and sugar was only 52 percent of the 1978 level, and in 1989 it was down to only 41 percent. The failure was the worst for the most crucial crop, cotton, which in the mid-1980s was still at only about one-half of the prerevolutionary level and then dropped further, to only 19 percent, in 1989. The decline in coffee production occurred more slowly, primarily the result of attacks by Contra forces. Much of Nicaragua's coffee-producing area lies within or close to the war zones, and the rebels selected coffee production as a particular target of their campaign of economic sabotage. By decade's end coffee area under cultivation was only 73 percent that of 1979. As a result of this trend of declining area under export production combined with increased grain cultivation, a historic shift occurred: The ratio of grain land to export crop land increased from 93 percent in 1978 to 259 percent in 1989.

But neither this reassurance nor the consolidation of the state farms was of benefit to much of the rural population. By early 1980 peasant discontent, especially as focused through the ATC, encouraged new policy initiatives dealing with rental relationships and the provision of credit. Government decrees that spring included a sharp reduction in land rents and the prohibition of sharecropping. At the same time, the allocation of credit to small and medium-sized producers expanded tremendously. Small producers received seven times more credit in 1980 than they had in 1978; altogether about one-half of small farmers received credit from the government in 1980, which had a notable impact on rural living standards and basic grain production (Collins 1986:52). The government also had other objectives: Subsidized credit rates were used to encourage the formation of cooperatives, with the ATC enlisted to promote their organization. Membership in the cooperatives boomed, up to as much as 60 percent of peasant households by June 1980 (Deere, Marchetti, and Reinhardt 1985:83) but in many cases only with the shakiest of peasant commitment.[6]

Stage Two: 1981–1984

Although the accomplishments of the policy initiatives of the first stage were substantial, they were incomplete. Pressures from the peasantry continued to mount, as did conflicts between the government and the agrarian bourgeoisie. Many rural people had yet to benefit much from the revolution, and many larger landowners were leaving land idle or running their operations at minimal production levels for reasons ranging from oppositional strategies to insecurity. Insufficient food production also continued to be a problem. To address these issues, an agrarian reform law was announced in July 1981.

The law attempted to reassure private owners by guaranteeing the right to private property and by not setting size limits on efficiently utilized landholdings. (In this respect, it was less radical than its Guatemalan and Salvadoran counterparts.) At the same time, rights were limited, too. Beneficiaries were prohibited from selling or subdividing the titles to their grants in order to prevent the concentration or fragmentation of holdings. The law permitted the confiscation of abandoned land and the expropriation of all idle, underutilized, or rented land on holdings above certain ceilings. Compensation for expropriated land was based on values declared for tax purposes over the preceding three years and was paid in agrarian reform bonds.

At the time of the law's announcement, officials estimated that up to 30 percent of the country's agricultural land could be expropriated under its provisions. The form this redistribution should take, however, occasioned much controversy among government officials and between them and representatives of peasants and rural workers. As the discussion advanced, the government agreed not to expand the state farm sector, which was now showing serious problems of falling productivity and escalating debts. Instead, a more communal socialist model prevailed, as most land was distributed to production cooperatives.[7] The program began slowly; then the pace increased in 1983, primarily in response to the growing threat from the Contra armies based in Honduras and Costa Rica. Financed by the United States, the Contras were finding greater receptivity among the conservative and disenchanted poor peasants living in outlying areas. Responding pragmatically, the Sandinista government awarded thousands of peasants in the war zones individual title to the land they occupied.

Altogether through July 1984, about 32 percent of rural families benefited directly from land redistribution and titling. However, the government did not always gain the credit from peasants that it believed it deserved. The land redistributed went to cooperatives—usually the peasants' least preferred choice, the production cooperatives. Government efforts continued to group individual farmers into the credit and service cooperatives. Land organized in the two forms of cooperatives more than tripled from 1981 to 1984, to almost one-fifth of all farmland, as Table 7.1 indicates; meanwhile, the share of land in the medium-small category of private farms (17 to 86 acres) was cut in half.

Stage Three: 1985–1990

Agrarian policy entered a new phase in 1985 in response to national defense needs and the difficulties of maintaining a multiclass coalition. The Contra forces had grown in strength to approximately 10,000–15,000 men, and the Reagan administration grew more belligerent in its public stance. By the end of 1984, it was estimated that the Contras had killed over 2,800 Nicaraguans, most of them noncombatants, and wounded more than 2,000 others. The most potent of the Contra forces, the Nicaraguan Democratic Front (FDN), operated out of Honduras, where it could easily strike across the border into north central Nicaragua, a remote, mountainous region whose deeply conservative peasants had been a stronghold of support for the Somozas and a number of whom were now siding with the Contras.[8]

Peasant support for the revolutionary regime was weakening in other regions as well. Despite the escalation of land grants, thousands of landless and land-poor peasant families remained. Dissatisfaction was especially acute in the Pacific region, where most of the land had remained in large export estates, either privately or state owned. In the country's most densely populated rural area (Masaya), for example, only 15 percent of the landless and land-poor families had received land. Declining support for the Sandinistas was demonstrated in peasants' low vote for the party's winning candidate in the 1984 presidential election (Daniel Ortega), their avoidance of the draft, and their decreasing participation in political ceremonies.

In response to such factors, the government made a number of changes in agrarian policy at middecade. Although the amount of land distributed fell in 1985, for the first time families organized in production cooperatives were less than a majority of recipients, and the following year for the first time less than a majority of the land went to these cooperatives. The year 1986 was also the peak for total amount of land distributed and number of families benefited. And it was the biggest year by far for individual recipients—about one-third of both reform land and families. The reform process then gradually came to an end. Redistributed land in 1987 was 56 percent of what it had been in 1986, and for 1988, the last year of the reform, it was only 18 percent. In these last two years, once again the production cooperatives were the preferred form of organization. Overall, the Nicaraguan reform benefited 77,000 families (outside of the state farms), 61 percent of which were in production cooperatives; only 11 percent of families received individual grants.[9]

To obtain more distributable land, some state farms were privatized in the war zones of the north, as were portions of other farms elsewhere (although often this would be the less productive land). Meanwhile, the government began in 1985 to purchase property from large landowners or to trade other properties with them, particularly in the Pacific region. In the following year, the agrarian reform law was modified to lower the ceiling on land that was free from expropriation from 850 down to 85 acres. Table 7.1 shows that the percentage of all land in the largest farms, state or private, thus declined at middecade, whereas the production cooperatives registered further growth.

Peasants also benefited from reductions in coercive government controls on their marketing of basic grains. The goals of adequate nutrition for the population and agricultural self-sufficiency for the country were embodied in the National Nutritional Plan (PAN) adopted in 1981 and in the development of the state's role in the marketing of staples. Through the Nicaraguan Agency for Basic Foods (ENABAS), the government controlled the import of foodstuffs and established consumer and producer staple prices. These policies registered notable success in the first years of the revolution. As Table 7.2 demonstrates, per capita consumption of

TABLE 7.2   Nicaragua: Index of per Capita Food Consumption, 1976/1978–1989
(1976/1978 = 100)

	1976/1978[a]	*1981*	*1984*	*1989*
Corn	100	78	82	74
Rice	100	219	197	146
Beans	100	89	114	86
Flour	100	190	123	61
Sugar	100	93	103	64
Beef	100	77	100	38
Chicken	100	128	100	107
Eggs	100	110	130	53
Calories	100	109	109	77
Protein	100	102	108	71

[a]Annual average.

SOURCE: Calculated from Nicaraguan government data collected by Utting
1991:45.

most foodstuffs exceeded prewar levels of 1981, and five years into the
revolution none of the items in this table were below prewar levels, with
the (important) exception of corn. It is significant that per capita caloric
consumption remained above prewar levels through 1986 and protein
consumption through 1985 (Utting 1991:45). But in the last part of the
decade, serious decline occurred for every item (with the exception of
rice) as the bottom fell out of the economy.

Given the country's financial straits, the subsidy for urban consumers
was considerable—almost 6 percent of the national budget in 1982
(Austin, Fox, and Kruger 1985:27). In the beginning prices were probably
adequate incentives for basic grain producers (mainly small and
medium-sized farmers). But after a few years growers, especially corn
producers, bitterly complained of declining real incomes. Regardless of
economic returns, farmers also resented government interference in what
had previously been their private marketing decisions. The replacement
of "exploitive" private grain merchants with "paternalistic" bureaucrats
was not necessarily an improvement from their perspective. It was to
such complaints that the government responded beginning in 1984 by reducing state controls, as explained more fully in the next section. But such
reforms were to be overshadowed by the collapse of the economy during
the last third of the decade.

Constraints on Revolutionary Policymaking

The accomplishments of Sandinista agrarian policy were considerable,
but they fell far short of the need. These shortcomings can be blamed in

part on disagreements within the leadership, policy errors, and misman-agement. In addition, Third World governments face numerous con-straints that limit the feasibility of significant change.[10] Furthermore, the Sandinista government confronted additional difficulties that are specific to small countries transgressing the boundaries of permissible policy es-tablished by a hegemonic power. Sandinista agrarian policy, then, was shaped and implemented within a context of considerable political and economic obstacles operating both domestically and internationally, just as they have been for the conservative administrations that followed in the 1990s. The economic factors can most fruitfully be discussed together; separate discussions of the domestic and the international political con-straints then follow.

Economic Constraints

A poor country to begin with, Nicaragua was devastated by the war against Somoza. Up to 50,000 people were killed in the last five years of the struggle, and another 100,000 were wounded—this out of a total popula-tion of only 2.5 million. Many of the deaths occurred not in combat but when Somoza unleashed his armed forces in indiscriminate urban attacks, including bombings by the air force. When the cost of this destruction is combined with both the massive capital flight that occurred during the war and the debt inherited from the dictator, the total comes to $4.1 billion, ac-cording to a UN study (Collins 1986:10; T. W. Walker 1981:41–42).

Nicaragua would need under any circumstances to maintain export earnings in order to cover the costs of its considerable imports. The huge expense of reconstruction, however, created an additional imperative for the recovery of those earnings from the serious declines they registered during the last months of the civil war. The diversification of exports was a long-term Sandinista policy goal, but these pressing short-term consid-erations meant that emphasis had to be placed on the traditional export commodities. Ironically, it was the development of these exports, espe-cially coffee, cotton, and beef, that revolutionary leaders blamed for the disruption of rural society—an argument substantiated in Part 1 of this study.[11] Once in power, the revolutionaries were committed to wide-spread reform that would give rural people access to sufficient land and employment. They also intended to reduce the country's dependence on imported food and ensure that all Nicaraguans, urban and rural, obtained nutritionally adequate diets. Serious tension soon developed, though, be-tween egalitarian objectives and the desire to diversify exports, on the one hand, and economic constraints on the other.

Aggravating this tension was the international economic context. All of the Central American economies contracted in the years after the Nicaraguan revolution; in 1979–1983 per capita GDP for the region declined by 14.7 percent (Conroy 1985:224).[12] Along with global recession, a major cause of this slump was deteriorating agricultural prices through the late 1970s and early 1980s. Consequently, restoring export production to the pre-1979 level would not be sufficient; previous levels would have to be surpassed just to achieve the same earnings. As a result of these trends, the external public debt as a percentage of export earnings grew catastrophically: from 181 percent of export earnings in 1978 to 826 percent in 1982 to an average of 3,200 for the last four years of the Sandinista period (and finally peaking at 4,781 percent in 1992).[13] Easing the short-term difficulties was substantial international assistance from the Soviet bloc and the European social democracies (as much as two or three times export earnings); but this, of course, just delayed the full impact of the problem. The program of egalitarian rural reform was therefore constrained by the imperative to restore export earnings, as can be seen most clearly in the reorganization of confiscated properties, the treatment of private cotton and coffee growers, and the response to rural labor shortages.

The farms the Sandinistas confiscated after taking power were almost all highly mechanized and were among the most important of the agricultural export producers. Policymakers believed that there was no alternative but to continue using them for export production. They were organized as large state farms because officials worried that if peasants were given control, they would probably switch production from export to food crops. Furthermore, top government officials had a Marxian commitment to transform "independent peasant producers into a proletarian class."[14] For these officials, even the production cooperatives were a less advanced form of social organization than the state farms.

However, most of export crop production remained in private hands, primarily with medium-sized and large producers. The tension between socialist ideology and dependence on the agrarian bourgeoisie for export earnings was especially great in the case of cotton, the country's most important earner of foreign exchange, the export crop suffering the greatest decline in production during and after the civil war, and (unlike coffee) a crop for which production decisions can be made on an annual basis. In theory this sector could have been nationalized and reorganized as part of the state farm system, but in practice such a move was impossible because the government was overburdened with organizing and administering the initial state production units and because of its desire to maintain national unity in face of the security threat from the United States. One purpose of the 1981 agrarian reform law was to reassure capitalist farmers; as long as they worked their land efficiently, they were not in danger of expropriation. Furthermore, the revolutionary government attempted to provide capitalist producers with sufficient incentives through the provision of credit and the establishment of purchase prices more generous than those offered to producers of other crops (as well as through the threat of expropriation for failure to produce).

If this dependence on the agrarian bourgeoisie was difficult for the Sandinistas, it was equally unpleasant for the planters. Colburn (1986:59) expresses it nicely: "Cotton producers are torn between the realization that 'there is money to be made in every tragedy' and Lenin's sobering adage that 'capitalists will make the very rope they will be hung by.'" Although many commercial growers continued with their plantings in order to protect their investments, many others left the country. Cotton cultivation partially recovered from the fivefold drop of 1978–1980, but only to about one-half of prerevolutionary levels before collapsing further to around just one-fifth in 1989.

Through its control of foreign trade and domestic prices, the government was able to determine growers' profit levels. If cotton growers complained that their profits were squeezed in order to maximize foreign exchange earnings going to the public treasury, it is not surprising that the Sandinistas were unsympathetic, especially since government policies were largely supportive of the growers and contrary to party ideology. The situation of coffee growers, however, was more complicated. Although larger farmers dominate coffee production, most producers have small holdings. As smallholders they are part of the poor majority that was the intended beneficiary of the revolution, but as coffee growers they experienced the same profit squeeze as the larger producers. Through the early 1980s, they complained of disincentives, as did large growers, because of insufficient profit levels. As the Contra war accelerated, the government was forced to face this problem, which it did in 1985, as discussed later in this chapter.

At the same time, export production and earnings were harmed by policies that did help the rural poor. In prerevolutionary Nicaragua, coffee and especially cotton growers depended on temporary workers to provide much of their labor during the harvest period. With the high rates of under- and unemployment, securing this seasonal labor was not difficult. In addition, growers imported Honduran and Salvadoran workers as needed. But after the revolution this cheap labor pool shrank. Many of the landless and land-poor received acreage. Poor farmers, who in the past had needed to supplement their incomes through seasonal labor, found their positions improved in the early years of the revolution by the large increase in available credit and by the higher prices paid for their crops. Moreover, the new government applied the minimum wage laws long on the books to rural employment, but it established a wage too low to attract sufficient labor; indeed, it was below the Honduran and Salvadoran levels. Neither did the wage keep pace with inflation in future years, especially in the cotton fields (although workers did benefit from the food, education, and health policies of the revolutionary government). Finally, as the Contra attacks escalated, a larger percentage of potential labor was absorbed by the unpopular draft.

Even when labor was available to export growers, it was not as "dependable" and "disciplined" as in the past. In place of the repressive presence of the national guard, workers expected the state to be at their side in their attempts to organize, win a fair wage, create decent working conditions, and free themselves from demeaning subservience to the *patrón* (boss). This rapid revolutionary transformation of the rural workforce was a major factor in many large landowners' decisions to decapitalize their holdings and leave the country with as much of their wealth as they could take. Meanwhile, the production imperative soon curbed the regime's revolutionary commitment. Work stoppages, strikes, and seizures of centers of production were prohibited by the vanguard of the socialist revolution in July 1981 in order to "combat labor indiscipline." The ATC was not much more supportive but instead often reflected the productionist concerns of the government rather than acting as the autonomous union voice of rural workers.

Certainly the challenges faced by state farm managers were severe. In addition to workers who often put in only two or three hours of minimal effort and broken machinery that could not be fixed because of lack of parts and skilled personnel, managers had to respond to the dictates of off-site bureaucratic planners that might be irrational for the enterprise itself. As one manager complained: "We have to produce cotton because this is what we are told to do. The plan says plant so many *manzanas* of cotton. And that is what we do. And so we are forced to lose money. We know it beforehand. But we must follow the directives that we are given" (quoted in Biondi-Morra 1993:74).

But these losses usually were covered by cheap credit from government financial institutions that in turn were fed by the central bank's printing presses—from 1983 to 1988 the government's average fiscal deficit ran close to one quarter of GDP (Arana 1997:83). A government survey in 1985 found that thirty of the forty-five state enterprises with appropriate financial data were operating at a loss; twenty-six of these were export producing, with cotton farms especially big losers—and this was after a big debt bailout in 1982 (Biondi-Morra 1993:61). These debt problems were compounded by a fascination with large agroindustrial development projects on the part of government leaders, usually the same ones with a preference for state farms. Undisciplined by market forces, these few projects consumed vast sums of scarce monies; indeed, just eight of these giants (for Nicaragua) received over half of all investment funds (Spoor 1995:60).

Under the weight of all of these forces, the economy broke. Per capita GDP fell steadily, so that by 1988 it was only 71 percent of its 1980 level (see Table 3.3), with under- and unemployment doubling to 32 percent from 1981 to 1989 (Enríquez 1997:38). Meanwhile inflation accelerated, from 300 percent in 1985 to 1,300 percent in 1986 and up to as much as 33,000 percent in 1988 (Arana 1997:82). The economic crisis meant not only falling living standards but also shortages of all supplies, including beans, rice, and sugar, and long waits in line for goods when they were in supply. Consequently, emigration increased, even among longtime supporters of the revolution.

To combat the hyperinflation, the Nicaraguan government instituted two packages of austerity measures in 1988 and another in January 1989. The harsh measures, which included a 20 percent cut in the budget, lay-offs of close to 10,000 state workers, wage cuts, and credit and money supply restrictions, were described as "far more severe" than many of those mandated by the International Monetary Fund, but without its financial help. Inflation did drop, but fears of recession later resulted in an easing up—and less success (*Envio,* June 1989:11–12 and August 1989: 10–11). This was the economic context, then, for the 1990 elections.

Policymakers' efforts to manage the economic crisis did not occur within a political vacuum, nor did the important economic choices earlier in the decade. Decisions about how to advance economic development and export earnings while pursuing redistributional goals were influenced not only by ideology and economic constraints but also by considerable political pressures.

Domestic Political Constraints

Peasant organization received substantial support from the Sandinistas during the struggle against Somoza and in the months after the revolutionary victory.[15] Before 1979 was over, the membership of the ATC had reached 59,000; by the end of 1980 it was over 100,000. Peasant mobilization was fully congruent with revolutionary aspirations, but it could also threaten regime objectives. Through the revolutionary struggle, the landless and land-poor were empowered to act, taking land either spontaneously or in actions organized by the ATC. These land takeovers jeopardized the government's program to reactivate export production, however, both by switching production to food crops and by diminishing the labor supply. In the months after taking power, the government thus attempted to discourage land takeovers, with some success. But as the months passed peasants grew restive, and takeovers increased in frequency.

The government came close to promulgating an agrarian reform in 1980, but in the end it did not do so because of pressures from two very different quarters. Relations between the Sandinistas and the bourgeoisie, always tense, came close to the breaking point that spring as the bourgeois representatives in the governing junta resigned amid growing concern within that sector over the concentration of power by the FSLN and the radicalization of the revolution. The strained alliance held for the time being, in part because of Sandinista reassurances concerning respect for property rights. It was certainly not the right time to announce a new agrarian reform program.

From the other side, the ATC was dissatisfied because of its insufficient involvement in the formulation of the proposed program. The union had included virtually all of the organized rural popular forces, making it very heterogeneous. In 1981 it split, with the National Union of Farmers and Ranchers (UNAG) created to represent small and medium-sized producers, leaving rural wage earners as the base for the ATC. For the government, the motive was largely tactical. The smaller producers had begun to join the agricultural producers' organization controlled by the larger commercial farmers, the Union of Nicaraguan Agricultural Producers (UPANIC), perceiving a greater commonality with other producers than with the rural laborers in the ATC. Obviously, their alliance with the agrarian bourgeoisie rather than with the rural proletariat ran counter to the regime's needs and strategy, and so the new organization was formed. This made the ATC more coherent as an organization but also cut its membership by over half.

Small and medium producers contributed about half of all agricultural production at the time. Within a year about 42,000 had joined the new organization; by 1984 UNAG represented about one-third of all agricultural producers; and by 1987 its members and their families constituted close to two-thirds of the peasant population (Luciak 1995:79–83, 103). As its membership increased and expanded into the ranks of the richer peasantry, the UNAG became the most autonomous popular organization in the country and grew more assertive in pressing the demands of its constituency, especially the need for more land redistribution. Land seizures continued, and reports from the field described a peasantry that could not be appeased much longer. Furthermore, basic food production still had not recovered fully from the civil war, a problem aggravated when the new Reagan administration eliminated credits for U.S. wheat purchases. In response to these various pressures, deliberations concerning the agrarian reform law were renewed in the spring of 1981, this time with the substantial involvement of the ATC and the UNAG.

Implementation of the reform was slow, though, for a variety of administrative and political reasons. Officials in the agricultural ministry generally preferred an orderly, socialist transformation of agriculture; they focused on the needs of the state farms and were committed to producer cooperatives as the best form for the organization of redistributed land to take. By contrast, peasants generally wanted land as soon as possible, and they wanted freedom to determine how to organize it—usually as individual holdings. The peasants' position was promoted by UNAG, which had increasing success as the Contra war escalated. Although the government remained committed to the objective of socialist transformation, a program of land titling was initiated in late 1982; most of the recipients were settlers with individual holdings in frontier regions, often in the war zones. As the fighting expanded, so did the program.

These pressures continued to escalate through the mid-1980s. The Contra forces grew in size and expanded their operations, reinforcing the government's need to secure the border region and to solidify its popular support. At the same time, disenchantment on the part of many peasants increased because the revolution had not brought them the hoped-for benefits, especially land and improved incomes. Many also bitterly resented the military draft instituted in 1983. Aggravating the ideological divide between the socialist Sandinista leadership and the culturally conservative and individualistic peasants of the mountainous border areas was that none of the leaders came from a rural, much less peasant, background and often regarded the peasantry as backward.

As discussed earlier, the pace and form of land redistribution were altered in 1985 in response to these pressures. But they could not match need, and by decade's end peasants were organizing their own land takeovers. Changes were also enacted to provide more attractive incentives to workers and producers. Wage increases and other material incentives instituted in 1985–1986 closed the gap between industrial and agricultural incomes for coffee workers and promoted increased productivity for all major export crops. State-set grain prices were increased to keep up with rapidly rising inflation, and then price controls were lifted on beans and corn, much to the satisfaction of peasant producers.[16] But inflation proved to be the winner: In the later part of the decade the increase in basic grain prices was only about one-half of the increase in the price of needed inputs and only one-third of the increase in manufactured consumer goods (Enríquez 1997:43). Further aggravating peasants were roadblocks the government instituted in 1986 to crack down on black market grain sales.

Nicaraguans and observers differ as to whether the Sandinista project of socialist transformation was in the best interest of the country. What is clear is that success would have been difficult under the best of circumstances. Instead, the Sandinistas came to power in a poor country following a destructive civil war and soon faced the implacable opposition of the most powerful country in the world.

International Political Constraints

Once the 1979 transition of power was completed in Nicaragua, the Carter administration reconciled itself to working with the revolutionary government.[17] Emergency aid was delivered and large appropriations for Nicaragua were requested from Congress. The continuation of U.S. influence and the desire to moderate the course of the revolution were paramount concerns, but the administration also argued explicitly for the need to work with, and for, social change. This approach altered substantially under the Reagan administration, first in rhetoric and then in substance, as Reagan was convinced that the Sandinistas were determined to establish a Marxist-Leninist regime in Nicaragua and to export its revolution throughout the region as an ally of the Soviet Union.[18] Implementation of the Reagan policy proceeded incrementally, however, because of a wary U.S. public, a skeptical Congress, and divisions within the administration's own ranks.

The first substantive step was taken in early 1981 when the United States discontinued further financial aid. Later economic sanctions included the use of considerable leverage to limit international financial assistance and the imposition of a complete trade embargo in 1985 (honored by no other country). More significant, the National Security Council approved in November 1981 a plan to build a counterrevolutionary force. Small groups of anti-Sandinistas were already forming in the region; U.S. financial and organizational support were critical to their viability. The initial appropriation was $19 million for a 500-man force. By 1983 the United States was known to have spent over $100 million in building a Contra force of 10,000–15,000. Further assistance was limited by growing congressional concern and vigilance; appropriations for fiscal years 1984 and 1986 were limited to $24 and $27 million, respectively (the second sum only for "humanitarian" purposes); no aid was approved for fiscal 1985. Congressional apprehension over Sandinista intentions also intensified, however. Caught between contradictory concerns, Congress in 1986 approved $100 million in new aid.

And then in October 1986 an airplane on an illegal covert mission to supply the Contras crashed in Nicaragua, and so did the Reagan policy. Investigations into the Iran-Contra affair eventually disclosed that contrary to congressional intent and action, the Reagan administration had raised money secretly to keep the Contras alive as a fighting force during the period that Congress had suspended such assistance. Under the direction of Colonel Oliver North, the operation to finance the Contras raised $34 million from other countries, $2.7 million from private individuals, and—the most scandalous part—$16.1 million from covert arms sales to Iran, all through actions later declared by congressional investigating committees to be based on "secrecy, deception, and disdain for the law" (U.S. Congress 1987:3–11). The ensuing controversy did considerable harm to the Reagan administration and especially to its ability to pursue a military solution in Nicaragua.

The consequences for Nicaragua of the Reagan policies were severe. It is clear the Contra war would never have assumed the dimensions that it did without U.S. backing. The Sandinista government estimated the war's economic cost at $17.8 billion—about nine times greater than the country's peak annual domestic production (Spalding 1994:213). Total casualties were around 60,000 by 1989, including an estimated 29,000 killed by the Contras (*Envio,* February 1989:16). Many were the victims of the Contras' deliberate policy of terrorism directed against the civilian population (Chamorro 1986). In addition, about .33 million Nicaraguan peasants were displaced from their homes by fighting, many forced to take refuge in squatter settlements or government relocation camps. As the conflict dragged on, political polarization heightened and civic morale deteriorated. The combined effects of these actions sorely aggravated the various economic and political constraints discussed earlier.

A key strategy of the Contras was economic sabotage. Particular targets were the vulnerable coffee crop (especially on agricultural cooperatives), agricultural technicians, and storage facilities for basic grains. The strategy was one not just of sabotage but also of terror; production was attacked both by direct destruction and by eliminating or terrorizing those who provided the labor. In the 1984–1985 season, for example, more than 200 coffee pickers were murdered and fifty-nine farms burned. By the war's end, some 6,500 UNAG leaders and members had been assassinated. Cooperative members in particular paid a high price, making up just under two-thirds of the Sandinista war dead (Luciak 1995:98–102).

The opposition of the Reagan administration reinforced the pressures from both the larger growers and the peasantry. Given the clash between the interests of the bourgeoisie and the ideological commitments of the Sandinistas, tensions were unavoidable. In light of the region's historical political patterns, it is an open question whether, left to itself, either group would have been willing to continue to compromise with the other rather than seeking its elimination as a serious political contender. Whatever possibilities there were for domestic reconciliation were greatly reduced by the Reagan administration's hostile policy toward the Nicaraguan government. The point has been well made by Gilbert (1986): "So long as the internal opposition had the hope that Washington would remove the FSLN, they had little incentive to seek any sort of accommodation with the regime. And so long as the FSLN saw the internal opposition as the disloyal ally of the contras and the Yankees, it had little incentive to offer any concessions toward accommodation" (p. 115).

The effect of U.S. policy and the Contra war on government-peasantry relations was contradictory, causing strain on the one hand and leading to beneficial policy changes on the other. Limited by the U.S. Congress and public in its ability to pursue its objectives more forcefully, the Reagan administration undertook what in essence was a war of attrition. Reinforcing the impact of economic hardship on popular support for the government was the military draft. After the program had been in effect for fifteen months, it was estimated that around 50,000 young men had fled the country, and thousands of others were in hiding. The draft also affected economic performance; whether in compliance, in flight, or in hiding, workers were in acutely short supply in the harvest of all principal crops, the result being decline in production (*NY Times*, March 19 and April 11, 1985).

A remarkable set of events brought the war to an end, as Central American leaders asserted their national and regional interests against those of the United States in a fashion unparalleled in the area's history. The war was a destabilizing threat to the rest of the region, especially for contiguous Costa Rica and Honduras. As it became clear that the Contras would not win, Honduras in particular needed a resolution that would remove the Contras from its territory. Meeting in Esquipulas, Guatemala, the Central American presidents agreed in August 1987 to a plan for national reconciliation, peace, and democratization in each country.[19] For Nicaragua, the plan called for an end to external assistance to the Contras in return for a Sandinista pledge to restore political freedoms that had often been abridged during the war. Although the government's performance was spotty, it made major efforts toward compliance. The Reagan administration, however, sought to undermine the accord through pressures on its regional allies and by attempting to keep the Contra army together by continuing the flow of "humanitarian" assistance.

Nonetheless, the Contras were finished as a real fighting force. Defeated militarily and unable to command sufficient support in the U.S. Congress, the Contras agreed in March 1988 to a cease-fire with the Sandinista government. Although small-scale attacks continued, the government had won the military battle. Time ran out on the Reagan administration in January 1989 as the Sandinistas outlasted their fierce opponent. The administration of George Bush was no kinder toward the Ortega government, but it was clear to observers that the new U.S. administration wanted a settlement of the conflict so that attention could be shifted to other policy concerns and continual costly battles with Congress could be avoided.

Within this new political context, the Central American presidents were able to formulate a more precise peace plan, which they signed in February 1989 at a meeting in El Salvador. This accord exchanged a Nicaraguan commitment to presidential elections by February 25, 1990, and specific electoral reforms for promises by the other presidents of a plan for the demobilization and relocation of the Contras and of verification mechanisms. Consequently, the struggle between Nicaraguans shifted to the electoral arena. Agreement on a common candidate to challenge President Ortega, though, was difficult. By 1989 the Sandinistas were opposed by twenty different political parties, including three to their left. Fourteen of these parties joined together in the United Nicaraguan Opposition (UNO), which eventually selected Violeta Barrios de Chamorro as its presidential candidate. Although she was an attractive candidate—the widow of the martyred publisher of *La Prensa* slain in 1978 and a short-term member of the first revolutionary junta—her political abilities at the time were unproven.

Regardless of who would win in 1990, the future of Nicaragua looked dismal. Either candidate would face a devastated economy and a bankrupt treasury, as well as a polarized nation. In an upset predicted by few, Nicaraguan voters selected Chamorro as the more promising hope. The voting majority apparently had little expectation of economic improvement or national reconciliation under a renewed Sandinista administration. For improvement, they were inclined to chance the alternative.

Unmaking the Revolution

The new Chamorro administration represented both a vastly different constituency as well as a completely different ideological vision of state and society from that of the Sandinistas. Nonetheless, in governing it confronted many of the same forces that constrained its predecessor. As a result and like its predecessor, the new government pursued a course of action more moderate than intended and expected. It also found itself facing ironic situations, such as relying on the army and police, still led by the FSLN, to control land invasions undertaken by demobilized Contra peasants. By the end of the term, although the Chamorro administration had some important successes, popular dissatisfaction was so great that her party was an inconsequential actor in the 1996 presidential elections. Why this was so can be seen by looking at the economic and political constraints Chamorro faced.[20]

The economy was in shambles when Chamorro entered office after several years of recession, exorbitant inflation, and escalating foreign debts. Nicaraguans wanted improvement, and they needed it fast. Yet economic realism dictated fiscal and monetary restraint, reinforced in this case by Chamorro's constituency's ideological conviction that the size and role of the state needed to be greatly limited. Chamorro had great success in reducing inflation, bringing it down from over 13,000 percent in 1990 to 866 percent in 1991 and all the way down to 3.5 percent in 1992; for the next four years it leveled off at an average of 13.2 percent (Arana 1997:83; Dye et al. 1995:9; *NotiSur,* January 17, 1997). But as is normally the case, a policy commitment to fight inflation did little for economic growth, at least in the short run. The economy did not begin growing until 1994, and in

1995 per capita GDP was still less than it had been in 1990. Consequently, unemployment in 1995 was double that of 1990 and as much as ten times that of 1984 (Arana 1997:83–84). Extreme poverty was estimated at over 50 percent in rural areas midway through Chamorro's term and close to 90 percent in zones where conflict continued (Dye et al. 1995:10).

In order to promote economic growth, the government in conventional fashion turned to the agro-export sector, especially cotton. Although the government's austerity policies, including the sharp curtailment of credit to smaller farmers, hit the poor majority hard, larger producers were provided incentives to activate production. Cotton export earnings had fallen steadily from the mid-1980s; the government did succeed in encouraging minor recovery of cotton production in 1990 and 1991 before the bottom fell out of the cotton market for the remainder of Chamorro's term. Fortunately, the other leading agricultural exports (coffee, meat, sugar) did recover from the across-the-board decline of 1992–1993, but total annual agricultural export earnings (led by coffee) for 1994–1995 still were only half of what they had been for 1977–1979.[21]

The government had to be concerned about export earnings because the foreign debt had reached crippling levels, indeed at times the highest on a per capita basis in the world. The debt also meant that Nicaragua required substantial international financial assistance, which then gave international creditors significant leverage with the government, ensuring that it would remain steadfast in pursuing austerity at home and trade liberalization abroad. In the early years of Chamorro's term, this assistance was primarily new loans to pay the debt; later Nicaragua was able to negotiate significant agreements with major creditors such as Russia and Germany for debt forgiveness and debt buyback at sharply discounted rates (as much as 92 percent). Such assistance was deemed necessary because the debt had become so unmanageable; in 1995 just the interest due was double annual export earnings (*Chronicle,* July 27, 1995).

The involvement of international actors was important because of the diversity of Chamorro's coalition, with her own position and that of her top advisers more moderate than that of most of the politicians who had brought her to office.[22] Fissures in her coalition quickly opened, and before long there was a substantial cleavage between Chamorro and the conservatives.[23] To the surprise of many, her government often negotiated with the Sandinistas and at crucial points gained majority congressional support with FSLN legislators against the conservative parties. Many in Chamorro's original coalition desired a rapid repeal of all Sandinista policies. Although she, too, opposed much of what the prior government had done, by her actions it would appear that her top priority as president was peace and national reconciliation, which necessarily meant a willingness to negotiate with the Sandinistas. Many observers regard the progress in this area as the most important accomplishment of her administration.

Among the most intractable issues that the Chamorro government dealt with, and the most significant for this study, were the related ones of the status of the agrarian reform of the 1980s and the reintegration of both former Contra and FSLN soldiers into civilian life. Conservatives and former owners of confiscated properties demanded that private property rights be reenshrined through a return of expropriated lands or at least adequate compensation. However, beneficiaries of the reform were adamant that they retain what they regarded as their just due, and they were well represented by organizations such as the FSLN, ATC, and UNAG. In addition, tens of thousands of peasants still had not received land but continued to press their cause. Most significant, as inducement for their demobilization, the Contras, almost all of them poor peasants, were promised land and assistance. As the national army was downsized, the government made similar commitments to these soldiers. Moving through these contradictory forces would be difficult under any circumstances; success at a minimum would require substantial resources, but of course these were lacking.

After the Sandinistas lost the February 1990 elections, their lame-duck congress passed a series of laws, including one that turned agrarian reform titles into individual property titles. But there was too little time remaining to implement the law. During her campaign Chamorro had promised to respect the holdings of the reform beneficiaries, but once in office she faced both substantial pressures from her right to return confiscated properties as well as mass actions, such as land invasions, from virtually all corners. Out of these conflicting pressures, the intermittent working relationship between Chamorro and the FSLN developed. The right, in turn, expanded its coalition by gaining substantial assistance from U.S. senator Jesse Helms, whose major leverage was his ability to hold up U.S. economic assistance for months at a time.

The outcome that slowly evolved and then was formalized by the property stability law of October 1995 was that reform beneficiaries were not dispossessed and prior owners were offered compensation. The major exception was the former state farms: 40 percent of the 800,000 acres were returned to former owners, 29 percent converted to worker cooperatives, 15 percent distributed to former Sandinista soldiers, and 14 percent distributed to former Contra soldiers (Everingham 1997:11). For the most part, the reform cooperatives were subdivided among members. However, the ongoing economic crisis has meant that many beneficiaries have not been able to hold on to their land and compensation has been inadequate from the viewpoint of prior owners. By mid-1995 about 60 percent of claims had been settled, but instead of money the claimants received fifteen-year bonds whose actual value has deteriorated rapidly (*Chronicle,* July 27, 1995).

More problematic have been the former soldiers. Simply put, they were promised more than the state could deliver. They, along with other discontented peasants, responded with land invasions, which averaged over 200 annually for the first three years of the administration and over fifty annually for the next two (Dye et al. 1995:26). The government did respond with land grants to thousands of soldiers and other peasants (although often in frontier areas on more marginal lands), but it was not rapid enough. Some former Contras (known as the *recontras*) took up arms again to pressure the government, as did some former national army soldiers (the *recompras*); some even joined forces together (becoming the *revueltos,* or "scrambled"). These efforts were directed at trying to force the government to make good on the promise of land. However, they also were for security purposes, as killing for revenge was a frequent occurrence in outlying areas; for example, some 212 Sandinista militants were said to have been killed in the northern zone in the four years after the election, and former Contras complained of constant harassment by the Sandinista-dominated army and police (*NotiSur,* April 22, 1994). Some of the armed groups degenerated into common criminal bands, further aggravating the security problems. Fighting was so bad in some northern areas that anarchy reigned, virtually paralyzing agricultural activity and leading to demands from producers for increased government security measures. Of growing concern were kidnappings of hundreds of producers held for ransom. Despite repeated negotiations and agreements, these rural conflicts outlived the Chamorro administration, and her successor confronted continued havoc caused by up to 1,000 *rearmados* (rearmed Contras and Sandinistas) in the northern mountains (*EcoCentral,* May 20, 1997).

As the election of October 1996 approached, Chamorro remained very unpopular, with twice as many Nicaraguans in one Gallup survey calling her administration's performance bad than those who rated it good. Although the economy had finally begun growing, the same survey found that two-thirds of those questioned portrayed their family's economic situation as worse than the year before (Butler et al. 1996:7–8). Turning against the centrist government, voters had polarized alternatives: Daniel Ortega once again as the Sandinista candidate and Arnoldo Alemán on the right. Again voters rejected the FSLN, giving Alemán an eleven-point presidential victory and his electoral coalition a five-seat edge over the Sandinistas (although not a majority) in the legislature. The combative head of the coffee growers' association during the Sandinista period, Alemán made his political mark as a populist mayor of Managua during the Chamorro years. This populist orientation continued during the election, even though his strongest backers included the hard right. Although

Alemán promised that he would respect the gains of the reform beneficiaries, after he took office he announced plans that would annul the land claims and titles of up to 300,000 rural families. Small farmers quickly took to the streets in April, followed by the FSLN. The confrontation ended when talks between Alemán and Ortega led to the establishment of special committees with diverse representation to examine the problem of confiscated property as well as other contentious issues. As the century closed, the question of who would control the land still occupied central stage in Nicaragua.[24]

Conclusion

The processes that created the agrarian systems of Central America also limited the ability of policymakers to alter those systems. Fueled by agro-export expansion and the spread of commercial agriculture, the agrarian transformations marginalized much of the peasantry, depriving many of their land and their self-sufficiency. Regimes that would seek seriously to address these problems are constrained in their ability to do so. The agrarian transformations of the past created and strengthened elites with vested interests in maintaining the resulting structures and with substantial power to protect them.

Sandinista agrarian policy consequently confronted the necessity of dealing with an agrarian bourgeoisie that had considerable incentives and resources to resist and frustrate the government. Reinforcing that group's position was the economy's dependence, at least in the short run, on agricultural exports, which meant its dependence as well on the cooperation of numerous medium-sized and large producers of coffee, cotton, and sugar, especially as world prices for those commodities deteriorated. But these economic imperatives needed to be balanced with the demands and needs of the rural majority. The consequences of the past agrarian transformations guaranteed that the revolutionary government would face insistent demands for land, not only from land-poor peasants but also from many of the landless rural laborers who dreamed of regaining their landed status, even if only in the form of a small plot.

However, there was a conflict between the socialist vision of the Sandinista leadership and the desires of much of the peasantry. Under different circumstances and with the support of the peasantry—won over time through improved benefits and education—the original Sandinista project of a gradual socialist transformation of the agrarian sector may have been successful. Balancing the conflicting pressures from the bourgeoisie and the peasantry while attempting to transform society along socialist lines would have been difficult under the most propitious conditions. These problems were seriously aggravated by the hostility of the United States and the Contra army it organized and financed. International economic and political constraints, then, conspired to frustrate the Sandinistas' attempt at a new type of agrarian transformation in Central America. Although the Sandinista government showed a unique responsiveness to peasant needs and demands, its capability to carry out its plans was limited. Between Sandinista policy errors and mismanagement and counterrevolutionary mobilization coupled with U.S. intervention, Nicaragua was set back by decades in its ability to provide for the basic needs of its population.

On a more positive note, Nicaraguan society and politics have been transformed forever by the popular mobilization that took place during the Sandinista period. In part promoted by the FSLN, peasant political activity was in other cases directed at changing Sandinista policy. What is important to see is that during each of the three post-Somoza administrations peasants organized against the agrarian policy of governments of the left, center, and right and forced significant compromises from each. There is strong support in Nicaragua for private property rights; a recent survey found 80 percent regarded such rights as inviolable (Butler et al. 1996:10). But this has a different meaning now than it did before the revolution. Today only about a quarter of Nicaraguan farmland is in large estates, about half of what it was before the revolution, whereas about 39 percent is in holdings of less than 87 acres, more than double the 1978 figure (Jonakin 1996:1188). It is clear that the rural majority intends to defend this more equitable distribution of the land. What they hope for is a government that understands *their* desires.

Notes

1. The major sources for this section are Black (1981), Berryman (1984), Booth (1985), Gould (1990), Millett (1977), Núñez Soto (1981), and T. W. Walker (1981).

2. The colonies were supported by substantial international assistance, such as that from the United States. This U.S. assistance became controversial during the late 1970s when questions arose whether the aid was actually beneficial to the poor and whether it should be used as leverage to influence Somoza's human rights performance (*Post*, October 24, 1977:29; Mudge 1979; Sigmund and Speck 1978; and U.S. Senate 1978).

3. For different views on the background of the FSLN, including its evolution, ideological and organizational disputes, and role in the overthrow of Somoza, see Black (1981), Booth (1985), Cuzán (1989, 1991), Everingham (1996), Hodges (1986), Kinzer (1991), Nolan (1984), Ryan (1995), and T. W. Walker (1981).

4. The most recent accounts of Sandinista agrarian policy are Biondi-Morra (1993), Enríquez (1991, 1997), Luciak (1995), Ryan (1995), Spalding (1994), Spoor (1995), and Utting (1991). Useful discussions among the extensive earlier literature can be found in Austin, Fox, and Kruger (1985); Barraclough (1983); Colburn (1986, 1990); Collins (1986); Deere and Marchetti (1981); Deere, Marchetti, and

Reinhardt (1985); FitzGerald (1985); Kaimowitz (1989); Kaimowitz and Stanfield (1985); Peek (1983); Reinhardt (1989); Spalding (1985); and Thome and Kaimowitz (1985). Many of these authors worked with the Sandinistas on agrarian policy.

5. See Chapters 3 and 4 for the specifics of these trends.

6. In the credit and service cooperatives (CCS), farmers owned the land individually but purchased inputs collectively and received assistance from the cooperative in obtaining credit and technical assistance. In the Sandinista production cooperatives (CAS), land and other resources were held collectively. The government favored the latter arrangement, peasants the former.

7. Annual government data on land distributed and families benefited by form of organization can be found in Enríquez (1997:111–112).

8. In addition to the sources listed previously, this section is also based on AWC (1985), Berman (1996), *Monitor* (October 7, 1986:12), Kinzer (1991), *NY Times* (January 23, 1985:A2 and March 19, 1985:A1 and 11).

9. Of the rest, 20 percent were grants received as part of credit and service cooperatives, with the other 8 percent to two other forms of cooperatives (Enríquez 1997:112).

10. This argument is most fully developed by Colburn (1986), who claims that "the uniformities of contemporary post-revolutionary regimes in small developing countries [such as Nicaragua] suggest that the parameters of choice are limited. Predictable decisions are thrust on revolutionary elites by circumstances beyond their control. Thus, the effect of leadership on events seems to be of degree (and perhaps sequence) and not of kind" (p. 23).

11. Agrarian reform minister Jaime Wheelock had written the leading agrarian history of Nicaragua before becoming the leader of one of the three factions of the FSLN (Wheelock Román 1980; also see Núñez Soto 1981).

12. In each of the four last years of the period 1979 to 1983, the performance of the Nicaraguan economy exceeded the regional average. However, the 1979 decline was so severe (25.9 percent) that the 22.5 percent growth in real GDP for this period was insufficient to bring the economy back to the level of 1978, which in turn was 7.2 percent below that of 1977 (Conroy 1985:224). On agricultural prices during this period, see Maxfield and Stahler-Sholk (1985:252) and Collins (1986:279).

13. For sources, see Figure 3.6. By 1995 debt as a percentage of export earnings had dropped to 1,706 percent—still four times greater than Honduras, its closest neighbor on this score.

14. Enríquez (1997:65). Especially helpful for this section were Biondi-Morra (1993); Colburn (1986); Colburn and De Franco (1985); Collins (1986); Deere, Marchetti, and Reinhardt (1985); Enríquez (1991, 1997); Gilbert (1985); Kaimowitz (1980); Luciak (1995); Sholk (1984); and Spalding (1994).

15. This section draws especially on Collins (1986); Deere, Marchetti, and Reinhardt (1985); Enríquez (1997); and Luciak (1995). Also see Colburn (1986), Deere and Marchetti (1981), *Envio* (August 1989), Gilbert (1985), and Thome and Kaimowitz (1985).

16. According to one economist, there "has emerged a quite remarkable consensus of the left, center, and right that governmental intervention in agricultural commodity markets has had undesirable results in almost every instance, in every country" (Bruce Gardner, quoted in Johnson and Schuh 1983:219).

17. Helpful in preparing this section have been Arnson (1993), *Envio* (March 1989), Gilbert (1986), Gutman (1988), Honey (1994), LeoGrande (1979, 1982, 1985), Kinzer (1991), Moreno (1990), Muravchik (1986–1987), and Schoultz (1984).

18. For arguments supporting this perspective, see Cuzán (1989), U.S. Department of State (1985b), and Valenta and Valenta (1984). Establishing the true intentions of the Reagan administration was difficult, both because of divisions within it (which Reagan typically would not settle) and because domestic and international laws discouraged admission of the intention to overthrow the government of another country. Nonetheless, Reagan came close to confessing such a goal during the first press conference of his second term when he stated, according to one report, "that his objective is to 'remove' the 'present structure' of the Government in Nicaragua" (*NY Times*, February 22, 1985:A1). In order to secure congressional support for aid to the Contras, he stated the opposite later in the year: "We do not seek the military overthrow of the Sandinista government or to put in its place a government based on supporters of the old Somoza regime" (*Post*, June 12, 1985:A1).

19. The plan is usually referred to as the Esquipulas Accord for the site of its signing or as the Arias Plan, in recognition of the leading role played by the president of Costa Rica, Oscar Arias, for which he was awarded the Nobel Peace Prize.

20. Sources for the Chamorro years include: Arana (1997), Butler et al. (1996), *Chronicle* (June 15 and November 2, 1995, and May 23, 1996), Dye et al. (1995), de Groot and Plantinga (1993), Jonakin (1996, 1997), *NotiSur* (April 29, May 6, and August 5, 1994), Spalding (1994), *Update* (May 22, 1992), and Walker (1997).

21. For the Sandinista period, annual total agricultural export earnings for the first five years averaged 68 percent of the 1977–1979 period and only 38 percent during the last three years (calculated from FAO data).

22. Her most important adviser was her son-in-law Antonio Lacayo. Essentially the relationship can be portrayed as Chamorro as head of state (but not figurehead) and Lacayo as day-to-day head of government.

23. Neither were the Sandinistas immune to fragmentation. Best symbolizing the split would be Sergio Ramírez, vice president under Daniel Ortega, who left the FSLN in 1995, forming a new social democratic party under whose banner he ran for president in 1996 (Butler et al. 1996).

24. On Alemán and his first half year in office, see Butler et al. (1996); *EcoCentral* (March 20, April 24, and July 24, 1997); and *NotiSur* (November 1, 1996, and January 17, 1997).

Chapter Eight

Honduras: The Limitations of Reform

Land tenure relations in Honduras before World War II were notably different from those in the rest of Central America. The peasants of Honduras did not experience the same demands for their land and their labor as did their counterparts elsewhere in the region (excluding Costa Rica). By midcentury, though, the situation began to change. Land pressures and conflicts increased as population growth and the expansion of commercial farming, especially for the export market, created land scarcities that resulted in agrarian conflict. In response, the government has since the early 1960s undertaken programs to reform land tenure relations, sometimes with the United States as a participant. These programs have included colonization, adjudication of land disputes, redistribution of property, and titling of landholdings.

This chapter's analysis of agrarian policy in contemporary Honduras demonstrates both the accomplishments and the limitations of reformism in situations of dire need. Many rural people have benefited from the reform programs, and rural dissatisfaction has been kept lower than it otherwise would have been. However, landlessness and rural unemployment are worse now than before the reforms were initiated. Even though Honduras escaped the devastation of the region's civil conflicts of the 1980s, it remains poorer on most indicators than its neighbors. Because of the way political power is distributed and the limitations of prevailing ideologies, the reforms have been too mild to respond adequately to the basic needs of many rural people. As a result, the future of Honduras is uncertain.

The Initiation of Agrarian Reform

Agrarian reform first came to Honduras in the early 1960s in response to both external stimuli, through the Alliance for Progress, and internal pressures. The most liberal Honduran president up to that point, Ramón Villeda Morales, established the National Agrarian Institute (INA) in 1961. The following year he gained congressional approval for an agrarian reform law that was aimed particularly at the fruit companies' uncultivated land, though it applied to all idle lands not fulfilling their social function (Fonck 1972; *International Labour Review* 1963). Villeda was one of the Latin leaders most in line with the Kennedy administration's progressive preferences, but his agrarian reform law was quite unpopular with the U.S. ambassador and leading U.S. legislators, not to mention the fruit companies. Ambassador Charles Burrows recalls that he told the Honduran president, "This is not a good law. It's going to cause you all kinds of trouble, and I think you ought to take a very, very close look at it" (Burrows 1969:14). Meanwhile, U.S. senators put pressure on the Kennedy administration to protect the interests of the fruit companies and to uphold the principle of adequate compensation, which meant, in the words of Senator Wayne Morse, payment in "hard, cold American dollars" (U.S. Congress 1962:21614–21620).

Standard Fruit indicated that it could live with the law, but United Fruit had no intention of doing so. It stopped its planting program, throwing many Hondurans out of work. At the same time, Villeda took a long-scheduled trip to the United States. Before returning to Honduras, he met with United Fruit officials, with whom he had a "very satisfactory conversation." He promised them a revised law that would be, in Burrows's (1969) words, "livable for private interests" (pp. 16–17). Before Villeda's trip, Burrows (1962) had written to the State Department, "I am sure that The Fruit Company is in an excellent position and can probably get much of what it wants from the Honduran government in terms of agrarian law revision, replacement of INA personnel or anything else. Please pass this on where it will do the most good" (p. 2). The revision was delivered, and the INA director was removed (Posas 1979:126).

On October 3, 1963, the eve of national elections scheduled to select his successor, Villeda was overthrown by a military coup. Although Burrows (1969:35–36) claims that the coup was unrelated to the agrarian reform, the probable victor in the election would have been the head of Villeda's party, viewed by many as a radical who would continue with his general reform program; this was undoubtedly a major cause of the coup.[1] More generally, large landowners, both domestic and foreign, were alarmed at the growing mobilization of peasants on the north coast and appreciated the value of the coup as a conservative reaction against the awakening of popular forces in the countryside.

The cause of agrarian reform largely disappeared in Honduras from the time of the coup until the late 1960s, just as it disappeared from the U.S. foreign policy agenda. The progressive rhetoric of 1961 reflected the abstract goals of intellectuals close to Kennedy; implementation of the U.S. role in the Alliance for Progress, however, was left to career officials with different perspectives and interests, including a need to be responsive to legislators. Many of the latter agreed with major economic elites that structural reform was unwise and even dangerous. As one high USAID official admitted to a researcher, "We were particularly shocked by Kennedy's endorsement of land reform and the implication that we would push it. None of us had the slightest intention of doing so in our capacities" (quoted in Olson 1974:111; also see Lowenthal 1973 and Montgomery 1984).

Furthermore, Central America's land-based elites, still dominant political forces in each of the countries, were not about to permit the implementation of reform measures that seriously threatened their privileged position. Consequently, agrarian reform for the United States became "technical modernization without structural reform" (Petras and LaPorte 1973:394). The United States encouraged passage of the original agrarian reform legislation in Central America, indirectly as well as directly in some cases, but effective implementation of that legislation disappeared as an objective of U.S. policy.

Settling Land Disputes

Disputes between peasants and large landowners increased during the 1960s, both because of rapidly growing rural populations and because of the dispossession of peasants by landowners attracted to new profit-making opportunities.[2] In response, peasants became more active in asserting their interests. By the later part of the decade, the government had begun to rule in their favor in land disputes.

Encouraged by the example of the Cuban revolution, serious peasant mobilization in Honduras began in the early 1960s in response to land disputes with a United Fruit Company subsidiary on the north coast. United Fruit, desiring to expand its activities into new ventures such as African palm and cattle raising, moved to evict peasants from lands that they rented, in some cases for decades. During the same period, it also cut its workforce in the area by half.

Peasants in southern Honduras had sent delegations to the capital as early as 1955 to defend their lands against encroachment by large landowners; in the 1960s those in the north took a new step. Peasants from the affected areas organized together in October 1961, forming the Central Committee of Peasant Unity (CCUC). They were assisted by leaders who had settled in the area after having been fired by United Fruit in the aftermath of a strike in 1954 that had important consequences for national as well as agrarian politics. After the meeting, they sent a letter to President Villeda that contrasted their landlessness with the vast, often uncultivated holdings of the fruit company and asked him to require that the land fulfill its social function.

Dissatisfied by the responses from the government and United Fruit, the CCUC initiated in early 1962 a campaign of recovering idle lands, as peasants occupied and began cultivating them. Up to 1,000 peasants also marched on the town of El Progreso, the first time peasants in Honduras had demonstrated in such large numbers in their own behalf. United Fruit ran cattle through some of their plantings in order to drive the invaders out; it also received some assistance toward this end from military forces stationed in the area. CCUC leaders were able to convince President Villeda to enjoin any further efforts to dispossess them, at least through the harvest. When United Fruit refused the resulting request of local authorities to remove its cattle from the disputed lands, the president sent a commission from the agrarian reform agency (INA) to work out a compromise.

The successes of CCUC were short-lived. It reorganized as the National Federation of Honduran Peasants (FENACH) in August 1962, but two months later its directors were arrested at a meeting and held incommunicado for nearly five days. They were released in face of their hunger strike and the pressure of their followers, who had gathered outside the building where they were held. After the coup of 1963, FENACH was destroyed; the leaders who were caught were jailed, its offices and archives were demolished, and its membership repressed. A few of the leaders took to the mountains to initiate armed struggle; they included Lorenzo Zelaya, its president and catalyst. A former labor leader at United Fruit and a communist militant, Zelaya was discovered with six comrades and killed in an armed confrontation in April 1965.

During its brief existence, the militant FENACH faced not only repression but also competition. Within two months of FENACH's formation, a new Honduran peasant federation was organized, the National Association of Honduran Peasants (ANACH). This explicitly anticommunist movement received substantial organizational assistance from the United States through the AFL-CIO and its Latin American arm, the Inter-American Regional Organization of Labor (ORIT). The more militant FENACH had an estimated membership of 15,000 in August 1962, and ANACH had 5,000 members at its formation two months later. The latter's membership was soon expanded by some 8,000 peasants who deserted FENACH because of the repression directed against it (Kincaid 1985:137). Despite its more moderate and anticommunist stance, ANACH was also immobilized by government repression in the first years following the 1963 coup. In 1966, when a new president of the federation became more outspoken, its financial sponsors forced his resignation. Accusing him of being a communist, they threatened to suspend all assistance if he did not resign (Posas 1981a:85–87).

The repressive mid-1960s were a time of rapid expansion of cotton planting and cattle raising in Honduras; the area harvested in cotton more than doubled between 1964 and 1966. Landowners were responding in part to new commercial opportunities but also to the threat of agrarian reform. Idle lands, or those rented to peasants for a long period, might at some point be subject to expropriation or peasant occupation. Meanwhile, INA received only minimal appropriations during this period. Not only was it indifferent to the plight of the peasantry, some even saw it as a protector of landed interests. Government-backed eviction increased, and the rental of land in areas of commercial expansion became virtually impossible.

Despite intermittent repression, by the end of the 1960s Honduran peasants had organized and were asserting themselves to a degree unparalleled in Central America and perhaps even in all of Latin America (Astorga Lira 1975:17). Catalyzed by the enclosure movement and land pressures discussed in Part 1, peasant mobilization was facilitated by a political opening that began with the appointment of a sympathetic INA director in 1967 and that was enlarged by both the popular opposition to fraudulent municipal elections in March 1968 and the fallout of the war with El Salvador in July 1969.

Outside agents for change played an important role in this mobilization as well. Similar in importance to Catholic Action in Guatemala was the radio school movement in southern Honduras. Facing Central America's lowest per capita population of priests in the country with the most difficult terrain, the Honduran Catholic Church developed a radio school network as a way of bringing literacy, education, and religious teaching to isolated rural communities. There were 7,250 students in 343 schools in 1962, and the numbers doubled by 1964 (White 1977:237). The program was placed in private hands so that international funding (especially USAID) could be obtained; these organizations, however, drew their inspiration from the Christian Democrats. As the program matured through the 1960s, it undertook more directly the successive commitments of peasant mobilization, organization, and support of confrontation with elite interests.

In the early 1960s, the program addressed the peasants' consciousness; in the words of one leader, "What we were trying to do was to influence the fundamental way of thinking of the campesino, change his individualism and fatalism and to orient him toward the community" (quoted in White 1977:243). This effort was followed by attempts to organize cooperatives, which came to receive greater priority than religious and literacy activities. Similar currents were moving in other parts of the church; consequently, there was a strong movement by 1964 whose goals were promoting "community-level action motivated by the communitarian values of Christianity" (White 1977:245). Furthermore, this movement created a communications system linking the countryside with modernizing forces and bypassing rural elites (White 1977:401). These activities contributed directly to peasant mobilization, then, by undermining the strength of traditional values and relationships of domination while offering the alternative of more cooperative, assertive values and organizations.

Such efforts by progressive Christians facilitated the formation in southern Honduras of peasant leagues, which grouped together in 1964 as the Social Christian Peasant Association of Honduras (ACASCH). After reorganization in the following years, it has been known as the National Peasant Union (UNC) since 1970. It was more militant than ANACH, and the competition between the two national peasant organizations for members and affiliates made both more aggressive than either probably would have been alone. A third national peasant organization also appeared in 1970, the Federation of Honduran Agrarian Reform Cooperatives (FECORAH), representing peasants settled in reform cooperatives.

As the peasant organizations became bolder, their major tactic was to stage land occupations. Most of their targets during the early 1960s were unoccupied lands owned by the fruit companies, but later in the decade their objectives were more likely to be land held by domestic interests that peasants claimed was public. Honduras is unique in Central America in that up to one-third of its area was still public as late as 1974 as either national or *ejidal* (community-owned) lands. When land became more scarce and valuable with population growth and commercialization, peasants claimed that large landholders illegitimately enclosed the public lands, often evicting peasants who had been working them. These evictions were the crucial factor in generating the peasant mobilization of the late 1960s. As White (1977) points out in his impressive study of this development, "The brutality of many of these evictions proved to be the catalyst in breaking down the friendly dependence on helpful patrons and developed a profoundly emotional opposition. The evictions were the sudden, sharp deprivation which moved campesinos to risk their lives in organizing to counter rural elites and protest before government authorities" (pp. 181–182).

Peasant pressure won the appointment of the agronomist Rigoberto Sandoval as the director of INA in 1967. Under his leadership, the agency's prevailing clientilistic operations were ruptured as he moved to professionalize it, in part by bringing in international technocrats. Furthermore, in late 1968 INA began to adjudicate land conflicts in favor of peasants. Lands proven to be national or *ejidal* were recovered and turned into communal peasant settlements. If the land in question was in fact legitimately privately owned, INA often purchased it for peasant settlements. Either way, the results electrified many peasant communities, accelerating further organization and occupations. By the late 1960s, the major peasant organizations claimed a combined membership of some 90,000 rural families. At the same time, government support for INA increased; its budget was enlarged in late 1968 by the issuance of bonds and by land sales. The group settlements also were supported by technical assistance and credits from the National Development Bank.

The most important action taken by the government, though, was the expulsion of many of the 300,000 or so Salvadorans who were occupying over half a million acres of Honduran land. This was one critical step that led to the short-lived Soccer War of 1969 in which Honduras humiliated El Salvador and the government gained some breathing room on the agrarian question.

Land Redistribution

With the election of a conservative president in June 1971, the leadership and policy of the INA were to change.[3] The settlement of disputes in favor of peasants virtually ceased, and those occupying private land were likely to be arrested. The opposition to reform by large landholders also solidified during this period. At times violence was employed against squatters. The results could be tragic, as when six peasants were killed at La Talanquera in Olancho in 1972. Peasants became more restive, and their hunger march on the capital in December 1972 was partially responsible for the coup that brought the newly populist military leader Oswaldo López Arellano back to power. Having explicitly aligned himself with popular classes before the coup, he soon issued an emergency land reform measure, Decree Law 8.[4] It was followed in January 1975 by an agrarian reform measure, Decree Law 170, which promised to distribute almost 1.5 million acres to 120,000 families in five years.[5]

The realities of political power put an end to the reforms. López was removed from power in April 1975 after it was revealed that United Brands (the former United Fruit) had paid a $1.25 million bribe to the Honduran government to encourage (successfully) a substantial reduction in a proposed increase in the banana export tax. López's power had already been diminishing, and the previous month he had been replaced as head of the armed forces by Juan Melgar Castro, who then succeeded him as president. Reform-oriented officials were able to hold on to a share of power until spring 1977, by which time most had been removed. Sandoval was brought back as the head of INA in October 1975, but his position was undercut by Melgar's appointment of a subdirector whose function was to restrain his boss (Ickis 1983:25).

The 1975 agrarian reform law established maximum landholding sizes and legitimated the expropriation of idle and underused lands. The law was published two weeks before it went into effect, and its application was delayed for over half a year because of the failure of Melgar's less-than-committed cabinet to approve the necessary implementing regulations. The delays provided large landholders with the time to subdivide property or to begin grazing cattle on it in order to establish use. Their interests were also advantaged by limitations placed on INA's ability to assess in the field the status of land use and by the law's appeals mechanism. INA decisions could be appealed to a special council, which, according to Posas (1979:101), well represented large landholders.

The delay in implementation of the law also provided its opponents with time to protest. Most notable were the activities of the National Federation of Farmers and Cattlemen (FENAGH), especially in the outlying department of Olancho. Ninety armed men from a FENAGH affiliate seized the regional office of the National Peasant Union on June 19, 1975. Then on June 25 six people were killed at a peasant training center in the department capital; and on the same day two foreign priests were murdered, their bodies discovered at the bottom of a well with those of seven other victims. The Catholic bishop was forced to flee the department (Anderson 1982:117–118; *Time* 1975:36). In a departure from procedures elsewhere in Central America, some of the guilty were tried and imprisoned; the commission that investigated the murders declared that they were part of a vast plan directed by FENAGH (Posas and del Cid 1981:211).

In the face of governmental delay and despite occasional violence, peasant mobilization, in the form of marches, demonstrations, and a record number of land occupations, increased throughout 1975. In early October the three major peasant organizations united and gave the government until the end of the month to respond to their need for land. When it did not, they launched massive, simultaneous land takeovers throughout the countryside, returning even when removed by the military. In the face of this unprecedented level of popular pressure, which also included organized urban interests, the Melgar government finally proposed a plan for the recovery and adjudication of public and idle private lands.

Although a substantial amount of land was redistributed, significant opposition to the agrarian reform remained within the government and on the part of economic elites, making implementation of the program very difficult. By early 1977 opponents of reform had clearly won: The last of the progressive military leaders were sent into "diplomatic exile," and in March Sandoval announced his resignation, citing the lack of government support for agrarian reform. During the remaining years of military rule, very little land was distributed, and most of that was through expensive colonization programs, often financed by loans from international donors.

When civilian government was restored in early 1982, the new INA director charged, according to one account, that the agency had been plundered "to such a degree that when the Liberal government arrived they found they had an institution that was completely ruined" (*La Prensa* 1982:3). The elected government (1982–1986) of Roberto Suazo Córdova pledged to satisfy peasants' needs, and the reform pace did quicken under his administration; once again, however, performance fell short of promises. In the first three years of Suazo's term, about 146,000 acres were distributed (Ruhl 1985:70), far below the original commitment of over 123,000 acres for 1983 alone (*La Prensa* 1983:4). It was not surprising, then, that peasant pressure through mass land occupations continued. The peasants' efficacy was depleted, though, by fragmentation; at least fourteen different groups claimed to speak for them in 1984.

Several positive features of the Honduran agrarian reform should be noted. Perhaps most significant is that there was considerable land redistribution in a nonrevolutionary situation and government intervention on the side of peasants in conflicts with larger landholders. Between 1962 and 1980, about 36,000 rural families benefited from the program (see Table 8.1); the number of beneficiaries through the 1970s was equivalent to about 22 percent of the landless and land-poor families in the mid-1970s (Ruhl 1984:55). Of course the reform had major political consequences. Ruhl (1984) points out that it "was very important symbolically because the program demonstrated the continued flexibility and reform potential of the Honduran government and fostered an 'incrementalist' policy orientation among the peasant organizations" (p. 55).

Despite its achievements, Honduran agrarian reform has fallen far short of both its stated goals and the country's needs. The peak of the reform process was reached in 1973–1974, according to all three indicators in Table 8.1: average number of families benefited, average amount of land awarded, and average size of the grants. The pace slackened after the promulgation of the 1975 law. Even at the end of 1980, the number of families benefited and the amount of land awarded were only one-sixth the law's stated goal; in addition, the average size of the grants had declined. By the late 1990s, Honduras has more landless families than before the implementation of Decree Law 8 began in late 1972. The grants of the Suazo administration of the 1980s, for example, met less than one-half of the need generated during its tenure (Ruhl 1985:73–74).

The redistribution of land in Honduras was facilitated by the large quantity of national and *ejidal* lands remaining in the country and by the

TABLE 8.1   Honduras: Land Distribution Under the Reform Process, 1962–1984

	Families Benefited		Land Awarded (hectares)		Average Grant per Family[a]
	Total	Annual Average	Total	Annual Average	
1962–1966	281	56	1,357	271	4.8
1967–1972	5,348	891	34,604	5,767	6.5
1973–1974	11,739	5,870	79,552	39,776	6.8
1975–1977	12,405	4,135	80,150	26,717	6.5
1978–1981	9,174	2,294	38,937	9,734	4.2
1982–1984	13,241	4,414	58,770	19,590	4.4
Total	52,188	2,269	293,370	12,755	5.6

[a]Land grants were often to groups, not individual families. Therefore this column does not give average annual size of grant but instead a measure of per-family size of grants.

SOURCES: Calculated from Morris 1984:101 and Ruhl 1985:70.

expulsion of Salvadoran settlers in 1969. Most of the land distributed was publicly owned. Furthermore, of the private land that was distributed, much was given by the fruit companies voluntarily or obtained through expropriations of holdings in less hospitable climates following the "Bananagate" disclosures that brought down the López government in 1975.

But in many cases the land distributed was in remote areas, divided into parcels of insufficient size, and of poor quality. Technical and credit assistance, including a $12 million loan initiated by USAID in 1974, was made available to the cooperative farms as part of the reform process, but the actual funds were difficult to obtain and often insufficient. For such reasons, the abandonment rate of reform farms has been high; by one estimate, some 40 percent of the original settlers already had left these settlements by the early 1980s (USAID 1982:4). Furthermore, the INA itself acknowledged that because it concentrated its efforts on the group settlements, the remaining 80 percent of the reform beneficiaries did not receive adequate technical assistance and financial support (Tiempo 1983:19a).

There was a close connection between agrarian reform in Honduras and the commercialization of agriculture. These reform projects, such as the huge Bajo Aguán (which by mid-1977 consisted of almost 4,000 families organized in eighty cooperatives), were advantaged over other peasant groups in the provision of credit, technical assistance, and infrastructure development. In 1981, for example, they were earmarked for about 65 percent of INA's support (even though they consisted of about 30 percent of the reform groups), with the basic grains sector receiving 8 percent (Stringer 1989:372). Much of this backing came from international donors, especially the Inter-American Development Bank and the United States.

In some cases the government required that such settlements devote themselves to export production.[6] Boyer (1982:192–194) cites the example of a reform settlement that attempted, after unpleasant experiences raising cotton and then melons, to return to raising grain and cattle. It was refused credits by the National Development Bank and by other creditors unless it returned to cotton production. Ironically, one USAID report (1983:6–7) points out that the land received by the reform sector "was most often land unsuited for intensive agricultural purposes," though it would be appropriate for livestock grazing.

Stabilizing the Countryside in the 1980s

In the 1980s, however, the philosophy of the Honduran and U.S. governments changed from supporting land distribution for group farms to supporting, as USAID (1982) phrased it, "an agrarian reform based on the principles of private property" (p. 6). Although it addressed the real and serious problems of a substantial number of rural families, this approach offered nothing for the growing number of landless peasants. This shift was, though, consistent with the philosophy of the new Reagan administration. More important, it was congruent with Honduras's role in the evolving U.S. geopolitical strategy for the region.

Landholders in Honduras typically lacked legal title to their land; USAID (1982:1) estimates that in the early 1980s three-quarters of farmers had insecure tenancy. Not only does the lack of title leave peasants vulnerable to dispossession by more powerful interests, but it also limits access to bank credits because a formal title is often necessary for collateral. Both insecurity and lack of credit, of course, constrain productivity. For such reasons, in recent years ambitious land titling programs have been undertaken, their expense largely underwritten by loans from the United States.

The small farmer titling project was based on a $10 million loan and a $2.5 million grant made by the United States in 1982. Its goal was 70,000 titles. Special targets of the program were small and medium-sized coffee growers, described by USAID as "very strong and politically conscious" (USAID 1982:5). Of the country's 48,000 coffee producers, about 95 percent had insecure titles to the land they worked. These farmers also benefited from a decree in 1981 that exempted coffee lands from the agrarian reform program and abolished previous restrictions against the granting of titles through the reform process to coffee holdings of under 13 acres.

Beneficiaries gained an important measure of security through this program, especially the less powerful among them. By the end of 1989, over 32,000 titles had been issued, 55 percent of them to holdings of less than 13 acres. Recipients believed that the value of their land increased more than untitled land did; they also obtained better access to credit (Stanfield et al. 1990:35–37). Credit has been especially important in recent years as coffee rust has become a major threat to coffee trees. Control of this disease is possible, but it requires a substantial investment most onerous for small farmers. In 1981 the United States initiated a five-year, $9.55 million program in Honduras to help coffee growers, including funds to combat coffee rust (USAID 1982:1–13).

Honduran and U.S. officials were concerned about stabilizing the Honduran countryside in the early 1980s as the FMLN insurgency spread in El Salvador to the southwest and the revolution radicalized in Nicaragua to the southeast. Stabilizing the frontier with Nicaragua was especially important as it became the primary staging area for the Contra war against the Sandinistas. The United States poured money into Honduras, particularly for the military (but much of it was lost to corruption). The effort succeeded; Honduras was a pillar of stability through the conflicts of the 1980s. But the military's position in society grew[7] and violence spread, both with adverse consequences for peasant political activity.

Honduran politics in the 1980s was far less violent than that of its neighbors, but within its own traditions it was a violent decade, with two serious rounds of political killings totaling 184 deaths, according to the official report of the human rights ombudsman (*NotiSur*, January 7, 1994). In the first period, some 123 people disappeared in Honduras during 1981–1984 (Americas Watch 1987:64), most at the hands of a secret military unit organized in 1980 that functioned as an official death squad. Former members of the unit have testified that the special interrogation and kidnapping teams of Battalion 316 detained, tortured, and killed over 100 suspected leftists in its network of secret jails in the early 1980s.[8]

This recourse to violence by the Honduran military corresponded to the initiation of the country's role as a staging base for the Contra war against Nicaragua and to the rise to power of General Gustavo Alvarez Martínez, who was the organizer of Battalion 316. The Contras began coalescing on Honduran soil in 1981 with Alvarez's encouragement, U.S. money, and Argentine trainers. Appropriately, Alvarez was the representative of the Honduran government to the joint staff organized to manage and coordinate the "secret war." He was even more helpful when he became the head of the armed forces in January 1982, working closely with the hard-line U.S. ambassador, John D. Negroponte. Alvarez was forced out of his post in March 1984, for reasons unrelated to these abuses. The human rights situation in Honduras improved substantially shortly after his departure.[9]

This encouraging record, though, was defiled by a resurgence of political violence beginning in 1986. As always, progressive activists were particular targets; as vigilantism spread, reputed criminals and delinquents were targeted as well. Significantly contributing to the growing insecurity in the country was the large Contra presence. Around 56,000 fighters and their dependents occupied an area of 279 square miles in Honduras with deleterious consequences. As Schulz and Schulz (1994) describe the situation: "Many communities had become uninhabitable because of fighting between the contras and the Sandinistas. . . . Assassinations, murders, armed robberies, kidnappings, torture, intimidation, property seizures, and cattle rustling had become a part of everyday life. Land mines were a constant danger. . . . Damage to the local economy was in the tens of millions of dollars" (pp. 170–171).

The violence continued into the new decade with the murders of five peasants in May 1991 in a controversy over a land occupation near Aqua Caliente. These deaths were then followed in the next few months by 13 peasants killed in fighting among peasant organizations themselves (Schulz and Schulz 1994:287–293).

Mass mobilization has always been difficult in Central America, but it was especially so given the war in Nicaragua and the deteriorating human rights situation. There was a minor leftist insurgency in Honduras in the early 1980s supported by Nicaragua and periodic leftist bombings and kidnappings. However, no sooner had the Honduran congress passed an antiterrorist law than peasants found that it was being applied against them as well. The UNC claimed in May 1982 that about fifty peasant leaders in the northwest were arrested and accused of being "subversives." The repression continued; in the fifteen months beginning in May 1983, 334 members of the UNC were jailed (Kincaid 1985:144; Schulz and Schulz 1994:80–83; *Tiempo* 1982:5).

After Alvarez was deposed, the repression lifted and the government was more willing to talk with leaders. But beyond negotiations, there was little government response. Meanwhile, the INA grew more bureaucratic, politicized, conservative, and corrupt. In turn the UNC, one of the two leading peasant organizations, moved in a conservative direction, leading to charges of its co-optation. Land invasions continued to be the major form of peasant action, but the peak had come in May 1987 with over 200 simultaneous land occupations by tens of thousands of peasants—and only minor results (Schulz and Schulz 1994:211–215).

In recent years the biggest problem for peasants, as for all Hondurans, has been the persistent economic crisis. When Rafael Callejas became president in 1990, per capita GNP had declined 13 percent over the past decade, and the budget deficit for the prior year was an unsustainable 12.5 percent of GNP (Schulz and Schulz 1994:273–274). The latter condition mandated an austerity program in order to maintain the flow of necessary international loans, but such programs invariably exacerbate the first condition. And so it did, as the poverty rate climbed to 72 percent in early 1992 (*Update*, March 12, 1992). Fiscal problems continued, however, so the next president, Carlos Roberto Reina, was required to initiate further austerity measures. He did have some success, bringing down the fiscal deficit and generating moderate growth. But inflation accelerated; the foreign debt continued to climb, with annual payments due greater than export earnings; and the currency faced rapid devaluations. Poverty inched up, with 54 percent of Hondurans said to be in "extreme" poverty (*Chronicle*, February 22, 1996; *EcoCentral*, October 3, 1996).

The economic program of the 1990s also included the controversial agricultural modernization law passed in 1992. This law symbolized the change in government policy from agrarian reform to the promotion of commercial agriculture and the parallel reduction in the role of the state in agriculture, as the government turned instead to market forces. Meanwhile the numbers—and even rates—of rural landlessness and poverty climb.

Conclusion

Agrarian reform has had a mixed history in Honduras. The first attempt at reform, the 1962 law, was in part both inspired by and aborted by external forces—elements of the U.S. government in both cases and also the United Fruit Company in the second. Even without those forces, the Honduran government undoubtedly did not at that time have the power (or the will) to implement meaningful land redistribution. At the end of the 1960s, however, substantial peasant mobilization altered the configuration of political power. Peasant dissatisfaction created new pressures on the government and new incentives for political leaders to espouse reformist policies. As a consequence, policies became more favorable to peasant interests, and first the National Agrarian Institute in the late 1960s and early 1970s and then the López Arellano government in 1973–1974 altered their orientations. The zenith of populist reformism passed quickly, however, as government leadership changed and the opposition of large landowners solidified. It is also important to recall that little domestically owned private land was redistributed. Peasants have been much less likely to succeed in their attempts to occupy and "recover" idle and underused private lands than in their efforts to claim disputed public lands.

This survey of agrarian policy in Honduras demonstrates the advantages and weaknesses of reformism in situations of dire need. The recipients of land, titles, and credit and marketing support often have enjoyed an improved material position, sometimes one substantially improved. The perceived responsiveness of the political system to their needs in turn has generated support for the system and for particular political officials. But at the same time, because structural reform has been beyond the will and capacity of political officials and outside of the interest of the United States, the problems of landlessness and near landlessness are at historic highs; the INA director estimated the number of landless rural families at 180,000 in early 1991 (*Update,* January 31, 1991). Thus far, then, reform programs have been unable adequately to address the structural causes of rural poverty and insecurity in Honduras.[10]

Notes

1. See Anderson (1982:113), Pearson (1980:302), Posas (1981b:22), and Shaw (1979:139). In addition, Schulz and Schulz (1994:31) emphasize the antipathy of the military toward the two Liberal Party leaders stemming from what the military saw as challenges to its institutional prerogatives.

2. Critical sources for this section are Posas (1979, 1981a, 1981b) and White (1977). For other sources on peasant mobilization during this period, see Kincaid (1985), Pearson (1980), Pfeil (1977), Ruhl (1984), Stringer (1989), and Volk (1981). For related discussions, see Anderson (1981), Durham (1979), MacCameron (1983), Morris (1984), Peckenham and Street (1985), Posas and del Cid (1981), and Schulz and Schulz (1994).

3. Major sources for this section are Posas (1979) and Ruhl (1984, 1985). For other sources on the agrarian reform, see Astorga Lira (1975), Hatch and Lanao Flores (1977), Schulz and Schulz (1994), Slutzky (1979), Stringer (1989), Tendler (1976), USAID (1982), and Volk (1981).

4. General López Arellano had become president in 1963 as an air force colonel and had served until 1971.

5. The U.S. government appears to have had little role in the original steps of the agrarian reform of the 1970s. The drafters of the 1975 law, though, were advised by consultants from the University of Wisconsin at Madison.

6. Nonetheless, for the entire reform sector during the mid-1980s basic grains (including sorghum) accounted for about 80 percent of total production (Ruhl 1985:71).

7. A new U.S. ambassador to Honduras, John Ferch, insisted on treating the civilian government rather than the military high command as the highest authorities in the country. He was removed from his position in June 1986, after only ten months at his post (Americas Watch 1987:122). The overbearing presence of the United States in Honduras had the unintended consequence of fueling anti-U.S. sentiment, intense expressions of which could be found across the political spectrum, especially in the latter 1980s (*NY Times,* April 9, 1988:6).

8. See especially *Baltimore Sun* (June 11–18, 1995), as well as Americas Watch (1984), Committee for the Defense of Human Rights in Honduras (1985), LeMoyne (1988), and *NY Times* (May 2, 1987:1). There have been numerous reports that the Central Intelligence Agency (CIA) and State Department knew of many of the kidnappings; the extent of U.S. knowledge of the torture and killings is a matter of some controversy; see Americas Watch (1987:114–121), *Baltimore Sun* (June 11–18, 1995), and Schulz and Schulz (1994:82–87). To the credit of the Honduran government, when relatives of some of the victims filed suit, the civilian administration of José Azcona Hoyo accepted the jurisdiction of the Inter-American Court of Human Rights. When the court in 1988 found the Honduran govern-

ment guilty in the 1981 disappearance of one of its citizens, the president's spokesman announced that the government "has no option but to respect the judgment fully" (*NY Times*, July 30, 1988:1). In 1995 charges were brought by the government against nine military officers for attempted murder of six students in 1982 (*NotiSur*, August 4, 1995).

9. See *Baltimore Sun* (June 11–18, 1995), *Post* (April 2:A15 and December 16, 1984:A27), Schulz and Schulz (1994:65–102), and WOLA 1987.

10. For a very different view, see the position of Fernando Lardizabal (1986), the former president of FENAGH.

Chapter Nine

Costa Rica: Toward Sustainable Development

The agrarian structure of Costa Rica historically has differed from that of other Central American countries; it is generally less stratified and less repressive. Consequently, the impact of the successive agrarian transformations on the lives of rural Costa Ricans has not been as severe as elsewhere in the region. Although rural Costa Rica has confronted many of the same issues as it neighbors, it has had a better chance at peaceful problem-solving and has avoided the violence of the rest of the region. This can be seen not only in its approach to traditional issues of agrarian politics, such as access to land, but also in its handling of environmental problems, which are reaching disastrous proportions throughout the region because of rapid population growth and the intensification of commercial agriculture.

Environmental degradation was explored briefly in Part 1 as one of the consequences of the region's postwar agrarian transformation. Environmental issues are examined in greater depth in this chapter because they have been the object of public policy in Costa Rica more so than in the rest of the area—in fact, more so than just about anywhere outside of rich industrial democracies. In recent years Costa Rica has been at the forefront of attempts to integrate conservation with improvement of rural living standards. President José María Figueres Olsen spoke in 1996, for example, of turning the country "into a pilot project of sustainable development," with Costa Rica "offering itself to the world as a 'laboratory' for this new development paradigm" (Figueres Olsen 1996: 190). The problems Costa Rica faces, though, are formidable; the results will be instructive for the rest of the region.

Traditional Agrarian Issues

The Initiation of Agrarian Reform

The foundation of Costa Rica's agrarian reform program was passed into law in 1961.[1] This action was primarily a reflection of domestic politics; indeed, serious governmental deliberation on agrarian reform began in the mid-1950s, with antecedent actions as far back as the turn of the century. Concern had grown as the population exploded at an alarming rate. Land pressures in the countryside led to increasing numbers of peasants taking matters into their own hands by occupying unused property, heightening rural tensions. In addition, the successful passage of agrarian measures was facilitated by Eisenhower's endorsement in 1960 of such reforms, Kennedy's more fervent support the following year, and especially the promise inherent in the Alliance for Progress of help from the United States to finance their implementation.

Costa Rican law authorizes the expropriation of unused private lands, but this has never been an important aspect of the country's reform process. In fact, many of the legislators who voted for the measure did not expect that it would be fully implemented, valuing it instead for symbolic purposes. The law requires full compensation for expropriated land; supreme court decisions in 1967 and 1969 mandated, respectively, that payment must be in cash, if so desired, and that it must be at full market value. Under such tight constraints, implementation of the law was restricted until 1970 to a series of colonization projects, which settled only 1,272 peasant families on 87,500 acres in often unsuccessful colonies, and to a very limited titling of land held by squatters who could prove legitimate possession (Seligson 1980a:126–131; 1984:31).

A primary impetus for passage of Costa Rica's agrarian reform law was the problem of squatters; it was estimated that the country had some 16,500 squatter families in the mid-1960s, a number that grew as the decade advanced. The conservative nature of the law, however, limited government action through the colonization program, especially under right-of-center governments. Therefore, in the second half of the decade the government relied on the adjudication of land disputes as its major response to the growing problem of rural conflict. When squatters could prove legitimate occupation, they were given legal titles. When they could not, they were offered an opportunity to relocate to one of the colonies, though in some cases the government bought the land in dispute for purchase by the squatter. Dealing with manifestations of the problem rather than the problem itself, this approach was not able to keep up with the growing number of squatters; in 1966–1969 only 2,093 families were settled with titles.

The Costa Rican agrarian reform entered its most active phase during the mid-1970s, centering for the first time on the expropriation of property. This activism came about because of both pressure from below and the electoral victory of the president who has demonstrated the greatest commitment to agrarian reform.[2] The pace of peasant land invasions intensified in the late 1960s and into the 1970s as a result of increasing land pressures, frustration over the minimal benefits of the reform program, and the encouragement of left-wing urban groups. Rural elites in turn increasingly called in the police to remove squatters. Indeed, a new rural police force was created in 1969 primarily to prevent land invasions; the expanding community of foreign growers sometimes employed their own private police forces. In the frontier regions of the country, "a potentially explosive sociopolitical situation" grew (Hall 1985:202; also see Salazar 1979:220–223).

The victor in the 1974 presidential election was Daniel Oduber of the National Liberation Party (PLN), the more progressive of Costa Rica's major parties. He had just barely lost the election in 1966, and then in 1970 he was defeated for his party's nomination by its hero of the 1948 "revolution," former president José Figueres. Figueres did little to advance the cause of agrarian reform, despite the deteriorating rural situation. But Oduber, long identified as a strong supporter of agrarian reform, secured the right for the agrarian reform agency to issue about $12 million in bonds. These were used as compensation for the expropriation of several large holdings, including some of those of the United Fruit subsidiary operating on the southern Pacific coast. Until this point United Fruit largely had escaped the reform, even though only about 14 percent of its almost 500,000 acres in Costa Rica was under cultivation at the start of the reform period.[3]

Costa Rica redistributed about 413,000 acres of land between 1962 and 1979, approximately 5.4 percent of all land in farms in 1973. The beneficiaries were 5,428 families, three-quarters of whom received their grants between 1975 and 1979. However, at the end of this period Costa Rica still had over 44,000 landless rural families and more than 18,000 land-poor families (Seligson 1984:34). Although agrarian reform in Costa Rica at this point had failed to keep pace with the growing need (and has done no better since), the results for those fortunate enough to have benefited should not be overlooked. Reform beneficiaries produce basic food crops with yields above the national averages; are satisfied with the progress they have made; participate at above national rates in both conventional political activities and cooperative activities; and compared to landless peasants are more trusting of government, more positively oriented toward the future, and more efficacious (Seligson 1980a:136–144; 1984:35–43).

When agrarian reform became a policy concern in Costa Rica, most of the existing farms had no titles, including up to 91 percent of those in remote areas (Sáenz and Knight 1971:1–7).[4] To address this insecurity, an ambitious land-titling program was undertaken, with much of the ex-

pense underwritten by loans from the United States. The Costa Rican titling program benefited 24,510 families by 1979. When this land is added
to that which was distributed by the government, the total area titled
equaled about one-quarter of the amount in farms in 1973. Coming into
the 1990s, though, about 60 percent of farms still lacked titles, creating frequent competing ownership claims (World Bank 1993a:10). Although titling programs do not address the fundamental problem of structural inequality and can in fact exacerbate it (by titling large properties), the
Costa Rican program has had positive benefits, as title recipients are more
likely to receive bank credits and technical assistance and to plant permanent crops (Seligson 1982:52–53).

Crisis and Recovery

The more conservative presidential candidate won in the 1978 election;
by the time the PLN returned to power in 1982 (and again in 1986), severe
financial crisis limited the country's ability to pursue its model of land redistribution through full compensation. The economy was on the brink of
collapse by 1982 because of rising oil prices, worldwide recession, satu-
rated export markets, and economic mismanagement. The crisis was then
compounded by the subsequent structural adjustment program mandated by international lenders and the resulting deepening of the local recession (Edelman 1985). Between 1980 and 1982, the terms of trade
dropped by 25 percent (largely coffee and bananas); the economy contracted by 11 percent; real wages fell by 27 percent and per capita income
by 14 percent; inflation climbed to over 90 percent; and the share of the
population below the poverty line, which is disproportionately high in
rural areas, jumped by 60 percent (Morley 1995:134–135). Rural unemployment and landlessness were further compounded in 1985 when
United Brands decided to close its Pacific coast banana operations, claim-
ing that following a long strike it could no longer compete successfully
with producers elsewhere (*Post*, January 16, 1985:15; also see Morsink-
Villalobos and Simpson 1980).

    In response to this threat to their economic security, peasant organiza-
tional activity increased, including a growing union movement. Especially important was the National Union of Small Agriculturists (UPA),
which by 1985 reached a membership of 16,000, more than double that of
any other rural union. After a period of petitions and demonstrations, the
union moved to highway blockages as an effective means of gaining the
government's attention and sometimes its positive action. On occasion it
also sponsored sizable land invasions (Anderson 1994:75–80, 101–106). As
a consequence of such assertive actions, by the mid-1980s many government officials and private observers portrayed the rural situation in Costa

Rica as "explosive" *(Libertad* 1985:4; *La Nacion* 1983:2a, 1984b:4a; *La Repúb-lica* 1983:21).

However, the government demonstrated a willingness to negotiate with union leaders and to concede to some of their demands. The leaders themselves became less confrontational (Anderson 1994:78). The resumption of economic growth certainly facilitated accommodation. Important as well was a huge jump in economic assistance from the United States, an increase directly related to President Reagan's geopolitical concerns, given Costa Rica's northern border with Nicaragua. Total U.S. assistance in 1983 equaled about 10 percent of Costa Rica's GDP, making it the recipient of the second highest per capita level of U.S. aid in the world for the next few years (Edelman 1985).

The PLN administration of President Luís Monge (1982–1986) did attempt to make good on its campaign slogan of "return to the land." Monge was aided by a new reform law, passed just before he assumed office, that increased the agrarian reform agency's revenues from tax collections. In his first fifteen months, the government acquired ninety farms (only one through expropriation) totaling about 90,000 acres and obtained options for sale to another 50,000 acres. This land was distributed to almost 5,000 families *(La Nacion* 1984a:16a). In the decade that followed, the government obtained another 75,000 acres for redistribution (Segura Bonilla et al. 1996:annex 6). Much of the land redistributed in the 1980s was in the northern zone, an area then still sparsely settled and therefore a worry to U.S. officials and some Costa Ricans as the war against Nicaragua escalated. The point is often made that for agrarian reform to succeed, recipients must get ample support in addition to land. That was certainly the case in this zone, as infrastructure (roads, electricity, schools, and even a USAID-financed ecolodge) soon followed.

As a consequence of this growth and policy responsiveness, Costa Rica was one of only four Latin American countries to reduce its poverty rate as well as to improve its distribution of income in the 1980s. The poverty rate dropped from the heights reached during the recession of the early 1980s and by 1989 had fallen below where it had been at the beginning of the period, even though per capita income had yet to regain its 1981 level. One reason for this rare accomplishment was the government's commitment to increasing the minimum wage as economic growth renewed. A second is that much of this growth was in agriculture, the sector of the economy that disproportionately employs the poor. As a result, when agricultural production expanded, so, too, did the wages of agricultural workers, thereby shrinking poverty in Costa Rica and the living standard gap between urban and rural areas (Morley 1995:115, 134–150, 184–188).

Labor shortages have recently become a growing problem for Costa Rican agriculture. In the early 1990s, for example, 15 to 20 percent of the coffee crop was not harvested because of worker shortages. At the time about one-third of agricultural workers were Nicaraguans escaping from the 60 percent unemployment at home. By 1997 only about a quarter of the coffee pickers were estimated to be Costa Rican and in the sugarcane fields only 10 percent. Government officials estimated Nicaraguans in the country to equal about 16 percent of the Costa Rican population and up to 30 percent of the economically active population. These figures indicate economic success for Costa Rica: Other sectors of the economy are growing rapidly enough and with more attractive living conditions to draw workers away from agriculture, even though agricultural wages have been increasing, too. However, the presence of tens of thousands of Nicaraguans desperate for work suppresses agricultural wages. Labor leaders charge that Nicaraguans often are paid below the minimum wage, with no benefits, and harassed into silence (*NotiSur*, February 10, 1995; *Tico Times*, October 1, 1993:6 and January 24, 1997:22).

Sustainable Development

Costa Rica once was blanketed by some of the world's most biologically rich forests, but deforestation, especially since about 1950, has left the country with few large blocks of forested land.[5] Indeed, Costa Rica suffered in some recent years from perhaps the highest deforestation rate in the world. Today forests cover only about a quarter of Costa Rica. With the frontier virtually gone, deforestation rates have declined, yet the less visible process of forest degradation continues at an alarming pace. Because much of the deforested land is not appropriate for agriculture, it is now degraded pasture. By one authoritative account, over one-half of the land cleared between 1966 and 1989 was appropriate only for forest (World Bank 1993a:3).

At the same time that the trees have been falling, Costa Rica has moved to protect its environment with one of the most ambitious systems of national parks and reserves in the world relative to population and area. Twelve percent of the country is under absolute (legal) protection in national parks and biological reserves, with another 15 percent of the country tightly regulated through different types of protected zones, but in which almost all of the land is privately owned. Actual conservation on the ground, however, is constrained by tight state resources and intense pressures on the land from banana, cattle, and timber enterprises and from a steadily expanding population.

Meeting the material needs of this population is as central to the concept of sustainable development as is the protection of the environment. This is well stated in the most common definition of the term, which comes from the 1987 World (Bruntland) Commission report, *Our Common*

Future: Sustainable development, it says, is "development that meets the needs of the present without compromising the ability of future generations to meet their own needs" (quoted in Weaver et al. 1997:34). The remainder of this chapter explores the environmental impacts of traditional land use practices and recent efforts in Costa Rica at building a more sustainable path of development.

Traditional Land Use Practices

Public policy until recently encouraged the conversion of forests to agricultural use through subsidies for various crops, such as protected prices, exemptions for input duties, and especially through credit policies. Deforestation has clearly been driven by the demand for more agricultural land rather than for timber. Indeed, up to 86 percent of cut timber from 1955 to 1973 either was burned or left to rot on site (Ashe 1978). Most forests were cleared for cattle grazing, which requires large extensions of land to be profitable. Generous tax credits and low interest loans granted irrespective of land capability or tenure and often subsidized by foreign agencies provided a strong stimulus for clearing land for cattle, as discussed in Chapter 3. Although the level of livestock credit has declined in recent years, it still represented 25 percent of all agricultural credit in Costa Rica in 1989 yet contributed only 10 percent to agricultural GDP (World Bank 1993a:14); by this point pastures covered about 47 percent of the national territory (Segura Bonilla et al. 1996:14).

In recent years banana expansion has been a bigger threat to forests than have cattle. This has been most true in the northern Atlantic lowlands, where thousands of acres of forest have been leveled to make way for new banana fields, in some cases right up to protected areas of great biological importance. Traditional banana cultivation methods also have been targeted for their adverse environmental consequences, ranging from heavy pesticide use to excessive waste production. For every ton of bananas produced in the early 1990s, over twice as much garbage was produced, almost half of which was nonbiodegradable. Other key crops are also major sources of pollution. In the drainage basin for the central plateau where most Costa Ricans live, 68 percent of the organic pollution in the mid-1980s came from coffee processing. Similarly, the country's largest orange concentrate plant is charged with polluting the local water supply. Recently, though, major cleanup efforts have been made in each area, with notably positive results concerning coffee-processing wastes (*Tico Times*, December 13, 1991; May 26 and July 7, 1995; July 11, 1997).

Deforestation in Costa Rica until recent years was constrained by neither law nor custom. The long history of expansion into virgin areas led Costa Ricans to perceive an abundant, almost limitless frontier; to develop a wasteful mentality toward soils, forests, and other resources; and to utilize slash-and-burn practices with little concern for conservation (Augelli 1987). Forestlands were considered worthless on the frontier. Holders of uncleared land paid higher taxes than those with cleared land. Needless to say, the larger biological services of forests, from the protection of soil and water quality to carbon sequestration, went largely unrecognized.

On the Costa Rican frontier, settlers generally occupied land by squatting. According to Spanish legal code, a settler could acquire land by peacefully and continuously occupying the land for at least ten years, after which the squatter could petition the Crown for a title. Throughout Latin America squatters demonstrate such peaceful and continuous possession by clearing, or "improving," the land. This practice was institutionalized in Costa Rica in 1941 with passage of a law that permitted possession of up to 741 acres on the frontier, as long as the occupant cleared at least half of the land and maintained cattle at the rate of one for every 12.4 acres. Such improvements yielded landholders possessory rights that they could sell and use as a basis for obtaining titles; most frontier settlers in the past, however, failed to register. Although the 1969 forestry law prohibited further spontaneous settlements, enforcement proved difficult in remote areas.

Privately owned lands throughout the country also have been the prey of squatters, especially in remote areas. Land-hungry peasants view forested land as "unused" land too inviting to ignore. The frontier culture reinforces a belief that they can take possession through their own hard work. Even when the owner can demonstrate satisfactorily to the courts possession of a legal title, the owner must reimburse the squatter for the "improvements" (i.e., forest destruction), including wages. This vulnerability discourages some landowners from maintaining forest stands or from reforesting previously cleared areas. Tenure insecurity often leads to deforestation. Landholders cannot be sure that they will not be evicted from the land before they can reap returns from it. So they clear the forest quickly to establish good-faith possession. The cattle that then usually replace crops on the degraded soil serve as collateral for bank loans.

An important example of these forces is the Osa Peninsula in the southwest corner of the country, which contains the largest remaining rain forest on the Central American Pacific coast. The Golfo Dulce Forest Reserve covers about 40 percent of the peninsula, serving as a buffer around Corcovado National Park. However, approximately one-third of the reserve's forest cover had been cut by the beginning of the 1990s, almost all in recent years. The typical survival strategy of the 8,000 residents of the reserve has consisted of selling timber and then using the cleared land for crops and cattle. Yet most of the reserve lands are suited for neither because of their steep slopes, fragile soils, and frequent precipitation. Heavy tropical rains pour down logging roads, skid trails, and cattle paths, washing away the soils and silting rivers. After two to three years of farming, the yields fall to such low levels that the farmer must clear new land once again.

Toward Environmental Protection

In the face of the rapid disappearance of its forests, the Costa Rican government launched a multifaceted approach. First, it created the impressive system of national parks beginning in 1969. Second, it established a complex regulatory framework governing forestry on privately owned lands through the forest law of 1969 and subsequent revisions. Third, it provided financial incentives for reforestation and later natural forest management. At some point in the 1980s, the rate of deforestation slowed (in part, though, because there were few accessible forests left to convert to agriculture). The regulatory framework undoubtedly also played a part in this partial success.

Under the new regulations, all tree cutting in Costa Rica requires a permit from the government. Before forested land can be cleared for agriculture, a technical study must prove that such land use is suitable. Even when the cutting is to be selective within a natural forest, the landholder must obtain a permit and pay a tax. In fact, a precondition for issuance of a permit in the latter case has been the approval of a management plan, which must be prepared by a forester registered with the government. The intent of these requirements is to ensure sustainable forestry and to protect landholders from squatters, since filing a management plan demonstrates active use of the land. However, the Costa Rican government—and especially its field personnel—have not had the resources or the requisite knowledge to provide the supervision required by this approach, and field personnel have been vulnerable to corruption.

Initiated in 1979, the more important incentives the Costa Rican government offered to maintain an adequate forest cover included income tax deductions, subsidized credit, and transferable bonds. The incentives worked: Close to 100,000 acres were reforested in the following thirteen years. Forced by a structural adjustment program to cut back public-sector spending, the government ended all of these reforestation incentives in 1995, with the exception of one program targeted to smallholders. Fortunately, timber prices have increased enough in recent years to make reforestation without subsidies profitable for at least largeholders.

How to best protect the remaining blocks of forests outside of the national parks has been the subject of much discussion in Costa Rica in recent years. Some emphasize these forests' importance for values other than forestry products (e.g., biodiversity, water quality, carbon sequestration, etc.). Others who instead stress forestry production are divided between those most interested in maximizing the productiveness of the sector as a whole (usually more oriented to the needs of larger producers) and those more interested in forestry as one means of creating adequate living standards for smallholders.

It has been a challenging time for those who seek forest protection through state regulation. Annual public deficits, growing domestic public debt, and monstrous international debts make it difficult to imagine the financing necessary for major statist approaches. Besides, key sources of international financing (i.e., the United States, World Bank, and Inter-American Development Bank) have conditioned assistance on scaling back the scope of the state.[6]

After much debate through the first half of the decade, in 1996 a new forestry law was passed, representing a compromise between conservationists and production-oriented groups and between larger producers and smallholders. The most important features of the law establish mechanisms for the participation of stakeholders in the forestry policymaking process and for the creation and distribution of subsidies for forest cover preservation. The subsidies are critical, since the law also prohibits any further conversion of private forested land to agricultural use (including plantations).

These forests are of incalculable value not just to Costa Rica but also to the global community. In the end, some believe this wider worth might be the key to their preservation. The financial return landholders get when they sell forest products does not include payment for the other benefits the forest provides, such as watershed and biodiversity preservation, carbon sequestration, and aesthetic values. Indeed, one study estimates that in the fullest measure of the value of Costa Rican forests, about 70 percent of that value accrues to the global community (World Bank 1993a:3–6; Kishor and Constantino 1994). It then follows, some argue, that up to 70 percent of the subsidy for sustainable forest management should come from the global community. Currently a number of carbon sequestration projects are being organized in Costa Rica, following the UN Framework Convention on Climate Change and a joint implementation agreement with the United States, but most of them await international investors. The major exception is the CARFIX carbon sequestration program, which provides annual payments to landowners participating in a sustainable forest management project adjacent to a major national park.[7]

In summary, the absence of a forest stewardship culture in traditional Costa Rica should be no surprise given that the once omnipresent forests were a barrier to economic activity (i.e., agriculture) rather than a source of economic value, just as was the case in the United States as it expanded to the west. Now the environmental awareness of Costa Ricans is growing, especially in urban areas but increasingly in the countryside as well. This normative change is a response to rapid deforestation and other environmental degradations and in part the consequent increasing material value of the remaining forests and other natural resources. The resulting shift in government policy has been substantial; whether it has been sufficient remains to be seen.

Contemporary Challenges

The challenge of sustainable development, though, is not just biological conservation but enhanced living standards for the human population. Significant contributors to this model of development include income from the preservation of forests, agriculture, and nonagricultural employment.

Much of the deforested land in Costa Rica, as previously indicated, cannot support sustainable agriculture because, for example, slopes are too steep. In these cases conservation and long-term economic values are congruent. The need, then, is to increase the economic value of forests so that landholders do not clear them for short-term gain and to encourage regeneration where they have. There are now a variety of nongovernmental organizations as well as government agencies working to this end in Costa Rica. The hope is to find better markets and prices for forest products, whether they are sustainably harvested timber from primary or regenerated forests or nontimber products that can be cultivated among the trees, such as black pepper and vanilla.

The economic value of forests also has increased in recent years with the growth of tourism. In the 1990s Costa Rica boomed as a site for both beach tourism and ecotourism; in 1994 tourism became the country's leading earner of foreign exchange. Many of these visitors want to see tropical forests and "exotic" wildlife. Although much of the income from tourism is captured by affluent, including foreign, interests, tourism does provide greater demand for services and create new employment opportunities for local communities, as well as bolster government revenues. At the same time, ecotourism has its costs. Some of the leading natural attractions in Costa Rica are now jeopardized by too many visitors and their infrastructure requirements. Once-isolated communities have been transformed forever by tourism, and not always in desirable ways. Finally, most of the jobs that are created are low-paying and usually involve servicing the needs of far more affluent visitors who are not always sensitive to the feelings of a proud people.

The promotion of nontraditional agricultural exports also could play an important part in a sustainable development strategy, assuming ecologically sound land use practices (a big assumption). This would require policies that ensure that ample benefits flow to small farmers. Unfortunately, as Part 1 documents, NTAEs in Central America invariably have been associated with the increasing concentration of critical resources in rural society, as remains true in contemporary Costa Rica. The benefits of public policies intended to promote NTAEs have disproportionately gone to larger interests, whereas monies for programs meant to serve smaller farmers have been reduced. Subsidies to NTAEs are justified to promote a new dynamic sector of the economy; subsidies to smaller farmers are cut because they are seen as economically inefficient. NTAE supporters seek niches in the global economy where Costa Rica might have a comparative advantage; basic grain producers have been left to compete with U.S. agribusiness. During the 1980s USAID provided about $110 million to Costa Rica for projects related to NTAEs and at the same time successfully pressured the government to reduce subsidies to production for the domestic market (Honey 1994:181–196).

Basic grain producers have opposed these policies, sometimes in coordinated and aggressive actions such as highway blockades and public building occupations. The cut in price supports and credit for grain production along with increasing competition from U.S. growers have been primary factors in the decline in the number of grain producers; for example, the number of rice farmers shrunk to one-quarter its former size in the six years to 1988. It is important to note, though, that most of these benefits went to larger producers and often were substantial, so much in the case of rice production that at times the state absorbed all of the risk (Edelman 1992:303–314).

The large-scale protests by grain producers of the late 1980s have not been repeated in the 1990s; more notable have been protests from coffee producers over high taxes (*Update*, August 3 and August 12, 1988; *Tico Times*, January 27, 1995:15). Because of large fiscal deficits (and intense pressures from international lenders), recent Costa Rican administrations have been intransigent on the need to cut subsidies and services as well as on the need to preserve government revenues (*Chronicle*, July 6 and September 14, 1995).

Finally, sustainable development requires diversifying employment opportunities beyond agriculture to industry. Here Costa Rica, with its more educated workforce and political stability, has a competitive edge in the global economy over most other lesser-developed countries. In 1981, 21 percent of household heads in Costa Rica had at least a secondary school education; by 1992 the rate had grown to 35 percent (Morley 1995:188). Indeed, the Association of American Chambers of Commerce in Latin America gave Costa Rica its highest ranking in both 1995 and 1996 for the best-trained and most productive labor force, as well as in the latter year to its justice system for its ability to render impartial decisions. For such reasons, increasing numbers of advanced technology companies have located in the country, most notably Intel, which broke ground in April 1997 on a new plant that will produce one-third of all of its microprocessors and provide employment for about 2,000. Similarly, when Motorola announced the expansion of its manufacturing plant to include 500 additional employees, the ability of the Costa Rican labor force to assimilate new technologies was given as an important reason. With such successes, by the mid-1990s industrial exports had increased to 28 percent of the country's total, following agricultural products, which were 43 percent.[8]

Conclusion

Agrarian politics in Costa Rica differ from that of the rest of the region. Rural Costa Ricans have not demonstrated the same organizational strength as their counterparts in Honduras, for example, nor the same political power nor policy successes. They have not shown the combativeness of some of their counterparts in the other three countries. Neither have they had the same intensity of reason for such activities. Rural Costa Ricans did not experience on the same mass scale the land dispossessions suffered by Honduran peasants nor the horrendous repression of El Salvador, Guatemala, and Nicaragua. In addition, these political differences are due to numbers; the percentage of the overall economically active Costa Rican population that is employed in agriculture is half that of Honduras (28 percent in 1983 and falling to 22 percent in 1993, whereas Honduras remained constant at 54 percent).[9] Finally, agrarian groups in Costa Rica must compete with many well-organized interests and face a more institutionalized state, one that is more stable and complex and less personalistic and permeable than it has often been in other Central American countries.

Indeed, from the early days of the colonial period, Costa Rica has been different from the other societies of Central America. Less sharply and rigidly stratified and less repressive, Costa Rica has been in a better position to respond to the challenges and opportunities of the twentieth century, in particular those of recent decades. Today the average Costa Rican, especially in rural areas, lives in greater freedom and equality than counterparts elsewhere in the region and is healthier, better educated, and more affluent. Certainly Costa Rica is far from a paradise; serious poverty and inequality do remain. But in its context the country's accomplishments are considerable.

Notes

1. This sections draws on the following works: Barahona Riera (1980), Edelman (1992), Hall (1985), Riismandel (1972), Rowles (1985), Sáenz and Knight (1971), Salazar (1962), and Seligson (1980a).

2. See Barahona Riera (1980), Hall (1985:202–204), Rowles (1985:213), and Seligson (1980a:131–135; 1980b:83, 98; 1984:30–31).

3. One of the most important colonies started in the mid-1960s, Bataan, was on 25,900 acres of land purchased from United Fruit for $549,414. Because the land was a former abaca (fiber) plantation, the price included substantial infrastructure.

4. Clarifying landownership has been problematic. Costa Ricans could homestead up to 30 hectares of public domain land as late as 1939. Often, though, these same remote, unused lands had been granted by the state years earlier to other individuals. A 1942 law allowed such absentee landowners to exchange land settled by homesteaders for other public lands. Sáenz and Knight (1971:11, 32–33) cite one study that claimed that twenty landowners obtained 512,000 hectares of public domain lands through such exchanges.

5. Much of this section is based on annual field research from 1991 to 1997 with Robert Gottfried of the University of the South Economics Department, as well as the following sources: Augelli (1987), Boza (1993), Carriere (1991), Hartshorn et al. (1982), Hedstrom (1986), Jones (1992), Lehmann (1992), Lutz and Daly (1991), Porras and Villarreal (1985), Segura Bonilla et al. (1996), Solórzano et al. (1991), Tropical Science Center (1992), Umaña and Brandon (1992), and World Bank (1993a).

6. USAID was especially heavy-handed with its pressure in Costa Rica during the 1980s, as were other elements of the U.S. government, in efforts to promote neoliberal economic reforms and to induce Costa Rican support for the U.S. war against Nicaragua (Honey 1994). By the 1990s little USAID financial assistance remained, except in the environmental area.

7. CARFIX receives offset payments from Wachovia Timberland Investment Management of Atlanta to support programs run by the Costa Rican NGO FUNDECOR in Braulio Carrillo National Park and its surrounding buffer zone.

8. Costa Rica Trade and Investment Center (CINDE), various press releases at <http://www.cinde.or.cr>.

9. See the UNFAO database at <http://www.fao.org>.

Chapter Ten

Conclusion: Land, Power, and Poverty

This study has argued that to understand properly the challenges facing agrarian society in contemporary Central America, one must view political dynamics in their socioeconomic context and from a historical perspective. Accordingly, the scope of this investigation has been broad, ranging from export development in colonial days to labor systems in the nineteenth century, from religiously inspired development work in the 1970s and revolutionary and counterrevolutionary armies in the 1980s to peacemaking in the 1990s. The purpose of this final chapter is to summarize the earlier arguments and to extend their conclusions. The following areas are examined: the impact of the major agrarian transformations, the sources of peasant mobilization, the responses by the region's governments, and the role of the United States.

Agrarian Transformations

A fundamental constraint that has continually plagued development-oriented Central American elites has been the inadequate size of domestic markets: There has been too little domestic demand to stimulate enough production to fuel rapid economic growth. A primary concern, then, has been to discover and develop exports for foreign markets. What elites have conveniently and consistently downplayed is the relationship between internal demand and social stratification. Colonial society was structured by a relatively few Spaniards dominating a much larger indigenous population for the purpose of extracting surplus for their own enrichment. The Indians, as conquered people, were the source of tribute and forced labor; they certainly were not copartners in the creation of a new society.

As decades and then centuries passed, new social groups arose, but society remained highly stratified. Consequently, elites continued to face the same dilemma: the establishment of healthy domestic markets would necessitate a change in the distribution and utilization of resources. Peasants would have to be allowed access to sufficient land and other resources to meet their needs and to produce surplus for their own disposal. Peasant labor then would no longer be so exploited through coercion, either legal or extralegal. In short, the system of domination implanted at the time of the conquest and reinforced across the succeeding centuries would have to be dismantled in order for robust domestic markets to evolve.

Production for export has offered elites a way around their dilemma, requiring neither social upheaval nor the diminution of elite privilege. Even better, it can be justified as in the best interest of society. The profits made from selling indigo, coffee, bananas, cotton, sugar, beef, or snow peas overseas could be plowed back into the economy, promoting economic development from which all groups could benefit. Self-interest, then, is reinforced by capitalist ideology and the doctrine of comparative advantage. The agro-export development model has appealed to reformist groups as well. Although they desire viable programs of widespread social reform, they usually lack the necessary power. When in office, they have therefore faced many of the same economic constraints as have elites.

Beyond furthering elite interests, though, the results of the agro-export development model in such stratified societies have been mixed. On the one hand, exports and economies have expanded and diversified. Incomes have grown not only for elites but also within the middle sectors and for some of the peasantry. On the other hand, the material and psychological interests of many rural people have been harmed—often severely—by the periodic export-fueled agrarian transformations, including that of the postwar period. Through physical force and market forces, elites have expropriated land and labor in order to further their objectives. The quantitative data provided in this study uphold the numerous descriptive reports from and about the region. The share of land devoted to export crops increased relative to that used for food crops in each country through the 1970s and continuing up to the present in Costa Rica, Guatemala, and Honduras. Consequently, per capita domestic production of basic foods has declined throughout the region (with the mixed exception of El Salvador), aggravating already serious malnutrition problems. As population has grown and land pressures intensified, peasants have been forced off their land. Because sufficient new employment opportunities have not been generated, both landlessness and unemployment have risen in rural areas, as have the ranks of the land-poor and the underemployed.

These findings do not contest the importance for countries with small economies to discover and expand nontraditional exports or the viability of the agro-export development model itself. The focus here is narrower: the consequences of agro-export development for countries with highly stratified agrarian systems.[1] When resources—be they land, capital, technology, knowledge, or credit—are highly concentrated, new economic opportunities invariably will be absorbed into these existing patterns rather than transform them. Central America in recent decades provides numerous examples of this basic social dynamic.

Because Central American agrarian elites across the centuries have consistently relied on coercion to obtain the land and labor necessary to pursue their objectives, their strategy could more accurately be termed "the repressive agro-export development model." Although important political changes had occurred in each country, elites were able as late as the 1970s to prevent innovations that would restructure their systems of domination. There were, of course, important variations among countries, depending on such factors as the nature of the indigenous civilizations at the time of the conquest, topography, climate, location, and the availability of land, labor, and capital. As a result, the most exploitive and repressive systems were created in Guatemala and El Salvador, followed by Nicaragua and then Honduras, with Costa Rica the least so.[2]

Peasant Mobilization

The first notable expression of peasant discontent in the postwar period occurred in Guatemala as the system of rural control loosened under the progressive governments of 1944–1954. Next, a substantial percentage of the peasantry was organized in Honduras by the late 1960s, and they continued to play a major role through the middle of the next decade. Indeed, the 1970s witnessed the awakening of the peasantry as a political force throughout the region. Rejecting submissiveness, increasing numbers of rural people asserted their interests through cooperatives, unions and other peasant organizations, political parties, and finally, revolutionary armies.

Three types of factors influence peasant mobilization. First, agrarian transformations erode economic security, upset traditional social relations, and weaken traditional value systems. Second, political organizers from outside of peasant communities provide needed sources of economic assistance, protection, organizational expertise, and new value systems. Third, the response of the state, especially the mix it chooses between reform and repression, has decisive consequences for the scope and intensity of mobilization.[3]

Each of these factors has been important in contemporary Central America. Peasants, especially indigenous communities, resisted the earlier agrarian transformations in the region, but in the end with little success. Then, as in the present period, the immediate cause of their resistance was the attack on their economic security. What is distinctive about the contemporary period is the critical role of the political factors, that is, the activities of outside organizers and government policies.

Among the most significant of the new political forces in rural Central America have been the religious workers. With easier access and greater legitimacy than other actors because of shared religious beliefs (and, in the case of priests, status), Catholic Church workers in each country have played a central role in peasant mobilization. Throughout the region, their efforts eroded the values and power relationships that perpetuated peasants' passivity. Whether those efforts were directly religious, socioeconomic, or political, they often served to foster the transformation of attitudes from fatalist to activist and to create new organizations that nurtured this transformation and facilitated its expression. Supported by this process, peasants took the lead in asserting their rights to a better life, participating in demonstrations, marches, and land invasions.

The efforts of church people were reinforced by those of secular actors. In Guatemala during the reform period of the 1950s, radical organizers and political party activists encouraged peasant organization. Similar actors in the 1970s were joined by development workers from other countries, often the United States. Urban leftists were also active during the 1970s and 1980s in the countryside of the other four nations. Especially prominent were the roles played in El Salvador by organizers from the popular organizations and in Nicaragua by the Sandinistas. Like the church workers, the secular activists brought a message and support that served to undermine traditional hierarchical relations and to facilitate popular organization. When combined with the subsistence crisis facing many rural people, these efforts led to the peasants' mobilization to defend and improve their position. The end results, however, were heavily dependent on the nature of each government's response to this popular threat to the status quo.

The World Conference on Agrarian Reform and Rural Development held in 1979 emphasized the importance of the participation of the rural poor to successful rural development (UNFAO 1992). The subjects of policy must be active in its formulation both in order to get policy right and to legitimate it to those who will be affected by it. However, organizations that sustain popular participation are critical not just for the articulation of interests but also for the defense of interests. No better example is provided than contemporary Nicaragua, where one of the major accomplishments of the revolution has been the enduring mobilization of the peasants, who forced changes in the agrarian policies of the last three administrations, ranging from the far left to the center-right to the right of the political spectrum. Also worthy of note is that the most assertive peasant organizations in the region today are in the three most repressive countries of the past, where such activities used to run the risk of death. The creation of a safer space for peasant political participation in El Salvador, Guatemala, and Nicaragua is one of the most significant benefits of the peace processes of the 1990s.

The Government Response

The government reaction to peasant mobilization and organization in postwar Central America ranges across the full spectrum of possibilities. In the traditional agrarian structure, the passivity of the peasantry was maintained through patron-client relationships and the submissive value systems they perpetuated. Power was concentrated and peasants had few alternatives, if any. Behind this stratified network stood the state. Should its coercive capability be required, it was ready to harass and intimidate potential rural leaders. Until recent decades, however, such preventative action was required only infrequently. Since then the Honduran state has been the most characteristic of this stance (except for the late 1960s and early 1970s). For most of the 1960s, peasant mobilization was discouraged through harassment and jailings. From the mid-1970s, Honduran administrations had to accept the existence of a well-organized peasantry, but the government has been able to hamper its activities by such tactics as the repeated jailings of peasant leaders in the 1980s. Fortunately, Honduran officials did not fall to the level of relying on the consistent use of torture and murder to enforce their will, as did some other regimes.

Governments and private groups were willing to move beyond preventative intimidation to the use of widespread violence in El Salvador, Guatemala, and Nicaragua in order to protect their interests. Repression, however, has not always worked as intended. Rather than beating the population back into submissiveness, repression in each country during the 1970s provoked further popular resistance. The reliance on unjustified violence stiffened the resolve of many people who were already in opposition to the regime and delegitimized it for numerous others, many of whom were politicized and radicalized as a result. When the villages and families of peasants were the victims of repression, many of the survivors moved into opposition out of rage and in self-defense.

As terrible as it was, at this stage the repression was not sufficient to protect the regimes of these three countries. Consequently, the governments escalated the violence, making it more indiscriminate and systematic. The application of widespread repression from 1980 to 1983 in El Salvador and to 1984 in Guatemala accomplished, for a time, its purpose. Although the revolutionary forces continued their struggles in both countries, the tens of thousands of murders in each were sufficient to destroy popular organizations and to restore fear and passivity to much of the countryside. In Nicaragua, by contrast, Somoza's willingness even to destroy parts of the nation's cities with his air force was not sufficient to save his regime. Although his forces killed on levels approaching those of the other two countries, his personalistic dictatorship had alienated all sectors of society and did not have the institutional capacity to implement state terrorism on the same systematic level.

At other times governments in Central America have promoted peasant mobilization and organization. The foremost examples are the active support given by the Arbenz government in Guatemala and especially the Sandinistas in Nicaragua. With this support, rural people felt free to assert their interests. Peasant organizations proliferated, and their memberships skyrocketed. Other governments have been permissive, especially in Costa Rica, where peasant mobilization is viewed favorably, but have offered little active support. Still other administrations are closer to neutral in their position, neither promoting nor inhibiting peasant organization. This is the stance that predominates through the region today; given recent history, this must be regarded as a positive development.

The most important factors that explain the stance a government will assume have been the level of perceived threat from popular mobilization, the degree of repression inherent in the agrarian system, and constraints on resources.[4] The scope of peasant mobilization is a major constituent of the perception of threat, but this reaction is conditioned by other elements as well. Particularly likely to heighten the elites' apprehension is when peasant mobilization is assisted by regime opponents, especially revolutionary forces. The extent to which regime and opponents are internationally isolated or supported also has played a role in the past.

Second, the cumulative impact of the earlier agrarian transformations resulted in more repressive systems in Guatemala, El Salvador, and to a lesser extent Nicaragua for reasons discussed throughout this study, such as the availability of exportable crops, land, labor, and capital. Consequently, these systems already had built into them a reliance on coercion and a disposition toward settling conflict through repression. Any level of peasant mobilization would thus be a greater danger to such a system than would a comparable level in Costa Rica or Honduras, and these societies also had a better-developed coercive capacity to deal with threats.

Finally, governments have varied in their access to resources with which to meet peasants' demands, especially the primary demand for land. Land distribution was facilitated in Guatemala in the 1950s and in

Honduras and Costa Rica up to the mid-1970s by the availability of public lands. Similarly, the early stages of the Sandinista reform were made easier by the flight of Somoza and his supporters, which created vast areas of public lands that could be used for revolutionary objectives at relatively low cost. Large tracts of unused or underused private lands have also made it easier to meet demands, especially if the acreage was owned by multinational corporations. Such foreign-owned lands were most plentiful, again, in Guatemala during the Arbenz reform and in Honduras and Costa Rica; underutilized domestically owned lands were important for the reforms in Guatemala and Nicaragua.

Taken together, these factors meant that Costa Rica and Honduras generally had less repressive structures to begin with as well as fewer constraints on the ability of committed governments to meet peasants' demands for land. Their regimes have been sufficiently responsive to hold rural discontent below the level that would represent a serious threat to the maintenance of the system. Whether this will remain true for Honduras, though, is one of the most challenging questions.

In Guatemala in the 1950s, the underutilized lands of the United Fruit Company and of domestic *latifundistas,* together with the national farms, were sufficient to permit a major redistribution without an attack on large-scale commercial agriculture. But by the 1970s the further expansion of commercial agriculture and population growth in Guatemala and El Salvador had created land pressures that intensified elite opposition to any serious consideration of agrarian reform or other needs of the peasantry. Given that both countries' systems were based on highly exploitive labor arrangements, mounting land pressures heightened the probability that peasant mobilization would be experienced as an intolerable threat to the status quo.

In Nicaragua, by contrast, land pressures were not as acute, nor was the labor system relatively as coercive. Furthermore, the Somoza dynasty had preempted the landowning class from exercising state power. These are some of the reasons the agrarian bourgeoisie in Nicaragua did not at first view the country's popular mobilization as the kind of threat it represented to their counterparts in Guatemala and El Salvador. Consequently, an antidictator alliance uniting all classes could form, encouraging revolutionary success.[5]

These variations in constraints are important to keep in mind when comparing the agrarian reforms of the five countries. As Table 10.1 indicates, the most far-reaching of the Central American reforms clearly has been the Nicaraguan. When workers on state farms are included among its beneficiaries, as they are in this table, then the percentage of the rural population reached by the reform was greatest in Nicaragua, followed by Guatemala under Arbenz, and then by El Salvador, Honduras, and Costa

TABLE 10.1   Central America: A Comparison of Agrarian Reform Programs

	Years Covered	Cropped Land[a] per Rural Person	Beneficiaries[b] as % of Rural Population	Land Distributed[c] Total Area	Land Distributed[c] As % of Farmland
Costa Rica	1962–1984	.37	1.1	637	13
El Salvador	1980–1984	.34	3.3	789	24
Guatemala	1952–1954	.44	4.6	1,800	27
Honduras	1962–1984	.94	2.2	725	6
Nicaragua	1979–1988	1.15	11.8	5,050	41

[a]Cropped land is arable land plus land under permanent crops for 1978 in hectares per person in rural areas. Calculated from IADS 1981:17.

[b]Beneficiaries are total number of recipients of distributed land in years covered; includes national lands as well as expropriated lands. Nicaragua includes workers on state farms (about 46 percent of total). With family members, true percentage of beneficiaries is much greater.

[c]Land distributed is total area in thousands of acres. Farmland combines 1980 estimates of arable land, land permanently under cultivation, and permanent pastureland from UNECLA 1983:601. Figures for distributed land (and beneficiaries) vary from year to year as reform lands are abandoned or state farms are redistributed to individuals (with the latter overstating the percentage of land redistributed in Nicaragua as that land gets double-counted).

SOURCES: For Costa Rica, *La Nación* 1984a:16a; Seligson 1984:34; for El Salvador, Reinhardt 1986:table 3; for Guatemala, Aybar de Soto 1978:181, 210; for Honduras, Morris 1984:101; Ruhl 1985:70; for Nicaragua, Enríquez 1991:table 4.1; Reinhardt 1986:table 3.

Rica. Because beneficiaries invariably have families, the reform sector is substantially larger than this percentage indicates; a multiplication factor of five or six people is commonly used. For the percentage of farmland distributed, the rankings are the same except for a reversal between Costa Rica and Honduras at the low end of the scale.[6]

There are important differences in the politics of the three major agrarian reforms in Central America. The Arbenz reform in Guatemala was facilitated by the availability of extensive unused lands on private and foreign-owned estates as well as by the government-operated national farms. As a result, it could be implemented without attacking productive commercial farms. But although domestic politics made the expropriation of foreign-owned lands relatively easier, United Fruit's ability to propagandize in the United States was a critical factor, leading to the overthrow of the Arbenz government and the undoing of the reform.

Only in El Salvador and Nicaragua, then, have large, productive commercial farms represented a substantial proportion of the lands redistributed—and in each case, under unique circumstances. Nicaragua is unique not only because of its revolutionary process but also because the prerevolutionary concentration of land in the hands of the Somoza family and a small number of its supporters allowed a revolutionary regime to redistribute land in its first years without attacking the agrarian bourgeoisie or having to face the problematic issue of compensation. In El Salvador, by contrast, meaningful reform was not possible without confronting the bourgeoisie. What is often overlooked in the criticisms of the Salvadoran reform is that it is the only case in Central America of the expropriation of a substantial number of large commercial farms in productive operation at the time.

The number of landless and land-poor peasants in the region increases constantly, as do the ranks of the rural unemployed and underemployed. Unfortunately, as the need for land redistribution has grown, so, too, has its difficulty. The "easiest" lands to expropriate and/or distribute—accessible public property and unused lands on large estates—are essentially gone. The conditions that gave rise to the peasant demands and movements discussed in this study will continue into the future, as, undoubtedly, will rural tensions and conflicts. The difficulties in the 1990s of meeting the land needs of the former combatants in El Salvador and Nicaragua are good indicators of the troubles that lie ahead.

Land redistribution in the past could be justified on grounds of both productivity gains and poverty alleviation. As commercial enterprises replace inefficient haciendas, however, it is less clear whether breaking largeholdings into multiple family farms leads to greater production. There are still, though, powerful arguments for land redistribution as a measure for combating rural poverty and inequality. Poverty can be alleviated by other broad-based development policies as well, and to be fully successful land redistribution must be accompanied by supportive credit and technical assistance programs. Nonetheless, agrarian reform remains the best approach for reducing rural poverty in such stratified societies as those in Central America. The problem with agrarian reform is not its appropriateness but rather the amount of political will and power required.[7]

The United States and Agrarian Reform

The case material presented in Part 2 indicates that U.S. policy toward the agrarian reforms of Central America in the postwar period has been a critical determinant of their fate. The stance of the United States has been the outcome of policymakers' perceptions of three factors; in order of increasing importance, these are (1) the nature of the reform itself, (2) the effect of the reform on the economic interests of U.S. corporations, and (3) the relationship of the reform to U.S. security concerns.

The agrarian reforms described in this study range from minor distributive programs with limited scope and few beneficiaries, such as colonization projects, to major land redistributions that adversely affect major economic actors and benefit large numbers of impoverished peasants. The distributive programs have been unproblematic for the United States; indeed, it has been the primary financial benefactor of many of them. They threaten neither vested economic interests nor the principle of private property, yet some of the needy are benefited and also, sponsors hope, immunized against the inducements of radical movements. The limitation of the distributive programs is that for the same reasons they are unproblematic, they are incapable of responding effectively to the growing issues of landlessness and near landlessness, as the case of Honduras so clearly demonstrates.

The redistributive programs have been a greater challenge to U.S. policymakers. The governments that implemented two of the three most thorough reforms incurred the enmity of the U.S. government and became the targets of U.S. counterrevolutionary efforts: Arbenz was overthrown in Guatemala and the Sandinista project severely damaged in Nicaragua. Neither this opposition nor U.S. support for the reform in El Salvador can be explained without reference to the other two factors, economic interests and security concerns.

For the most part, Central American agrarian reforms have not affected U.S. economic interests. Neither in Nicaragua nor in El Salvador did lands falling within the scope of the reforms include any notable holdings of North American companies. Nor in Costa Rica has reform seriously affected the sizable holdings of the fruit companies. However, the threat to the United Fruit/United Brands holdings in both Guatemala and Honduras was central to the demise of reform efforts in each country. Although it is questionable whether domestic forces would have allowed serious implementation of the 1962 Honduran reform, any such effort was precluded by successful United Fruit opposition. The company was also triumphant in its battle against the Guatemalan government in the early 1950s, though, as argued earlier, U.S. intervention in Guatemala is explicable in terms of the perceived communist threat, not direct economic motives. Nevertheless, it remains true that no agrarian reform that threatened serious harm to major U.S. economic interests has been successful in Central America.

This does not mean that lands owned by U.S. interests cannot be expropriated. In Honduras in 1975, United Brands lost 57,000 acres and Standard Fruit 84,000 acres to a government expropriation order. This action came at the peak of several years of increasing peasant mobilization, including growing numbers of land invasions and occupations. It is significant that the action was taken by a conservative military commander who had recently replaced a populist military leader. The expropriations were not presented as an attack on the fruit companies but rather as part of a package of moves intended to defuse an explosive situation. Furthermore, the fruit companies were at a point of extreme vulnerability; only months before, it had been disclosed that United Brands had bribed the previous government into reducing the banana export tax. A year later, when the director of the agrarian reform institute attempted further fruit company expropriations, his actions were overturned and he was forced out of office.

In the cases of the three redistributive land reforms, U.S. policy was a function of a more fundamental concern, the security of the United States as perceived by policymakers. The Arbenz government was attacked not because it was conducting an agrarian reform but because the nature of that reform reinforced the perception of top U.S. officials that Guatemala was falling to the communists. To the Reagan administration, the situation in Nicaragua was similarly "clear" from the beginning: The Sandinistas were communists and thus inherently a threat to the United States and the rest of Central America. Questions concerning the necessity or justice of the Nicaraguan reform were secondary, perhaps even irrelevant.

In El Salvador, in contrast, the United States was the sponsor of a reform that benefited about a quarter of the rural poor. This undertaking, unique for the United States in Central America, was also the result of security concerns. Both the Carter and Reagan administrations believed that the only hope of preventing the left from coming to power lay in preempting its issue of agrarian reform while giving firm support to a government of "the center."

An analysis of the Central American cases in light of the security interests of the United States leads, then, to the following set of conclusions. The fundamental determinant of policy toward agrarian reform in Central America is U.S. security interests as policymakers see them. Major redistributive agrarian reforms will be supported only when they are viewed as furthering the security interests of the United States; but this is an uncommon occurrence. If no major security interests are seen as relevant, then policy will be determined by the nature of the reform and by economic considerations.

In more general terms, the results of this study correspond to those of other analyses of U.S. policy toward Latin America. They are particularly congruent with Blasier's (1976) account of the U.S. response to revolutionary change, which explains U.S. reconciliation to two revolutions (those in Mexico and Bolivia) and opposition to two others (those in Guatemala and Cuba). In the first two cases, revolutionary leaders were willing to compromise with the United States; in the second pair, they were not. Washington in turn found that it could best advance its security interests (excluding from the hemisphere a great-power rival) by accommodating itself to revolutionary change in Mexico and Bolivia. In this context, the most interesting comparison is that of Bolivia with El Salvador.

In 1953 the Eisenhower administration reconciled itself to a progressive regime in Bolivia that had nationalized the tin mines and was conducting an extensive land reform. One of the crucial actors was the president's brother, Milton Eisenhower, who explained that "rapid peaceful social change is the only way to avert violent revolution in Bolivia" (quoted in Blasier 1976:133). The Bolivian government made major efforts to facilitate the perception that it was not only uninfluenced by communism but even a bulwark against such a threat. As a result of this accommodation, U.S. influence in Bolivia increased significantly, and the course of the revolution was moderated. Between 1952 and 1964, U.S. economic assistance to Bolivia averaged more per capita than that to any other country (Blasier 1976:144). However, Bolivia's position as the second lowest-ranking country in the Western Hemisphere in per capita GNP (after Haiti) remained unchanged until 1992, when Honduras and Nicaragua fell below it. Although it would be a mistake to overstate the comparison, U.S. motivations and policy approaches were similar in Bolivia and El Salvador. Perceived U.S. interests were protected more successfully than the quality of life was improved for impoverished Bolivians and Salvadorans.

The dilemma for advocates of major land redistribution in Central America is clear. Substantial redistributive programs attack the fundamental interests of powerful groups, which will use their power to oppose major reforms. The result will be considerable political conflict. Because compensation in cash at market value is not feasible for widespread expropriations, such reforms can be portrayed as attacks on the principle of private property. Consequently, their opponents can find receptive audiences in the United States for claims that the reforms are socialist in nature and harmful to economic development. The credibility of the opponents' case has been strengthened when they could point to self-identified Marxists in positions of power in Central America, such as Guatemala in the 1950s and Nicaragua in the 1980s.

The preeminent influence of anticommunism in U.S. policy toward the region constrained the possibilities in the past for major land redistribution. Therefore the demise of communism worldwide removes a substantial obstacle to progressive change in Central America. Furthermore, individual corporations have less ability now to influence U.S. policy than did United Fruit in the 1950s. For both reasons, it is possible to imagine a more open response by the United States to redistributive reforms in the future. Yet the countervailing factor cannot be overlooked: Any future redistribution would have to target productive commercial farms, unlike the easier target of the underutilized hacienda lands of the past.

Conclusion

Agrarian society in Central America today is less inequitable and repressive than it was just a few decades ago. Reform and its threat have eliminated many of the largest estates, especially those that do not utilize their land productively. Economic development has greatly reduced rural poverty in Costa Rica, and land redistributions in El Salvador, Honduras, and Nicaragua have benefited tens of thousands of peasant families in each country. Peasants, along with the rest of their fellow citizens, have been able to choose between meaningful alternatives in relatively free and fair elections since the mid-1980s. Nonetheless, unless agrarian society is transformed along more equitable lines, the number of people whose land, employment, and income are insufficient will continue to grow. Until such a transformation occurs, the contradictions of rural society will continue to generate political conflicts that at times will threaten the stability of societies and perhaps even that of the region.

However, the 1980s in Central America retaught a series of tragic lessons about social change. First, socioeconomic structures are hard to change. Second, they are especially hard to change in small countries when the beneficiaries of those structures enjoy the support (whatever the reasons) of a hegemonic great power. Third, the consequences of sociopolitical conflict are not an abstraction but are measured by the blood, tears, death, and anguish of real individuals—by the hundreds of thousands.

The price could have been even more. Amid the analysis of systems and states, the accomplishments of individuals can be lost. How much greater the tragedy would have been without the courageous work of human rights monitors, schoolteachers, priests and other church workers, agricultural advisers, democratic politicians, health workers, labor and peasant organizers, and thousands of others working under dangerous conditions. It is the continuing efforts of such individuals that create new opportunities for change in Central America. Their sacrifices, including the lives of many, represent one reason why more just outcomes are warranted.

Notes

1. FitzGerald (1991:3) makes the point well: The issue is not the agro-export model itself but "the social organisation of production and exchange involved." Also see Carter et al. (1996:34).

2. For more extended treatments of the importance of such factors for inter-country variations, see, among others, Chinchilla (1983), Gudmundson (1995), Stone (1983), and Vilas (1995).

3. The seminal discussions of the first factor are Paige (1975), Scott (1976), and Wolf (1969). Significant analyses of the second factor include Migdal (1974), Popkin (1979), Scott (1985), and Singelmann (1981). For the third factor, see Brockett (1993), McClintock (1984), Skocpol (1982), and Tilly (1978).

4. For a more complete consideration, see Brockett (1991a).

5. A good discussion along these lines is Midlarsky and Roberts (1985).

6. These results are for 1980 data on area for Guatemala. If 1950 data are used, the Arbenz reform distributed about 36 percent of farmland, very close to the Nicaraguan accomplishment (itself more likely to be overstated, as explained in note c of Table 10.1).

7. For relevant discussions, see Carter and Barham (1996), as well as de Janvry (1989), Dorner (1992), Thiesenhusen (1995), and Tomich et al. (1995).

References

Adams, Dale W., Douglas H. Graham, and J. D. Von Pischke (1984). *Undermining Rural Development with Cheap Credit.* Boulder, CO: Westview Press.

Adams, F. Gerard, and Jere R. Behrman (1982). *Commodity Exports and Economic Development.* Lexington, MA: Lexington Books.

Adams, Richard N., ed. (1957). *Political Changes in Guatemalan Indian Communities: A Symposium.* New Orleans: Middle American Research Institute.

_____ (1968–1969). "The Development of the Guatemalan Military." *Studies in Comparative International Development,* 4(5), 91–114.

_____ (1970). *Crucifixion by Power: Essays on Guatemalan National Social Structure, 1944–1966.* Austin: University of Texas Press.

Adelman, Irma (1980). "Income Distribution, Economic Development and Land Reform." *American Behavioral Scientist,* 23(3), 437–456.

Adelman, Irma, and Sherman Robinson (1978). *Income Distribution Policy in Developing Countries: A Case Study of Korea.* Stanford, CA: Stanford University Press.

Adler, John H., Eugene R. Schlesinger, and Ernest C. Olson (1952). *Public Finance and Economic Development in Guatemala.* Stanford, CA: Stanford University Press.

Aguilera Peralta, Gabriel (1979). "The Massacre at Panzós and Capitalist Development in Guatemala." *Monthly Review,* 31(7), 13–24.

Alas, Higinio (1982). *El Salvador: ¿Por qué la insurrección?* San José, Costa Rica: Permanent Secretariat of the Commission for the Defense of Human Rights in Central America.

Alexander, Robert J. (1974). *Agrarian Reform in Latin America.* New York: Macmillan.

Allen, Roy, Claudia Dodge, and Andrew Schmitz (1983). "Voluntary Export Restraints as Protection Policy: The U.S. Beef Cases." *American Journal of Agricultural Economics,* 65(2), 291–296.

América Indígena (1974). 43(2).

Americas Watch (1984). *Honduras: On the Brink. A Report on Human Rights Based on a Mission of Inquiry.* New York: Americas Watch, Lawyers Committee for International Human Rights, and Washington Office on Latin America.

_____ (1987). *Human Rights in Honduras: Central America's "Sideshow."* New York: Americas Watch.

_____ (1988a). *Closing the Space: Human Rights in Guatemala, May 1987–October 1988.* New York: Americas Watch.

_____ (1988b). *Nightmare Revisited 1987–88.* New York: Americas Watch.

_____ (1991). *El Salvador's Decade of Terror: Human Rights Since the Assassination of Archbishop Romero*. New Haven, CT: Yale University Press.

Americas Watch Committee [AWC] (1982). *Human Rights in Guatemala: No Neutrals Allowed*. New York: AWC.

_____ (1983). *Creating a Desolation and Calling It Peace*. New York: AWC.

_____ (1984, January 26, February 6). *Protection of the Weak and Unarmed: The Dispute over Counting Human Rights Violations in El Salvador*. Reprinted in U.S., House Committee on Foreign Affairs. *The Situation in El Salvador*. Hearings Before Subcommittees on Human Rights and International Organizations and on Western Hemisphere Affairs. 98th Congress, 2nd session, 291–342.

_____ (1985). *Violations of the Laws of War by Both Sides in Nicaragua 1981–1985*. New York: AWC.

Americas Watch Committee and American Civil Liberties Union (1982). *Report on Human Rights in El Salvador*. New York: Random House.

Amnesty International [AI] (1977). *The Republic of Nicaragua*. London: AI.

_____ (1981a). *"Disappearances": A Workbook*. New York: AI.

_____ (1981b). *Guatemala: A Government Program of Political Murder*. New York: AI.

Anderson, Charles W. (1961). "Politics and Development Policy in Central America." *Midwest Journal of Political Science*, 5(4), 332–350.

Anderson, Ken, and Jean-Marie Simon (1987). "Permanent Counter-Insurgency in Guatemala." *Telos*, 73, 9–46.

Anderson, Leslie (1994). *The Political Ecology of the Modern Peasant: Calculation and Community*. Baltimore, MD: Johns Hopkins University Press.

Anderson, Thomas P. (1971). *Mantanza: El Salvador's Communist Revolt of 1932*. Lincoln: University of Nebraska Press.

_____ (1981). *The War of the Dispossessed: Honduras and El Salvador, 1969*. Lincoln: University of Nebraska Press.

_____ (1982). *Politics in Central America*. New York: Praeger.

Arana, Mario (1997). "General Economic Policy." In Thomas W. Walker, ed., *Nicaragua Without Illusion*. Wilmington, DE: Scholarly Resources.

Arias, Arturo (1985). "El Movimiento Indígena en Guatemala: 1970–1983." In Daniel Camacho and Rafael Menjívar, eds., *Movimientos populares en Centroamérica*. San José, Costa Rica: Editorial Universitaria Centroamericana.

Arnson, Cynthia J. (1993). *Crossroads: Congress, the President and Central America, 1976–1993*. 2nd ed. University Park: Pennsylvania State University Press.

Arroyo, Gonzalo (1978). "Agriculture and Multinational Corporations in Latin America." In Vilo Harle, ed., *Political Economy of Food*. Farnborough, England: Saxon House, Teakfield.

Ashe, Jeffery (1978). *Rural Development in Costa Rica*. New York: ACCION International.

Associated Press [AP] (1981, May 5). "Military Aid Favored to Guatemala by State Department If It Is Sought." *Chattanooga (TN) Times*, A6.

Astorga Lira, Enrique (1975). *Evaluación de los asentamientos y cooperativas campesinas en Honduras*. Tegucigalpa: National Agrarian Institute.

Augelli, J. P. (1987). "Costa Rica's Frontier Legacy." *The Geographical Review*, 77, 1–15.

Austin, James, Jonathan Fox, and Walter Kruger (1985). "The Role of the Revolutionary State in the Nicaraguan Food System." *World Development*, 13(1), 15–40.

Aybar De Soto, José M. (1978). *Dependency and Intervention: The Case of Guatemala in 1954.* Boulder, CO: Westview Press.

Baer, Donald E. (1973). "Income and Export Taxation of Agriculture in Costa Rica and Honduras." *Journal of Developing Areas,* 8(1), 39–54.

Baloyra, Enríque (1982). *El Salvador in Transition.* Chapel Hill: University of North Carolina Press.

Barahona Riera, Francisco (1980). *Reforma agraria y poder político.* San José: Editorial Universidad de Costa Rica.

Barham, Bradford, Mary Clark, Elizabeth Katz, and Rachel Schurman (1992). "Nontraditional Agricultural Export in Latin America." *Latin American Research Report,* 27(2), 43–82.

Barkin, David (1982). "The Impact of Agribusiness on Rural Development." In Scott McNall, ed., *Current Perspectives in Social Theory,* Vol. 1. Greenwich, CT: JAI Press.

Barkin, David, Rosemary L. Batt, and Billie De Walt (1990). *Food Crops vs. Feed Crops: Global Substitution of Grains in Production.* Boulder, CO: Lynne Rienner.

Barraclough, Solon (1970). "Agricultural Policies and Strategies of Land Reform." In Irving L. Horowitz, ed., *Masses in Latin America.* New York: Oxford University Press.

_____ (1973). *Agrarian Structure in Latin America.* Lexington, MA: Lexington Books.

_____ (1983). *A Preliminary Analysis of the Nicaraguan Food System* (Report No. 83.1). Geneva: United Nations Research Institute for Social Development.

Barry, Tom (1986). *Guatemala: The Politics of Counterinsurgency.* Albuquerque, NM: Inter-Hemispheric Education Resource Center.

Bauer Paíz, Alfonso (1956). *Cómo opera el capital yanqui en Centroamérica (El caso de Guatemala).* Mexico City: Editorial Ibero-Americana.

Belli, Pedro (1970). "Farmers' Response to Price in Underdeveloped Areas: The Nicaraguan Case." *American Economic Review,* 60(2), 385–392.

_____ (1977). "Bitter Lemons: The Central American Experience in the Export of Fruits and Vegetables." *Baylor Business Studies,* 8, 23–33.

Berger, Susan A. (1992). *Political and Agrarian Development in Guatemala.* Boulder, CO: Westview Press.

Berman, Paul (1996). "In Search of Ben Linder's Killers." *New Yorker,* September 23, 58–81.

Berry, R. Albert, and William R. Cline (1979). *Agrarian Structure and Productivity in Developing Countries.* Baltimore, MD: Johns Hopkins University Press.

Berryman, Philip (1984). *The Religious Roots of Rebellion.* Maryknoll, NY: Orbis.

Betancur, Belisario, Reinaldo Figueredo Planchart, and Thomas Buergenthal (1993). *From Madness To Hope: The Twelve-Year War in El Salvador; Truth for El Salvador.* New York: United Nations.

Biondi-Morra, Brizio N. (1993). *Hungry Dreams: The Failure of Food Policy in Revolutionary Nicaragua, 1979–1990.* Ithaca, NY: Cornell University Press.

Blachman, Morris J., and Kenneth E. Sharpe (1988–1989). "Things Fall Apart in El Salvador." *World Policy Journal,* (6)1, 107–139.

Black, George (1981). *Triumph of the People: The Sandinista Revolution in Nicaragua.* London: Zed.

_____ (1983a). "Garrison Guatemala." *NACLA Report on the Americas*, 17(1), 2–35.

_____ (1983b). "Guatemala—The War Is Not Over." *NACLA Report on the Americas*, 17(2), 2–38.

_____ (1985). "Under the Gun." *NACLA Report on the Americas*, 19(6), 10–24.

Blasier, Cole (1976). *The Hovering Giant: U.S. Responses to Revolutionary Change in Latin America*. Pittsburgh: University of Pittsburgh Press.

Blutstein, Howard I., Elinor C. Betters, Deborah H. Lane, Jonathan A. Leonard, and Neda Walpole (1971). *Area Handbook for Honduras*. Washington, DC: U.S. Government Printing Office.

Bonner, Raymond (1984). *Weakness and Deceit: U.S. Policy and El Salvador*. New York: Times Books.

Booth, John A. (1980). "A Guatemalan Nightmare: Levels of Political Violence, 1966–1972." *Journal of Interamerican Studies and World Affairs*, 22(2), 195–220.

_____ (1985). *The End and the Beginning: The Nicaraguan Revolution*. 2nd ed. Boulder, CO: Westview Press.

Booth, John A., and Mitchell Seligson (1979). "Peasants as Activists: A Reevaluation of Political Participation in the Countryside." *Comparative Political Studies*, 12(1), 29–59.

Bowen, Gorden (1983). "U.S. Foreign Policy Toward Radical Change: Covert Operations in Guatemala, 1950–1954." *Latin American Perspectives*, 10(1), 88–102.

_____ (1985). "The Political Economy of State Terrorism: Barrier to Human Rights in Guatemala." In George W. Shepherd Jr. and Ved P. Nanda, eds., *Human Rights and Third World Development*. Westport, CT: Greenwood Press.

Boyer, Jefferson C. (1982). "Agrarian Capitalism and Peasant Praxis in Southern Honduras." Ph.D. dissertation, University of North Carolina, Chapel Hill.

Boza, Mario A. (1993). "Conservation in Action: Past, Present, and Future of the National Park System of Costa Rica." *Conservation Biology*, 7(2), 239–247.

Braun, Joachim von, and Maarten D. C. Immink (1994). "Nontraditional Vegetable Crops and Food Security Among Smallholder Farmers in Guatemala." In Joachim von Braun and Eileen Kennedy, eds., *Agricultural Commercialization, Economic Development, and Nutrition*. Baltimore, MD: Johns Hopkins University Press.

Braun, Joachim von, and Eileen Kennedy, eds. (1994). *Agricultural Commercialization, Economic Development, and Nutrition*. Baltimore, MD: Johns Hopkins University Press.

Brintnall, Douglas E. (1979). *Revolt Against the Dead: The Modernization of a Mayan Community in the Highlands of Guatemala*. New York: Gordon and Breach.

Brockett, Charles D. (1990). *Land, Power, and Poverty: Agrarian Transformation and Political Conflict in Central America*. Boston: Unwin Hyman.

_____ (1991a). "Sources of State Terrorism in Rural Central America." In P. Timothy Bushnell, ed., *State Organized Terror: The Case of Violent Internal Repression*. Boulder, CO: Westview Press.

_____ (1991b). "The Structure of Political Opportunity and Peasant Mobilization in Central America." *Comparative Politics*, 23(3), 253–274.

_____ (1992). "Measuring Political Violence and Rural Inequality in Central America." *American Political Science Review*, 86(1), 169–176.

_____ (1993). "A Protest-Cycle Resolution of the Repression/Popular-Protest Paradox." *Social Science History*, 17(3), 457–484.

Brooks, Joseph J. (1967). "The Impact of U.S. Cotton Policy on Economic Development: The Cases of El Salvador and Nicaragua." *Public and International Affairs*, 5, 191–214.

Brown, Antoinette B. (1983). "Communication." *Culture and Agriculture*, 21, 8, 18.

Brown, Marion (1971). "Peasant Organization as Vehicle of Reform." In Peter Dorner, ed., *Land Reform in Latin America: Issues and Cases*. Madison: University of Wisconsin Land Tenure Center.

Browning, David (1971). *El Salvador: Landscape and Society*. Oxford: Clarendon Press.

——— (1983). "Agrarian Reform in El Salvador." *Journal of Latin American Studies*, 15(2), 399–405.

Buckley, Tom (1984). *Violent Neighbors: El Salvador, Central America and the United States*. New York: Times Books.

Bulmer-Thomas, Victor (1987). *The Political Economy of Central America Since 1920*. Cambridge: Cambridge University Press.

——— (1994). *The Economic History of Latin America Since Independence*. New York: Cambridge University Press.

Burbach, Rodger, and Patricia Flynn (1980). *Agribusiness in the Americas*. New York: Monthly Review Press.

Burgos-Debray, Elizabeth, ed. and trans. (1984). *I, Rigoberta Menchú: An Indian Woman in Guatemala*. London: Verso.

Burke, Melvin (1976). "El Sistema de plantación y la proletarización del trabajo agrícola en El Salvador." *Estudios Centroamericanos*, 31, 473–486.

Burrows, Charles R. (1962, November 18). Letter to Edward M. Rowell, Department of State. Dorchester, MA: John F. Kennedy Library. Presidential office files, countries, box 18.

——— (1969, September 4). Recorded interview by Dennis J. O'Brien. Dorchester, MA: John F. Kennedy Library. Oral History Program.

Butler, Judy, David R. Dye, and Jack Spence, with George Vickers (1996). *Democracy and Its Discontents: Nicaraguans Face the Election*. Cambridge, MA: Hemisphere Initiatives.

Caballero, José María (1984). "Agriculture and the Peasantry Under Industrialization Pressures: Lessons from the Peruvian Experience." *Latin American Research Review*, 19(2), 3–42.

Cabarrús, Carlos R. (1983). *Génesis de una revolución: análisis del surgimiento y desarrollo de la organización campesina en El Salvador*. Mexico City: Ediciones de la Casa Chata.

Cambranes, Julio C. (1985). *Coffee and Peasants: The Origins of the Modern Plantation Economy in Guatemala, 1853–1897*. South Woodstock, VT: Plumsock Mesoamerican Studies.

Campos, Jose Edgardo, and Hilton L. Root (1996). *The Key to the Asian Miracle: Making Shared Growth Credible*. Washington, DC: Brookings Institute.

Cardenal, Fernando (1976, June 8). "Prepared Statement." U.S., House, Committee on International Relations. *Human Rights in Nicaragua, Guatemala, and El Salvador: Implications for U.S. Policy*. Hearings Before Subcommittee on International Organizations. 94th Congress, 2nd session, 17–29.

Cardona, Rokael (1978). "Descripción de la estructura y económica del agro Guatemalteco 1954–1975." *Política y Sociedad*, 6(July-December), 5–43.

Cardoso, Ciro F. S. (1977). "The Formation of the Coffee Estate in Nineteenth-Century Costa Rica." In Kenneth Duncan and Ian Rutledge, eds., *Land and Labour in Latin America*. London: Cambridge University Press.

Carias, Marco, and Daniel Slutzky (1971). *La Guerra inutil, análisis socio-económico del conflicto entre Honduras y El Salvador*. San José, Costa Rica: Editorial Universitaria Centroamericana.

Carmack, Robert M. (1983). "Spanish-Indian Relations in Highland Guatemala, 1800–1944." In Murdo MacLeod and Robert Wasserstrom, eds., *Spaniards and Indians in Southeastern Mesoamerica*. Lincoln: University of Nebraska Press.

_____, ed. (1988). *Harvest of Violence: The Maya Indians and the Guatemalan Crisis*. Norman: University of Oklahoma Press.

Carriere, Jean (1991). "The Crisis in Costa Rica: An Ecological Perspective." In David Goodman and Michael Redclift, eds., *Environment and Development in Latin America: The Politics of Sustainability*. Manchester: Manchester University Press.

Carter, Michael R., and Bradford L. Barham (1996). "Level Playing Fields and *Laissez Faire*: Postliberal Development Strategy in Inegalitarian Agrarian Economies." *World Development*, 24(7), 1133–1149.

Carter, Michael R., Bradford L. Barham, and Dina Mesbah (1996). "Agriculture Export Booms and the Rural Poor in Chile, Guatemala, and Paraguay." *Latin American Research Review*, 31(1), 33–66.

Carter, W. E. (1969). *New Lands and Old Traditions: Kekchi Cultivators in the Guatemalan Lowlands*. Gainesville: University of Florida Press.

Carvajal, Manuel J. (1979a). *Bibliography of Poverty and Related Topics in Costa Rica*. Washington, DC: U.S. Agency for International Development.

_____ (1979b). *Report on Income Distribution and Poverty in Costa Rica*. Washington, DC: U.S. Agency for International Development.

Central America Report [CAR] (1986). "UPEB No Match for Banana Companies." *Central America Report*, April 25, 114–115.

Central American Information Office [CAMINO] (1982). *El Salvador: Background to the Crisis*. Boston: CAMINO.

Chamorro, Edgar (1986, January 9). "Terror Is the Most Effective Weapon of Nicaragua's 'Contras.'" Letter to the editor. *New York Times*, A22.

Chapin, Norman (1980). "A Few Comments on Land Tenure and the Course of Agrarian Reform in El Salvador." In *El Salvador: Agrarian Reform Organization Project Paper*, Annex IIA, *A Social Analysis*. Washington, DC: U.S. Agency for International Development.

Checchi, Vincent (1959). *Honduras: A Problem in Economic Development*. New York: Twentieth Century Fund.

Chenery, Hollis (1979). *Structural Change and Development Policy*. Washington, DC: World Bank.

Chernow, Ron (1979). "The Strange Death of Bill Woods." *Mother Jones*, May, 32–41.

Chinchilla, Norma Stoltz (1983). "Interpreting Social Change in Guatemala: Modernization, Dependency, and Articulation of Modes of Production." In Ronald H. Chilcote and Dale L. Johnson, eds., *Theories of Development: Mode of Production or Dependency?* Beverly Hills, CA: Sage.

Chomsky, Aviva (1996). *West Indian Workers and the United Fruit Company in Costa Rica, 1870–1940*. Baton Rouge: Louisiana State University Press.

Clairmonte, Frederick F. (1975). "Bananas." In Cheryl Payer, ed., *Commodity Trade of the Third World.* New York: Wiley.

Clark, Mary A. (1995). "Nontraditional Export Promotion in Costa Rica: Sustaining Export-Led Growth." *Journal of Inter-American Studies and World Affairs,* 37(2), 181–223.

_____ (1997). "Transnational Alliances and Development Policy in Latin America: Nontraditional Export Promotion in Costa Rica." *Latin American Research Review,* 32(2), 71–98.

Colburn, Forrest D. (1982). "Current Studies of Peasants and Rural Development: Application of the Political Economy Approach." *World Politics,* 34(3), 437–449.

_____ (1986). *Post-Revolutionary Nicaragua: State, Class, and the Dilemmas of Agrarian Policy.* Berkeley: University of California Press.

_____ (1990). *Managing the Commanding Heights: Nicaragua's State Enterprises.* Berkeley: University of California Press.

Colburn, Forrest D., and Silvio De Franco (1985). "Privilege, Production and Revolution: The Case of Nicaragua." *Comparative Politics,* 17(3), 277–290.

Colby, Benjamin N., and Pierre L. vanden Berghe (1969). *Ixil Country.* Berkeley: University of California Press.

Colindres, Ana Marie (1993). "Non-Traditional Exports in Guatemala." In Wim Pelupessy and John Weeks, eds., *Economic Maladjustment in Central America.* New York: St. Martin's Press.

Collazo-Davila, Vincente (1980). "The Guatemalan Insurrection." In Bard E. O'Neill, William R. Heaton, and Donald J. Alberts, eds., *Insurgency in the Modern World.* Boulder, CO: Westview Press.

Collins, Joseph (1986). *Nicaragua: What Difference Could a Revolution Make?* 3rd ed. New York: Grove Press.

Committee for the Defense of Human Rights in Honduras (1985). *Human Rights in Honduras 1984.* Washington, DC: Washington Office on Latin America and World Council of Churches.

Conroy, Michael E. (1985). "Economic Legacies and Policies: Performances and Critique." In Thomas W. Walker, ed., *Nicaragua: The First Five Years.* Boulder, CO: Westview Press.

Conroy, Michael E., Douglas L. Murray, and Peter M. Rosset (1996). *A Cautionary Tale: Failed U.S. Development Policy in Latin America.* Boulder, CO: Lynne Rienner.

Conway, H. McKinley, Jr. (1963). *El Salvador: A "Bright Spot" in Central America.* Atlanta: Conway Publications.

Corbo, Vittorio, Ann O. Krueger, and Fernando Ossa, eds. (1986). *Export-Oriented Development Strategies: The Success of Five Newly Industrializing Countries.* Boulder, CO: Westview Press.

Cuzán, Alfred G (1989). "The Nicaraguan Revolution: From Autocracy to Totalitarian Dictatorship?" *Journal of Interdisciplinary Studies,* 1(1/2), 183–204.

_____ (1991). "Resource Mobilization and Political Opportunity in the Nicaraguan Revolution: The Praxis." *American Journal of Economics and Sociology,* 50(1), 71–83.

Daines, Samuel R. (1977). "Analysis of Small Farms and Rural Poverty in El Salvador." Report prepared for the U.S. Agency for International Development, San Salvador.

Davidson, John R. (1976a). *The Basic Village Education Project in Guatemala*. Washington, DC: U.S. Agency for International Development, Manpower Development Division.

———— (1976b). *The Rural Credit and Cooperative Development Project in Guatemala*. Case Studies in Development Assistance No. 1. Washington, DC: U.S. Agency for International Development.

Davis, L. Harlan (1973). "Foreign Aid to the Small Farmer: The El Salvador Experience." *Inter-American Economic Affairs*, 29(1), 81–91.

Davis, L. Harlan, and David E. Weisenborn (1981). "Small Farmer Market Development: The El Salvador Experience." *Journal of Developing Areas*, 15(3), 404–415.

Davis, Shelton H. (1983a). "Introduction." In Julie Hodson, ed., *Voices of the Survivors: The Massacre at Finca San Francisco, Guatemala*. Cambridge, MA: Cultural Survival and Anthropology Resource Center.

———— (1983b). "The Social Roots of Political Violence in Guatemala." *Cultural Survival Quarterly*, 7(1), 4–11.

———— (1983c). "State Violence and Agrarian Crisis in Guatemala." In Martin Diskin, ed., *Trouble in Our Backyard: Central America and the United States in the Eighties*. New York: Pantheon.

Davis, Shelton H., and Julie Hodson (1982). *Witnesses to Political Violence in Guatemala: The Suppression of a Rural Development Movement*. Boston: Oxfam America.

Deere, Carmen (1982). "A Comparative Analysis of Agrarian Reform in El Salvador and Nicaragua." *Development and Change*, 13(1), 1–41.

Deere, Carmen, and Peter Marchetti (1981). "The Worker-Peasant Alliance in the First Year of the Nicaraguan Agrarian Reform." *Latin American Perspectives*, 8(2), 40–73.

Deere, Carmen, Peter Marchetti, and Nola Reinhardt (1985). "The Peasantry and the Development of Sandinista Agrarian Policy, 1979–1984." *Latin American Research Review*, 20(3), 75–109.

de Groot, Jan P., and Jan Plantinga (1993). "The Future of Agrarian Reform in Nicaragua." In Wim Pelupessy and John Weeks, eds., *Economic Maladjustment in Central America*. New York: St. Martin's Press.

De Janvry, Alain (1981). *The Agrarian Question and Reformism in Latin America*. Baltimore, MD: Johns Hopkins University Press.

———— (1989). "Farm Structure, Productivity, and Poverty." In George Horwich and Gerald J. Lynch, eds., *Food, Policy, and Politics: A Perspective on Agriculture and Development*. Boulder, CO: Westview Press.

Dessaint, Alain Y. (1962). "Effects of the Hacienda and Plantation System on Guatemala's Indians." *América Indígena*, 22(4), 323–354.

Dewitt, R. Peter (1977). *The Inter-American Development Bank and Political Influence*. New York: Praeger.

Diskin, Martin (1982). "1982 Supplement." In Laurence R. Simon and James C. Stephens Jr., *El Salvador Land Reform, 1980–1981: Impact Audit*. Boston: Oxfam America.

———— (1984a, January 26, February 6). "The Direction of Agrarian Reform in El Salvador." In U.S., House, Committee on Foreign Affairs. *The Situation in El Salvador*.

Hearings Before Subcommittees on Human Rights and International Organizations and on Western Hemisphere Affairs. 98th Congress, 2nd session, 87–128.

_____ (1984b, January 26, February 6). "Prepared Statement." In U.S., House, Committee on Foreign Affairs. *The Situation in El Salvador*. Hearings Before Subcommittees on Human Rights and International Organizations and on Western Hemisphere Affairs. 98th Congress, 2nd session, 84–86.

_____ (1989). "El Salvador: Reform Prevents Change." In William C. Thiesenhusen, ed., *Searching for Agrarian Reform in Latin America*. Winchester, MA: Unwin Hyman.

_____ (1996). "Distilled Conclusions: The Disappearance of the Agrarian Question in El Salvador." *Latin American Research Review*, 31(2), 111–126.

Dorner, Peter, ed. (1971). *Land Reform in Latin America: Issues and Cases*. Madison: University of Wisconsin Land Tenure Center.

_____ (1972). *Land Reform and Economic Development*. Baltimore, MD: Penguin.

_____ (1992). *Latin American Land Reforms in Theory and Practice*. Madison: University of Wisconsin Press.

Dosal, Paul J. (1985). "Accelerating Dependent Development and Revolution: Nicaragua and the Alliance for Progress." *Inter-American Economic Affairs*, 38(3), 75–96.

_____ (1993). *Doing Business with the Dictators: A Political History of United Fruit in Guatemala, 1899–1944*. Wilmington, DE: Scholarly Resources.

Dozier, Craig L. (1958). *Indigenous Tropical Agriculture in Central America*. Washington, DC: National Academy of Sciences.

Duncan, Kenneth, and Ian Rutledge, eds. (1977). *Land and Labour in Latin America: Essays on the Development of Agrarian Capitalism in the Nineteenth and Twentieth Centuries*. London: Cambridge University Press.

Dunkerley, James (1982). *The Long War: Dictatorship and Revolution in El Salvador*. London: Junction Books.

Durham, William (1979). *Scarcity and Survival in Central America*. Stanford, CA: Stanford University Press.

Dye, David R., Judy Butler, Deena Abu-Lughod, and Jack Spence, with George Vickers (1995). *Contesting Everything, Winning Nothing: The Search for Consensus in Nicaragua, 1990–1995*. Cambridge, MA: Hemisphere Initiatives.

Ebel, Roland H. (1964). "Political Change in Guatemala: Indian Communities." *Journal of Inter-American Studies*, 6(1), 91–104.

_____ (1988). "When Indians Take Power: Conflict and Consensus in San Juan Ostuncalco." In Robert M. Carmack, ed., *Harvest of Violence: The Maya Indians and the Guatemalan Crisis*. Norman: University of Oklahoma Press.

Edelman, Marc (1985). "Back from the Brink." *NACLA Report on the Americas*, 19(6), 37–46.

_____ (1992). *The Logic of the Latifundio: The Large Estates Of Northwestern Costa Rica Since the Late Nineteenth Century*. Stanford, CA: Stanford University Press.

El-Ghonemy, M. Riad (1990). *The Political Economy of Rural Poverty: The Case for Land Reform*. New York: Routledge.

Ellis, Frank (1983). *Las Transnacionales del banano en Centroamerica*. San José, Costa Rica: Editorial Universitaria Centroamericana.

Enríquez, Laura J. (1991). *Harvesting Change: Labor and Agrarian Reform in Nicaragua, 1979–1990*. Chapel Hill: University of North Carolina Press.

_____ (1997). *Agrarian Reform and Class Consciousness in Nicaragua.* Gainesville: University Press of Florida.

Everingham, Mark (1996). *Revolution and Multiclass Coalition in Nicaragua.* Pittsburgh: University of Pittsburgh Press.

_____ (1997). "Agrarian Reform, Neo-Liberal Adjustment and Democracy in Central America and East Africa." Paper presented at the meeting of the Latin American Studies Association, April 17–19, 1997, Guadalajara, Mexico.

Faber, David (1993). *Environment Under Fire: Imperialism and the Ecological Crisis in Central America.* New York: Monthly Review Press.

Falla, Ricardo (1978). *Quiché rebelde.* Guatemala City: Editorial Universitaria de Guatemala.

_____ (1994). *Massacres in the Jungle: Ixcán, Guatemala, 1975–1982.* Boulder, CO: Westview Press.

Feder, Ernest (1977). *Strawberry Imperialism.* The Hague: Institute of Social Studies.

_____ (1981)."The World Bank–FIRA Scheme in Action in Tempoal, Veracruz." In Rosemary E. Galli, ed., *The Political Economy of Rural Development: Peasants, International Capital, and the State.* Albany: State University of New York Press.

Fei, John C. H., Gustav Ranis, and Shirley W. Y. Kuo, with Yu-Yuan Bian and Julia Chang Collins (1979). *Growth with Equity: The Taiwan Case.* New York: Oxford University Press.

Ffrench-Davis, Ricardo, and Ernesto Tironi (1982). *Latin America and the New International Economic Order.* London: Macmillan.

Fields, Gary S. (1980). *Poverty, Inequality, and Development.* New York: Cambridge University Press.

Figueres Olsen, José María (1996). "Sustainable Development: A New Challenge for Costa Rica." *SAIS Review* (Winter/Spring), 187–202.

FitzGerald, E. V. K. (1985). "Agrarian Reform as a Model of Accumulation: The Case of Nicaragua Since 1979." *Journal of Development Studies,* 22(1), 208–225.

_____ (1991). "Introduction: The Central American Agro-Export Economy— Issues and Debates." In Wim Pelupessy, ed., *Perspectives on the Agro-Export Economy in Central America.* Pittsburgh: University of Pittsburgh Press.

Fletcher, Lehman B., Eric Graber, W. C. Merrill, and E. Thorbecke (1970). *Guatemala's Economic Development: The Role of Agriculture.* Ames: Iowa State Press.

Fonck, Carlos O. (1972). "Modernity and Public Policies in the Context of the Peasant Sector: Honduras as a Case Study." Ph.D. dissertation, Cornell University, Ithaca, NY.

Forché, Carolyn, and Philip Wheaton (1980). *History and Motivations of U.S. Involvement in the Control of the Peasant Movement in El Salvador.* Washington, DC: Ecumenical Program for Interamerican Commitment in Action.

Foreign Agriculture (1960). "Costa Rica's Livestock Industry." *Foreign Agriculture,* 12, 15–16.

Forster, Cindy (1994). "The Time of Freedom: San Marcos Coffee Workers and the Radicalization of the Guatemalan National Revolution, 1944–1954." *Radical History Review,* 58, 35–78.

Fox, John W. (1978). *Quiché Conquest: Centralism and Regionalism in Highland Guatemalan State Development.* Albuquerque: University of New Mexico Press.

Galli, Rosemary E. (1981). "Colombia: Rural Development as Social and Economic Control." In Rosemary E. Galli, ed., *The Political Economy of Rural Development: Peasants, International Capital, and the State.* Albany: State University of New York Press.

Garnier, Leonardo, Gladys González, and Jorge Cornick (1988). "Costa Rica: Las vicisitudes de una política bananera nacional." In Edelberto Torres-Rivas and Eckhard Deutscher, eds., *Cambio y continuidad en la economía bananera.* San José, Costa Rica: Facultad Latinoamericana de Ciencias Sociales.

Gayoso, Antonio (1970). *Land Reform in Guatemala.* Washington, DC: U.S. Agency for International Development.

Ghose, Ajit Kumar (1983). *Agrarian Reform in Contemporary Developing Countries.* Boston: St. Martin's Press.

Gilbert, Dennis (1985). "The Bourgeoisie." In Thomas W. Walker, ed., *Nicaragua: The First Five Years.* Boulder, CO: Westview Press.

_____ (1986). "Nicaragua." In Morris J. Blachman, William M. LeoGrande, and Kenneth Sharpe, eds., *Confronting Revolution: Security Through Diplomacy in Central America.* New York: Pantheon.

Gleijeses, Piero (1991). *Shattered Hope: The Guatemalan Revolution and the United States, 1944–1954.* Princeton, NJ: Princeton University Press.

Goldberg, Ray A. (1981). "The Role of the Multinational Corporation." *American Journal of Agricultural Economics,* 63(2), 367–374.

Goldberg, Ray A., and Leonard M. Wilson (1974). *Agribusiness Management for Developing Countries—Latin America.* Cambridge, MA: Ballinger.

Gómez Leonel, and Bruce Cameron (1981). "American Myths." *Foreign Policy,* 43, 71–78.

Gondolf, Ed (1981). "Community Development Amidst Political Violence: Lessons from Guatemala." *Community Development Journal,* 16(3), 228–236.

González B., Rodrigo (1993). *El Regimen de tenencia de la tierra en Costa Rica.* Heredia, Costa Rica: Editorial de la Universidad Nacional.

Gordon-Ashworth, Fiona (1984). *International Commodity Control: A Contemporary History and Appraisal.* New York: St. Martin's Press.

Gott, Richard (1971). *Guerilla Movements in Latin America.* New York: Doubleday.

Gould, Jeffry (1990). *To Lead as Equals: Rural Protest and Political Consciousness in Chinandega, Nicaragua, 1912–1979.* Chapel Hill: University of North Carolina Press.

Graber, Eric S. (1980). *Income Distribution, Employment and Social Well-Being in Guatemala: A Survey.* Washington, DC: U.S. Agency for International Development.

Griffin, Keith (1978). *International Inequality and National Poverty.* New York: Macmillan.

Griffith, William J. (1965). *Empires in the Wilderness: Foreign Colonization and Development in Guatemala, 1834–1844.* Chapel Hill: University of North Carolina Press.

Grindle, Merilee S. (1986). *State and Countryside: Development Policy and Agrarian Politics in Latin America.* Baltimore, MD: Johns Hopkins University Press.

Gudmundson, Lowell (1983). "Costa Rica Before Coffee: Occupational Distribution, Wealth Inequality, and Elite Society in the Village Economy of the 1840s." *Journal of Latin American Studies,* 15(2), 427–452.

_____ (1986). *Costa Rica Before Coffee: Society and Economy on the Eve of the Export Boom*. Baton Rouge: Louisiana State University Press.

_____ (1995). "Lord and Peasant in the Making of Modern Central America." In Evelyne Huber and Frank Safford, eds., *Agrarian Structure and Political Power: Landlord and Peasant in the Making of Latin America*. Pittsburgh: University of Pittsburgh Press.

Guess, George M. (1979). "Pasture Expansion, Forestry, and Development Contradictions: The Case of Costa Rica." *Studies in Comparative International Development*, 14(1), 42–55.

Gutman, Roy (1988). *Banana Diplomacy: The Making of American Policy in Nicaragua, 1981–1987*. New York: Simon and Schuster.

Hall, Carolyn (1985). *Costa Rica: A Geographical Interpretation in Historical Perspective*. Boulder, CO: Westview Press.

Handy, Jim (1984). *Gift of the Devil: A History of Guatemala*. Boston: South End Press.

_____ (1994). *Revolution in the Countryside: Rural Conflict and Agrarian Reform in Guatemala, 1944–1954*. Chapel Hill: University of North Carolina Press.

Harness, Vernon L., and Robert D. Pugh (1970). *Cotton in Central America*. Foreign Agricultural Service Publication No. M–154. Washington, DC: Department of Agriculture.

Harrison, Peter D., and B. L. Turner (1978). *Pre-Hispanic Maya Agriculture*. Albuquerque: University of New Mexico Press.

Hartshorn, Gary, et al. (1982). *Costa Rica: Country Environmental Profile; A Field Study*. San José, Costa Rica: Tropical Science Center.

Hatch, John K., and Aquiles Lanao Flores (1977, August 19). "An Evaluation of the AIFLD/HISTADAUT Project Proposal to Assist Peasant Federations." Paper prepared for U.S. Agency for International Development, Washington, DC.

Hatch, L. Upton, Glenn C. W. Ames, and L. Harlan Davis (1977). *Small Agricultural Producers Credit Programs: El Salvador; A Case Study*. Case Studies in Development Assistance No. 3. Washington, DC: U.S. Agency for International Development.

Hedström, Ingemar (1986). *Somos parte de un gran equilibrio: la crisis ecológica en Centroamérica*. San José, Costa Rica: Departamento Ecuménico de Investigación.

Hemphill, Alan K. (1976). "Livestock Prospects Mixed in Central America—Mexico." *Foreign Agriculture*, 14, 29.

Herring, Hubert (1964). *A History of Latin America from the Beginning to the Present*. New York: Knopf.

Herring, Ronald J. (1983). *Land to the Tiller: The Political Economy of Agrarian Reform in South Asia*. New Haven, CT: Yale University Press.

Hewitt De Alcantara, Cynthia (1973–1974). "The Green Revolution as History: The Mexican Experience." *Development and Change*, 5(2), 25–44.

_____ (1976). *Modernizing Mexican Agriculture: Socioeconomic Implications of Technological Change, 1940–1970*. Geneva: United Nations Research Institute for Social Development.

Hildebrand, John R. (1969). *Economic Development: A Latin American Emphasis*. Austin, TX: Pemberton Press.

Hillman, Jimmye S. (1981). "The Role of Export Cropping in Less Developed Countries." *American Journal of Agricultural Economics*, 63(2), 375–383.

Hodges, Donald C. (1986). *Intellectual Foundations of the Nicaraguan Revolution.* Austin: University of Texas Press.

Holland, Barbara J. (1973). *The Dynamics of Health: Nicaragua.* Washington, DC: U.S. Government Printing Office.

Honey, Martha (1994). *Hostile Acts: U.S. Policy in Costa Rica in the 1980's.* Gainesville: University of Florida Press.

Hough, Richard, John Kelley, Steve Miller, Russell DeRossier, Fred L. Mann, and Mitchell A. Seligson (1983). *Land and Labor in Guatemala: An Assessment.* Washington, DC: U.S. Agency for International Development and Development Associates.

Hoy, Don R. (1984). "Environmental Protection and Economic Development in Guatemala's Western Highlands." *Journal of Developing Areas,* 18(2), 161–176.

Huizer, Gerrit (1972). *The Revolutionary Potential of Peasants in Latin America.* Lexington, MA: Lexington Books.

Human Rights Watch/Americas (1996). *Guatemala: Return to Violence.* New York: Human Rights Watch/Americas.

Ickis, John C. (1983). "Structural Responses to New Rural Development Strategies." In David C. Korten and Felipe B. Alfonso, eds., *Bureaucracy and the Poor.* West Hartford, CT: Kumarian Press.

Immerman, Richard H. (1982). *The CIA in Guatemala: The Foreign Policy of Intervention.* Austin: University of Texas Press.

Inter-American Development Bank [IDB] (1976). *Informe general sobre el desarrollo agropecuario y rural de El Salvador.* Washington, DC: IDB.

_____ (various years). *Economic and Social Progress in Latin America.* Washington, DC: IDB.

International Agricultural Development Service [IADS] (1981). *Agricultural Development Indicators.* New York: IADS.

International Bank for Reconstruction and Development [IBRD] (1953). *The Economic Development of Nicaragua.* Baltimore, MD: Johns Hopkins University Press.

International Institute of Agriculture (1947). *The World's Coffee.* Rome: UN Food and Agricultural Organization.

International Labour Review [ILR] (1963). "Agrarian Reform Law in Honduras." *International Labour Review,* 87(6), 573–580.

International Work Group for Indigenous Affairs [IWGIA] (1978). *Guatemala 1978: The Massacre at Panzós.* Copenhagen: IWGIA.

Jacoby, Erich H. (1971). *Man and Land: The Fundamental Issues in Development.* New York: Knopf.

Jiménez, Dina (1985). "El Movimiento campesino en Guatemala: 1969–1980." In David Camacho and Rafael Menjívar, eds., *Movimientos populares en Centroamérica.* San José, Costa Rica: Editorial Universitaria Centroamericana.

Johnson, D. Gale, and G. Edward Schuh (1983). *The Role of Markets in the World Food Economy.* Boulder, CO: Westview Press.

Johnson, Kenneth F. (1972). "Guatemala: From Terrorism to Terror." *Conflict Studies,* 23, 4–17.

_____ (1973). "On the Guatemalan Political Violence." *Politics and Society,* 4(1), 55–83.

Johnston, Bruce F., and William C. Clark (1982). *Redesigning Rural Development: A Strategic Perspective*. Baltimore, MD: Johns Hopkins University Press.

Jonakin, Jon (1996). "The Impact of Structural Adjustment and Property Rights Conflicts on Nicaraguan Agrarian Reform Beneficiaries." *World Development*, 24(7), 1179–1191.

_____ (1997). "Agrarian Policy." In Thomas W. Walker, ed., *Nicaragua Without Illusion*. Wilmington, DE: Scholarly Resources.

Jonas, Susanne (1991). *The Battle for Guatemala: Rebels, Death Squads, and U.S. Power*. Boulder, CO: Westview Press.

Jones, Chester Lloyd (1966, originally published 1940). *Guatemala: Past and Present*. New York: Russell & Russell.

Jones, Jeffrey R. (1984). "The Central American Energy Problem: Anthropological Perspectives on Fuelwood Supply and Production." *Culture and Agriculture*, 22(Winter), 6–9.

_____ (1992). "Environmental Issues and Policies in Costa Rica: Control of Deforestation." *Policy Studies Journal*, 20(4), 679–694.

Kaimowitz, David (1980). "Nicaraguan Coffee Harvest 1979–80: Public Policy and the Private Sector." *Development and Change*, 11(4), 497–516.

_____ (1989). "The Role of Decentralization in the Recent Agrarian Reform." In William C. Thiesenhusen, ed., *Searching for Agrarian Reform in Latin America*. Winchester, MA: Unwin Hyman.

_____ (1995). "Land Tenure, Land Markets, and Natural Resource Management by Large Landowners in the Petén and the Northern Transversal of Guatemala." Photocopy, San José, Costa Rica.

_____ (1996). *Livestock and Deforestation in Central America in the 1980s and 1990s: A Policy Perspective*. Jakarta: International Food Policy Research Institute.

Kaimowitz, David, and David Stanfield (1985). "The Organization of Production Units in the Nicaraguan Agrarian Reform." *Inter-American Economic Affairs*, 39(1), 51–78.

Karnes, Thomas L. (1978). *Tropical Enterprise: The Standard Fruit and Steamship Company in Latin America*. Baton Rouge: Louisiana State University Press.

Karush, G. E. (1978). "Plantations, Population, and Poverty: The Roots of the Demographic Crisis in El Salvador." *Studies in Comparative International Development*, 8(3), 59–75.

Kay, Cristóbal (1995). "Rural Development and Agrarian Issues in Contemporary Latin America." In John Weeks, ed., *Structural Adjustment and the Agricultural Sector in Latin America and Caribbean*. New York: St. Martin's Press.

Keene, Beverly (1980). *Export-Cropping in Central America*. Background Paper No. 43. Washington, DC: Bread for the World.

Kent, George (1984). *The Political Economy of Hunger*. New York: Praeger.

Kepner, Charles David, Jr., and Jay Henry Soothill (1967, originally published 1935). *The Banana Empire: A Case Study of Economic Imperialism*. New York: Russell & Russell.

Kessing, Donald B. (1981). "Exports and Policy in Latin American Countries: Prospects for the World Economy and for Latin American Exports, 1980–90." In Warner Baer and Malcolm Gillis, eds., *Export Diversification and the New Protectionism*. Champaign: University of Illinois Press.

Kincaid, Douglas (1985). "'We Are the Agrarian Reform: Rural Politics and Agrarian Reform." In Nancy Peckenham and Annie Street, eds., *Honduras: Portrait of a Captive Nation*. New York: Praeger.

_____ (1987). "Peasants into Rebels: Community and Class in Rural El Salvador." *Comparative Studies in Society and History*, 29(3), 466–494.

King, Russell (1977). *Land Reform: A World Survey*. Boulder, CO: Westview Press.

Kinzer, Stephen (1991). *Blood of Brothers: Life and War in Nicaragua*. New York: G. P. Putnam's Sons.

Kishor, Nalin, and Luis Constantino (1994). "Sustainable Forestry: Can It Compete?" *Finance and Development*, 31(4), 36–39.

Koo, Hagen (1987). "The Interplay of State, Social Class, and World Systems in East Asian Development: The Cases of South Korea and Taiwan." In Frederic C. Deyo, ed., *The Political Economy of the New Asian Industrialists*. Ithaca, NY: Cornell University Press.

Krasner, Stephen D. (1978). *Defending the National Interest*. Princeton, NJ: Princeton University Press.

Kriesberg, Martin, Ervin Bullard, and Wendell Becraft (1970). *Costa Rican Agriculture: Crop Priorities and Country Policies*. Washington, DC: U.S. Department of Agriculture.

Kusterer, Kenneth C., Maria Regina Estrada De Batres, and Josefina Xuyá Cuxil (1981). *The Social Impact of Agribusiness: A Case Study of ALCOSA in Guatemala*. Evaluation Special Study No. 4. Washington, DC: U.S. Agency for International Development.

LaBarge, Richard A. (1968). "Impact of the United Fruit Company on the Economic Development of Guatemala, 1946–1954." In Richard H. LaBarge, Wayne M. Clegern, and Oriol Pi-Sunyer, *Studies in Middle American Economics*. New Orleans: Tulane University, Middle American Research Institute.

LaFeber, Walter (1984). *Inevitable Revolutions: The United States in Central America*. New York: Norton.

Laird, Larry K. (1974). "Technology Versus Tradition: The Modernization of Nicaraguan Agriculture, 1900–1940." Ph.D. dissertation, University of Kansas, Lawrence.

Landsberger, Henry A., and Cynthia N. Hewitt (1970). "Ten Sources of Weakness and Cleavage in Latin American Peasant Movements." In Rodolfo Stavenhagen, ed., *Agrarian Problems and Peasant Movements in Latin America*. New York: Doubleday Anchor.

Lappé, Frances Moore, and Joseph Collins (1978). *Food First: Beyond the Myth of Scarcity*. New York: Ballantine.

Lardizabal, Fernando (1986). "Myths and Realities: Agricultural Policy or Agrarian Reform?" In Mark B. Rosenberg and Philip L. Sheperd, eds., *Honduras Confronts Its Future*. Boulder, CO: Lynne Rienner.

Lassen, Cheryl A. (1980). *Landlessness and Rural Poverty in Latin America: Condition, Trends, and Policies Affecting Income and Employment*. Ithaca, NY: Cornell University Center for International Studies.

Lassey, William R., James Huffman, Bertha Clow, Layton Thompson, Clive Harston, and Mary Mobley (1969). "The Lake Izabal Area of Guatemala: Communication, Social Change and Agricultural Development." Photocopy, Montana State University Center for Planning and Development, Bozeman.

Lawyers Committee for International Human Rights and Americas Watch Committee [LCIHR-AWC] (1984). *El Salvador's Other Victims: The War on the Displaced*. New York: LCIHR-AWC.

Lehmann, Mary P. (1992). "Deforestation and Changing Land-Use Patterns in Costa Rica." In Harold K. Steen and Richard P. Tucker, eds., *Changing Tropical Forests*. Durham, NC: Forest History Society.

LeMoyne, James (1988). "Testify to Torture." *New York Times Magazine* (June 5), 44–47.

LeoGrande, William M. (1979). "The Revolution in Nicaragua: Another Cuba?" *Foreign Affairs*, 58(1), 28–50.

_____ (1981). "Land Reform and the El Salvador Crisis." *International Security*, 6(1), 27–52.

_____ (1982). "The United States and the Nicaraguan Revolution." In Thomas W. Walker, ed., *Nicaragua in Revolution*. New York: Praeger.

_____ (1985). "The United States and Nicaragua." In Thomas W. Walker, ed., *Nicaragua: The First Five Years*. Boulder, CO: Westview Press.

LeoGrande, William M., and Carla Anne Robbins (1980). "Oligarchs and Officers: The Crisis in El Salvador." *Foreign Affairs*, 58(4), 1084–1103.

Lethander, Richard W. (1968). "The Economy of Nicaragua." Ph.D. dissertation, Duke University, Durham, NC.

Libertad (San José) (1985, July 19–25). "Landless Peasants Stage Protest in Front of INA." In U.S. Joint Publications Research Service, *JPRS Reports*, No. LAM–85–079–90.

Linares, Olga F. (1979). "What Is Lower Central American Archeology?" *Annual Review of Anthropology*, 8, 21–43.

Lindo-Fuentes, Héctor (1990). *Weak Foundations: The Economy of El Salvador in the Nineteenth Century*. Berkeley: University of California Press.

Lofchie, Michael F., and Stephen K. Commins (1982). "Food Deficits and Agricultural Policies in Tropical Africa." *Journal of Modern African Studies*, 20(1), 1–25.

Long, Norman, and David Winder (1981). "The Limitations of 'Directive Change' for Rural Development in the Third World." *Community Development Journal*, 16(2), 82–87.

Lovell, W. George, and Christopher H. Lutz (1994). *Demography and Empire: A Guide to the Population History of Spanish Central America, 1500–1821*. Boulder, CO: Westview Press.

Lowenthal, Abraham F. (1973). "United States Policy Toward Latin America: 'Liberal,' 'Radical,' and 'Bureaucratic' Perspectives." *Latin American Research Review*, 8(3), 3–26.

Luciak, Ilja A. (1995). *The Sandinista Legacy: Lessons from a Political Economy in Transition*. Gainesville: University Press of Florida.

Lungo Uclés, Mario (1995). "Building an Alternative: The Formation of a Popular Project." In Minor Sinclair, ed., *The New Politics of Survival: Grassroots Movements in Central America*. New York: Monthly Review Press.

Lutz, Ernst, and Herman Daly (1991). "Incentives, Regulations, and Sustainable Land Use in Costa Rica." *Environmental and Resource Economics*, 1, 179–194.

McCamant, John (1968). *Development Assistance in Central America.* New York: Praeger.

MacCameron, Robert L. (1983). *Bananas, Labor, and Politics in Honduras: 1954–1963.* Syracuse, NY: Maxwell School of Citizenship and Public Affairs, Syracuse University.

McCann, Thomas (1976). *An American Company: The Tragedy of United Fruit.* New York: Crown.

McClintock, Cynthia (1984). "Why Peasants Rebel: The Case of Peru's Sendero Luminoso." *World Politics,* 37(1), 48–84.

McClintock, Michael (1985a). *The American Connection.* Vol. 1: *State Terror and Popular Resistance in El Salvador.* London: Zed.

_____ (1985b). *The American Connection.* Vol. 2: *State Terror and Popular Resistance in Guatemala.* London: Zed.

McCreery, David J. (1976). "Coffee and Class: The Structure of Development in Liberal Guatemala." *Hispanic American Historical Review,* 56(3), 438–460.

_____ (1983). *Development and the State in Reform Guatemala, 1871–1885.* Athens: Ohio University Press.

_____ (1994). *Rural Guatemala, 1760–1940.* Stanford, CA: Stanford University Press.

MacLeod, Murdo J. (1973) *Spanish Central America: A Socioeconomic History, 1520–1720.* Berkeley: University of California Press.

MacLeod, Murdo J., and Robert Wasserstrom, eds. (1983). *Spaniards and Indians in Southeastern Mesoamerica.* Lincoln: University of Nebraska Press.

McSpirit Alas, Stephanie (1994). "Agrarian Change and Peasant Revolution in El Salvador and Guatemala." Ph.D. dissertation, State University of New York, Buffalo.

Manz, Beatrice (1988). *Refugees of a Hidden War: The Aftermath of Counterinsurgency in Guatemala.* Albany: State University of New York Press.

Marshall, C. F. (1983). *The World Coffee Trade.* Cambridge: Woodhead-Faulkner.

Martz, John D. (1956). *Communist Infiltration in Guatemala.* New York: Vantage Press.

Maxfield, Sylvia, and Richard Stahler-Sholk (1985). "External Constraints." In Thomas W. Walker, ed., *Nicaragua: The First Five Years.* Boulder, CO: Westview Press.

May, Rachel A. (1993). "The Effects of Political Violence on the Development of Popular Movements: Guatemalan Campesino Organizations, 1954–1985." Ph.D. dissertation, Tulane University, New Orleans.

May, Stacy, and Galo Plaza (1958). *The United Fruit Company in Latin America.* New York: National Planning Association.

Meier, Gerald M., ed. (1984). *Leading Issues in Economic Development.* 4th ed. New York: Oxford University Press.

Merrill, William C. (1974). *The Long-Run Prospects for Increasing Income Levels in Guatemala's Highlands.* Guatemala City: National Council for Economic Planning.

Metrinko, Monika (1978, October 16). "Exports Fuel Growth of Central America's Beef Production." *Foreign Agriculture,* 16, 2–3.

Meyer, Carrie A. (1989). *Land Reform in Latin America: The Dominican Case.* New York: Praeger.

Midlarsky, Manus I., and Kenneth Roberts (1985). "Class, State, and Revolution in Central America: Nicaragua and El Salvador Compared." *Journal of Conflict Resolution*, 29(2), 163–193.

Migdal, Joel S. (1974). *Peasants, Politics, and Revolution: Pressures Toward Political and Social Change in the Third World*. Princeton, NJ: Princeton University Press.

Miles, Sara, and Bob Ostertag (1989a). "D'Aubuisson's New ARENA." *NACLA Report on the Americas*, 23(2), 14–39.

_____ (1989b). "FMLN's New Thinking." *NACLA Report on the Americas*, 23(3), 15–38.

Millett, Richard (1977). *Guardians of the Dynasty*. Maryknoll, NY: Orbis.

Minkel, Clarence W. (1967). "Programs of Agricultural Colonization and Settlement in Central America." *Revista Geográfica*, 66, 19–53.

Molina Chocano, Guillermo, and Ricardo Reina (1983). *La Evolución de la pobreza rural en Honduras*. Publication No. PREALC1223. Santiago, Chile: International Labour Organisation.

Monteforte Toledo, Mario (1972). *Centro América: subdesarrollo y dependencia*. Vol. 1. Mexico City: National Autonomous University of Mexico.

Montes, Segundo (1980). *El Agro salvadoreño (1973–1980)*. San Salvador: University of Central America.

Montgomery, John D. (1984). "United States Advocacy of International Land Reform." In John D. Montgomery, ed., *International Dimensions of Land Reform*. Boulder, CO: Westview Press.

Montgomery, Tommie Sue (1995). *Revolution in El Salvador*. 2nd ed. Boulder, CO: Westview Press.

Mooney, Joseph P. (1984). "Was It Worsening of Economic and Social Conditions That Brought Violence and Civil War to El Salvador?" *Inter-American Economic Affairs*, 38(2), 61–69.

Morales Velado, Oscar A., et al. (1988). *La Resistencia no violenta ante los regimenes salvadoreños que han utilizado el terror institucionalizado en el periodo 1972–1987*. San Salvador: University of Central America.

Moreno, Dario (1990). *U.S. Policy in Central America: The Endless Debate*. Miami: Florida International University Press.

Morley, Samuel A. (1995). *Poverty and Inequality in Latin America: The Impact of Adjustment and Recovery in the 1980's*. Baltimore, MD: Johns Hopkins University Press.

Morley, Sylvanus G., and George W. Brainerd (1983). *The Ancient Maya*. 4th ed. Revised by Robert J. Shaver. Stanford, CA: Stanford University Press.

Morris, James A. (1984). *Honduras: Caudillo Politics and Military Rulers*. Boulder, CO: Westview Press.

Morsink-Villalobos, Jennifer, and James R. Simpson (1980). "Export Subsidies: The Case of Costa Rica's Banana Industry." *Inter-American Economic Affairs*, 34(3), 69–86.

Mosk, Sanford A. (1955). "The Coffee Economy of Guatemala, 1850–1918: Development and Signs of Instability." *Inter-American Economic Affairs*, 9(3), 6–20.

Mudge, Arthur W. (1979). "A Case Study in Human Rights and Development Assistance: Nicaragua." *Universal Human Rights*, 1(4), 93–102.

Munro, Dana G. (1918). *The Five Republics of Central America*. New York: Oxford University Press.

Muravchik, Joshua (1986–1987). "The Nicaraguan Debate." *Foreign Affairs*, 65(2), 366–382.

Murphy, Brian (1970). "The Stunted Growth of Campesino Organizations." In Richard N. Adams, ed., *Crucifixion by Power.* Austin: University of Texas Press.

Murray, Douglas L. (1994). *Cultivating Crisis: The Human Cost of Pesticides in Latin America.* Austin: University of Texas Press.

Myers, Norman (1981). "The Hamburger Connection: How Central America's Forests Became North America's Hamburgers." *Ambio*, 10(1), 3–8.

La Nación (San José) (1983, June 2). "Government to Distribute Land to 10,000 Families." In U.S. Joint Publications Research Service, *JPRS Reports*, No. 83830–61.

_____ (1984a, April 5). "IDA Responds." In U.S. Joint Publications Research Service, *JPRS Reports*, No. LAM–84–067–41.

_____ (1984b, May 14). "Peasant Occupation of Farm Land Continues in Southern Region." In U.S. Joint Publications Research Service, *JPRS Reports*, No. LAM–84–079–63.

Nairn, Allan, and Jean-Marie Simon (1986, June 30). "Bureaucracy of Death." *New Republic*, 13–17.

Nathan Associates (1969). "Agricultural Sectoral Analysis for El Salvador: Summary." Paper prepared for the government of El Salvador.

Naylor, Robert A. (1967). "Guatemala: Indian Attitudes Toward Land Tenure." *Journal of Inter-American Studies*, 9(4), 619–640.

Newfarmer, Richard S. (1983). "The Private Sector and Development." In John P. Lewis and Valeriana Kallab, eds., *U.S. Foreign Policy and the Third World: Agenda 1983.* New York: Praeger.

Newson, Linda (1982). "The Depopulation of Nicaragua in the Sixteenth Century." *Journal of Latin American Studies*, 14(2), 253–286.

_____ (1985). "Indian Population Patterns in Colonial Spanish America." *Latin American Research Review*, 20(3), 41–74.

Nolan, David (1984). *The Ideology of the Sandinistas and the Nicaraguan Revolution.* Coral Gables, FL: University of Miami, Graduate School of International Studies.

North, Liisa (1985). *Bitter Grounds: Roots of Revolt in El Salvador.* 2nd ed. Toronto: Between the Lines.

North American Congress on Latin America [NACLA] (1974). "Guatemala: Breaking Free." *NACLA's Latin America and Empire Report*, 8(3).

Norton, Chris (1985, November-December). "Build and Destroy." *NACLA Report on the Americas*, 26–36.

Norton, Roger D. (1992). "Integration of Food and Agricultural Policy with Macroeconomics Policy: Methodological Consideration in a Latin American Perspective." Rome: FAO.

Núñez Soto, Orlando (1981). *El Somocismo y el model capitalista agro-exportador.* Managua: National Autonomous University of Nicaragua.

Olson, Gary L. (1974). *U.S. Foreign Policy and the Third World Peasant: Land Reform in Asia and Latin America.* New York: Praeger.

Orellana, Sandra L. (1984). *The Tzutjil Mayas: Continuity and Change, 1250–1630.* Norman: University of Oklahoma Press.

Organization of American States [OAS] (1966). *Domestic Efforts and the Needs for External Financing for the Development of Nicaragua*. Washington, DC: OAS, Inter-American Committee on the Alliance for Progress.

_____ (1974). *Situation, Principal Problems and Prospects of the Economic Development of Guatemala*. Washington, DC: OAS, Inter-American Economic and Social Council.

_____ (1975). *Situation, Principal Problems and Prospects for the Integral Development of El Salvador*. Washington, DC: OAS, Inter-American Economic and Social Council.

Oshima, Harry T. (1993). *Strategic Processes in Monsoon Asia's Economic Development*. Baltimore, MD: Johns Hopkins University Press.

Paige, Jeffery M. (1975). *Agrarian Revolution: Social Movements and Export Agriculture in the Underdeveloped World*. New York: Free Press.

_____ (1983). "Social Theory and Peasant Revolution in Vietnam and Guatemala." *Theory and Society*, 12(6), 699–737.

_____ (1985). "Cotton and Revolution in Nicaragua." In Peter Evans, Dietrich Rueschemeyer, and Theda Skocpol, eds., *State Versus Market in the World-System*. Beverly Hills, CA: Sage.

_____ (1996). "Land Reform and Agrarian Revolution in El Salvador: Comment on Seligson and Diskin." *Latin American Research Review*, 31(2), 127–139.

Parsons, James J. (1965) "Cotton and Cattle in the Pacific Lowlands of Central America." *Journal of Inter-American Studies*, 7(2), 149–159.

Parsons, Kenneth H. (1976). *Agrarian Reform in Southern Honduras*. Research Paper No. 67. Madison: University of Wisconsin Land Tenure Center.

Pastor, Robert A. (1982, July 20 and 22). "Agricultural Development in the Caribbean Basin." Prepared statement in U.S., House, Committee on Foreign Affairs. *Agricultural Development in the Caribbean and Central America*. Hearings Before Subcommittee on Inter-American Affairs. 97th Congress, 2nd session, 75–106.

Paus, Eva, ed. (1988). *Struggle Against Dependence: Nontraditional Export Growth in Central America and the Caribbean*. Boulder, CO: Westview Press.

Payer, Cheryl (1975). *Commodity Trade of the Third World*. New York: Wiley.

Payeras, Mario (1983). *Days of the Jungle: The Testimony of a Guatemalan Guerrillero, 1972–1976*. New York: Monthly Review Press.

Pearse, Andrew (1980). *Seeds of Plenty, Seeds of Want: Social and Economic Implications of the Green Revolution*. Oxford: Clarendon Press.

Pearson, Neale J. (1969). "Guatemala: The Peasant Union Movement, 1944–1954." In Henry Landsberger, ed., *Latin American Peasant Movements*. Ithaca, NY: Cornell University Press.

_____ (1980). "Peasant Pressure Groups and Agrarian Reform in Honduras, 1962–1977." In William P. Avery, Richard E. Lonsdale, and Ivan Völgyes, eds., *Rural Change and Public Policy*. New York: Pergamon Press.

Pearson, Ross (1963a). "Land Reform, Guatemalan Style." *American Journal of Economics and Sociology*, 22(2), 225–234.

_____ (1963b). "Zones of Agricultural Development in Guatemala." *Journal of Geography*, 62(1), 11–22.

Peckenham, Nancy, and Annie Street, eds. (1985). *Honduras: Portrait of a Captive Nation*. New York: Praeger.

Peek, Peter (1983). "Agrarian Reform and Rural Development in Nicaragua, 1979–1981." In Ajit K. Ghose, ed., *Agrarian Reform in Contemporary Developing Countries*. New York: St. Martin's Press.

Pelupessy, Wim, ed. (1991). *Perspectives on the Agro-Export Economy in Central America*. Pittsburgh: University of Pittsburgh Press.

Perera, Victor (1993). *Unfinished Conquest: The Guatemalan Tragedy*. Berkeley: University of California Press.

Petras, James F., and Robert LaPorte Jr. (1973). *Cultivating Revolution: The United States and Agrarian Reform in Latin America*. New York: Random House/Vintage.

Pfeil, Ulrike (1977). "Peasant Mobilization and Land Reform: A Theoretical Model and a Case Study (Honduras)." Master's thesis, University of Florida, Gainesville.

Place, Susan E. (1981). "Ecological and Social Consequences of Export Beef Production in Guanacaste Province, Costa Rica." Ph.D. dissertation, University of California, Los Angeles.

Plant, Roger (1978). *Guatemala: Unnatural Disaster*. London: Latin American Bureau.

Popkin, Samuel L. (1979). *The Rational Peasant*. Berkeley: University of California Press.

Porras, Anabelle, and Villarreal, Beatriz (1985). *Deforestación en Costa Rica*. San José: Editorial Costa Rica.

Posas, Mario (1979). "Política estatal y estructura agraria en Honduras (1950–1978)." *Estudios Sociales Centroamericanos*, 8, 37–116.

―――― (1981a). *Conflictos agrarios y organización campesina*. Tegucigalpa: Editorial Universitaria.

―――― (1981b). *El Movimiento campesino hondureño: una perspectiva general*. Tegucigalpa: Editorial Guaymuras.

Posas, Mario, and Rafael Del Cid (1981). *La Construcción del sector público y del estado nacional en Honduras, 1876–1979*. San José, Costa Rica: Editorial Universitaria Centroamericana.

La Prensa (San Pedro Sula, Honduras) (1982, September 28). "Agrarian Reform Discussed at Peasants Meeting." In U.S. Joint Publications Research Service, *JPRS Reports*, No. 82258–89.

―――― (1983, January 18). "Land Occupation Denounced." In U.S. Joint Publications Research Service, *JPRS Reports*, No. 83020–88.

Prisk, Courtney E., ed. (1991). *The Comandante Speaks: Memoirs of an El Salvadoran Guerilla Leader*. Boulder, CO: Westview Press.

Prosterman, Roy L. (1981). "El Salvador Debate: Real Facts and True Alternatives." *Food Monitor*, 24, 13–19.

―――― (1982, August 9). "The Unmaking of a Land Reform." *New Republic*, 21–25.

―――― (1983). "The Demographics of Land Reform in El Salvador Since 1980." In James W. Wilkie and Stephen Haber, eds., *Statistical Abstract of Latin America*, Vol. 22. Los Angeles: University of California Latin American Center.

Prosterman, Roy L., and Jeffrey M. Riedinger (1987). *Land Reform and Democratic Development*. Baltimore, MD: Johns Hopkins University Press.

Prosterman, Roy L., Jeffrey M. Riedinger, and Mary N. Temple (1981). "Land Reform and the El Salvador Crisis." *International Security*, 6(1), 53–74.

Puchala, Donald J., and Jane Stavely (1979). "The Political Economy of Taiwanese Agriculture." In Raymond F. Hopkins, Donald J. Puchala, and Ross B. Talbot, eds., *Food, Politics, and Agricultural Development*. Boulder, CO: Westview Press.

Quiros Guardia, Rodolfo (1973). *Agricultural Development in Central America: Its Origin and Nature.* Research Paper No. 49. Madison: University of Wisconsin Land Tenure Center.

Ramos, Hugo H., and Walter Adams (1993). "Effects of the Structural Adjustment Program on the Demand and Consumption of Basic Grains in El Salvador." Paper prepared at the University of Kansas, Manhattan, for USAID.

Reinhardt, Nola (1989). "Contrasts and Congruence in the Agrarian Reforms of El Salvador and Nicaragua." In William C. Thiesenhusen, ed., *Searching for Agrarian Reform in Latin America.* Boston: Unwin Hyman.

La República (San José) (1983, July 24). "Land Ownership." In U.S. Joint Publications Research Service, *JPRS Reports*, No. 84297–13.

Reutlinger, Shlomo, and Harold Alderman (1980). "The Prevalence of Calorie-Deficient Diets in Developing Countries." *World Development*, 8(5/6), 399–411.

Riismandel, John N. (1972). "Costa Rica: Self-image, Land Tenure, and Agrarian Reform, 1940–1965." Ph.D. dissertation, University of Maryland, College Park.

Ross, Delmer G. (1975). *Visionaries and Swindlers: The Development of the Railways of Honduras.* Mobile, AL: Institute for Research in Latin America.

Roux, Bernard (1978). "Expansión del capitalismo y desarrollo del subdesarrollo: la integración de América Central en el mercado mundial de la carne de vacuno." *Estudios Sociales Centroamericanos*, 1, 8–34.

Rowles, James P. (1985). *Law and Agrarian Reform in Costa Rica.* Boulder, CO: Westview Press.

Ruhl, J. Mark (1984). "Agrarian Structure and Political Stability in Honduras." *Journal of Interamerican Studies and World Affairs*, 26(1), 33–68.

_____ (1985). "The Honduran Agrarian Reform Under Suazo Córdova." *Inter-American Economic Affairs*, 39(2), 63–81.

Ryan, Phil (1995). *The Fall and Rise of the Market in Sandinista Nicaragua.* Montreal: McGill-Queen's University Press.

Saenz Maroto, Alberto (1970). *Historia agrícola de Costa Rica.* San José: University of Costa Rica.

Sáenz P., Carlos, and C. Foster Knight (1971). *Tenure Security, Land Titling and Agricultural Development in Costa Rica.* San José: University of Costa Rica.

Salazar, José M. (1962). *Tierras y colonización en Costa Rica.* San José: Ciudad Universitaria.

_____ (1979). "Política agraria." In Chester Zelaya, ed., *Costa Rica Contemporánea*, Vol. 1. San José: Editorial de Costa Rica.

Sanderson, Steven E. (1986). *The Transformation of Mexican Agriculture.* Princeton, NJ: Princeton University Press.

Satterthwaite, Ridgway (1971). "Campesino Agriculture and Hacienda Modernization in Coastal El Salvador: 1949 to 1969." Ph.D. dissertation, University of Wisconsin, Madison.

Schlesinger, Stephen, and Stephen Kinzer (1983). *Bitter Fruit: The Untold Story of the American Coup in Guatemala.* New York: Doubleday.

Schmid, Lester (n.d.). "Some Effects of U. S. Foreign Policy Upon Farmers and Other Rural People of Guatemala." Mimeograph, University of Wisconsin Land Tenure Center.

Schoultz, Lars (1983). "Guatemala: Social Change and Political Conflict." In Martin Diskin, ed., *Trouble in Our Backyard: Central America and the United States in the Eighties.* New York: Pantheon.

_____ (1984). "Nicaragua: The United States Confronts a Revolution." In Richard Newfarmer, ed., *From Gunboats to Diplomacy: New U.S. Policies for Latin America.* Baltimore, MD: Johns Hopkins University Press.

Schulz, Donald E., and Deborah Sundloff Schulz (1994). *The United States, Honduras, and the Crisis in Central America.* Boulder, CO: Westview Press.

Schwartz, Norman B. (1978). "Community Development and Cultural Change in Latin America." *Annual Review of Anthropology, 7,* 235–261.

Scott, James C. (1976). *The Moral Economy of the Peasant: Rebellion and Subsistence in Southeast Asia.* New Haven, CT: Yale University Press.

_____ (1985). *Weapons of the Weak: Everyday Forms of Peasant Resistance.* New Haven, CT: Yale University Press.

_____ (1990). *Domination and the Arts of Resistance: Hidden Transcripts.* New Haven, CT: Yale University Press.

Segura Bonilla, Olman, Miriam Miranda Quiros, Robin Gottfried, and Luis Gamez Hernandez (1996). "Políticas del sector forestal en Costa Rica." Report prepared for Consejo Centroamericano de Bosques y Areas Protegidas, Heredia, Costa Rica.

Seligson, Mitchell (1980a). *Peasants of Costa Rica and the Development of Agrarian Capitalism.* Madison: University of Wisconsin Press.

_____ (1980b). "Trust, Efficacy and Modes of Political Participation: A Study of Costa Rican Peasants." *British Journal of Political Science,* 10(1), 75–98.

_____ (1982). "Agrarian Reform in Costa Rica: The Impact of the Title Security Program." *Inter-American Economic Affairs,* 35(4), 31–56.

_____ (1984). "Implementing Land Reform: The Case of Costa Rica." *Managing International Development,* 1(2), 29–46.

_____ (1995). "Thirty Years of Transformation in the Agrarian Structure of El Salvador, 1961–1991." *Latin American Research Review,* 30(3), 43–74.

_____ (1996). "Agrarian Inequality and the Theory of Peasant Rebellion." *Latin American Research Review,* 31(2), 140–158.

Sexton, James D., ed. (1985). *Campesino: The Diary of a Guatemalan Indian.* Tucson: University of Arizona Press.

Shane, Douglas (1980). "Hoofprints in the Forest." Report, U.S. Department of State, Washington, DC.

Shaw, Royce Z. (1979). *Central America: Regional Integration and National Political Development.* Boulder, CO: Westview Press.

Shepherd, Philip (1985). "Wisconsin in Honduras: Agrarian Politics and U.S. Influence in the 1980s." In Nancy Peckenham and Annie Street, eds., *Honduras: Portrait of a Captive Nation.* New York: Praeger.

Sherman, William L. (1979). *Forced Native Labor in Sixteenth Century Central America.* Lincoln: University of Nebraska Press.

Sholk, Richard (1984). "The National Bourgeoisie in Post-Revolutionary Nicaragua." *Comparative Politics,* 16(3), 253–276.

Sigmund, Paul, and Mary Speck (1978, October 4, 5, and 6). "Virtue's Reward: The United States and Somoza, 1933–1978." Prepared statement in U.S., Senate,

Committee on Foreign Relations. *Latin America.* Hearings Before Subcommittee on Western Hemisphere Affairs. 95th Congress, 2nd session, 204–217.

Simon, Laurence R., and James C. Stephens Jr. (1982). *El Salvador Land Reform, 1980–1981: Impact Audit.* 2nd ed. Boston: Oxfam America.

Singelmann, Peter (1981). *Structures of Domination and Peasant Movements in Latin America.* Columbia: University of Missouri Press.

Skocpol, Theda (1982). "What Makes Peasants Revolutionary?" *Comparative Politics,* 14(3), 351–375.

Slutzky, Daniel (1979). "Notas sobre empresas transnacionales, agroindustriales y reforma agraria en Honduras." *Estudios Sociales Centroamericanos,* 8, 35–48.

Smith, Carol A. (1978). "Beyond Dependency Theory: National and Regional Patterns of Underdevelopment in Guatemala." *American Ethnologist,* 5(3), 574–617.

⸺ (1984a). "Does a Commodity Economy Enrich the Few While Ruining the Masses? Differentiation Among Petty Commodity Producers in Guatemala." *Journal of Peasant Studies,* 11(3), 60–95.

⸺ (1984b). "Local History to Global Context: Social and Economic Transitions in Western Guatemala." *Comparative Studies in Society and History,* 26(2), 193–228.

⸺ (1990). "The Militarization of Civil Society in Guatemala's Economic Reorganization as a Continuation of War." *Latin American Perspectives,* 17(4), 8–41.

Smith, Robert S. (1956). "Forced Labor in the Guatemalan Indigo Works." *Hispanic American Historical Review,* 36(2), 319–328.

Smith, T. Lynn, ed. (1965). *Agrarian Reform in Latin America.* New York: Knopf.

Smyth, Frank (1988–1989). "Consensus or Crisis? Without Duarte in El Salvador." *Journal of Interamerican Studies and World Affairs,* 30(4), 29–52.

Sobhan, Rehman (1993). *Agrarian Reform and Social Transformation: Precondition for Social Transformation.* London: Zed.

Sojo, Carlos (1992). *La Mano visible del mercado.* San José, Costa Rica: CRIES.

Solórzano Raúl, Ronnie de Camino, and Richard Woodward (1991). *Accounts Overdue: Natural Resource Depreciation in Costa Rica.* Washington, DC: World Resources Institute and Tropical Science Center.

Spalding, Rose J. (1985). "Food Politics and Agricultural Change in Revolutionary Nicaragua, 1979–82." In John C. Soper and Thomas C. Wright, eds., *Food, Politics, and Society in Latin America.* Lincoln: University of Nebraska Press.

⸺ (1994). *Capitalists and Revolution in Nicaragua: Opposition and Accommodation, 1979–1993.* Chapel Hill: University of North Carolina Press.

Spence, Jack, George Vickers, and David Dye (1995). *The Salvadoran Peace Accords and Democratization: A Three Year Progress Report and Recommendation.* Cambridge, MA: Hemisphere Initiatives.

⸺ (1997). *Chapultepec: Five Years Later—El Salvador's Political Reality and Uncertain Future.* Cambridge, MA: Hemisphere Initiatives.

Spielmann, Hans O. (1972). "La Expansión ganadera en Costa Rica." *Revista Geográfica,* 77, 57–84.

Spoor, Max (1995). *The State and Domestic Agricultural Markets in Nicaragua.* New York: St. Martin's Press.

Stanfield, David, Edgar Nesman, Mitchell Seligson, and Alexander Coles (1990). "The Honduras Land Titling and Registration Experience." Mimeograph, University of Wisconsin Land Tenure Center.

Stanley, William (1996). *The Protection Racket State: Elite Politics, Military Extortion, and Civil War in El Salvador.* Philadelphia: Temple University Press.

Stannard, David E. (1992). *American Holocaust: Columbus and the Conquest of the New World.* New York: Oxford University Press.

Stoll, David (1993). *Between Two Armies in the Ixil Towns of Guatemala.* New York: Columbia University Press.

Stone, Samuel (1983). "Production and Politics in Central America's Convulsions." *Journal of Latin American Studies,* 15(2), 453–469.

Stonich, Susan C. (1993). *"I Am Destroying the Land": The Political Ecology of Poverty and Environmental Destruction in Honduras.* Boulder, CO: Westview Press.

Storrs, K. Larry (1990). "El Salvador Highlights, 1960–1990: A Summary of Major Turning Points in Salvadoran History and U.S. Policy." Washington, DC: Library of Congress, Congressional Research Service.

Strasma, John (1989). "Unfinished Business: Consolidating Land Reform in El Salvador." In William C. Thiesenhusen, ed., *Searching for Agrarian Reform in Latin America.* Winchester, MA: Unwin Hyman.

Strasma, John, Peter Gore, Jeffrey Nash, and Refugio Rochin (1983). "Agrarian Reform in El Salvador." Paper prepared by Checchi & Co. for U.S. Agency for International Development, Washington, DC.

Streeten, Paul (1974). "World Trade in Agricultural Commodities and the Terms of Trade with Industrial Goods." In Nurul Islam, ed., *Agricultural Policy in Developing Countries.* New York: Wiley.

_____ (1990). "Comparative Advantage and Free Trade." In Azizur Rahmankhan and Rehman Sobhan, eds., *Trade Planning and Rural Development.* London: Macmillan.

Stringer, Randy (1989). "Honduras: Toward Conflict and Agrarian Reform." In William C. Thiesenhusen, ed., *Searching for Agrarian Reform in Latin America.* Winchester, MA: Unwin Hyman.

Strouse, Pierre A. D. (1970). "Instability of Tropical Agriculture: The Atlantic Lowlands of Costa Rica." *Economic Geography,* 46(1), 78–97.

Tai, Hung-Chao (1974). *Land Reform and Politics: A Comparative Analysis.* Berkeley: University of California Press.

Tax, Sol (1963). *Penny Capitalism: A Guatemalan Indian Economy.* Chicago: University of Chicago Press.

Taylor, James Robert, Jr. (1969). *Agricultural Settlement and Development in Eastern Nicaragua.* Research Paper No. 33. Madison: University of Wisconsin Land Tenure Center.

Tendler, Judith (1976). *Intercountry Evaluation of Small Farmer Organizations: Final Report [on] Ecuador and Honduras.* Washington, DC: U.S. Agency for International Development.

Thiesenhusen, William C. (1981). "El Salvador's Land Reform: Was It Programmed to Fail?" *Christianity and Crisis,* 41(8), 133–137.

_____, ed. (1989). *Searching for Agrarian Reform in Latin America.* Winchester, MA: Unwin Hyman.

_____, (1995). *Broken Promises: Agrarian Reform and the Latin American Campesino.* Boulder, CO: Westview Press.

Thome, Joseph, and David Kaimowitz (1985). "Agrarian Reform." In Thomas W. Walker, ed., *Nicaragua: The First Five Years.* Boulder, CO: Westview Press.

Thrupp, Lori Ann (1995). *Bittersweet Harvests for Global Supermarkets: Challenges in Latin America's Agricultural Export Boom.* Washington, DC: World Resources Institute.

Tiempo (San Pedro Sula, Honduras) (1982, May 5). "Peasants' Union Protests Arrests in Northwest." In U.S. Joint Publications Research Service, *JPRS Report,* No. 80872–122.

_____ (1983, October 24). "Most Agrarian Reform Beneficiaries Fail to Receive Assistance." In U.S. Joint Publications Research Service, *JPRS Report,* No. 84872–122.

Tilly, Charles (1978). *From Mobilization to Revolution.* Reading, MA: Addison-Wesley.

Time (1968, January 26). "Guatemala: Caught in the Crossfire," 23.

_____ (1975, August 18). "Blood and Land," 36.

Timmer, C. Peter (1982). "Appropriate Technology, Food Production, and Rural Development: The Rural Sector from a Food Policy Perspective." In Ray A. Goldberg, ed., *Research in Domestic and International Agribusiness Management,* Vol. 3. Greenwich, CT: JAI Press.

Tomich, Thomas P., et al. (1995). *Transforming Agrarian Economies: Opportunities Seized, Opportunities Missed.* Ithaca, NY: Cornell University Press.

Torres, James F. (1979). *Income Levels, Income Distribution, and Levels of Living in Rural Honduras: A Summary and Evaluation of Qualitative and Quantitative Data.* Washington, DC: U.S. Agency for International Development.

Torres Rivas, Edelberto (1971). *Interpretación del desarrollo centroamericano.* San José, Costa Rica: Editorial Universitaria Centroamericana.

_____ (1993). *History and Society in Central America.* Austin: University of Texas Press.

Torres-Rivas, Edelberto, and Eckhard Deutscher, eds. (1988). *Cambio y continuidad en la economía bananera.* San José, Costa Rica: Facultad Latinoamericana de Ciencias Sociales.

La Tribuna (Tegucigalpa) (1983, November 23). "Japanese Agricultural Development Aid." In U.S. Joint Publications Research Service, *JPRS Report,* No. LAM–84–006.

Tropical Science Center (1992). "Forest Policy for Costa Rica." Paper prepared for the Ministry of Natural Resources, Energy, and Mines, San José, Costa Rica.

Trudeau, Robert H. (1984). "Guatemala: The Long-Term Costs of Short-Term Stability." In Richard Newfarmer, ed., *From Gunboats to Diplomacy: New U.S. Policies for Latin America.* Baltimore, MD: Johns Hopkins University Press.

_____ (1993). *Guatemalan Politics: The People Struggle for Democracy.* Boulder, CO: Lynne Rienner.

Trudeau, Robert H., and Lars Schoultz (1986). "Guatemala." In Morris J. Blachman, William M. LeoGrande, and Kenneth Sharpe, eds., *Confronting Revolution: Security Through Diplomacy in Central America.* New York: Pantheon.

Tulchin, Joseph S., with Gary Bland (1992). *Is There a Transition to Democracy in El Salvador?* Boulder, CO: Lynne Rienner.

Tuma, Elias (1965). *Twenty-Six Centuries of Agrarian Reform.* Berkeley: University of California Press.

Umaña, Alvaro, and Katrina Brandon (1992). "Inventing Institutions for Conservation: Lessons from Costa Rica." In Sheldon Annis, ed., *Poverty, Natural Resources and Public Policy in Central America*. New Brunswick, NJ: Transaction.

United Nations (various years). *Statistical Abstract*. New York: UN.

United Nations, Development Programme [UNDP] (various years). *Human Development Report*. New York: Oxford University Press.

United Nations, Economic Commission for Latin America [UNECLA] (1950). *The Economic Development of Latin America and Its Principal Problems*. Lake Success, NY: United Nations Department of Economic Affairs.

_____ (1979). *Transnational Corporations in the Banana Industry of Central America*. N.p.: UNECLA.

_____ (1983). *Statistical Yearbook for Latin America*. New York: UNECLA.

United Nations, Food and Agriculture Organization [UNFAO] (1992). *Organization and Management of Agricultural Development for Small Farmers*. Economic and Social Development Paper 20, Rev. 1. Rome: FAO.

_____ (various years). *Production Yearbook*. Rome: FAO.

United States, Agency for International Development [USAID] (1970, March 27). "$3 Million Aid Loan to Help Small Farmers in Guatemala." Press release.

_____ (1982). *Honduras, Project Paper: Small Farmer Titling*. Washington, DC: USAID.

_____ (1983). *Honduras, Project Paper: Small Farmer Livestock Improvement*. Washington, DC: USAID.

_____ (1984). *Honduras, Project Paper: Export Promotion and Services*. Washington, DC: USAID.

_____ (1985). *Latin America and the Caribbean*. Vol. 1. Congressional presentation, fiscal year 1986, annex 3. Washington, DC: USAID.

United States, Agency for International Development, Office of Housing (1980). *Urban Poverty in Guatemala*. Washington, DC: USAID.

United States, Congress (1962, October 2). *Congressional Record*. Washington, DC: U.S. Government Printing Office.

_____ (1987). *Report of the Congressional Committees Investigating the Iran-Contra Affair*. Washington, DC: U.S. Government Printing Office.

United States, Department of Agriculture, Foreign Agricultural Service [USDA] (various years). *Attaché Reports*. Washington, DC: USDA.

United States, Department of State (1954). Office Memorandum: "ARA Monthly Report for July." 714.00/8–454. U.S. National Archives.

_____ (1955). Despatch 48: "U.S. Assistance to Guatemala in FY1955." 814.00-TA/7–2255. U.S. National Archives.

_____ (1983, April). "El Salvador's Land Reform." *GIST*. Washington, DC: Department of State, Bureau of Public Affairs.

_____ (1984, January 26, February 6). *Report on Status of Land Reform in El Salvador*. Reprinted in U.S., House, Committee on Foreign Affairs. *The Situation in El Salvador*. Hearings Before Subcommittees on Human Rights and International Organizations and on Western Hemisphere Affairs. 98th Congress, 2nd session, 291–342.

_____ (1985a). "El Salvador's Land Reform." *GIST*. Washington, DC: Department of State, Bureau of Public Affairs.

_____ (1985b)."*Revolution Beyond Our Borders*": *Sandinista Intervention in Central America*. Washington, DC: Department of State.

United States, General Accounting Office [GAO] (1994). *El Salvador: Implementation of Post-war Programs Slower Than Expected*. Washington, DC: GAO.

United States, House (1981a, February 25, March 24, April 29). Committee on Appropriations. *Foreign Assistance Legislation for Fiscal Year 1982*. Parts 1 and 2. Hearings Before Subcommittee on Foreign Operations. 97th Congress, 1st session.

_____ (1981b, July 14, 21, 28). Committee on Foreign Affairs. *The Caribbean Basin Policy*. Hearings Before Subcommittee on Inter-American Affairs. 97th Congress, 1st session.

_____ (1981c, July 30). Committee on Foreign Affairs. *Human Rights in Guatemala*. Hearings Before Subcommittee on Inter-American Affairs. 97th Congress, 1st session.

_____ (1982, February 2, 23, 25; March 2). Committee on Foreign Affairs. *Presidential Certification on El Salvador*, Vol. 1. Hearings Before Subcommittee on Inter-American Affairs. 97th Congress, 2nd session.

_____ (1984, January 26, February 6). Committee on Foreign Affairs. *The Situation in El Salvador*. Hearings Before Subcommittees on Human Rights and International Organizations and on Western Hemisphere Affairs. 98th Congress, 2nd session.

_____ (1985a, February 20). Committee on Foreign Affairs. *Developments in Guatemala and U.S. Options*. Hearings Before Subcommittee on Western Hemisphere Affairs. 99th Congress, 1st session.

_____ (1985b, March 5, 19). Committee on Foreign Affairs. *Foreign Assistance Legislation for Fiscal Years 1986–87*. Part 6. Hearings and Markup Before the Subcommittee on Western Hemisphere Affairs. 99th Congress, 1st session.

United States, Senate (1978, October 4, 5, 6). Committee on Foreign Relations. *Latin America*. Hearings Before Subcommittee on Western Hemisphere Affairs. 95th Congress, 2nd session.

Utting, Peter (1991). *Economic Adjustment Under the Sandinistas: Policy Reform, Food Security, and Livelihood in Nicaragua*. Geneva: United Nations Research Institute for Social Development.

Valenta, Jiri, and Virginia Valenta (1984). "Soviet Strategy and Policies in the Caribbean Basin." In Howard J. Wiarda, ed., *Rift and Revolution: The Central America Imbroglio*. Washington, DC: America Enterprise Institute.

Valverde, Victor, Reynaldo Martorell, Victor Mejia-Pivaral, Hernan Delgado, Aaron Lechtig, Charles Teller, and Robert E. Klein (1977). "Relationship Between Family Land Availability and Nutritional Status." *Ecology of Food and Nutrition*, 6(1), 1–7.

Valverde, Victor, Isabel Nieves, Nancy Sloan, Bernard Pillet, Fredrick Trowbridge, Timothy Farrell, Ivan Beghin, and Robert E. Klein (1980). "Life Styles and Nutritional Status of Children from Different Ecological Areas of El Salvador." *Ecology of Food and Nutrition*, 9(3), 167–177.

Veblen, Thomas T. (1978). "Forest Preservation in the Western Highlands of Guatemala." *Geographical Review*, 68(4), 417–434.

Vilas, Carlos M. (1995). *Between Earthquakes and Volcanoes: Market, State, and the Revolutions in Central America*. New York: Monthly Review Press.

Volk, Steven (1981). "Honduras: On the Border of War." *NACLA Report on the Americas*, 15(6), 2–37.

Walker, Thomas S. (1981). "Risk and Adoption of Hybrid Maize in El Salvador." *Food Research Institute Studies*, 18(1), 59–88.

Walker, Thomas W. (1981). *Nicaragua: The Land of Sandino*. Boulder, CO: Westview Press.

_____, ed. (1985). *Nicaragua: The First Five Years*. Boulder, CO: Westview Press.

_____, ed. (1997). *Nicaragua Without Illusions: Regime Transition and Structural Adjustment in the 1990's*. Wilmington, DE: Scholarly Resources.

Warnken, Philip F. (1975). "The Agricultural Development of Nicaragua: An Analysis of the Production Sector." Mimeograph, University of Missouri, Columbia.

Warren, Kay B. (1978). *The Symbolism of Subordination: Indian Identity in a Guatemalan Town*. Austin: University of Texas Press.

Washington Office on Latin America [WOLA] (1979). *El Salvador: Human Rights and U.S. Economic Policy*. Washington, DC: WOLA.

_____ (1983). *Guatemala: The Roots of Revolution*. Washington, DC: WOLA.

_____ (1987). *Police Aid and Political Will*. Washington, DC: WOLA.

Wasserstrom, Robert (1975). "Revolution in Guatemala: Peasants and Politics Under the Arbenz Government." *Comparative Studies in Society and History*, 17(4), 443–478.

Watanabe, John M. (1992). *Maya Saints and Souls in a Changing World*. Austin: University of Texas Press.

Weaver, Fredrick Stirton (1994). *Inside the Volcano: The History and Political Economy of Central America*. Boulder, CO: Westview Press.

Weaver, James H., Michael T. Rock, and Kenneth Kusterer (1997). *Achieving Broad-Based Sustainable Development: Governance, Environment, and Growth with Equity*. West Hartford, CT: Kumarian Press.

Webre, Stephen (1979). *José Napoleón Duarte and the Christian Democratic Party in Salvadoran Politics, 1960–1972*. Baton Rouge: Louisiana State University Press.

Weeks, John (1985). *The Economies of Central America*. New York: Holmes & Meier.

_____ (1986). "An Interpretation of the Central American Crisis." *Latin American Research Review*, 21(3), 31–54.

Weir, David, and Mark Schapiro (1981). *Circles of Poison*. San Francisco: Institute for Food and Development Policy.

West, Robert C., and John P. Augelli (1976). *Middle America: Its Lands and Peoples*. 2nd ed. Englewood Cliffs, NJ: Prentice-Hall.

Wheelock Román, Jaime (1980). *Imperialismo y dictadura: crisis de una formación social*. 5th ed. Mexico City: Siglo Veintiuno Editores.

Whetten, Nathan L. (1961). *Guatemala, the Land and the People*. New Haven, CT: Yale University Press.

White, Alastair (1973). *El Salvador*. New York: Praeger.

White, Richard A. (1984). *The Morass: United States Intervention in Central America*. New York: Harper & Row.

White, Robert A. (1977). "Structural Factors in Rural Development: The Church and the Peasant in Honduras." Ph.D. dissertation, Cornell University, Ithaca, NY.

Wilken, Gene C. (1987). *Good Farmers: Traditional Agricultural Resource Management in Mexico and Central America*. Berkeley: University of California Press.

Wilkie, James W., and Manuel Moreno-Ibáñez (1984). "New Research on Food Production in Latin America Since 1952." In James W. Wilkie and Adain Perkal, eds., *Statistical Abstract of Latin America*, Vol. 23. Los Angeles: University of California Latin American Center.

Williams, Robert G. (1986). *Export Agriculture and the Crisis in Central America*. Chapel Hill: University of North Carolina Press.

_____ (1994). *State and Social Evolution: Coffee and the Rise of National Government in Central America*. Chapel Hill: University of North Carolina Press.

Wilson, Charles Morrow (1968, originally published in 1947). *Empire in Green and Gold: The Story of the American Banana Trade*. New York: Greenwood Press.

Wilson, Richard (1991). "Machine Gun and Mountain Spirits: The Cultural Effects of State Repression Among the Q'eaqhi' of Guatemala." *Critique of Anthropology*, 11(1), 33–61.

Wolf, Eric R. (1969). *Peasant Wars of the Twentieth Century*. New York: Harper & Row.

Woodward, Ralph Lee, Jr. (1976). *Central America: A Nation Divided*. New York: Oxford University Press.

_____ (1984). "The Rise and Decline of Liberalism in Central America." *Journal of Interamerican Studies and World Affairs*, 26(3), 291–312.

World Bank (1978). *Guatemala: Economic and Social Position and Prospects*. Washington, DC: World Bank.

_____ (1993a). "Costa Rica Forestry Sector Review: Discussion Draft." Paper prepared by the Agriculture and Natural Resource Operations, Mexico and Central America.

_____ (1993b). *The East Asian Miracle: Economic Growth and Public Policy*. New York: Oxford University Press.

World Development Forum (1985). Washington, DC: Hunger Project.

Wortman, Miles L. (1982). *Government and Society in Central America, 1680–1840*. New York: Columbia University Press.

Wynia, Gary W. (1972). *Politics and Planners: Economic Development Policy in Central America*. Madison: University of Wisconsin Press.

Newspapers and Newsletters

Chronicle	(*Chronicle of Latin American Economic Affairs**)
EcoCentral	(*Central American and Caribbean Political Economy and Sustainable Development**)
Envio	(Managua)
Monitor	(*Christian Science Monitor*)
NotiSur	(*Latin American Political Affairs**)
NY Times	(*New York Times*)
Post	(*Washington Post*)
Tico Times	(San José, Costa Rica)
Times of the Americas	(Miami)
Update	(*Central American Update**)

*Publications of Latin American Data Base, University of New Mexico.

Index